The Knopf Collectors' Guides to American Antiques

Robert Bishop & William C. Ketchum, Jr.
Series Consultants

A Chanticleer Press Edition

Folk Art

Paintings, Sculpture & Country Objects

Robert Bishop, Judith Reiter Weissman,
Michael McManus, and Henry Niemann

With photographs by Schecter Me Sun Lee

Alfred A. Knopf, New York

This is a Borzoi Book
Published by Alfred A. Knopf, Inc.

Published in the United States by Alfred A. Knopf, Inc., New York, and simultaneously in Canada by Random House of Canada Limited, Toronto. Distributed by Random House, Inc., New York.

Prepared and produced by
Chanticleer Press, Inc., New York.

Color reproductions by Nievergelt Repro AG, Zurich, Switzerland. Type set in Century Expanded by Dix Type Inc., Syracuse, New York. Printed and bound by Dai Nippon Printing Co., Ltd., Tokyo, Japan.

First Printing

Library of Congress Catalog Number: 82-48945
ISBN: 0-394-71493-8

Contents

Acknowledgments

This book was a joint effort that would have been impossible without the expert assistance of my three co-authors: Judith Reiter Weissman, who wrote the section on country household objects; Michael McManus, who dealt with sculpture; and Henry Niemann, who wrote about the paintings.

I want to express my appreciation to all the institutions, galleries, and individuals for making their collections available to us, particularly the Museum of American Folk Art, where Claire Hartman patiently arranged for photography. Barbara Johnson not only allowed us access to her splendid collection of scrimshaw but also helped write about it. I am also grateful to Sanford Smith of the Smith Gallery, who provided transparencies and information about his marine paintings, and to Nancy Druckman of Sotheby's. Schecter Me Sun Lee, assisted by John P. Bellacosa, spent months photographing most of the folk art in this book.

William C. Ketchum, Jr., was invaluable in helping to select the pieces to be photographed, commenting on the manuscript, and compiling the price guide. Patricia L. Coblentz reviewed the text and made many valuable suggestions. Robert Shaw of the Shelburne Museum and John Farrand, Jr., of Chanticleer Press advised on the decoy section. John Kremitske and Marcia Lawther copy-edited the text.

I am especially grateful to Paul Steiner and the staff of Chanticleer Press: Gudrun Buettner and Susan Costello, who developed the idea for the series; Michael Goldman, who, with the assistance of Constance V. Mersel, edited and coordinated this guide through completion; Milton Rugoff, who helped polish the text; Carol Nehring, who supervised the art and layouts; and Helga Lose, who directed the production of the book. Finally, I want to thank Charles Elliott, senior editor at Alfred A. Knopf, for his encouragement and support.

Robert Bishop

About the Authors, Photographer, and Consultants

Robert Bishop
Director of the Museum of American Folk Art in New York City since 1976, co-author Robert Bishop is a well-known writer, lecturer, and teacher in the fields of American art and antiques. His more than thirty books include *The Knopf Collectors' Guide to Quilts, Coverlets, Rugs & Samplers*, *American Folk Sculpture*, and *Folk Painters of America*. Dr. Bishop established this country's first master's degree program in Folk Art Studies at New York University, and is on the editorial boards of *Antique Monthly*, *Art & Antiques*, and *Horizon* magazines.

Judith Reiter Weissman
Co-author Judith Reiter Weissman is a freelance writer and lecturer whose specialty is American folk art and textiles. The author of many articles and a contributor to *The Knopf Collectors' Guide to Quilts, Coverlets, Rugs & Samplers*, Dr. Weissman has been a guest curator at the Museum of American Folk Art and is on the faculty of the graduate program in Folk Art Studies at New York University.

Michael McManus
Michael McManus, a co-author of this guide, has a master's degree in Folk Art Studies from New York University. He has written articles about folk sculpture and is planning an exhibition of American folk art that will travel to the People's Republic of China.

Henry Niemann
A collector of twentieth-century folk paintings, co-author Henry Niemann is studying folk art in the graduate program at New York University.

Schecter Me Sun Lee
Schecter Lee is a New York-based freelance photographer whose works have been published in national and international magazines. Among his most recent books are *American Folk Dolls*, published by Alfred A. Knopf, as well as *Pottery and Porcelain*, a new volume in *The Knopf Collectors' Guides to American Antiques*.

William C. Ketchum, Jr.
A member of the faculty of The New School for Social Research, consultant William C. Ketchum, Jr., is also a guest curator at the Museum of American Folk Art in New York City and a consultant to several major auction houses. Dr. Ketchum has written 18 books, including *Pottery and Porcelain* in *The Knopf Collectors' Guides to American Antiques*. He is an associate editor of *Antique Monthly*.

Patricia L. Coblentz
Consultant Patricia L. Coblentz has written several books with Robert Bishop, including *American Decorative Arts*, and lectures frequently on folk art. Formerly she was the assistant director of the Museum of American Folk Art and editor of the museum's magazine, *The Clarion*.

Preface

Once neglected by collectors and scholars, folk art has become one of the most popular and exciting fields in American art and antiques. Whether portraits, baskets, decoys, cigar-store figures, or painted tin trays, these pieces are colorful and evocative expressions of the American cultural mainstream. Interest in folk art has reached every segment of the population, including connoisseurs who shop at elegant galleries, experts tracking down the identities of anonymous artists, and amateur collectors decorating their homes in a country style with the household objects that are often called "primitives" today.

But interest has not always been so great. Early in this century, few people were drawn to folk art, though some collectors of antiques bought folk paintings and sculpture as decorative accessories for colonial furniture. In the 1920s, however, many artists discovered American folk art; their enthusiasm started a trend that was continued by modern-art collectors. This confirms the paradox that a taste for the primitive is often a product of sophistication. Today folk art is collected by all kinds of people who not only appreciate its artistic merit but who also wish to preserve our rich cultural heritage.

The first collectors specialized in early paintings, sculpture, and fine handmade objects. As interest has grown, the field has expanded; thus, today's collectors are just as likely to seek out factory-made weathervanes, cast-iron implements, or the works of living craftsmen, painters, and sculptors. Increasing popularity has caused the prices of folk art to rise, often dramatically, and today some paintings by well-known artists sell for six-figure sums. Yet because this is a relatively new field, many kinds of works, particularly those from the late 19th and early 20th centuries, are readily available and often inexpensive.

This book covers nearly every type of folk art made from the time of the Revolutionary War to the 1980s. To help collectors identify the objects they find, the pieces illustrated in this guide are arranged by subject or function rather than by period, decoration, style, or material. Each entry describes a representative work and tells where, when, by whom (if known), and of what materials it was made. In addition, it provides historical background along with practical hints, including what to look for and what to avoid. A general essay, How to Evaluate Folk Art, summarizes these hints and includes information on fakes and reproductions. To acquaint collectors with what they can expect to pay, the Price Guide in the appendix lists current price ranges for the types of folk art illustrated. The high prices listed for some works may be the result of their rarity, fine workmanship, or current appeal; low prices may indicate undervalued areas worth investigating. Thus, this guide will help readers to assemble a distinctive collection of American folk art and to expand their appreciation of its diversity, charm, and beauty.

A Simple Way to Identify Folk Art

"The art of the common man," as folk art is sometimes called, is remarkably varied in type, material, style, age, and value. It includes pieces traditionally deemed folk art, such as primitive 19th-century paintings, shop figures, and handmade boxes, as well as a wide variety of useful country-style objects, such as kitchen utensils and baskets.

To help collectors identify, date, and assess the value of the works they encounter, we have chosen more than 360 examples for picture-and-text coverage. Pieces in several mediums, however, such as textiles and pottery, are found in other books in this series. In presenting the range of American folk art, this guide includes not only the most common types available, but also rare and outstanding examples that are important for an understanding of the development of American folk art. So that works can be found quickly, paintings and sculpture are organized visually according to subject, and utilitarian objects by function. This organization is further explained by the Visual Key. Collectors who are seeking information about a particular artist or craftsman may also refer to the Checklist of Artists and Craftsmen in the back of the book, which will direct them to illustrated works.

An introductory essay, What Is Folk Art?, describes the scope and characteristics of the field. Essays on folk paintings, folk sculpture, and country household objects, together with the brief essays at the beginning of each section of color plates, sketch the history of the various types of folk art. The essay called How to Evaluate Folk Art provides hints about authenticating, dating, and judging works in many mediums; this is followed by an illustrated section showing comparisons of similar paintings, sculpture, and household objects, pointing out how to determine which are good, better, or best. The Checklist of Artists and Craftsmen provides information on approximately 200 important creators of folk art, including many whose works are not featured in the book. Finally, the up-to-date Price Guide lists price ranges for all the folk art illustrated in this volume.

Using these tools—photographs, descriptions, essays, and tables—both beginners and connoisseurs will find, we hope, that this book makes collecting folk art more enjoyable and rewarding.

What Is Folk Art?

"Folk art" is today used as an umbrella term for numerous artistic forms and utilitarian objects in a wide variety of mediums and from every period of American history; it ranges from primitive paintings and sculpture to baskets, wooden kitchenware, factory-made weathervanes, and even modern-day outdoor "junk sculpture." It has been subject to many different definitions over the years, largely because it refers to a relatively new field in which discoveries are constantly being made.

Some Generalizations
The term "folk art" combines what in Europe is often called "folk craft," meaning handmade everyday household objects having traditional decoration, with "naive art," referring to such paintings as those by Henri Rousseau and, in America, by Edward Hicks and Grandma Moses. It also brings together numerous transplanted cultural traditions, including those of the Pennsylvania Germans and Spanish-speaking people of the Southwest. Though primarily a provincial art originating in rural America, much folk art was produced in towns. It includes "women's work" such as quilting as well.

In contrast to the "fine arts," folk art is the art of the people. Its creators, often anonymous or now forgotten, were either self-taught amateurs working for their own pleasure, or paid artisans and painters with varying degrees of training and skill. Folk paintings and sculpture are characterized by a direct style, bold colors, strong design, and immediate, uncomplicated meaning. Often, folk painters and sculptors selected themes, particularly religious and patriotic ones, shunned by many academically trained artists; some also expressed negative social attitudes, including racial prejudices. When utilitarian objects such as painted tinware, ships' figureheads, shop signs, and household utensils have been made by craftsmen of imagination and aesthetic vision, they too are considered folk art.

Carousel horse. Stein and Goldstein. Painted wood, glass, and horse hair. Brooklyn. c. 1900

Although sometimes considered a "charming postscript" to American art, folk art is actually in the mainstream of American culture. Its appeal is often nostalgic—evoking images of a less troubled world—or highly decorative, with its bright colors, flattened perspective, and simple arrangement of forms. But while much folk art is clearly derivative, it is often original and exciting, and as powerful as the finest academic art.

The First Collectors
American folk art was first acknowledged and collected in the 1920s by American artists returning from study in Europe, where the art of primitive peoples was causing great excitement. At the time, no gallery in any American art museum was devoted to native folk art. The first major museum exhibitions in this field took place in the 1930s. Since then specialized museums and galleries have proliferated across the country.

Modern Folk Art
Many experts and collectors limit the definition of folk art to work produced in the century between American independence in 1776 and the fourth quarter of the 19th century, when rampant industrialization caused a decline in handwork. Indeed, many types of paintings and objects were essentially 19th-century phenomena. But the creation of folk art never ceased. Since the Second World War, there has been much disagreement about whether modern works can be genuine folk art. Even when fashioned in relative cultural isolation, modern pieces are usually quite different from older folk art. Though most traditionalists reject 20th-century works, preferring pieces with the mellow patina only age can produce, a new breed of collectors now accepts many of them as true folk art. For them, the age of a piece is of little consequence, and our evolving folk heritage is as rich and diverse as ever.

The Peaceable Kingdom. *Edward Hicks. Oil on canvas. Newtown, Pennsylvania. c. 1847.*

Folk Painting

The appreciation of American folk painting calls for an open mind and a perceptive eye. The traditional criteria for judging art must be set aside, since the subtleties of formal composition, sophisticated techniques, and realistic detail and perspective were seldom, or only accidentally, achieved by America's folk masters.

Although many painters were indeed anonymous, untrained, itinerant, and artistically naive, in recent years dozens have been identified and credited with large bodies of work. It is also now known that not all were itinerant or lacking in basic artistic training, and that many of them earned their living by painting.

Portraits

In the 17th and 18th centuries, having your portrait "taken" was a sign of being cultured and successful. These works were either English in style, focusing on the sitter's face, or Dutch, striving for a realistic spatial arrangement. From about 1800 to 1840, a vigorous American style of portrait painting was developed by countless artists who traveled from village to village and recorded the likenesses of country folk. These painters may have lacked technical competence, but they displayed a keen power of observation and an intuitive sense of design.

Landscape, Historical, Religious, and Still-Life Paintings

Folk landscapes and seascapes became most popular in the 19th century. To express their love for their country, artists recorded every aspect of the land, from midwestern farms to thriving industrial towns and bustling seaports. Folk artists, particularly recent immigrants, celebrated their freedom in historical and nationalistic paintings. Most popular were idealized portraits of George Washington and other political heroes. As one Russian visitor to America, Paul Svinin, observed in the early 19th century: "It is noteworthy that every American considers it his

Portrait of Major Andrew Billings. *Beardsley Limner. Oil on canvas. New England. c. 1785.*

sacred duty to have a likeness of Washington in his home, just as we have images of God's saints."

Religion has always been a major inspiration for folk artists. Probably the most famous American folk painting—surviving in about sixty versions—is Edward Hicks's *The Peaceable Kingdom,* illustrating the prophecy in the book of Isaiah (11:6) that the wolf, lamb, leopard, and kid would lie down together when the Messiah comes. In the 19th century, innumerable religious artworks were created in the academies where young girls of good families were sent to learn polite arts such as music, needlework, and watercolor painting. Students at these schools also produced thousands of romantic watercolor landscapes, still lifes (also called theorems, so named for the stencils used to make them), reverse paintings on glass, as well as mourning, tinsel, and sandpaper pictures.

20th-Century Paintings

Folk painters have continued to play an important part in American art in the 20th century. They fall into several broad categories. Among the best known are the "memory painters," such as Grandma Moses and Mattie Lou O'Kelley, whose vibrant, animated scenes depict fast-disappearing life-styles. "Obsessive," or "isolate," painters work in a cultural vacuum and create highly personal, visionary paintings that are often raw and abrasive in style and obsessive in their repetitions of certain themes. "Neo-naives" are professionally trained artists who self-consciously work in a primitive style, and are thus considered by many collectors not to be true folk artists.

Hoosick Valley (from the Window). *Grandma Moses. Oil on masonite. Hoosick Falls, New York. 1946.*

Folk Sculpture

When the first comprehensive exhibition of American folk sculpture was shown at the Newark Museum in 1931, viewers were surprised and impressed by these beautiful utilitarian objects. Sculpture has since become the most widely collected form of folk art.

Gravestones, Weathervanes, and Shop Signs

American folk sculpture first appeared in the Southwest, where 16th-century Spanish colonists and Indians who had been converted to Catholicism made religious carvings. On the East Coast, 17th-century English and Dutch settlers developed their own sculptural forms—grave markers, weathervanes, and trade signs.

Grave markers are the earliest remaining pieces of dated American folk sculpture, with the finest examples being created in New England. At first carved with symbols of time, death, or rebirth, by the 18th century some stones also bore portraits of the deceased.

Weathervanes were very important to the early colonists, since many of their occupations depended on the weather. Vanes were at first handcrafted of wood or shaped metal in either silhouette or three-dimensional forms. By the mid-19th century, most vanes were made in factories, where improved technology eventually made all handwork unnecessary.

Trade signs or figures, appearing in nearly every town, had to be both eye-catching and self-explanatory because most people could not read. The cigar-store Indian met these requirements perfectly, since Indians had come to be associated with tobacco. As literacy rose, flat painted signs with written messages also became prevalent.

Figureheads and Scrimshaw

Carved embellishments for ships are nearly as old as the

Bird trees. Painted wood and wire. Probably Pennsylvania. c. 1875.

shipping industry. Until the mid-18th century, American-made figureheads generally followed animal forms popular in England. American carvers then began to use human figures that symbolized a vessel's name or perhaps represented a member of the shipowner's family.

Other nautical art includes scrimshaw—articles fashioned from whale teeth (also called ivory) or whalebone by sailors on long voyages. Some objects, such as the engraved whale teeth, were purely decorative; others, such as pie crimpers, were both aesthetically pleasing and utilitarian.

Decoys, Whirligigs, and Decorative Carvings

Wildfowl decoys, which lured birds within shooting range, originated at least 1,000 years ago among the Indians in the Southwest. When demand for food, availability of guns, and an interest in hunting for sport increased in the 19th century, large numbers of decoys were created from materials such as wood, cork, rubber, metal, and canvas. At first made by hand, by the 1890s they were also being mass produced.

German-speaking immigrants brought their woodcarving skills to America, where they settled primarily in Pennsylvania. They carved not only utilitarian objects but also ornamental sculptures, as well as some of the earliest American whirligigs, outdoor toys activated by the wind. The finest folk sculptures from Pennsylvania are perhaps the eagles, roosters, and other creatures fashioned by Wilhelm Schimmel in the second half of the 19th century.

Modern folk sculptors derive their themes from a variety of sources, including nature, everyday life, and the Bible. This material is often highly influenced by the artists' memories, viewpoints, and feelings. Religious fervor motivates many, such as Edgar Tolson of Kentucky, well known for his series of carvings entitled *The Fall of Man*.

Expulsion. *Edgar Tolson. Painted wood. Campton, Kentucky. c. 1969.*

Country Household Objects

It is difficult today to comprehend the routine tasks faced by early Americans. Women's domestic duties, in particular, were arduous until late in the 19th century, when some tasks, such as making cloth, were taken over by factories, and others, such as tending fires, became unnecessary. Household chores required a variety of tools and equipment, which were sometimes so well designed or handsomely decorated that they are today considered folk art. These objects provide clues about early, primarily country life-styles.

The Early Years
Utility was the prime consideration in colonial life, and thus virtually every object had to be functional. Even so, society measured an individual not only by his social or political position but also by the quantity and quality of his furnishings and household possessions. Because England discouraged the development of colonial industries, most raw materials and many objects were imported. It is rare, for instance, to find iron, brass, or copper utensils from before 1800 that can definitely be proven to be of American origin. By the time of the Revolution, however, more than eighty ironworks were operating in Pennsylvania, where rich deposits of ore had been discovered. Most iron household goods were fashioned by local blacksmiths. Lighting devices, roasters, toasters, trivets, and fireplace accessories were integral parts of every kitchen hearth. Brass, bronze, and copper were used to a more limited extent.

Life Around the Fireplace
From the pieces shown in this book it is evident that the fireplace, called "the altar of family living," was extremely important in the early American home. Most 17th- and 18th-century dwellings were heated by a cavernous central fireplace. Pots, ladles, andirons, trivets, and other tools used at a fireplace

Compote of mixed fruit. Painted chalkware. United States. c. 1890.

were often stylishly embellished; unfortunately, few of these early objects have survived. Parlors and bedchambers usually contained small fireplaces, but these seldom provided sufficient heat for physical comfort. Warming pans, foot warmers, and certain kinds of stoves all helped warm rooms that had meager or no sources of heat.

Lighting Devices
The fireplace was a major source of light as well as heat. Until the Victorian period, lighting devices changed little; most people used grease and fat lamps. Candles were expensive; candlemaking eventually developed into an important industry, but in rural areas candles were still often made at home in small molds. Despite the introduction of many alternatives, candles remained the primary source of artificial light in most American homes until the introduction of kerosene in about 1850.

Household Chores
Cooking, making cloth, and washing clothing were time-consuming occupations that were considered strictly women's work. In general, the American diet was monotonous, and the utensils for preparing and serving food were rudimentary. Simple wooden or earthenware bowls, plates, and spoons were used for eating, and in rural households these basic forms remained unchanged through the 19th century. Many trays, coffeepots, and other implements began to be made from tin in the mid-18th century. Because tin was far less expensive than silver or pewter, tinware became very popular in the 19th century; it was painted, often quite colorfully, to prevent rusting.
Except for those who could afford imported cloth, Americans depended on homemade fabric for their clothing and bedcovers. Women had to turn raw fiber into cloth, using wheels to spin the

Hanging candle box. Painted pine. Connecticut River Valley. c. 1800.

thread, winders and swifts to measure it, and looms to weave the thread into fabric.

Laundering was particularly strenuous; women carried water for boiling and rinsing from pump or well to stove and then tub, scrubbed the garments by hand, wrung them out, and then hung the wet clothing outdoors to dry.

Boxes, Baskets, and Agricultural Tools

Early Americans depended largely on boxes and baskets to store or carry objects. Boxes were generally wooden and often painted or carved or decorated in other ways. They were used to hold anything from candles and knives to handkerchiefs and jewelry. Baskets were indispensable for many farming activities, from sowing to harvesting. Lighter and more delicate ones were used inside the house for storing many of the same kinds of objects as boxes.

Although part of the population lived in East Coast cities and midwestern boom towns in the early and mid-19th century, most of America remained rural, and agriculture was the chief occupation. Wooden pitchforks, hand-hewn rakes, and other tools were strictly utilitarian, but because of their bold designs some are today admired for their aesthetic qualities.

The Flowering

While most 19th-century country people lived simple lives, they often showed a true concern for elegance and beauty. This led to a great proliferation of folk art, beginning about 1800 and lasting until the last quarter of the century, when mass production made sturdy inexpensive objects available to every household. Most Americans were fascinated by the possibilities of mass production. Factory-made kitchenware and weathervanes replaced the one-of-a-kind productions of an earlier day. Nonetheless, creative individuals, or those artisans living in relative isolation, such as the Shakers, continued to turn out household objects worthy of being called folk art, and some craftsmen still do so today.

Pennsylvania Germans and Shakers

Some of the most beautiful pieces of utilitarian folk art came from ethnic or communal settlements. During the 18th and early 19th centuries, groups of immigrants, such as the Swedish in the Delaware River Valley and the Dutch in the Hudson River Valley, transmitted Old World cultural and artistic traditions from one generation to another. The most important of these folk traditions were those of the German-speaking immigrants who settled mainly in Pennsylvania; regardless of whether they came from Germany, Austria, Holland, Switzerland, Moravia, or Silesia, they were lumped together as "Pennsylvania Dutch." Their lives revolved around the home, and they richly embellished every object in it.

Of the many communal societies, none lasted as long as the Shakers, who established more than twenty villages from New England to Indiana and Kentucky in the late 18th and 19th centuries. Shaker beliefs led to the elimination of "superfluities" in life and in craftsmanship. Whatever they fashioned was plain and durable, and strict doctrines governed the design of much of their output. In the second half of the 19th century, many Shaker furnishings and objects were made for public sale, and thus their superb designs influenced other craftsmen and made a lasting impact on American folk art.

How to Evaluate Folk Art

The works embraced by the term "folk art"—paintings, sculpture, and utilitarian objects—are incredibly diverse. Although to an extent these types must be evaluated using different guidelines, there are fundamental criteria that apply to all: authenticity, condition, quality of design, and attribution. Here the general criteria are explored first, followed by a discussion of the guidelines particular to each material and type of folk art. Sample illustrated comparisons of paintings, sculpture, and household objects follow on pages 24 through 29.

Authenticity

Many kinds of folk art are faked, altered, or reproduced, in particular rare and valuable pieces. Fakers almost always try to simulate signs of age and wear and conceal evidence of recent manufacture. Except for some extremely well-executed examples that may fool even the experts, most fakes display some telltale inconsistency in design, material, construction, or detail that may be discovered through comparison with documented works.

Just as common as outright fakes are authentic pieces that have been altered to enhance their value: a European painting of a ship may have had an American flag painted over a foreign one; colorful pigments may be added to a piece of engraved scrimshaw; or a work may bear a forged signature.

Though not intended to deceive, reproductions are another potential problem for collectors. Their manufacture has long been a legitimate business, and most reproductions are clearly labeled as such. But labels may fall off or be removed deliberately, and then the copies may be mistaken for originals. Particularly deceptive are those reproductions that have been made with "aged" surfaces.

The best protection against these pitfalls is a knowledge of construction or execution, materials, and typical decoration. Also vital is an understanding of the effects of aging on various materials and types of work. Moreover, knowing how a utilitarian object was used will tell a collector where it should show signs of wear; for example, a field basket should be worn on its bottom and handles, and an andiron should display wear on its feet and discoloration from fire on its rear parts. Uniform wear over the entire surface of a functional piece is usually a sign of trickery, since wear occurs at different rates on an object's protected and exposed areas.

Having judged that a piece is authentic, a collector should also verify its nationality. American folk art is usually more valuable to American collectors than comparable imported examples. European pieces may often be recognized by materials not native to America or by atypical, usually more elaborate, forms and decoration.

Condition and Restoration

The desirability of virtually any piece of folk art depends on its condition. Though a mellow patina is an asset and ordinary signs of age are acceptable, major damage or excessive wear will lessen the value of a piece substantially.

An object in its original condition with paint or finish intact is, of course, preferable to a restored one. But if a piece is damaged, careful restoration will generally recoup some of its lost value. Over-restoration, however, diminishes the appeal and value of a piece of folk art in any medium. Whether a piece should be restored, and if so, how extensively, can be a perplexing

 question since it depends on the collector's taste, the type and value of the object, and the cost and quality of the restoration. In general, restoration is acceptable if it increases the basic integrity of a piece. A collector should therefore seek a restorer who has experience in repairing the type of object in question.

Attribution and Quality of Design
An artist's signature or a firm attribution to a maker adds greatly to the value of a work; an uncertain or questionable attribution is of doubtful value. It is therefore important to check the documentation upon which an attribution is based.
Knowing the identity of the artist or craftsman who created a work is, of course, an asset, yet even the best-known and most highly respected folk artists executed some unsuccessful works. A piece must always be judged not only by who made it but by the quality of its design, execution, and, again, condition.

Paintings

Dating
Paintings may often be dated by the clothing, furniture, buildings, ships, or accessories pictured in them. Carpets and other floor coverings are particularly useful; ingrain carpets, for instance, were not manufactured until the 1830s. Theorem pictures can sometimes be dated by the style of the baskets or glass containers depicted in them.
If you suspect that a painting was inspired by a print, try to trace the source in books about popular printmakers and in newspaper advertisements of the period. Identifying its source may help date the painting.
Some modern naive painters execute works on old objects, such as breadboards or trays; this practice may make such paintings appear older than they really are.

Attribution
When attempting to identify the artist who painted a picture, study such details as the modeling of facial features, the way in which hands are executed, and the placement of the figure on the canvas. Compare these details to the treatment of comparable ones in signed or attributed portraits. The work of many artists is marked by certain stylistic qualities or idiosyncrasies that may help in attributing unsigned work to them.
Paintings are not always signed on the front, so look for a signature on the back, the stretchers under the canvas, and the parts of the painted surface covered by the frame. If the handwriting of the signature differs from that on documented works, it may signal that the painting is a fake.

Alterations and Restoration
An ultraviolet light, often called a black light, will help detect alterations on a painting, since areas with added paint will glow differently than those with original paint. These lamps are available at most art-supply stores.
Works in certain mediums are particularly prone to damage and should be carefully examined before purchase. For instance, pastel or sandpaper pictures are easily damaged and difficult to repair; they should always be matted carefully so that they will not rub against the glass or stick to it. Reverse paintings on glass are also very prone to damage and nearly impossible to restore. Because certain types of cardboard and paper contain a high acid content that tends to eat away at pigments, some collectors avoid paintings on these materials. Works on tin are difficult to restore if the paint has flaked or the metal has rusted.

Watercolors fade easily, particularly if exposed to bright sunlight, and they are costly to restore. Canvas board is also difficult to repair; moreover, the corners are fragile and are easily crushed. Paintings on oilcloth often peel or flake. Paintings on board can be difficult or impossible to restore if the board is warped or the paint flaking. A canvas with flaking paint, however, may be reconditioned by applying hot wax to its back; the wax passes through the canvas and holds flaking particles in place. Moreover, the canvas can be removed from its stretchers and fixed to a new canvas backing with glue or heated wax. Such relining does not seriously affect the market value of a painting if substantial paint loss has not already occurred. These difficult and expensive processes should be attempted only by an expert. Canvas may become slack over the years, but restretching it is a minor task; wooden pegs, or "keys," may be inserted into the stretcher joints to pull the sagging canvas taut. Early frames have sometimes been backed with old boards, which can seriously discolor watercolors; such boards should be removed and replaced by acid-free board. Similarly, old matting should be replaced by acid-free matting.

Wood

Many kinds of folk art are made of wood: decoys, boxes, some weathervanes, whirligigs, religious carvings, shop figures, decorative animal sculptures, carousel carvings, figureheads, gameboards, canes, and a variety of household utensils. Each type requires a different set of guidelines for dating and evaluation, but certain generalizations can be made.

Signs of Age

Determining the date of a wooden carving or utensil is often difficult because wood is relatively soft and ages quickly from use and exposure to the elements. A whirligig or decoy that has stood outdoors for a few years or a spoon that has been in constant use for only a short time may easily appear much older than it is, particularly since a traditional design may well have been copied by a later craftsman. One characteristic of wood is that it dries as it ages, so that over the decades pieces become lighter in weight and satiny in texture. In addition, wood shrinks across the grain as it ages, causing, for instance, a circular bowl to become slightly oval. Kitchen utensils used over a long period of time should have stains or retain odors from the foods they have held; and chopping bowls should have hundreds of small cuts and scratches from knives.

Some signs of age are quite subtle. The soft mellow look, or patina, that wood acquires from exposure to air, smoke, dirt, and gentle friction is highly desirable. Though dyes and stains are sometimes used to simulate the darkened tones of an authentic patina, it is impossible to duplicate it exactly. Objects such as decoys are sometimes deliberately left outdoors for a few years to develop an attractive patina.

Painted surfaces also acquire a look of age. Original paint is a great asset, but many pieces have been repainted over the years, so paint must be studied carefully. The colors of old paint darken and become subdued, and the paint itself becomes brittle and crazed from the evaporation of its natural oils. The crazing that characterizes old paint is sometimes faked by applying intense heat to new paint, but simulated cracks are generally larger.

More obvious signs of age, such as wear, should accompany an overall patina. Paint and wood should be worn and chipped along edges, on protruding carved parts, and wherever a piece is most often handled. Old wood carvings that have long been exposed to the elements are likely to become weathered and extensively cracked. This condition is acceptable on figureheads, cigar-store Indians, and other carved figures, provided it does not occur in a crucial area, such as the face.

Dating

The type of decoration, materials, hardware, and tool marks may help date a piece. Over the centuries, American carvers have used the same kinds of woods; however, if plywood is used on a piece, it is undoubtedly from the late 19th or 20th century. Additional materials, such as wallpaper or newspaper used as lining inside a box, may help date a piece.

Tool marks sometimes also provide clues to the date of early folk art. The undersides or insides of an object are the best places to look for such marks, since these areas were usually left unsmoothed and unfinished. If saw marks are straight and parallel, the wood was probably cut with a handsaw; curved marks indicate the use of a rotary circular saw, which did not become common until the 1840s. Similarly, surfaces that are slightly uneven or have slight ridges were probably planed by hand, whereas smooth surfaces were accomplished with power-driven planes, which date from no earlier than the mid-19th century.

Hardware

Also helpful in dating are the nails, screws, and pegs used on most objects made of more than one piece of wood; other hardware, such as hinges, was used on objects with movable parts. Nails sometimes served as an integral part of a design, for instance, as the beaks on decoys.

Many early pieces were joined with hardwood pegs; in contrast, machine-made dowels were used on late 19th-century objects. Hand-forged nails made before 1800 have squarish, unevenly tapered shanks, sharp points, and large, imperfectly rounded heads. Machine-cut nails, used from about 1810 to 1890, have square or rectangular heads, rectangular, unhammered bodies tapering only on two sides, and blunt ends. Machine-made steel-wire nails, with the familiar round head and body, were perfected in the 1880s.

Screws made in the 17th and 18th centuries have an uneven spiral thread, blunt end, and only a slight taper. Machine-cut screws, used in the first half of the 19th century, have a more even thread and a round head. Modern screws, recognizable by uniform thread and a pointed end, became common after 1850.

Splint and Wicker

Although collectors should seek baskets in good overall condition, appropriate signs of age should also be evident. Splint and wicker (usually willow rods) become dry and brittle with age. They generally darken to a hickory-brown color, but this is sometimes faked by dyeing a new basket with tea. Baskets should be worn, particularly on the bottom, rim, and handle. Old paint should be worn and crazed, while dyes and stains often fade unevenly from exposure to sunlight.

Splint that varies in thickness and width was cut by hand rather than machine and suggests a date of manufacture prior to 1880. If uniform in width and thickness, the splint was cut by machine in one of the many factories that flourished about the turn of the century. A nailed rim instead of a wrapped one, as well as the use of nails or wire, is generally another sign of factory work.

Iron

It takes a good deal of experience to determine the date of iron objects because they age subtly and designs usually changed little over the decades. Early wrought iron generally has a hard, dark, shell-like rust on the surface. Iron rusts slowly and irregularly, so pitting should be uneven; chemically induced rusting will appear too uniform when examined with a magnifying glass. Reproductions are sometimes artificially rusted, giving them an orange-brown hue; this fake rust may rub off on the hands.

Cast-iron pieces display either casting seams or, if the seams have been smoothed, file marks. Old file marks should be broad, irregular, and shallow; modern grinders produce closely spaced, sharp lines. Iron objects should show signs of wear: for instance, andiron feet should be scraped and flattened, blades of tools should be thinned down from years of sharpening, and hinges should be worn. Iron objects used at a fireplace or oven should be slightly distorted in shape and reddish-gray in color on those parts held in the fire.

Reproductions that have been formed in a mold recently made from an old worn object rather than cast from an original mold may be recognized by blurred or missing details. Old paint on an iron object should be brittle and have hairline cracks from aging.

Tin

Old tin, like other metals, should be discolored and worn unevenly because of varying degrees of handling and exposure. A uniform patina may have been produced with acid, lye, or even paint or lacquer. Solder should turn its own distinctive color from aging. Older tinware will generally have thicker lines or larger dabs of solder than more recent work.

Original oil paint and lacquer on old tinware should show a network of hairline cracks and scratches, and should be more worn on exposed areas. Old paint should be brittle and may be flaking. New touchups on old paint will appear as noticeable splotches under ultraviolet light.

Copper

Copper weathervanes have been frequently reproduced, repaired, altered, and faked over the years. An old copper vane should be worn, oxidized, and weathered. Paint, if present, should be crazed. Examining a vane with an ultraviolet light will reveal repairs, such as patched bullet holes, and replaced parts, such as ears or tails.

Scrimshaw

Because they are valuable, scrimshaw objects have also often been faked or altered. Engravings or colorful pigments may have been added, so compare them to those on documented pieces. Look for cohesive designs and consistent execution.

Antique pieces will have acquired a patina that ranges from yellow to beige. New objects are sometimes stained with tea, oil, tobacco juice, or manure, or heated to change their color. Subtly tinted, plastic versions may also be passed off as vintage scrimshaw. Under an ultraviolet light, an early whale tooth will glow a mottled yellow, while a new one will often have a brown or blue hue; whalebone will glow white; plastic will not glow at all. Plastic will melt if poked with a hot needle, whalebone will not.

Good, Better, and Best: Paintings

Good

This simple portrait is quite charming and attractive, but certain characteristics diminish its value. Most notably, neither its artist nor subject has been identified. Although it is known to have been handed down in the Webber family of Mount Vernon, Maine, and probably depicts a member of that family, this information does not add substantially to the painting's desirability. Its flat spatial arrangement, inconsistent lighting, and limited palette would make it too primitive for many collectors. Since interesting accessories and rich scenery are prized in folk paintings, this child's simple dress and few possessions as well as the plain background are drawbacks. Moreover, the unknown artist failed to capture the character of his sitter. The fact that this painting is on a panel instead of canvas does not affect its value; it would, however, were the wood warped or the paint flaking, since a panel is difficult to restore.

Better

A well-conceived design and the inclusion of accessories are among the strengths of this portrait, though its painter and sitter are unknown. The figure of the girl successfully dominates the composition. The colorful rug and the guitar increase the aesthetic appeal of the portrait; moreover, the rug helps to date the work, and the guitar adds to its individuality and verisimilitude. Since guitars were valuable possessions in the early 19th century, the one shown here was probably intended to suggest the wealth of this girl's family. The fact that the instrument is cut off at the edge of the picture, however, could be seen as a shortcoming. A rich palette of strong colors is much preferable to the muddy brown tones used here, particularly in the girl's facial features. In spite of this, the characterization is vivid and the subject comes to life.

Best

This folk masterpiece is outstanding in many ways. It is by a well-known artist, Isaac Sheffield, who signed and dated it on the back, as well as identified the sitter—a two-year-old who had died two months before this posthumous work was completed. Such full documentation adds greatly to the value of this painting, as does its impressive provenance and record of exhibitions. Moreover, its design, palette, and characterization—altogether as important as its signature—are quite strong. Since collectors of folk art prize works that provide a wealth of information about the way people lived in the past, the carefully executed dress, pantaloons, shoes, purse, bonnet, and toys in this portrait heighten its appeal. The landscape in the background, though it tells nothing about the young girl or her family, does enhance the overall composition.

Portrait of a Girl with Basket. *Artist unknown. Oil on panel. Mount Vernon, Maine. c. 1835.*

Portrait of a Girl with Guitar. *Artist unknown. Oil on canvas. New England. c. 1835.*

Portrait of Mary Ann Wheeler. *Isaac Sheffield (d. 1845). Oil on panel. Stonington, Connecticut. 1835.*

Good, Better, and Best: Sculpture

Good

The archangel Gabriel, God's messenger, appears in many 19th-century weathervanes, which are silhouette or three-dimensional forms made in either metal or wood. Collectors generally prefer metal vanes because they tend to be more detailed and more durable. Moreover, because wooden vanes have had a low survival rate, those extant are often in poor condition despite being relatively new—usually from the late 19th or early 20th century.

The wooden silhouette vane shown here has a bold yet simple overall shape. Its surface, though nicely weathered, retains little of its original paint. Its handsome design is weakened, however, by the propeller fitted to the trumpet, since this element distracts from the undulating shape of the piece. Such a propeller, often placed on vanes of this type in the late 19th century, would deter purists from adding this otherwise fine example to their collections.

Better

The design of this sheet-metal vane is both vigorous and graceful. Its surface, which was either never painted or, more likely, has lost all of its paint, is handsomely textured from weathering. The metal braces serving as structural supports—common on vanes, such as this one, that have been cut from a single sheet of metal—do not diminish its appeal: these braces are a reminder that, like much folk art, weathervanes were functional objects. The sensitive craftsman of this piece, moreover, has managed to integrate the possibly obtrusive braces into the overall design.

Best

This archangel Gabriel weathervane would surely satisfy even the most demanding collector. The beautiful and exciting design is enhanced by original painted decoration that is still intact, a rarity on such an early piece. Its skillful maker cut away around the body so as to produce an almost lacy openwork pattern of wings, arms, legs, flowing sash, and trumpet. Though complex, this piece is well balanced and would therefore have functioned accurately as a wind indicator: the wings would have caught even the slightest breezes, causing the figure to shift accordingly. More than simply a fine craftsman, the unknown maker of this piece was obviously an artist, with the talent to create a masterpiece that transcends both time and place.

Archangel Gabriel weathervane. Pine and iron. New England. c. 1875–1900.

Archangel Gabriel weathervane. Sheet and wrought iron. New England. c. 1850–75.

Archangel Gabriel weathervane. Painted sheet iron. New England. c. 1840.

Good, Better, and Best: Household Objects

Good

Many kinds of lighting devices were invented or improved during the 19th century. The increased availability of candles and thin sheets of tin led to the creation of thousands of chandeliers, which were employed in nearly every American home. These chandeliers varied considerably in quality.

This particular example is distinguished by its straightforward, utilitarian design. Because of the thinness of the tin, stiff wires were rolled into the metal of the arms and main body. This chandelier was meant merely to be functional; its shape is graceless and it lacks added decoration such as punched designs. Nonetheless, its primitive quality would undoubtedly appeal to some collectors.

Better

The delicate central frame and arms of this chandelier are handsomely designed and well balanced. Unfortunately, this gracefulness was achieved at the expense of solid construction. A heavier-gauge metal and more substantial central frame would have produced a sturdier, more utilitarian piece. Nevertheless, collectors who value stylishness more than utility would be attracted to this example.

Best

This unique chandelier is, like much of the finest folk art, both beautiful and highly functional. It was probably meant to be used in a hall: the candles remained lit at night so that a family member going to another part of the house, most likely a bedchamber, could unhook one of the suspended lanterns and light the way; in the morning, the lantern could be reattached to the chandelier. The overall design of this chandelier is very appealing, and the arrangement of the convex supports on top makes it quite sturdy.

Chandelier. Tin. New England. c. 1800–50.

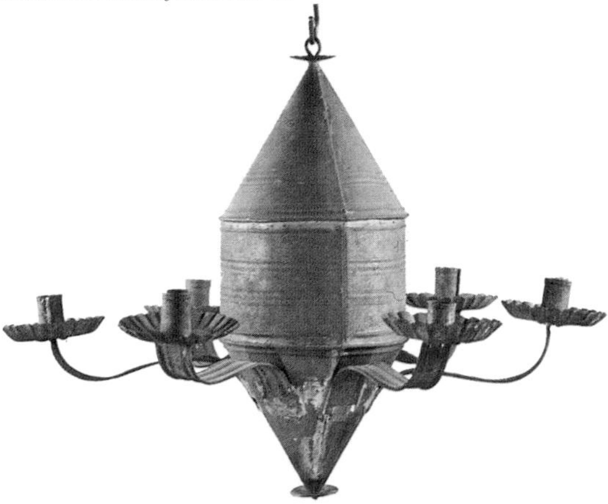

Chandelier. Tin. New England. c. 1800–50.

Chandelier. Tin. New England. c. 1800–50.

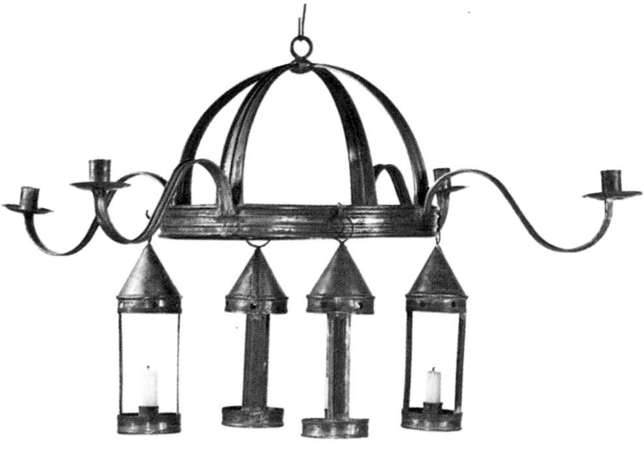

How to Use This Guide

The simple steps outlined below should make it easy for you to identify, date, and evaluate any piece of folk art you find.

Preparation

1. Familiarize yourself with the organization of this book by turning to the Visual Key. The 360 plates are divided into 14 groups, according to subject or function. There are 4 groups of paintings and 5 each of sculpture and household objects. Similar pieces within each division are grouped together, such as portraits of children or kitchen utensils with handles.
2. Read the introductory essays on the history of folk painting, folk sculpture, and household objects for an overview of the field. Also read the brief commentary that introduces the section of plates in which your piece belongs.
3. Thoroughly examine the piece you wish to identify, noting its materials, construction, style, decoration, and if it bears a signature or manufacturer's mark.

How to Identify Your Piece

1. Begin with the Visual Key. Find the symbol that stands for your object and then turn to the entries listed above it. Narrow your choice to the single color plate most like your object, either in subject or function or in style or decoration. Read the text to confirm your identification.
2. If you do not find an object that closely resembles yours, consult the List of Plates by Material. Turn to the entries that discuss objects made from the same material as your piece. These will often provide hints about dating and evaluating objects in that medium.
3. If you know who made your piece, look for the maker's name in the index. Read the entry for any piece by that artist, craftsman, or manufacturer, even if that work differs from yours in form or material. Also turn to the Checklist of Artists and Craftsmen, which provides information on about 200 well-known individuals, including many not discussed elsewhere in the book.
4. If you need still more information about your piece, look through the section of plates in which it belongs for works similar to yours.

For paintings: Look for similarities in style, execution, and composition, as well as elements, such as furniture and clothing, that provide clues for dating and identification.

For sculpture: Read the entries on those objects resembling yours in style and execution, and in construction and decoration.

For household objects: Look for objects that are either constructed or decorated like your piece, then read the entries on them.

5. Next read the essay How to Evaluate Folk Art, which discusses how authenticity and aesthetic qualities are judged and also provides hints on how to recognize fakes, reproductions, and alterations. The illustrated essays called Good, Better, and Best show how to apply the points discussed in How to Evaluate Folk Art.

Using the Price Guide

1. Read the essays in the Price Guide explaining the factors that affect prices.
2. Find the market value for the illustrated work that is most closely related to your piece in subject, style, or function.

Information-at-a-Glance

Each color plate in this guide is accompanied by a full description pointing out the significant features that help identify the work. The titles given for many of the paintings and some sculpture are their known or conventionally accepted titles; those given for household objects and some undocumented artworks are generic or descriptive. The plate number is repeated in the Price Guide and, where applicable, in the Checklist of Artists and Craftsmen. Technical terms are defined in the glossary.

Description
The description covers the essential components of a work. For paintings or figural sculpture, the most important or striking elements are described first. In descriptions of human figures, "left" and "right" refer to the subject's perspective. The description of a utilitarian object covers its general shape, decoration, and, where important, construction. This paragraph also indicates if a work is signed, dated, or otherwise inscribed.

Materials and Dimensions
This section notes the materials utilized in the work illustrated. Dimensions are always measured in inches and at the widest or tallest point. A base or stand is included in the measurements only if it is original or an integral part of the sculpture or object it supports.

Artist, Locality, and Period
This category indicates where and when the work was created. If the identity of the artist or craftsman is known, it is also given, along with birth and death dates. For mass-produced objects, manufacturers are indicated whenever possible.

Comment
Here we provide information about the history of the specific work or the general type illustrated, including notes on the artist or craftsman, information on construction techniques, and descriptions of related examples and common variations.

Hints for Collectors
These tips point out what to look for and what to avoid, what factors affect value, how to detect fakes, reproductions, and alterations, and the most reliable signs of age and authenticity. Hints are also given on caring for folk art and displaying collections.

Visual Key

The folk art in this guide is divided into 14 groups: 4 groups of paintings, 5 of sculpture, and 5 of country and various household objects. A symbol for each group appears at the left, along with a description of the types of works covered in that category. Symbols of representative works included in the group are shown at right, with relevant plate numbers above them. The overall group symbol is repeated at the beginning of the section concerning that group and in the Price Guide.

Portraits (*Plates 1–32*)
Paintings and drawings of people have always epitomized folk art. Those in this section span 200 years, from the 1770s to 1970s, with most dating from 1800 to 1850. They were executed in oils, watercolors, pastels, or crayon, on canvas, paper, board, glass, or even ivory. The subgroups are: 1) children; 2) women; 3) silhouettes; 4) men.

Landscapes and Seascapes (*Plates 33–66*)
Artists' interpretations of their environment—rural, urban, or marine—comprise a long tradition that remains strong today. The subgroups are: 1) landscapes; 2) views of cities or villages; 3) harbor scenes; 4) marine paintings.

Historical and Religious Paintings (*Plates 67–89*)
This group includes: 1) depictions of historical events, political leaders, or patriotic allegories; 2) memorial, or mourning, pictures; 3) biblical scenes; 4) fracturs, i.e., German-style watercolors of religious, documentary, or whimsical subjects.

Still Lifes and Animal Pictures (*Plates 90–105*)
Diverse both in subject and materials, the types of works in this group were produced primarily in the 19th century. They are: 1) tinsel pictures and *scherenschnitte* (or cutouts); 2) theorems, i.e., stenciled still lifes; 3) calligraphic drawings; 4) animal images, some of them modern.

1–10

11–21

21–22

22–32

33–36, 41–42, 45–53

37–40, 43–44

54–56,

57–66

67–69, 71–75

76–79

80–83

70, 84–89

90–93

94–97

99–103

98, 100–105

Signs, Architectural Elements, and Flat Sculpture
(*Plates 106–126*)
Most of the pieces shown here are flat and either painted or inscribed. These varied objects include: 1) flat, painted shop signs with lettering; 2) 3-dimensional trade signs; 3) architectural elements, such as finials and gates; 4) figural sculpture carved in low relief and painted; 5) painted or carved fireboards; 6) gravestones; 7) engraved scrimshaw, such as whale teeth and plaques.

Sculpture of People (*Plates 127–157*)
The human figure is the single most common subject for sculpture, as it is for paintings. Almost all the examples in this section are naive or stylized representations meant to be ornamental; some types, such as cigar-store Indians and doorstops, are also utilitarian. The subgroups are: 1) heads and busts; 2) religious representations; 3) large full-length figures; 4) small full-length figures.

Whirligigs and Weathervanes (*Plates 158–179*)
The whimsical pieces in this section range from simple figural weathervanes to complex wind toys with whirling figures, buldings, propellers, and gears. They are divided into the following groups: 1) single-figure whirligigs; 2) multifigure whirligigs; 3) human-shaped weathervanes; 4) animal-shaped weathervanes.

Animal Sculpture (*Plates 180–210*)
Nearly every kind of animal—from cats and frogs to eagles and elephants—has served as the subject of folk sculpture. Over the years, such pieces have been fashioned of metal, wood, plaster of Paris, stone, and whale ivory. Some were functional, serving as banks, inkwells, targets, or mill weights, but just as many were purely decorative. The subgroups are: 1) fish and whales; 2) reptiles and amphibians; 3) miscellaneous animals; 4) cats and dogs; 5) horses; 6) birds.

106–109

110–112

113–115

116–118

119–120

121–122

123–126

127–133

134–138

139–140, 143–145, 148–157

141–142, 146–147

158, 160–163

159, 164–167

168–169, 173

170–179

180–183

184–187

188–190, 196–198

191–195

Animal Sculpture (*Plates 180–210*)
–continued.

Decoys and Lures (*Plates 211–230*)

These waterfowl, shorebird, fish, and turtle images, unlike those in the previous section, were meant for use by hunters and fishermen to attract their prey. Though strictly utilitarian originally, many are now prized for their sculptural qualities. Most are made of carved and painted wood, though some inexpensive pieces are of hollow metal. The subgroups are: 1) turtles; 2) waterfowl; 3) shorebirds; 4) fish.

Baskets and Containers (*Plates 231–262*)

Ever since the Indians began weaving them centuries ago, baskets have been used by Americans to store and carry an endless variety of items. Traditional materials include splint, willow, and sweet grass, but basketlike containers have also been made of such innovative, nonwoven materials as bentwood, iron wire, and even bottle caps or cloves strung together. The subgroups are: 1) baskets with a center handle; 2) covered baskets; 3) baskets with side handles; 4) open bowl-shaped baskets; 5) containers in nonwoven materials; 6) baskets in unusual forms, such as eel traps and doll cradles.

Boxes and Shelves (*Plates 263–288*)

Boxes have always played an important part in American households, and many folk artists created highly individualized, painted or carved examples. Some were designed to hold specific kinds of items, such as tools, writing accessories or jewelry, but most were all-purpose. Display cases and hanging shelves, often quite distinctive and colorful, are also included here. The subgroups are: 1) rectangular boxes, mostly painted; 2) circular and oval boxes, some by Shaker craftsmen; 3) elaborate boxes and display cases, including some tramp art; 4) hanging containers and shelves.

199–201

202–210

211

212–220

221–226

227–230

231–233, 239–242

232, 241–249

234–235, 237–238, 257

236, 250–252

239, 241, 249–250, 252–253, 256–259

254–255, 260–262

263–270, 273, 279–280

271–272, 274–278

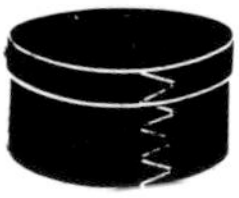

272–273, 281–284

285–288

Kitchenware (*Plates 289–320*)
Early kitchen utensils, almost all used in the preparation and serving of food, were often handsomely designed and decorated as well as utilitarian. Made of carved wood, painted tin, whalebone, or wrought or cast iron, even the plainest pieces were generally given some mark of individuality by their makers. The subgroups are: 1) bowls and trays; 2) dippers and serving spoons; 3) containers for liquids, salt, or spices; 4) molds for cookies, butter, or candles; 5) utensils with handles, such as waffle irons, knives, and rolling pins; 6) wrought-iron stands, toasters, and grills.

Heating, Lighting, and Other Household Items (*Plates 321–338*)
Most objects in this section were used for heating or lighting purposes and are therefore of metal. Carved wooden picture frames and painted or carved gameboards are also illustrated here. The subgroups are: 1) cooking or warming devices, such as ovens and bed-warming pans; 2) fireplace accessories; 3) lighting devices, such as lamps, cressets, and chandeliers; 4) picture frames; 5) gameboards.

Spinning and Washing Implements, Canes, and Miscellaneous Tools (*Plates 339–360*)
This diverse section features household utensils used for making yarn or cloth, as well as for sewing or laundering clothes. Also included here are agricultural tools, canes, and even fishing spears and bootjacks. The subgroups are: 1) spinning, winding, and sewing devices; 2) laundry implements and miscellaneous pieces; 3) farm tools; 4) canes.

289–292

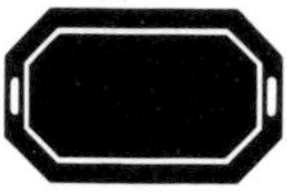

293–296, 313

297–300

301–306

307–316

317–320

321–324

325–328

329–332

333–334

335–338

339–344

345–351, 353, 359

352, 354–355

356–358, 360

Portraits

Portraits were among the first paintings created by the itinerant folk artists who traveled throughout the colonies in the 17th and 18th centuries. Their subjects were members of the upper and merchant classes, for whom such works were status symbols as well as records for posterity. The major artistic influence on these works was traditional English and Dutch portraiture.

The Heyday
From 1800 to 1840 the folk painter was a ubiquitous figure in the new republic, serving the growing middle class as well as the wealthy. As European influences waned, a more primitive, two-dimensional American style of portraiture developed, notable for its vigor and variety. To compensate for their lack of formal training, folk artists developed stylistic shortcuts, such as the broad strokes of Ruth and Samuel Shute and the pointillist dots Erastus Salisbury Field used to depict intricate lace. Shading was rare, generally appearing only on complex paintings. Having little knowledge of human anatomy, folk artists concentrated on faces; bodies often appear misshapen and lacking in perspective, and arms, hands, and feet are poorly rendered or concealed. Painted backgrounds are either a solid color or filled with conventional draperies, furnishings, and window-framed landscapes. Among the most interesting early portraits are those that include elements of social history or everyday life, such as detailed clothing, personal accessories, and scenery.

Traditional Materials
Most portraits were painted in oils on canvas, but many were executed on wooden panels or boards; still others were painted on paper, glass, and even ivory. Watercolors were also used throughout the first half of the 19th century, but relatively few such paintings have survived. Pastels were also employed, though less frequently. Silhouettes, easily executed and inexpensive, were a very popular form of portraiture; these were often embellished with watercolor depictions of clothing and accessories.

Later Portraits
With the growing popularity of daguerreotypes in the 1840s, the demand for paintings quickly dwindled. Portraits became a luxury, done by professionals almost exclusively for the wealthy. 20th-century folk artists have created portraits less frequently than their 19th-century predecessors. Many modern portraits do not depict a specific sitter. Some recent works have been created with such untraditional materials as crayons and felt-tip markers.

1 Memorial miniature in locket

Description
Oval gilt locket with portrait of blond-haired girl in white dress with blue trim, sitting on blue cushion. Holding small white dog under left arm and flowers in both hands. Reddish-brown and white tasseled drapery above and at sides. Brown wood floor; pale blue background.

Materials and Dimensions
Oil on ivory. Gilt frame. Height (without frame): 2¾″. Width: 2⅛″.

Artist, Locality, and Period
Unidentified. New England. c. 1820–30.

Comment
Early newspaper advertisements indicate that many portraitists who worked in large format also painted miniatures. In general, miniatures cost substantially less than full-size paintings since they required less time to execute. Memorial miniatures, like the early one shown here, were especially popular during the Victorian period because they allowed their wearers to display their bereavement in public. Most miniatures were executed on thin sheets of ivory, which were encased in gold or silver frames, further enhancing their value as jewelry. This example was probably painted by a schoolgirl to memorialize a sister.

Hints for Collectors
Finding a metal frame or locket for an unframed ivory miniature may be very difficult. Moreover, if the ivory is slightly curled at the edges, which is generally the case, it may be impossible to frame the piece without splitting it. It is usually best to set an old piece of ivory in a large frame with a mat, so the glass does not press against the painting and crack it. A fine original locket adds considerably to the value of a piece.

2 Dorman Theodore Warren

Description
Young boy with brown hair, blue eyes, and pink complexion, wearing red dress trimmed with white lace on collar and sleeves. Holding wicker basket of fruit. Seated on burgundy sofa. Olive-green background. Labeled on back.

Materials and Dimensions
Oil on panel. Height: 27¼″. Width: 22½″.

Artist, Locality, and Period
Attributed to Zedekiah Belknap (1781–1858), Townsend, Massachusetts. c. 1829.

Comment
Belknap painted portraits of this child's parents, using the same palette but more shading. This artist was an itinerant painter who had to travel throughout the countryside to find business, since his technique was less finished than that of academically trained artists in the Boston area.

Hints for Collectors
Like that of many folk painters, Belknap's work is uneven in quality; at his best, few artists excelled him, while at his worst, his pictures were drab records of colorless farm folk. Although this picture has great charm, the modeling of the body is careless and the subject lacks strong characterization. The fact that Belknap painted some works on wooden panels and others on canvas does not affect their value. This portrait is more valuable than both portraits of the sitter's parents combined, primarily because depictions of children are in great demand.

3 Portrait of a Child

Description
Young girl with pale complexion, pink dress, and yellow necklace. Her right shoe held in her left hand, a doll in her right. Seated on lush green hillside with scattered red flowers; broken tree trunk with hanging grapes. Ship under full sail visible against background of blue sky with wispy clouds.

Materials and Dimensions
Oil on canvas. Height: 26¾″. Width: 21¾″.

Artist, Locality, and Period
Attributed to William Matthew Prior (1806–73), Maine. c. 1830–40.

Comment
Prior spent most of his youth as an itinerant artist traveling through New England. Born and raised in Maine, he finally settled in Boston and lived his last 34 years there. He preferred doing landscape paintings and reverse paintings on glass, but financial need forced him to execute portraits. In his later years, Prior painted portraits of deceased persons, particularly children; the portrait shown here may have been such a memorial picture, with the broken tree symbolizing a severed life.

Hints for Collectors
The size and style of Prior's portraits depended on the prices his clients were willing to pay. If a prospective sitter had only $1, for instance, Prior would execute a small picture on cardboard "without shade"; $8 to $10 bought a large portrait on canvas "without shade," such as that shown here; and for $25 he would provide a finished, finely executed likeness. Collectors today are most attracted to the folk-art quality of Prior's pictures on cardboard and to his larger portraits "without shade"; these always bring higher prices than his more academic paintings.

4 Young Child with Black and White Cat

Description
Young child with short brown hair, dark eyes, red lips, and rosy cheeks, wearing red dress and necklace. Holding white sock in left hand near bare left foot; brown shoe and white sock on right foot. Seated on brown, red, and green carpet; petting black cat with white markings. Left shoe in foreground. Brown and red drapes at sides, with black background in between.

Materials and Dimensions
Oil on canvas. Height: 31¼″. Width: 25″.

Artist, Locality, and Period
Unidentified. c. 1830–50.

Comment
Carpets and other floor coverings can often help date paintings. Prior to the mid-18th century, Turkish or Oriental carpets were seldom used on floors since they were very expensive; instead they were generally placed on tables in the homes of the wealthy. A tough canvaslike material painted to imitate Turkish carpets was often used in the 17th, 18th, and early 19th centuries. Ingrain carpets like the one in this picture were not manufactured until the 1830s. These were woven of predyed wool, generally in hues of red, green, white, and, occasionally, brown. Folk artists often had difficulty depicting carpets in perspective, which lends a naive charm to a picture.

Hints for Collectors
Any well-executed folk painting is enhanced in value if it contains an attractive animal. Paintings with cats inevitably bring larger sums of money than those with dogs, birds, or any other animals.

5 Portrait of a Girl with Basket

Description
Young girl with fair skin, dark eyes, and short brown hair, wearing brown Empire-style dress with short sleeves and red trim, pale bloomers, and red shoes. Olive-green wicker basket in left hand. Standing on emerald-green base against mottled black background.

Materials and Dimensions
Oil on wood panel. Height: 34″. Width: 18¼″.

Artist, Locality, and Period
Unidentified. Mount Vernon, Maine. c. 1835.

Comment
During the early years of American portraiture, artists usually concentrated more on the sitter's face than on any other element. The face in this portrait, for example, is quite expressive, even though there is no consistent source of light, little understanding of anatomy, a flat spatial arrangement, and slight concern for the background. The hands, always difficult to render successfully, are typically camouflaged or hidden.

Hints for Collectors
For a keen-eyed, adventurous collector, an unsigned painting selling for a relatively modest price may well be a rewarding prospect for investment. Provenance, exhibition history, and any other available documentation should, of course, be evaluated before a purchase is made. Sometimes the same idiosyncratic element or technical deficiency present in several paintings known to be from a particular area or period may lead to the identification of a previously unknown artist. Since folk art is a relatively new field of scholarship, researchers frequently are able to make such identifications.

6 Mary E. Kingman

Description
Young girl with brown hair, blue eyes, pink lips, and pale complexion, wearing red brocade dress trimmed with white lace, white bloomers, red necklace, and black shoes. Brown wicker basket, with red apple, hanging over right arm; plums on branch in right hand; single plum in left. Standing beside white lattice and potted plant. Background of green trees, foliage, and rolling hills. Pink and blue sky. Signed, dated, and inscribed on back.

Materials and Dimensions
Oil on canvas. Height: 42″. Width: 29″.

Artist, Locality, and Period
Susan C. Waters (1823–1900), probably New York State. 1845.

Comment
A native of Binghamton, New York, Waters grew up in Friendsville, Pennsylvania. She earned her tuition at a women's academy by executing drawings for its natural history classes. Working as an itinerant painter in southern New York from 1843 to 1845, she moved next to Iowa and then to New Jersey. She became known for her still lifes and animal portraits, some of which were exhibited at the Philadelphia Centennial Exposition. This portrait reveals her careful attention to detail, such as the brocade pattern on the child's dress.

Hints for Collectors
This artist often included geraniums in her compositions, an unusual convention that helps collectors to recognize her paintings. Portraits showing the entire subject are less common than three-quarter-length views and usually fetch considerably larger sums.

7 Boy with a Parrot

Description
Full-length side view of boy with brown hair and delicately tinted features, wearing striped blue suit with white ruff and black shoes. Holding parrot in right hand. Standing on grassy knoll with green trees and bluish rolling hills in distance. Stained.

Materials and Dimensions
Watercolor and ink on paper. Height: 7½″. Width: 6¼″.

Artist, Locality, and Period
Attributed to Jacob Maentel (c. 1763–1863), Pennsylvania. c. 1815.

Comment
Born in Germany, Maentel is said to have served as physician to Napoleon before immigrating to America. He often presented his subjects in full-length side views against interior backgrounds or country landscapes of the type shown here. By 1830 most of his subjects were depicted at a three-quarter angle and with far more detail.

Hints for Collectors
Many folk-art historians maintain that some works once attributed to several different artists were in fact executed by Maentel, and they are attempting to trace the path of his wanderings through Pennsylvania, Maryland, and Indiana in an effort to solve the mystery. New discoveries may cause the value of a painting to appreciate or decline, so collectors should try to keep abreast of the latest research concerning a particular artist. Maentel's paintings with elaborately decorative backgrounds and delicately drawn hands and facial features arouse more interest than his simple profile figures in landscapes.

8 Young Boy Feeding Rabbits

Description
Boy with brown hair, dark eyes, and pale complexion, wearing black suit with white ruffled collar and gold buttons. Standing on lawn and feeding leaves to 2 spotted rabbits. Yellow path leading to white gate and pine trees protecting tan stone castle in distance. Lawn roller to left of gate; wall at far right. Sky in shades of blue. Signed and dated.

Materials and Dimensions
Oil on canvas. Height: 17″. Width: 15½″.

Artist, Locality, and Period
John Bradley (d. 1874), New York State or Connecticut. 1831.

Comment
Little is known about Bradley except that he painted portraits and miniatures and that he worked in New York and Connecticut from 1830 to 1840. Attributing a painting to him is problematical because he is thought to have alternated between using the signatures "I. Bradley," as on the example shown here, "J. Bradley," and "I. H. J. Bradley."

Hints for Collectors
Unusual details may make a folk painting difficult to identify. For example, though some might believe that this picture is English because of the buttressed castle with turrets in the background, such details do occur in paintings by American artists, who frequently relied upon European prints for their designs. Rabbits are also an unusual detail in American folk paintings; a collector with a special fondness for this animal would pay dearly for this example.

9 Young Boy with Toy Cat

Description
Boy, pictured to waist, with auburn hair, blue eyes, and pink complexion, wearing navy-blue coat with oversize white ruffled collar and gray buttons. Left hand holding brown toy cat with red collar and yellow base. Shaded olive background.

Materials and Dimensions
Oil on canvas. Height: 24½″. Width: 19″.

Artist, Locality, and Period
Unidentified. c. 1830–40.

Comment
Portraits are the most common type of American folk painting. Experts estimate that more than half the 19th-century portraits of children are memorial pictures, since infant mortality was quite common. Artists charged high prices for memorial pictures, often twice their normal fees. Pets or toys were frequently included in such pictures to soften the sorrowful effect of these works. The child in this picture holds a "pipsqueak," a 3-dimensional toy mounted on a kind of bellows that produced an animal sound when squeezed.

Hints for Collectors
While portraits have always had great appeal for serious collectors, they are not of as much interest to the general public. Portraits of children are usually more expensive than those of adults, and those with elaborate backgrounds or with details such as toys or children's furniture are always in greatest demand and thus the most costly.

10 Boy and Girl

Description
Blond boy sitting in black chair, wearing black frock coat and trousers and white shirt with oversize collar, and holding open book in right hand. To his right, blond girl in tan dress and bloomers, holding same book with right hand. Beige carpet with red and black floral design; tan book on carpet behind chair. Table with dark covering, book, and mementos on it. Draped red curtain. Shaded tan and black background.

Materials and Dimensions
Oil on canvas. Height: 47″. Width: 39″.

Artist, Locality, and Period
Attributed to Joseph Whiting Stock (1815–55), New England. c. 1840–50.

Comment
Stock was born in Springfield, Massachusetts. His legs were paralyzed in an accident when he was 11 years old; in 1839 he was badly burned. In spite of these hindrances, he traveled extensively during his career, and his talent flourished. Most of his portraits are set in pleasant landscapes or in comfortable domestic environments such as this one. Sensitivity and tenderness are hallmarks of his work. He frequently painted 2 or more sitters, generally members of the same family, in a single picture.

Hints for Collectors
Stock was an exceedingly prolific painter; his journal lists more than 900 pictures painted between 1842 and 1846. When an artist has left such a large body of work, it is often possible to deduce a basic list of characteristics that may help identify paintings not previously attributed to him. Portraits of multiple subjects are generally more valuable than those of a single sitter.

11 The Tow Sisters

Description
2 black-haired girls with arms around each other, seated on multihued upholstered chair in front of window with opened drapes. One wears yellow dress with red and black flowers and red trim. The other, seated on arm of chair, wears pink dress with black dots and yellow trim. Yellow curtain with red and black pattern at right, pink curtain with black print at left. Vase of flowers on red and yellow windowsill. Black floor and off-white sky. Signed, dated, and inscribed below.

Materials and Dimensions
Watercolor on paper. Height: 14¾″. Width: 12″.

Artist, Locality, and Period
MaryAn Smith (life dates and locale unknown). 1854.

Comment
Though very little is known about this artist, her formidable talents are clear in this double portrait. With a limited palette of pink, yellow, red, green, and black used in simply outlined shapes, she created an image that successfully conveys the refinement and sensitivity of her subjects. The "Tow" in the title may be a misspelling of "Two."

Hints for Collectors
This remarkable watercolor has often been referred to as "a prototype Matisse" because of its bold colors and stark modernity. The colors are still bright, which adds significantly to its market value. Pieces of such unusual design and execution, however, tend to be more highly prized by collectors who like modern art than by those who revere works with a look of age.

12 Lady in Yellow Dress Watering Roses

Description
Woman with curly brown hair, dark eyes, red lips, and rosy complexion, wearing yellow and red dress and red bonnet. Standing on lawn and watering red roses planted in yellow basket; watering can painted blue outside and red inside. Spotted dog seated behind her. Green grass and foliage; brown tree trunk at right. Cream-colored background.

Materials and Dimensions
Watercolor on paper. Height: 9¾″. Width: 7¾″.

Artist, Locality, and Period
Attributed to Elizabeth Glaser (life dates unknown), Baltimore. c. 1830.

Comment
Elizabeth Glaser probably studied in a women's academy, for her work reflects the training offered in these seminaries during the first half of the 19th century. Several of her inscribed pieces mention a suburb of Baltimore—Fredericktown—where she may have lived. This artist is as well known for her needlework and verses as for her watercolors and drawings.

Hints for Collectors
When folk art, such as this watercolor, can be attributed to a specific artist whose style is known from several extant works, its value generally increases greatly, provided that it has artistic merit and is in good condition. That a piece is by a well-known artist or is well documented is by itself insufficient reason for purchase; the quality of the painting is always the prime consideration.

13 Fräulein

Description
Woman with brown hair, rouged cheeks, blue eyes, and pink "Cupid's bow" lips, wearing showy red hat with blue plumes, low-cut red dress with puffed sleeves and black trim, lace collar, and elaborate necklace of green jewels. Black background.

Materials and Dimensions
Oil on glass. Height: 13″. Width: 9½″.

Artist, Locality, and Period
Unidentified. Probably Pennsylvania. c. 1840–60.

Comment
During the late 17th and 18th centuries, American interest in Oriental artworks reached fever pitch. The technique of reverse painting on glass had come to Europe from the Orient during the early 17th century, and within 50 years it had reached the New World. Painting on glass required artists to reverse their procedure; outlines were painted first, followed by highlights and shadows, then main figures, and finally the background. After the paint dried, a protective coat of white paint was applied, and the glass was framed with the unpainted surface facing front.

Hints for Collectors
Because of their extreme fragility, reverse paintings on glass are rare; documented examples are even rarer. Since American artists frequently copied portraits of fashionable women from European lithographs, proof of American origin can be difficult. Only those examples that can be positively identified as American will command substantial prices. If the wooden frame is original, a sliver of wood can be analyzed to determine its source by species and, therefore, the probable geographical origin of the painting; unfortunately, this is an expensive process that few laboratories will perform for private collectors.

14 Eliza Gordon Brooks

Description
Woman with blue eyes and curled brown hair adorned with tortoiseshell combs, wearing white-belted black dress with white lace trimming, gold earrings, brooch, and wedding band. Seated in yellow chair with painted decoration. Rose in right hand. Streaked blue background. Inscribed on back.

Materials and Dimensions
Watercolor and pencil on paper. Gilt paper. Height: 25″. Width: 19¼″.

Artist, Locality, and Period
Attributed to Ruth (1803–82) and Samuel (1803–36) Shute, Peterboro, New Hampshire. c. 1832–33.

Comment
Ruth Shute and her husband Samuel each painted many portraits, but most successful were their collaborations, like the one seen here. Ruth probably executed the penciled designs, and Samuel completed them with watercolors. No works dating from before their marriage in 1827 are known; Ruth continued to paint after Samuel's death in 1836. This portrait is distinctive for the sensitive facial features and the bold colorful streaking of the blue background.

Hints for Collectors
An artist's mature style is not always valued highest in the marketplace. Ruth Shute, like several early American folk painters, perfected her technical skills and produced largely academic works late in her career. Today's collectors, however, prefer the earlier folk paintings she executed with her husband, such as this example, over her mature efforts. The inscription behind this portrait, identifying its subject, approximate date, and origin, increases its value.

15 Woman in a Mulberry Dress

Description
Woman with brown hair, blue eyes, pink lips, and pale complexion, wearing dark dress with white lace pelerine and cuffs, pink bow, long earrings, and brooch. Seated on sofa, with her hands folded on top of book in lap. Column to her left; red curtain and gold tassel drawn to reveal landscape of water, trees, mountains, and blue and white sky.

Materials and Dimensions
Oil on canvas. Height: 33⅛″. Width: 27″.

Artist, Locality, and Period
Attributed to Isaac Sheffield (1798–1845), New England. c. 1830–40.

Comment
Sheffield is a folk painter admired today for his decorative style. His handsome sitters are placed in elegant interiors featuring conventional details such as sumptuous draperies and classical architectural elements. His portraits are often criticized, however, for lack of in-depth characterization of their subjects.

Hints for Collectors
Almost all folk artists were self-taught or had very limited training, and once they developed a stylistic formula, they generally continued to use it. They also tended to use the same color scheme again and again. When attempting to identify the artist responsible for a picture, scrutinize all details, including the modeling of eyes, ears, nose, and mouth, the way in which hands are executed, and the placement of the figure on the canvas. Compare these details with the treatment of sitters in attributed portraits.

16 Lauriette Ashley Adams Peck

Description
Woman with brown hair and eyes, red lips, and rosy complexion, wearing brown dress with large white lace pelerine, gold chain, locket, and brooch. Seated at end of sofa with exposed top rail. Open book in right hand, small stalk of flowers in left. Column in front of red curtain drawn to reveal landscape.

Materials and Dimensions
Oil on canvas. Height: 35¼″. Width: 29″.

Artist, Locality, and Period
Attributed to Erastus Salisbury Field (1805–1900), New York City or Connecticut River Valley. c. 1840.

Comment
Field's life spanned almost the entire 19th century, lasting a full 95 years. His only known teacher was the painter Samuel F. B. Morse—better known today as the inventor of the telegraph—with whom he studied for 3 months in 1824. Field's finest portraits were executed during the first half of his career. Like many folk artists, Field often portrayed his relatives; the sitter shown here was his second cousin. After his wife's death in 1859 he concentrated on historical and biblical paintings. His portraits display distinctive composition and palette.

Hints for Collectors
Field was a prolific painter; nearly 1,000 of his pictures are known. His later portraits do not bring the high prices commanded by his early ones; they reflect the influence of photography and are marred by an almost photographic style that supplanted his individualistic artistry. When attempting to identify a painting as Field's, look for short pointillist brush strokes. Also, examine the back of the canvas: small blue splotches, caused by his primer, will often be visible there.

17 Woman in Chippendale Side Chair

Description
Woman with brown hair and eyes and rosy complexion, wearing gray dress, white ruff, gold necklace, black lace shawl, and white bonnet. Seated in Chippendale side chair, holding book on her lap in left hand. Brown background.

Materials and Dimensions
Oil on canvas. Height: 29¼″. Width: 23″.

Artist, Locality, and Period
Attributed to J. Brown (active 1800–35), Massachusetts. c. 1800.

Comment
Brown's works are rare and not very well known. He is important, however, because he seems to have influenced many younger artists, such as Ammi Phillips. The picture shown here has been attributed through stylistic similarities to the few signed works by Brown.

Hints for Collectors
Paintings that reveal information about early American life are of sociological as well as aesthetic interest. This sitter's modified Empire-style dress, an American interpretation of a French design, was probably inspired by engravings of European fashions; these engravings were especially popular in port towns, where residents tried to keep abreast of foreign styles. The lace shawl might have been imported, as newspaper advertisements at the beginning of the 19th century abound in offerings of similar apparel. Because this is such a handsome painting, it would probably sell for a high price.

18 Lady from Maine

Description
Waist-length portrait of lady with brown hair, blue eyes, red lips, and rosy complexion, wearing lace bonnet with blue ribbon, and black dress with lace collar held by brooch. Right hand holding red object to breast. Brown background. Signed and dated on stretcher.

Materials and Dimensions
Oil on canvas. Height: 30½″. Width: 25″.

Artist, Locality, and Period
John Brewster, Jr. (1766–1854), Maine. 1820.

Comment
A deaf-mute from birth, Brewster was an itinerant painter who left his hometown of Hampton, Connecticut, in 1846 and traveled throughout that state as well as Massachusetts, New Hampshire, and Maine over a period of nearly 50 years. He is best known for his portraits and miniatures, which display fine brushwork, clarity of vision, and sensitive characterization.

Hints for Collectors
A painting is always more valuable when it is signed and dated. Not all painters signed their canvases on the front, so it is wise to check the stretchers and the back of a painting; Brewster, for instance, frequently penciled his name on the top stretcher, as on this portrait. The signature sometimes provides a clue to a faked painting, so always compare the handwriting with that on other works by the artist. A collector should obtain a written guarantee of authenticity from the dealer when purchasing a painting as expensive as this portrait.

19 Old Woman

Description
Elderly woman with blue eyes and pale complexion, wearing black dress and bow over white blouse, and frilly white bonnet with gray ribbon. Seated in wooden chair. Gray background.

Materials and Dimensions
Pastel on cardboard. Height: 25½″. Width: 18⅜″.

Artist, Locality, and Period
Unidentified. Probably New England. c. 1835.

Comment
One of the first artists in America to work in the pastel medium was Henrietta Johnston (died c. 1728) of Charleston, South Carolina. Though several 18th-century portraitists are known to have earned their living by making pastel pictures, the great majority of existing pastel portraits are from the 19th century. This example is noteworthy because it includes a country Queen Anne chair with a yoke-shaped top rail, a type popular in the Hudson Valley, on Long Island, and on the Connecticut shore from about 1720 to 1850. Well-rendered accessories such as this chair often help date a painting.

Hints for Collectors
Pastel pictures are not especially popular with collectors because they can be easily damaged and are difficult to repair. They must be carefully matted so that the pastel does not touch the glass. It is quite difficult to locate a competent conservator for this medium, so condition is all-important when considering the acquisition of such a work.

20 The Gossips

Description
2 gray-haired elderly women seated in wooden chairs. Woman at right wearing tan dress, blue apron, brown shawl, and glasses. Woman at left wearing green dress and gray apron and holding book in her lap; crazy quilt draped over back of chair. 3 pots of geraniums on windowsill. Wall with door at left; at right, calendar book dated 1915 hanging from mirror decorated with feathers.

Materials and Dimensions
Oil on canvas. Height: 22⅝″. Width: 32″.

Artist, Locality, and Period
Unidentified. New England. c. 1915.

Comment
Some art collectors prefer pictures that convey a story. Few 20th-century genre paintings are as evocative as the example shown here, perhaps based on an earlier lithograph or print.

Hints for Collectors
In general, collectors should seek to acquire only those paintings that are in excellent condition. Many pictures suffer substantial paint loss, and restoration requiring a skilled conservator can be expensive. Protective varnish that has become discolored, however, can be easily lifted off and inexpensively replaced by a conservator. But restoration influences the market value of a painting significantly, since an overly restored piece will find few buyers. The canvas shown here needs restretching; this slackness can sometimes be remedied by inserting "keys," or small wooden pegs, into the stretcher joints, causing them to spread and pull the sagging canvas taut.

21 Silhouette

Description
Waist-length profile of a woman, with cutout head topped by comb and 3 painted curls. Painted ruffled collar with pale pink bow; dress with puffed sleeves and shoulders, in blue with darker blue lines, and pink and white belt. Beige background.

Materials and Dimensions
Cut paper and watercolor on paper. Fabric. Height: 3⅛″. Width: 2¾″.

Artist, Locality, and Period
Unidentified. c. 1830–40.

Comment
The large number of Americans unable to afford painted portraits of themselves were able to have silhouettes like the one shown here executed for them inexpensively and quickly. Silhouettes were often achieved by sitting an individual between a light, usually a candle, and a piece of paper tacked to a wall. The sitter's shadow was then traced, cut out, and mounted. Though silhouettes became obsolete when daguerreotype photographs became popular in the 1840s, they continued to be made into the 20th century.

Hints for Collectors
Silhouettes were cut by so many artists that they are plentiful today. Those that are signed or that can be attributed to known craftsmen are the most expensive, but many reasonably priced anonymous pieces are available. A single silhouette does not bring as much in the marketplace as it would if it were part of a family group. Furthermore, silhouettes of famous people such as George Washington (made long after their death) are quite valuable, but much more subject to faking.

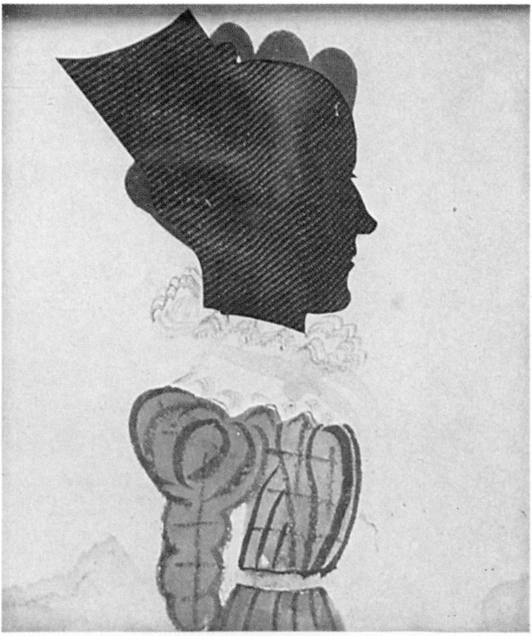

22 Silhouette

Description
Bust-length profile of a man in a ruffled collar, cut out to reveal black fabric behind. Painted hair. Tan background.

Materials and Dimensions
Cut paper and watercolor on paper. Fabric. Height: 4¼″. Width: 3¼″.

Artist, Locality, and Period
Unidentified. c. 1830–50.

Comment
The earliest silhouettes tend to be simplest—a cutout profile mounted on background paper. Another technique, called "hollow cutting," used the outer contour of the paper rather than the cutout silhouette itself; this contour was then backed with dark paper or cloth, as seen in this example. An instrument called a pantograph was often used to reduce the size of the sketched silhouette prior to cutting. Besides busts, artists executed silhouettes of full-length figures, groups, ships, and trains.

Hints for Collectors
Silhouettes embellished with watercolor details, such as colorful bonnets, clothing, and accessories, always command the highest prices. A silhouette retaining its original painted and decorated frame is most desirable. Because silhouettes are easily faked, a frame should be examined to see if its backing has been removed. Additional nail holes where the backing has been nailed into the frame may well indicate that the silhouette previously has been opened and tampered with.

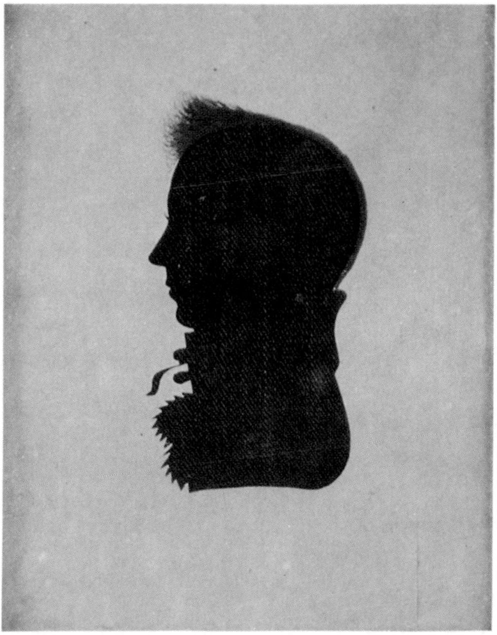

23 Archer Payne, Jr.

Description
Man with black hair, brown eyes, and ruddy complexion, wearing greenish-brown coat, black trousers, and white vest and jabot. Holding brown rifle in right hand, left hand resting on tan dog's head. Dead brown squirrel lying near large black hat. Brown tree trunk at right. Pink and blue cloudy sky.

Materials and Dimensions
Oil on canvas. Height: 41¾″. Width: 35¾″.

Artist, Locality, and Period
Attributed to the Payne Limner (life dates unknown), Goochland County, Virginia. c. 1791.

Comment
Very little is known about the man who is today identified only as the Payne Limner (early painters were called limners). 10 paintings of various members of the Archer Payne family have been handed down in the Payne family and have been attributed to a single artist who, for want of a signature, has been named after this family. In their diaries, several members of the Payne family refer to this artist's talents as well as his fondness of alcohol. His subjects tend to be imbued with a look of kindness and tranquillity. His portraits uniformly maintain a pleasing palette, and his technical abilities seem superior to those of most of the limners of his time.

Hints for Collectors
Documented 18th-century American folk paintings from the South are very rare and valuable, and those backed up with specific information about the sitter and his personality bring particularly high prices. This painting would undoubtedly appeal to a collector who is a hunter.

24 John Jackson

Description
Man with graying hair and sideburns, brown eyes, lined forehead, and ruddy complexion, wearing black coat, gray and black vest, and white shirt and cravat. Brown background. Signed and dated in pencil.

Materials and Dimensions
Oil on board. Height: 21⅜". Width: 16⅜".

Artist, Locality, and Period
Sheldon Peck (1797–1868), Vermont. c. 1820.

Comment
Peck was a self-taught artist whose earliest paintings were done in Vermont. His palette brightened after 1828, when he moved to New York State. Later he settled in Illinois, then still a frontier; here he became a wealthy landowner but continued to paint. He repeatedly used several decorative motifs, such as the rabbit's-paw design seen on the vest of the man in this painting. He worked quickly but paid great attention to detail; his technique is marked by long brush strokes flanked by shorter ones. This very early portrait displays his simple style and characteristic use of large areas of solid color.

Hints for Collectors
Peck is one of America's great masters of folk art. His style changed considerably over the years, and collectors prefer works from certain periods. The simple early portraits from Vermont, often painted on board as is this example, are not as popular as his paintings from New York and Illinois, which are generally larger and done on board or canvas. His last and by far most complex pictures, often including several members of a family, are generally painted on canvas and are most sought after.

25 Man with a Pipe

Description
Balding man with white hair, blue eyes, and ruddy complexion, wearing black robe with rolled collar and high-necked white stock. Holding white pipe in right hand and draping right arm over top of red chair; left hand inserted under coat at chest. Black background.

Materials and Dimensions
Oil on canvas. Height: 30″. Width: 24″.

Artist, Locality, and Period
Attributed to Ammi Phillips (1788–1865), Connecticut, Massachusetts, or New York. c. 1830.

Comment
Ammi Phillips is known to have worked in 3 distinct styles. His early paintings, dating approximately from 1812 to 1819, reveal a light, colorful palette and simple charm. By contrast, his portraits of the 1820s and early 1830s, such as this example, are marked by rigid poses, severe facial expressions, and somber colors. His works from after 1835 again show a more graceful stylization and richer tonalities. Phillips always paid close attention to detail; his rendering of fabric is particularly striking. While their poses are often awkward or stylized, his sitters are given a certain nobility. Backgrounds are almost always plain.

Hints for Collectors
Though almost unknown before the early 1960s when several art historians discovered the full extent of his work, Phillips is today probably the best known of all American folk painters. About 500 of his works have been identified, and more will certainly be attributed to him in the future. His portraits from his earliest period are among the most valuable of any folk paintings.

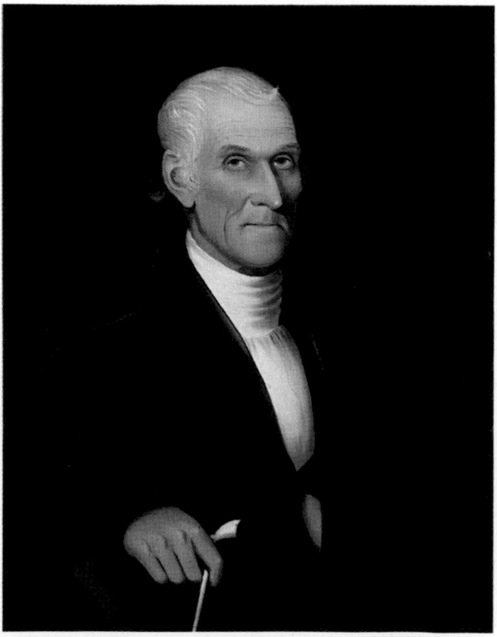

26 Reverend Ebenezer Gay, Sr.

Description
Man with dark eyes and thick eyebrows, wearing clerical garb of black frock, white collar, and white shoulder-length wig. Holding red book in right hand. Background of tasseled red-brown drapery and shelves of books.

Materials and Dimensions
Oil on canvas. Height: 38″. Width: 29″.

Artist, Locality, and Period
Attributed to Winthrop Chandler (1747–90), Suffield, Connecticut. 1773.

Comment
Chandler, best known for his stylish portraits and overmantels, was also a skilled carver, gilder, and illustrator. One of his first and most important commissions was the portrayal of Reverend Ebenezer Devotion, who, like the clergyman seen here, was shown against a background of books, a device characteristic of Chandler's work. Although an active artist, Chandler suffered financial difficulties during the final 15 years of his life and is thought to have repaid debts to family members with portraits.

Hints for Collectors
Few 18th-century paintings are attributable to a specific artist. When a handsome work by a well-known painter reaches the marketplace, it almost always arouses great interest and fetches a high price at auction. Chandler's paintings, although unsigned, may be attributed on the basis of stylistic similarities to documented works. Also characteristic are the full-face or slightly turned position of the sitter and the presence of a symbolic object, such as a sword for a military man. Many are framed in plain black molding, often with gilded decoration.

27 Sea Captain

Description
Sea captain with dark chinstrap beard, hair, and eyes, wearing black tie and frock coat and white shirt; gold watch fob hanging across chest. Red and gold telescope cradled in arm. Shipboard setting, with rigging at left. Distant sailing ships and shoreline under blue sky with orange sunset.

Materials and Dimensions
Oil on canvas. Height: 27⅛″. Width: 22¼″.

Artist, Locality, and Period
Attributed to Sturtevant J. Hamblen (active 1830–56), Massachusetts. c. 1830.

Comment
This artist was the youngest of 4 brothers descended from a line of New England artisans; his grandfather and father were both painters. Because photographers had begun to usurp the role of portrait painters, in 1856 he started a haberdashery with an older brother.

Hints for Collectors
Portraits frequently include objects related to the personal or professional life of their subjects. The telescope and nautical background in this portrait indicate that its unidentified sitter was a sea captain. It is often difficult to distinguish Hamblen's portraits from those by his more famous brother-in-law, William Matthew Prior, because Hamblen studied with Prior and acquired some of his stylistic characteristics, and because both artists seldom signed their works. Hamblen's portraits, however, often lack the academic polish of many of Prior's works. To compensate for his artistic limitations and to justify his prices, Hamblen included many personal effects and great amounts of detail on large canvases.

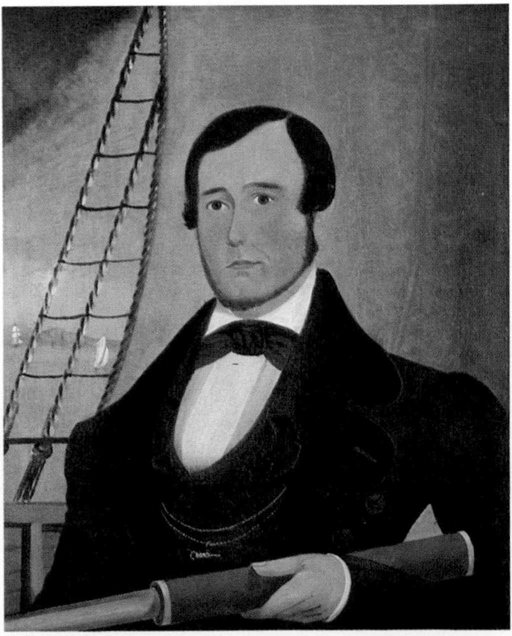

28 Captain Sylvanus Sampson

Description
Man with gray eyes and brown hair, wearing black frock coat and white jabot. Left hand inside coat at waist; right hand holding calipers. Background of brown and green drapery and window opening onto marine view of sailing vessel under cloudy blue sky. Accompanied by signed bill of sale.

Materials and Dimensions
Oil on canvas. Height: 37″. Width: 25″.

Artist, Locality, and Period
Rufus Hathaway (1770–1822), Duxbury, Massachusetts. 1793.

Comment
Hathaway was an itinerant New England painter until he married Judith Winsor in 1795 and became a physician in order to provide for his family. He painted sporadically thereafter, and only 20 or so works, mostly portraits and miniatures, are known. During the year that Hathaway painted Captain Sampson, he executed a portrait of Sampson's father-in-law that was almost identical in pose, dress, and background. Though much of Hathaway's work is crude, boldness of design, as shown in this example, distinguishes his paintings.

Hints for Collectors
Hathaway's work has a strength of characterization prized by collectors of early folk paintings. That the subject of this portrait was a sea captain is indicated by a sailing ship seen through the window in the background. This conventional symbolic representation of profession appeals to some collectors, who are usually willing to pay handsomely for paintings with it.

29 Gentleman Seated Between Tables

Description
Man with dark hair and pale complexion, wearing black frock coat, white shirt, and blue collar. Right hand folded over left hand holding book. Seated in brown chair between 2 tables and painted only to waist level. Small brown table topped by blue cloth and books at right; black table with books and inkwell at left. Plain background.

Materials and Dimensions
Watercolor and pencil on paper. Height: 7⅞″. Width: 7⅞″.

Artist, Locality, and Period
Attributed to Jane A. Davis (active 1827–55), New England. c. 1840.

Comment
One of many watercolor artists in New England during the 1830s and 1840s, Davis worked mostly in Rhode Island and Connecticut. This is one of her most complex paintings. The odd spatial arrangement of the sitter between 2 tables and the use of empty space beneath him give this picture an unusual charm. Davis also occasionally painted ivory miniatures.

Hints for Collectors
Never dismiss a work of art because it is different from pieces that are more familiar. Davis used a personal perspective in this watercolor; because this portrait is so unusual, it would probably command a high price. A dealer should be able to explain why a particular painting is important, as well as how it relates to other works by the same artist and to works by other artists of the same period. The dealer should also be able to supply the provenance for a piece, as well as direct a collector to books, articles, and original documentation bearing on the painter and the painting.

30 Frank Peters, the Tailor

Description
Elderly man with white hair, black-rimmed glasses, blue eyes, swarthy complexion, and stern expression, wearing off-white shirt and dark gray vest. Yellow cloth measuring tape hung around neck; hands folded across stomach. Mottled gray background. Signed.

Materials and Dimensions
Oil on canvas. Height: 28″. Width: 20″.

Artist, Locality, and Period
Joseph P. Aulisio (1910–74), Stroudsburg, Pennsylvania. 1965.

Comment
Because they fail to understand the nature of modern primitives, many collectors maintain that 20th-century folk paintings bear little relationship to those of earlier centuries. The portrait from 1965 shown here is, like many recent pieces, quite similar in both composition and execution to folk portraits from earlier periods. This folk masterpiece is remarkable for its straightforward style and strong characterization. Aulisio worked in a dry-cleaning store and began painting only toward the end of his life. He first gained recognition when he won a prize in a regional show at the Everhart Museum in Scranton, Pennsylvania.

Hints for Collectors
Modern folk art generally is not well represented in museums, but there are important examples in a few public collections, such as the High Museum of Art in Atlanta, the Museum of American Folk Art in New York City, the Museum of International Folk Art in Santa Fe, and the American Museum at Bath, England. However, many major collections are in private hands; viewings of them may sometimes be arranged with the help of a local museum curator.

31 Black Man

Description
Black man with Afro hairdo and large black eyes with red pupils, wearing white shirt with blue stripes and yellow trim. White background with penciled vertical striping. Signed and dated.

Materials and Dimensions
Crayon, felt-tip marker, and pencil on paper. Height: 15⅞″. Width: 12⅞″.

Artist, Locality, and Period
Inez Walker (1911–), New York State. 1976.

Comment
Born in Sumter, South Carolina, Inez Walker began to draw in the early 1970s while in prison in New York. She was granted an early parole in 1974, partially because of the success of her artistic endeavors. Since her release, she has been a migrant farm worker in upstate New York and has continued to draw, sometimes signing her work "Inez Nathaniel-Walker." Speaking of her childlike, energetic style, she has said, "I don't look at nothing to draw by. Just make 'em myself. I can't look at nobody and draw."

Hints for Collectors
Like so many folk artists who work in an "obsessive" or compulsive style, Inez Walker has produced an extraordinary number of pictures. All things being equal, works by a prolific artist tend to be a wiser investment than those by an artist with a small output, since the former come onto the market and into auction houses with a certain regularity that guarantees continued attention by collectors.

32 Black Man

Description
Black farmhand with black and lavender eyes, pale green nose, prominent grayish-pink lips, and irregular white streaks on cheeks. Wearing helmetlike blue hat with orange lining, green overalls with white suspenders, and pink shirt with white-trimmed collar. Gray background. Signed on back.

Materials and Dimensions
Watercolor on cardboard. Height: 13¾″. Width: 9¾″.

Artist, Locality, and Period
Rance "Bone" Maddov, Jr. (1963–), Alabama. 1976.

Comment
This striking portrait of a black field hand was painted with pigments made from plants and herbs grown adjacent to the young artist's house. Because it was executed on cardboard, which contains a heavy acid content that eats away the pigments, this painting may fade or deteriorate in a few years. For this reason, many collectors will not purchase a picture on cardboard.

Hints for Collectors
Black folk art received national and international attention in a remarkable exhibition entitled *Black Folk Art in America: 1930–1980*, organized in 1982 by the Corcoran Gallery of Art in Washington, D.C. Such an exhibition ensures high visibility for artists represented in it, as well as a probable escalation in the value of their works. Inclusion in important private collections further enhances the worth of an artist's works. Black folk paintings with notable ethnic flavor are generally most desirable.

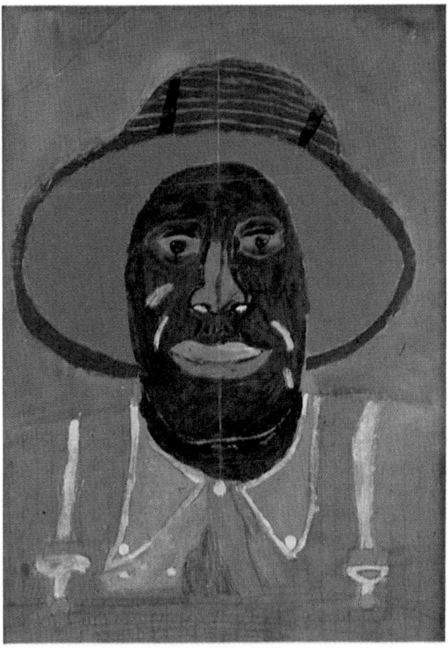

Landscapes and Seascapes

Landscapes and seascapes first appeared in the English and Dutch colonies in America during the last decades of the 17th century, with struggling self-taught "landskip" painters inspired primarily by European prints. These two genres had greatly increased in popularity by the mid-19th century, when the demand for them surpassed that for painted portraits. Since then, landscapes and seascapes have been the most common subjects for folk painters.

Landscapes
Early 19th-century folk landscapes, such as those by Thomas Chambers, reflected the Romantic tendencies prevalent in European art and in the work of professionally trained American artists. In contrast to these idealized, bucolic scenes was another kind of landscape, one that expressed the more literal, pragmatic view of nature held by most mid-19th-century Americans, who wanted art celebrating the achievements of their country. Thus, such painters as Paul Seifert, Charles Hofmann, and Fritz Vogt depicted houses, estates, farmlands, and towns, recording them for posterity in simple, honest styles. Local mills, factories, and historical monuments such as Mount Vernon were also popular subjects.

The rendering of detail was of utmost importance in these paintings, which were often executed in watercolors because of the practicality of that medium. The technique of watercolor painting was widely known, since it was taught in the flourishing schools for young women.

In the 20th century most folk landscapes have been "memory paintings," that is, scenes recalled from an artist's past rather than copied from nature; notable among these "memory painters" are Grandma Moses and Mattie Lou O'Kelley. Like the works of earlier painters, their crowded landscapes lack realistic perspective and lighting but are unified by the artist's personal vision and sense of design. The younger landscape painters of today often freely juxtapose objects or events at will, working from remembered impressions, imagined events, or even several old photographs.

Seascapes
Marine paintings grew in popularity in the early 19th century, when sea captains and ship owners commissioned "portraits" of their vessels. Many marine artists were professional painters, often working in the busy New York harbor and along the Hudson River. Although even the smallest details of the sailing ships and steamboats were painstakingly rendered, the crisp contours and often highly stylized figures, waves, and backgrounds place these seascapes squarely in the realm of folk art.

Since the turn of the 20th century, when the heyday of sailing vessels ended, most folk painters have relied on memory or vintage photographs or prints for such marine subjects as the *Titanic* or ships from the First or Second World War. Even though artists continue to execute nautical paintings and collectors avidly seek old examples, the genre is less popular today than the landscape.

33 Mural

Description
Mural detail of red-roofed white house and orchard on hill, separated from gray and brown barn by V-shaped fence. Background of pale green hills with dark trees. Tree in foreground at left with arching branches. Some paint loss.

Materials and Dimensions
Watercolor on plaster. Height (entire mural): 93½″. Width: 176½″.

Artist, Locality, and Period
Rufus Porter (1792–1884). Originally from the Captain Samuel Benjamin House (demolished) in Winthrop, Maine. c. 1830–35.

Comment
Born in Massachusetts, Porter first worked as a shoemaker's apprentice and later as a house and sign painter, primarily in Maine. In 1816, he became an itinerant portrait painter, traveling as far south as Virginia. His works include silhouettes, portraits, landscapes, and large murals. A true renaissance man, Porter was also an author and editor; he founded *Scientific American* magazine, taught drumming, managed a dancing school, and worked as an inventor, drawing up plans for a horseless carriage and a "flying ship."

Hints for Collectors
Porter murals are scattered throughout northern New England, many still in the buildings in which they were executed; they command substantial prices because few come onto the market. Old murals are occasionally discovered when wallpaper is removed. Specialists can remove murals from the original sites and reinstall them in new dwellings or museums, but the process is difficult and costly, so anyone contemplating such a project should obtain an estimate beforehand.

34 River View

Description
River with small white sailboat. Grassy knoll in foreground, with bare brown tree, evergreens, autumnal foliage, and shrubs. Brown cliffs in background at right. Pastel-blue sky with variegated clouds.

Materials and Dimensions
Oil on artist's board. Height: 8⅛". Width: 7⅞".

Artist, Locality, and Period
Unidentified. The Northeast. c. 1850–80.

Comment
It is often easy to confuse modest efforts by "Sunday painters" with those of true folk artists. Folk painters, however, usually have a force and vitality seldom achieved by most of their semiprofessional colleagues. The painting shown here falls into the first category, for it is not quite an academic painting nor is it truly a folk painting. Nonetheless, it might well be of interest in the marketplace, for not all collectors limit themselves to true folk art.

Hints for Collectors
Collectors' tastes vary considerably, so that a picture that does not suit one group may appeal to another. A painting such as this one—bought for a few dollars at a house sale in Maine—would not interest most serious folk art collectors but may attract general collectors. It is of prime importance to select a painting that you will be happy to live with, even if you hope eventually to resell it.

35 Romantic Landscape

Description
Brown castle on rocky shore, with blue and green foliage in front. At left, 2 large trees with gnarled roots. Man and woman at water's edge in foreground. Blue mountains in distance. White cumulus clouds in blue sky. Stained at top.

Materials and Dimensions
Watercolor on paper. Height: 15⅞". Width: 20".

Artist, Locality, and Period
Unidentified. Vicinity of Sturbridge, Massachusetts. c. 1830–50.

Comment
Academies or seminaries for women flourished after the American Revolution and throughout the 19th century. These schools trained students in pursuits thought suitable for young women. This landscape is typical of the European-inspired romantic paintings created in such institutions. Landscapes similar in design and execution have been discovered in central Massachusetts, suggesting that they originated in the same local finishing school.

Hints for Collectors
While this modest watercolor and others like it, probably painted by a group of associated artists, are generally of great interest to art historians, collectors are seldom particularly enthusiastic about them. A painting does not necessarily increase in value because, like this landscape, it has been extensively published or written about. However, if it is a major piece, its value will be significantly enhanced if it is included in important publications.

36 Hunters in a Hudson River Landscape

Description
Dramatically lit landscape at sunset, diagonally bisected by tree-lined gorge, with yellow hotel, the Catskill Mountain House, in mountainous background. 2 hunters on narrow promontory in foreground; standing hunter in yellow coat, blue trousers, and brown hat, with gun in right hand; seated hunter in red coat and brown hat. River in background. Pink clouds in blue sky.

Materials and Dimensions
Oil on canvas. Height: 18″. Width: 24″.

Artist, Locality, and Period
Attributed to Thomas Chambers (c. 1808–65), New York. c. 1840.

Comment
Chambers was born in England but came to America in 1832. He painted landscapes from 1834 until his death. Although he occasionally based his work on other artists' renditions or on contemporary engravings, he added personal touches such as bold colors and broad brushstrokes. The painting shown here illustrates this: the building on the cliff, called the Catskill Mountain House, had been depicted at virtually the same angle in an 1825 painting by Thomas Cole, and the same general theme had been explored by Jasper Francis Cropsey and others.

Hints for Collectors
Best known as a marine painter, Chambers's harbor views and riverscapes are among his most highly sought-after works. He is particularly admired for his dramatic and skillful treatment of light and shadow, as in this painting. Since he used nearly identical figures in many of his paintings, their presence may help to attribute an unidentified example.

37 View of the Genesee Falls When Sam Patch Took His Last Leap in 1829

Description
Waterfalls with city behind, including church towers, mills, covered bridge, trees, and houses. Small man at right, with arms outstretched, about to leap from platform built on land between falls. River in foreground. Sky with streaks of clouds. Title inscribed below.

Materials and Dimensions
Charcoal on sandpaper, or marble-dust paper. Height: 13″. Width: 18¼″.

Artist, Locality, and Period
Unidentified. Probably Rochester, New York. c. 1829–60.

Comment
Sam Patch, the subject of this sandpaper drawing, was a famous 19th-century falls jumper. Barely visible in the upper right-hand corner, he is poised a moment before his death during an exhibition jump at Genesee Falls in Rochester, New York, in 1829. Pictures detailing 18th- or 19th-century daily life or historical events are always of interest, and the whimsical quality of this particular work makes it irresistible.

Hints for Collectors
Collectors are always attracted to pictures of this type and are generally willing to pay a premium for them. Of special interest in this example is the rich detail of the town in the background: a covered bridge spans the river, and numerous mills and granaries line the water's edge, taking advantage of water-generated power. Such historical details always enhance a painting's desirability. Be careful when removing old protective glass from a sandpaper drawing, since part of the design may have adhered to the glass.

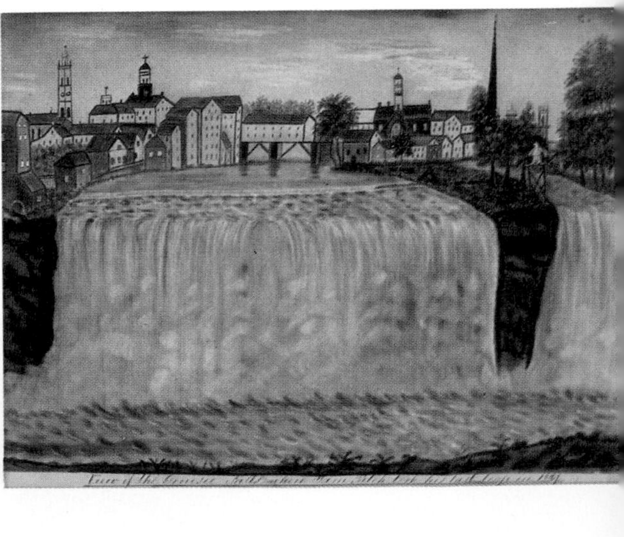

38 Slater Mill

Description
5 buildings on left forming angle with spillway on right. Brown stone building, followed by 2 white and 2 tan buildings, one with cupola. Dark river; dark green trees with sunlit tops. Pale blue sky with puffy clouds.

Materials and Dimensions
Oil on canvas. Height: 20″. Width: 27″.

Artist, Locality, and Period
Unidentified. Pawtucket, Rhode Island. c. 1873.

Comment
Cotton fabric was manufactured at Slater Mill, one of the many textile factories that sprang up in small towns in New England during the 19th century. Textile production was a mainstay of the local economy, and a mill was therefore a landmark worthy of being the subject of a painting. Many wealthy mill owners commissioned paintings of their buildings or of themselves. The unidentified creator of this work distinguished himself from other folk painters by the skillful way he drew attention to the light source and showed reflections of the sunlit treetops in the water.

Hints for Collectors
Local museums and historical societies are likely to be particularly interested in paintings of regional industry; the richer the detail, the more valuable the picture. The artistic merit of such pieces, however, may vary widely, and collectors should choose paintings that are aesthetically pleasing as well as historically informative.

39 Oswego Starch Factory

Description
View of red and blue factory buildings with red smokestacks and white roofs. Center railroad track with black train. Green trees, tan roads, and horses and buggies. River at left. City buildings and hills in background. Inscribed across bottom.

Materials and Dimensions
Watercolor and ink on woven paper. Height: 36⅛". Width: 53¼".

Artist, Locality, and Period
Unidentified. New York State. c. 1848–70.

Comment
Industrialists and businessmen in the 19th century occasionally documented their success by commissioning large paintings of their factories and other buildings, done on canvas, paper, or zinc. These paintings, particularly the watercolors on paper, were difficult to execute because they required a precision many folk artists could not achieve. Watercolor paintings of this size and quality are rare, since such large sheets of high-quality paper were not readily available in most areas. This example may have been a trade sign or decoration in a factory office.

Hints for Collectors
Because they were often framed without glass or were used as signs in sunny windows, most large architectural watercolors are faded or damaged. Seek examples with bright colors. Watercolors may be restored even if substantial portions of the paper are missing, but this is an expensive process and requires the talents of an expert. Before selecting a restorer, ask him to show you samples of his work or to provide names of previous clients or other references.

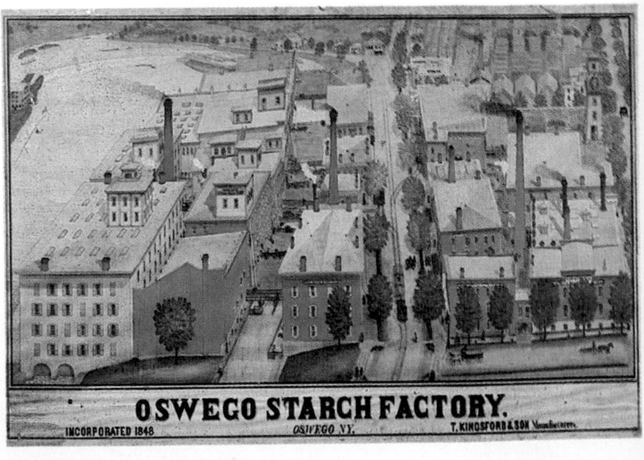

40 View of the Schuylkill County Almshouse Property

Description
Almshouse property with red residences to right of road, and yellow farm buildings, 2 blue and brown houses, and orchard to left; some buildings topped by white cupolas. Horses and wagon on road; people near intersection. White picket fences surround fields. White clouds in blue sky. Shield with stars and stripes at top center, and inscription "THE UNION FOREVER" below it. Painted border. Title and inscription along bottom. Signed and dated.

Materials and Dimensions
Oil on canvas. Height: 30″. Width: 41¾″.

Artist, Locality, and Period
Charles C. Hofmann (1821–82), Schuylkill County, Pennsylvania. 1881.

Comment
Hofmann emigrated from Germany in 1860 and settled in Reading, Pennsylvania. He often portrayed the almshouses to which he committed himself because of a drinking problem. He worked on canvas and after 1877 on zinc-coated tin as well. Though his painting career spanned more than 15 years, he remained a vagrant all his life and was in constant financial difficulty due primarily to his alcoholism.

Hints for Collectors
Paintings of almshouses are especially popular with a certain group of collectors today and usually create much excitement when they come onto the market. Collecting tastes change from decade to decade, however, and these shifts affect market value. The paintings that Hofmann executed on tin may be especially difficult to restore if the paint is flaking or the metal rusted.

41 Residence of Lemuel Cooper

Description
Farmstead with brown house, yellow barn, and several outbuildings surrounded by yellow and beige farm lands. In foreground, man driving horse-drawn hay wagon, another on hay rake; hunter and dog nearby. Grazing cattle. Dark green trees on pale green hills in distance; flag on hill at right. Blue clouds in streaked sky. Inscribed, signed, and dated along bottom.

Materials and Dimensions
Watercolor, oil, and tempera over pencil on woven paper. Height: 21⅞″. Width: 28″.

Artist, Locality, and Period
Paul A. Seifert (1840–1921), Plain, Wisconsin. 1879.

Comment
From the 1870s to 1915, the German-born watercolor artist Paul Seifert recorded in great detail many of the farmsteads near his home in Wisconsin. Because he preferred glowing metallic paints for details such as the sun and clouds, he often worked on cardboard or paper rather than on canvas. The mixed mediums give his pictures an added dimension and a luminescence rarely seen in folk paintings.

Hints for Collectors
Seifert displayed a clarity of vision seldom equaled in American landscape painting. He achieved this effect through carefully selected colors, the use of mixed mediums, and a remarkable attention to detail. His paintings are also much admired for what they tell us about midwestern farm life. All of these qualities combine to make Seifert's works extremely popular with collectors and therefore costly.

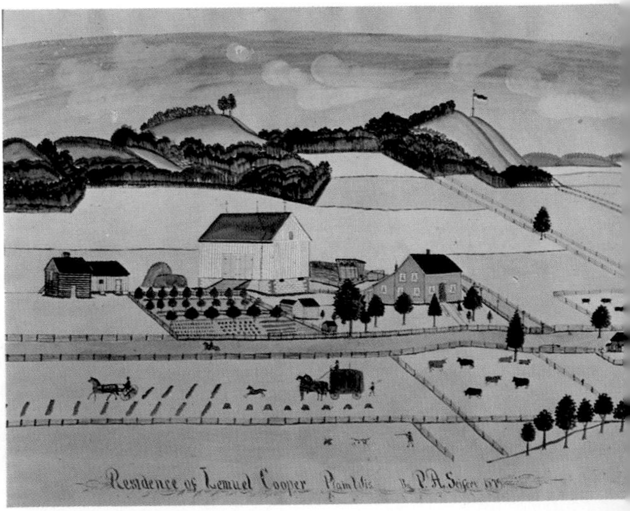

42 Residence of Mr. and Mrs. John H. Abel

Description
Farmstead with orange barn and small outbuildings at left of road; at right, 2-story white wooden house with green shutters, slate roof, 4 chimneys, and porch. Beehives to right of house. Lawn with people and animals; stone fence near road, with horse-drawn wagon. Trees mostly in background. Pale sky with suggestion of clouds. Signed, dated, and inscribed.

Materials and Dimensions
Crayon and pencil on paper. Height: 17½". Width: 23¾".

Artist, Locality, and Period
Fritz G. Vogt (active 1850–1900), Stone Arabia, New York. 1894.

Comment
Vogt worked in and around Albany, New York, during the last decade of the 19th century. He specialized in farmstead views, often recording the buildings in great detail and sometimes excluding or merely sketching in people and animals. He frequently used a straightedge to achieve a striking linear effect in his work.

Hints for Collectors
Admired for his skill as a graphic artist, Vogt worked in pen or pencil on paper, only occasionally embellishing his drawings with crayon or watercolor; those with color generally sell for double or triple the price of comparable black-and-white works. An original frame may be backed with old boards, which should be removed and replaced by the acid-free board available at art-supply stores.

43 Street Scene

Description
Turn-of-the-century view of New York City thoroughfare, with numerous figures, Broadway trolley, horse-drawn coach, bicycles, and vegetable cart; also delivery, police, and farm wagons. 5 colorful commercial façades, one marked "1881." Arching tree and telephone poles and wires along cobblestone road. Blue-gray sky. Signed and dated.

Materials and Dimensions
Acrylic on canvas. Height: 23⅝". Width: 35½".

Artist, Locality, and Period
Katherine Jakobsen (1951–), New York City. 1979.

Comment
One of today's highly acclaimed naive painters, Jakobsen grew up in Michigan and drove a small truck delivering Good Humor ice cream before she turned to painting. Some of her pictures are recollections of her early childhood; others are based on old photographs of urban scenes or on newspaper articles. Besides lovingly drawn landscapes and charmingly detailed childhood scenes, she is well known for fracturs.

Hints for Collectors
Many contemporary naive painters experiment with new paints and painting surfaces as they appear in art-supply stores. If you have an opportunity to discuss a work of art with its creator, ask about materials used; some materials are not stable enough to survive over a long period. Since a painting will fade seriously if exposed to strong light, it should never be hung in direct sunlight.

Jackson Square

Description
Yellow church flanked by 2 yellow buildings, each with lamppost to left; people on street in front. Memorial statue of General Andrew Jackson on horseback, set in park having trees, shrubs, grass, flowers, birds, and benches. Sewer and drain labeled. Blue sky with white birds flying within hollow cloud shapes. Signed and dated.

Materials and Dimensions
Acrylic on board. Height: 13⅝″. Width: 19½″.

Artist, Locality, and Period
Philo "Chief" Willey (1886–1980), New Orleans. 1974.

Comment
Like many 20th-century folk artists, Willey turned to painting in his old age. A retired fire chief—hence his nickname—he was immensely prolific, producing over 1,000 pictures during his lifetime. His oil paintings, childlike in style, are characterized by the use of bold primary colors. He also executed whimsical pencil-and-crayon sketches of scenes from his childhood as well as of New Orleans—depicted in the painting here—where he lived in his later years.

Hints for Collectors
When selecting folk paintings, look for strong designs and bold combinations of colors, for such works, regardless of age or provenance, are most likely to appreciate in value. Moreover, the style should be typical of the artist's work, as is the case with this example. A painting executed in a technique rarely used by the artist is usually less valuable. Paintings by "the Chief" are beginning to appear in museum collections and special exhibitions, which should add substantially to their value.

45 Carriage Maker

Description
Large brown building with sign reading "CARRIAGE MAKER." Open doors reveal men working at forge on ground floor and other activities above. Ramp leading to second floor. Wheel rack and wheels protruding from third floor. Carriages, buggies, horses, and people in gold-colored parking lot in foreground. Blue stream winding through green background past houses and trees. Signed.

Materials and Dimensions
Oil on canvas. Height: 19¾″. Width: 23½″.

Artist, Locality, and Period
T. Follett (active c. 1970–), New York City. 1980.

Comment
Folk paintings depicting early tradesmen appeal strongly to some collectors. This modern picture shows a carriage shop, where horse-drawn vehicles were produced and repaired. A forge was an important part of any well-organized shop, and a typical 19th-century example is visible here. Older artists who paint images recalled from their childhood usually fill their canvases with abundant details. When younger painters, such as the creator of this example, attempt pictures of scenes they never witnessed, they frequently rely on early photographs, prints, or lithographs for details.

Hints for Collectors
While folk paintings may be a valid medium for recapturing the past, one must bear in mind that they have been filtered through the artist's imagination. When buying a painting partly for its storytelling quality, try to determine whether the artist was recording facts or using artistic license; historically accurate paintings will command higher prices.

46 Reding's Mill

Description
Brown mill with light-colored stone base and waterwheel on blue river; several people in or near mill. Bridge in foreground with seated fisherman; nearby horse-drawn cart heading down a path. Another fisherman wading opposite mill; 2 fishermen in distant boat where river divides. Rich landscape of trees and grass. Blue sky with hazy white and pink clouds. Signed.

Materials and Dimensions
Oil on canvas. Height: 29½″. Width: 40″.

Artist, Locality, and Period
Edward Larson (1931–), Joplin, Missouri. c. 1979.

Comment
Some artists today, though professionally trained, prefer to work in a primitive style reminiscent of the best folk art; they are sometimes referred to as "neo-naives." Their works tend to be skillfully designed and exhibit a sophisticated color balance not often achieved by true folk painters. Edward Larson, one of these neo-naive artists, is also a quilt designer and sculptor. The landscape shown here displays his ability to blend several perspectives in a single picture, as well as his use of the unnatural, uniform lighting typical of many folk painters.

Hints for Collectors
It is sometimes difficult to distinguish modern folk art from other kinds of contemporary art. The work of neo-naive painters is one such area of confusion and debate. Its creators are generally of little interest to folk art collectors, many of whom consider them opportunists who paint only to satisfy public demand. There is, however, a substantial market for neo-naives among other art collectors. The finest neo-naive paintings often command prices far greater than those of comparable folk paintings.

47 Farm Scene

Description
Blue house with red roof and details; yellow couch on porch; brownish path leading to door. Blue and red horse grazing in foreground near white birdbath and apple trees. Hay wagon, red barn, blue chicken coop, and spotted cow in background. Landscape of meadows, fences, trees, and flowers. Blue sky with yellow and white patches. Signed and dated.

Materials and Dimensions
Acrylic on board. Height: 5¾″. Width: 9¼″.

Artist, Locality, and Period
Malcah Zeldis (1931–   ), New York City. 1980.

Comment
Born in New York of Jewish parents, Zeldis grew up in poverty in Detroit, where her father was a "Sunday painter." She began painting at age 16, but her work matured only after she visited Israel in the 1950s to rediscover her heritage. She judges a painting by how well it "tells the story." The farm scene shown here depicts rural life from an urban dweller's point of view. Her work provides a distinctive interpretation of 20th-century life in its bold unblended colors and direct approach.

Hints for Collectors
Zeldis's much-admired works have been eagerly purchased by museums and collectors of avant-garde art, suggesting that her paintings will continue to rise substantially in value. Still, some collectors find her palette harsh in its unblended colors and lack of shading. Many of her pictures are painted on masonite, a popular modern material that is easily scratched; in most cases such damage can easily be repaired by a professional.

48 Dream of a Nudist Camp Wedding

Description
Rustic nudist camp seen from above, with naked people enjoying the sun. 7 bathers in pool at center; flagpole nearby. Couple being married by robed figure in lower right corner, near woman painting a portrait. Sunbathers and strollers. 3 white birds. White house with red roof at center right. Green grass crisscrossed with gray paths. Stylized forest with snowcapped gray mountain peaks beyond. Narrow blue sky with white cloud wisps. Signed.

Materials and Dimensions
Acrylic on canvas. Height: 28″. Width: 32″.

Artist, Locality, and Period
Gustav Klumpp (1902–80), Brooklyn, New York. 1978.

Comment
Gustav Klumpp was one of the few recent folk artists who took the female nude as a central theme in his work. He achieved critical acclaim for a picture exhibited at the Brooklyn Museum, although he had not begun to paint until he retired. His paintings have since been acquired by museums around the world. In his own words: “My paintings speak for themselves. There is some kind of action, comical or something interesting, in it. I am not fond of dull paintings of landscapes or otherwise.”

Hints for Collectors
Some collectors of 19th-century folk paintings do not respond to 20th-century works. Collectors of modern art, on the other hand, are often attracted to 20th-century folk art. Fine contemporary folk painting is rapidly increasing in value. Before buying works by modern folk artists, try to find out if any were commissioned: this suggests early interest from collectors and often indicates there is already some demand for their paintings.

49 Picking Blackberries by the Creek

Description
Summertime view of southern village, with white church and white barn connected by road with red covered bridge at midpoint. 2 parallel creeks. Several farmsteads with brightly painted houses and barns. Footbridge over stream in foreground, with people picking berries on both banks. Horse-drawn carts, animals, cotton fields, green trees and grass, and red-tinged sky. Signed and dated.

Materials and Dimensions
Acrylic on canvas. Height: 23⅝″. Width: 35½″.

Artist, Locality, and Period
Mattie Lou O'Kelley (1907–), Maysville, Georgia. 1978.

Comment
Mattie Lou O'Kelley is one of the most important creators of naive paintings working today. Her vibrantly colored, animated scenes are much admired for the wealth of detail they provide about rural American life-styles that are rapidly disappearing.

Hints for Collectors
This artist is also well known for her watercolor paintings, which are primarily landscapes and still lifes. The most important of these are her "dot" pictures, rendered in a pointillist style similar to that of the French painter Georges Seurat. O'Kelley was in her early seventies when her paintings were first discovered by the public; at the time she thought she was the only artist ever to paint in this dot style, for like many folk painters she was unfamiliar with artworks of the past. The dot watercolors, usually done on paper, command only about one-quarter of the price fetched by her oils or acrylics on canvas. Even less costly, though beautiful in their own right, are her watercolor still lifes.

50

On a Sunday Afternoon

Description
New England winter scene with large gold-colored farmhouse, red barn, and 2 gray silos beyond. Horse-drawn sleigh filled with children in foreground. Blue stream with arched stone bridge at right, surrounded by children ice skating. Children and chickens wandering in snow. Evergreens and bare brown trees. White steepled church and red house in distance. Blue sky with pink and white clouds. Signed.

Materials and Dimensions
Acrylic on canvas. Height: 29½″. Width: 39½″.

Artist, Locality, and Period
Rose Labrie (1916–), Portsmouth, New Hampshire. c. 1979.

Comment
American folk art of the 20th century did not attract broad public attention until the 1930s and 1940s. Grandma Moses and other painters who depicted scenes from their childhood were most popular. "Memory painters"—artists, such as Rose Labrie, who recapture personal recollections on canvas—remain the focus of most collections of modern folk art.

Hints for Collectors
Several modern-day folk artists—notably Grandma Moses, Mattie Lou O'Kelley, and Katherine Jakobsen—have attracted the attention of scholars and publishers. In some cases, the artists themselves have created autobiographical books in which their narrative pictures play a major role. Labrie is a well-known writer of children's books, which she illustrates with her own paintings. The market value of a painting in one of her books is usually 50 to 100 percent greater than that of an unpublished picture.

51 Sledding

Description
Stylized view, in combined perspective, of village with snow-covered slope topped by regular rows of pines; slope continues downward as a street on which people are sledding. Reindeer at peak. Village scene includes houses, municipal building, tin shop, grocery store, automobiles, and trees with snow-covered branches. Puffy white clouds in blue sky on top and sides. Signed and dated.

Materials and Dimensions
Acrylic on canvas. Height: 35½″. Width: 23½″.

Artist, Locality, and Period
Ruth Hunter Perkins (1911–   ), Pennsylvania. 1979.

Comment
Ruth Hunter Perkins, sometimes called "Ma" Perkins, rekindled a childhood interest in painting when she and her husband were running a small restaurant specializing in chicken dinners. Her work was successful from the start: her naive-style paintings have appeared in publications and museum exhibitions, and she has developed a following among collectors. Stimulated by her efforts, her husband Cy, who had always believed himself lacking in artistic ability, tried painting in a similar style. While he has enjoyed a modest success, his wife's works have been most eagerly sought by collectors.

Hints for Collectors
Ruth Perkins has a unique way of expressing what she sees. She is most admired for her ability to combine several perspectives imaginatively in a single painting and still produce a work that is visually unified, as demonstrated by the example shown here. Her work, though still modestly priced, is likely to appreciate substantially.

52 Woman Shoveling Snow

Description
Winter scene of 2 gray clapboard houses with snow-covered roofs and white trim. Woman in coat and hat shoveling snow near fence opening; dog on path to house. Another figure in doorway. Bare snow-covered trees and bushes. Distant mountains with hunter and dog. Snowy foreground and gray background.

Materials and Dimensions
Charcoal on sandpaper, or marble-dust paper. Height: 17″. Width: 21″.

Artist, Locality, and Period
Unidentified. c. 1850–1900.

Comment
So-called sandpaper drawings, such as the one shown here, were usually drawn with charcoal on paper that had been covered with adhesive and sprinkled with a rough powder of marble dust. The medium was easy to manage, inexpensive, and "artistic" at the same time. All kinds of subjects were executed in such drawings. This example is particularly appealing because it resembles the work of the 20th-century painter Marc Chagall.

Hints for Collectors
Sandpaper pictures were produced in vast quantities, so only those that are well executed, historically significant, or especially charming are valuable. They are often in poor condition, with the charcoal drawings badly scuffed. A spray can of charcoal fixative, available in most art-supply stores, can be used to make a sandpaper drawing relatively permanent; pictures should be sprayed carefully to avoid build-up of fixative. An over-restored sandpaper drawing loses much of its charm and value. When framing this type of drawing, it is best to use a mat so that the picture will not be damaged by rubbing against the glass.

53 Mount Vernon

Description
Mount Vernon on hill overlooking Washington's tomb; stone-and-iron gate at entrance to tomb. Rolling hills with trees having white highlights on foliage. River at right with white sailboats. Streaks of white clouds in gray sky.

Materials and Dimensions
Charcoal on sandpaper, or marble-dust paper. Height: 14¼″. Width: 20″.

Artist, Locality, and Period
Unidentified. c. 1850–1900.

Comment
This picture was based on a print, a practice begun in the early 18th century when European prints began to appear in America. Prints served as inspiration for budding folk artists, who freely adapted compositions and rearranged details for their own purposes. In the 19th century, when the technique of lithography had been perfected, almost anyone could afford inexpensive prints. Currier & Ives produced an extraordinary variety of lithographs aimed at a broad market. Among their most popular subjects were scenes from the life of George Washington, Civil War battles, and other historic events. The Currier & Ives seasonal lithographs of Mount Vernon and the tomb of George Washington were copied by many artists of the Victorian era, who were attracted to their sentimentality.

Hints for Collectors
Sandpaper, or marble-dust, pictures vary greatly in quality. Look for examples in which the images are clearly defined. There are hundreds of sandpaper paintings of the tomb of George Washington, so be selective.

54 Morris Street and the Strand

Description
View of Chesapeake harbor with large yellow inn at lower right. White ferry and several sailboats on dark blue water winding through scene. Shipyard, houses, inns, toll booth, and shops selling bait, waterfowl, crabs, or oysters; many with signs. Hills in distance. Geese flying across unpainted sky. Inscribed on back.

Materials and Dimensions
Oil on board. Height: 23″. Width: 32⅞″.

Artist, Locality, and Period
Joyce Basye (1947–), Bowie, Maryland. 1981.

Comment
Like Grandma Moses, Katherine Jakobsen, and Mattie Lou O'Kelley, Joyce Basye is a self-taught artist who specializes in rustic scenes. Landscapes, much sought after by collectors of contemporary folk art, frequently appreciate more rapidly than do paintings of other subjects. The artist inscribed the back of this scene with a brief history of the ferry depicted. Such inscriptions add to the personal appeal of a work.

Hints for Collectors
Many contemporary naive painters attempt to enhance the value of their works by executing them on old objects, a practice that may confuse some collectors. Basye, for instance, chose to paint this picture on a late 19th-century breadboard, which makes this recent creation look older than it really is. Whether new or old, a painting should be judged more by the quality of its composition and execution than by its age.

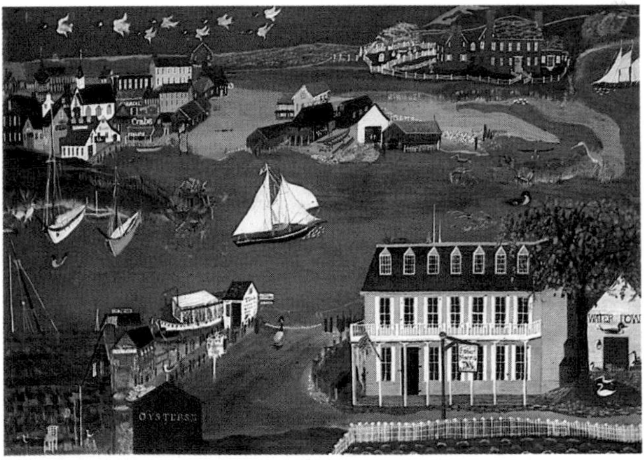

55 The Lighthouse

Description
Harbor scene with white lighthouse on distant hill at mouth of river. Shore with white and tan trees and yellow and green houses. 4 sailing ships and tugboat floating on rust-colored water. Fishermen on wharf at lower right. Birds on water and hovering in russet sky. Signed.

Materials and Dimensions
Oil on board. Height: 17″. Width: 21⅛″.

Artist, Locality, and Period
Earl Cunningham (1893–1978), St. Augustine, Florida. c. 1950.

Comment
Born in Maine and eventually settling in Florida, Cunningham was a tinker and junk dealer by trade. He owned a boat and often salvaged wood from the ocean, which he used in many of the more than 500 paintings he executed. His paints came from a local five-and-dime store.

Hints for Collectors
Most naive painters, no matter when they worked, developed a distinctive palette. Cunningham's paintings are characterized by rich dark colors with striking contrasts. Like so many folk artists, he used whatever materials were at hand. If you are purchasing an unframed picture, it is unlikely that a ready-made frame bought in an art-supply store will fit it exactly, since these are usually available only in standard sizes. Custom-made frames offer a wider selection of styles and, if well made, a better fit, but these are more expensive than pre-cut frames.

56 Harbor Scene on Cape Cod

Description
Steamboat and 3 sailing vessels, 2 flying the American flag. Choppy blue sea. Land on both sides with houses in muted colors; yellow church on left, yellow windmill and brown lighthouse on right. Gray mountains under overcast sky.

Materials and Dimensions
Oil on board. Mounted on aluminum. Height: 22¼″. Width: 31½″.

Artist, Locality, and Period
Unidentified. Massachusetts. c. 1890–1900.

Comment
Careful scrutiny of details can sometimes provide clues helpful in dating a painting. For example, a ship in the background of the painting shown here has sails as well as a smokestack and is therefore capable of being propelled by wind or steam power; since such dual-powered vessels began to disappear around 1900, this painting was probably completed before that date. Although the unknown artist who painted this harbor scene lacked technical adeptness, his sense of color and design more than compensates for this.

Hints for Collectors
During the 1950s and 1960s, many conservators believed that mounting a painting on a sheet of aluminum with either wax or glue was one of the best methods of preservation. Unfortunately, this sometimes later caused the paint to crack and fall off. Separating a picture from its aluminum backing and remounting it on canvas allows it to breathe, thus extending its life. Although this can be easily accomplished if the picture has been wax-mounted, it often cannot be done without damage if the work was mounted with glue. If wax was used, white areas will reveal a slight yellowing when examined in sunlight.

57 The Sarah Passing Flushing

Description
Clipper ship under full sail, with multicolored hull, 3 masts, and 4 jibs. American flag at stern; French flag atop mainmast; blue flag with white star atop foremast. Bluish-green water; pale, faintly cloudy sky. Sailing ships in background. Shore of Flushing, New York, at left. Inscribed across bottom.

Materials and Dimensions
Oil on glass. Height: 22″. Width: 28¾″.

Artist, Locality, and Period
Probably imported from China for the American market. 1849.

Comment
During the late 18th and throughout the 19th century, commerce between the Orient and American ports increased dramatically. Americans admired Oriental goods for their fine craftsmanship and exotic character. Countless Chinese pictures were exported to both England and America, including the now-famous "hong" pictures depicting the great warehouses and storage facilities in Chinese ports of call, as well as portraits of famous Chinese traders. Such pictures often adorned the headquarters of American merchant princes. Many sea captains commissioned Oriental artists to depict their vessels. Both the style and the medium—reverse painting on glass—suggest this painting of the *Sarah* is of Chinese origin.

Hints for Collectors
A picture's country of origin plays a significant part in its value. An American folk painting will almost always bring substantially more in the American marketplace than will a European work. But Chinese export pictures, particularly reverse paintings on glass, generally command a premium when they depict American ships or scenes.

58 Sailboat and Steamship

Description
Large black sailing ship having 3 sails and 4 jibs and flying the American flag. Distant gray steamship at right, with single stack. Small sailboats farther off on the horizon. Dark choppy water, with small island in distance. Light blue sky filled with hard-edged white and gray clouds.

Materials and Dimensions
Oil on sailcloth. Height: 19½″. Width: 36½″.

Artist, Locality, and Period
Attributed to Captain Cooke (life dates unknown), probably New England. c. 1915.

Comment
Little is known about the painter Captain Cooke (not to be confused with Captain James Cook, who explored the Pacific 150 years earlier), except that he grew up in Canada, had moved by the 1880s to New Bedford, Massachusetts, and was the harbor master of the port of Miami, Florida, toward the end of his life. The painting shown here has been attributed to Cooke largely because it was recently sold by a man whose grandfather was one of Cooke's friends.

Hints for Collectors
Paintings documenting American history—particularly those with a subject rich in adventure, such as the sailing vessel shown here—have special appeal to many collectors. The identification of the artist of a painting may increase its value tenfold or more; if a signature is not visible, the frame should be removed to see whether one is hidden under its lip. Most dealers will have thoroughly examined paintings before they sell them; inexperienced dealers, however, may overlook something.

59 The America off the Battery

Description
Clipper ship *America* with black hull, 2 masts, 4 white sails, and 11 sailors. Light blue flag atop aft mast and American flag atop aft rigging. Sailboats in distance. New York harbor with Battery in background. Sky filled with orange and gray clouds and smoke; greenish waves with whitecaps. Signed.

Materials and Dimensions
Oil on board. Height: 8″. Width: 10″.

Artist, Locality, and Period
James E. Buttersworth (1817–94), West Hoboken, New Jersey. c. 1846.

Comment
Buttersworth, along with the Bard brothers, was one of the first marine painters to achieve recognition among collectors. He was born in London, where his father, Thomas, was a well-known painter. In the 1840s he moved to New Jersey and began work on a series of lithographs, primarily of clipper ships, for Currier & Ives. Most of his paintings are undated, and though he painted for almost 50 years, his early and later styles are virtually indistinguishable. Many works, including the one shown here, are quite small-scale, making their precise detail extraordinary.

Hints for Collectors
Check the flags in ship paintings carefully, since fakers frequently paint American flags over European ones to make the pictures more valuable to American collectors. Such alterations may be easily detected through the use of a black light, generally available in art-supply stores. With their broad expanses of sky and water, older marine paintings are especially difficult to restore, because it is nearly impossible to match 19th-century pigments that have discolored.

60 The Mary P. Bates

Description
White single-deck fishing boat at sea. Brown cabin astern, with billowing smokestack and American flag flying; small forecastle with name inscribed above. Ship's name also on side, both fore and aft. White mast and rigging. 3 sailors aboard ship; 7 fishermen in white longboats floating alongside. Distant ships and land off stern. Whitecapped greenish waves; blue sky with white and pink clouds. Signed and dated.

Materials and Dimensions
Oil on canvas. Height: 25½″. Width: 35½″.

Artist, Locality, and Period
Charles Sidney Raleigh (1830–1925), New Bedford, Massachusetts. 1878.

Comment
English-born C. S. Raleigh was a mariner before settling in New Bedford, where in 1877 he began painting ships' portraits for their wealthy owners. Many of his works depict dramatic episodes, such as harpooning whales or rounding Cape Horn. He was meticulously accurate in detail, carefully blending tones on sails and in waves and delicately painting a ship's rigging with brushes containing only 2 or 3 hairs.

Hints for Collectors
Raleigh's paintings can be recognized by their distinctive style and details, such as the subtle shading of water and sky. More naive than the works of marine artists such as Antonio Jacobsen and Fred Pansing, Raleigh's paintings may often be found in galleries specializing in folk or in maritime art; their primitive charm appeals to collectors specializing in either area.

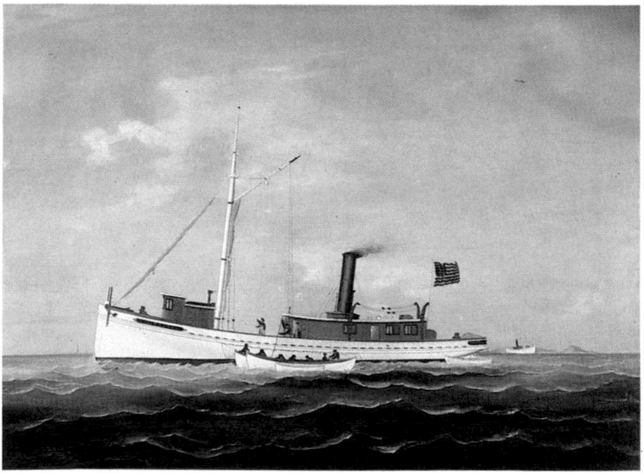

61 The Reindeer

Description
Paddle-wheel steamboat with 2 decks and the name "REINDEER" painted on side. Large black smokestack flanked by smaller vents. White flagpole topped by golden eagle at fore and aft. Prow bearing red and blue flags with initial "R" encircled by 13 stars; stern bears American flag and red flag with ship's name. Similar steamship at right and 2 sailboats at left, set against wooded, autumnal riverbank; background with mountains, blue sky, and white clouds. Name of ship's commander below. Signed, dated, and inscribed.

Materials and Dimensions
Oil on canvas. Height: 34″. Width: 56″.

Artist, Locality, and Period
James Bard (1815–97), New York City. 1852.

Comment
Bard's paintings of steamboats and sailing vessels provide an incomparable record of New York shipping during the 19th century. A prolific artist, he produced well over 1,000 paintings (about 450 have survived), which are characterized by great attention to detail. The depiction of the *Reindeer* is an exceptional example of his linear style and vibrant palette.

Hints for Collectors
James and his twin brother John collaborated for about 20 years. Since James's technique did not change after John's death in 1856, it is believed that James was the dominant creative force. Like most folk artists, he made little attempt to compete with his professionally trained contemporaries. His paintings are easily identified by their simple broadside perspective (almost always portside), naive backgrounds, stippled water, and primitive human figures.

62 The Connecticut

Description
White steamship in three-quarter view, having large side wheel and 4 levels with people. 2 billowing black smokestacks. 8 flags and banners, including one with ship's name and another reading "PROVIDENCE LINE FOR BOSTON." Dark blue sea with distant sailboats; sky in blue and white. Signed and dated.

Materials and Dimensions
Oil on canvas. Height: 30″. Width: 50″.

Artist, Locality, and Period
Antonio Jacobsen (1850–1921), Hoboken, New Jersey. 1889.

Comment
Born in Denmark, Jacobsen came to America as a young man and received his first commission to paint a ship's portrait in 1875. Like most fine marine paintings, his works are admired for their accurate detail; as the only surviving records of some vessels, many are invaluable sources of information to marine historians. The vitality and vibrant colors of his painted schooners and clipper ships make them extremely popular with collectors.

Hints for Collectors
Jacobsen worked rapidly and was very prolific, helped partly by his switch late in his career from canvas to composition board, which allowed pictures to dry more quickly. His paintings on board have a luminous quality that some collectors prefer to the flatter look of his earlier works, which were done on canvas. A work on board, however, is more difficult to restore. When considering the purchase of a work in this medium that requires extensive restoration, add an estimate of this cost to the purchase price before deciding.

63 The City of Lowell

Description
White steamship with 2 billowing black smokestacks and 3 levels with people. "CITY OF LOWELL" painted on side. Blue flag flying on bow, and American flag at stern. In background, steamship with rigging and single smokestack off bow and sailboat off stern. Hazy blue sky with gray clouds; dark blue waves. Signed.

Materials and Dimensions
Oil on canvas. Height: 30″. Width: 60″.

Artist, Locality, and Period
Fred Pansing (1844–1912), Hoboken, New Jersey. c. 1885.

Comment
New York harbor was the most frequent setting for Pansing's marine portraits, as for the works of many of his contemporaries, including Frederick S. Cozzens, Samuel Ward Stanton, James and John Bard, and James Buttersworth. After his early years as a sailor, Pansing turned primarily to sign painting for a livelihood, with commissioned ship's portraits becoming an ever-larger part of his output. He also occasionally decorated circus wagons. Later he designed lithographs, usually head-on views of ships based on photographs he had taken. The little port city of Hoboken was home to dozens of ship painters, who shared various stylistic consistencies and a concern for detail.

Hints for Collectors
Few art historians have focused on marine painting as yet, so available reference material is comparatively meager. One of the best ways to ascertain the age of an unsigned, unlabeled, and undated marine painting is to identify the design of its ship and determine when such vessels were commonly in use. Establishing the function of that ship will make it easier to locate illustrations of similar vessels in books on nautical history.

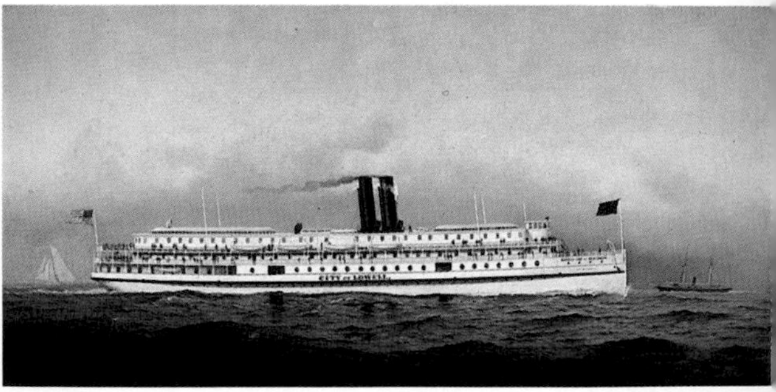

64 The Titanic

Description
Ocean liner shown in combined side and top views. Black hull; 4 black stacks trailing smoke, flanked by 2 masts with rigging. Flags at stern and bow, with name "TITANIC" on bow. Steeply tilted green upper deck with white railings and red pool. Greenish whitecapped waves; blue sky with hazy white clouds.

Materials and Dimensions
Oil on oilcloth with paper collage. Height: 15⅛". Width: 33⅛".

Artist, Locality, and Period
James Crane (life dates unknown), Ellsworth, Maine. c. 1968.

Comment
Like many folk artists, Crane did not begin to paint until his later years. Another trait shared by Crane and many other folk artists is the use of any available materials: it is not unusual to find some of Crane's poetic New England landscapes and ship paintings executed on a bedsheet, discarded plywood, or the wall of a house. His works are admired for their bold images and the way they combine several perspectives within a single view. The painting shown here exhibits another characteristic of much naive art: no single consistent light source illuminates the subject.

Hints for Collectors
Though some of Crane's pictures were executed on cardboard or canvas, more were painted on oilcloth. Unfortunately, as time passes, the paint tends to peel or flake off the oilcloth. When selecting any folk painting, beware of overly restored examples or fragile pieces requiring extensive restoration. These may be worth only a small fraction of the price they might otherwise command.

65 Destroyer

Description
Pale brown destroyer bearing number 158 and set in oval seascape. 4 smokestacks in center; 3 guns on bow, in center, and at stern. 2 masts connected by rigging; flagpole. Cabin on foredeck. 3 lifeboats. Portholes toward bow and stern. Depth-charge rack at stern. Dark blue sea. Green sky with pale clouds and large sun.

Materials and Dimensions
Oil on board. Height: 12″. Width: 20″.

Artist, Locality, and Period
Unidentified. The Northeast. c. 1918–25.

Comment
The tradition of ship painting has continued from the 19th into the 20th century. The painting shown here depicts an American destroyer launched in 1918 and sunk by a German U-boat in 1943. Its unknown artist executed it on the bottom of an oval serving tray. Quite often folk painters work with whatever materials are at hand—burlap, tin, stoneware, to name just a few—rather than buy canvases. This particular artist was probably a sailor who had served on the destroyer he painted in such detail.

Hints for Collectors
20th-century naive paintings are seldom costly unless they are executed by well-known artists such as Grandma Moses or Mattie Lou O'Kelley. The price of a painting will depend on its decorative quality and popular appeal. No matter what its subject, if a painting is not appealing, it will most likely sell for a small sum. Modest paintings like the example illustrated may be found in flea markets and at small antiques shows where less expensive folk art is sold.

66 Shooting the Polar Bear in the Arctic

Description
Polar bear crouching on iceberg, facing group of armed hunters, 2 on nearby ice floe and 3 in rowboat. Second polar bear in distance at left. Ship, powered by both sails and steam, visible on horizon at center. Grayish icebergs and dark icy water fill view. Dull gray sky with faint white clouds and pink glow on horizon.

Materials and Dimensions
Oil on canvas. Height: 15¼″. Width: 21⅛″.

Artist, Locality, and Period
Unidentified. c. 1880.

Comment
Historical folk paintings depicting adventurous frontier lifestyles are of great interest to collectors. During the 19th and early 20th centuries, for example, New England sea captains sailed to the Arctic. Their often lengthy voyages gave crew members time for pursuits such as painting and scrimshaw carving. The painting shown here was probably done by a seaman, since its realistic details suggest firsthand observation.

Hints for Collectors
Because folk artists often had no formal training whatsoever, they frequently failed to prepare their canvas by adequately sizing or priming it. When the canvas is not so prepared, it usually dries out, causing the paint to bubble and flake. If this starts to occur, the canvas can be removed from its stretchers and fixed to a new canvas backing with heated wax. Such relining does not seriously affect the market value of a painting if substantial paint loss has not already occurred. This is an expensive process and one that should be attempted only by an expert.

Historical and Religious Paintings

Folk artists were often inspired by historical or religious figures or events, with results ranging from the highly original work of well-known artists to schoolgirls' copies of contemporary prints. Some were based on firsthand observation and, though primitive in technique, faithfully presented the artist's own environment; others were imaginative renderings of exotic landscapes or allegorical themes.

Historical Paintings
Political, military, and other significant historical subjects particularly fascinated folk artists who had immigrated to America. Among the most popular subjects have been presidents —notably Washington and Lincoln—and Revolutionary and Civil War heroes, as well as the activities of political parties and factions.
From the late 18th to mid-19th centuries, young women studying in academies often painted or drew likenesses of famous Americans by copying popular prints. With the exception of these copied designs, figures in most historical works were crudely painted caricatures. Such pictures were executed not only on canvas, paper, and wood, but on glass as well, since reverse painting on glass became a popular technique in the early decades of the new republic.

Memorial Pictures
A new genre, the memorial (or mourning) picture emerged in America in the first years of the 19th century. Many of the earliest examples commemorate the death of Washington in 1799. Though some were sold, memorial pictures were generally created by young women as presents for bereaved relatives or friends. At first they were done in needlework, but watercolor-on-paper soon became the primary medium; ivory miniatures in lockets were also common. Artists relied on such standard symbols as a weeping willow and a grieving woman near a tomb.

Religious Paintings
Events in the life of Christ have been the most common religious subjects for folk painters, but stories from the Old Testament have also frequently served as inspiration. A renewal of interest in religious concerns was fostered by the women's academies of the 19th century, where students painted an untold number of watercolors of pious subjects such as the Annunciation or allegorical figures of Hope or Virtue. Religious folk painting still flourishes today, with most works reflecting a highly idiosyncratic or "obsessive" style; many are said to be based on divine revelation.

Fracturs
The German-speaking immigrants who settled chiefly in Pennsylvania brought with them a watercolor tradition called fractur (from the German *Fraktur*, an ornate kind of Gothic script), which can be traced to medieval illuminated manuscripts. Though some works date back to the early 18th century, the fractur style reached its peak in America during the first half of the 19th century. These highly stylized, vivid watercolors record events or depict spiritual themes or whimsical subjects; they usually include a verse in German as well as standard motifs like tulips, hearts, and doves. Birth and baptismal certificates, family records, and penmanship exercises are the most common forms; other, mainly decorative fracturs were glued inside chests or boxes or painted in books.

67 The Destruction of a Church in Bath, Maine

Description
Left: White church topped by large steeple with weathervane, American flag, and clock. Fire in rear downstairs window. People at windows; others running toward church, and some battering at wall with tree trunk. Boards falling out of windows. Village green with houses and trees alongside church. Green lawn with pools of water. Blue sky slightly overcast. *Right:* Same scene some hours later, church engulfed in red, orange, and yellow flames giving off black smoke. Red foreground reflecting fire. People standing at distance from church, holding American flag at right. Darker sky with white clouds and crescent moon.

Materials and Dimensions
Oil on canvas. Height: 17½″. Width: 24″.

Artist, Locality, and Period
Attributed to John Hillings (d. 1894), Bath, Maine. c. 1854.

Comment
These paintings depict the burning of a Roman Catholic church by members of a secret society known as the Know-Nothings; during the 1840s and 1850s, this extremely nativistic group combated all "foreign" influences, particularly Roman Catholic immigrants. 4 other pairs of paintings of this scene have been discovered, and though there are slight variations in design, all 5 sets were probably executed by the same artist, John Hillings.

Once he had established a successful design, he simply repeated it, much as William Matthew Prior depicted George and Martha Washington on many reverse paintings on glass. The pictures shown here may have been commissioned by people involved in the incident; experts are uncertain whether Hillings witnessed the fire or worked from firsthand descriptions. The fact that other sets of these paintings exist does not lower their value.

Hints for Collectors
Because of the historical information they provide, paintings of everyday life in the 19th century attract many collectors. The village green and houses in the pictures shown here, for instance, present a survey of northern New England architecture. Originally such pictures had little monetary value compared with portraits; thus few were produced and the type is relatively rare today. Examples filled with detailed activity and executed in bright colors are of great interest and value. It is always important to determine whether a work was executed by someone who witnessed the scene. Firsthand depictions, as opposed to those based on newspaper or magazine illustrations, are almost always more desirable.

68 Painted political pin

Description
Brown cabin with American flag. 2 men shaking hands in foreground. Farmer, plow, bale of hay, and cannon at right. Grass with brown patches. River and trees in background. Pale sky inscribed "Harrison & Reform." Brass frame with triangular indentations.

Materials and Dimensions
Watercolor and ink on ivory. Brass frame. Height (without frame): ⅝". Width: ¾".

Artist, Locality, and Period
Unidentified. c. 1840.

Comment
Many collectors specialize in political material such as buttons, ribbons, broadsides, and ephemera from election campaigns. There are other collectors who avidly seek furniture, clothing, and personal items associated with political leaders from George Washington to John F. Kennedy. This pin, from William Henry Harrison's "Log Cabin and Hard Cider" campaign for the presidency, is unusual because it is also a fine piece of decorative jewelry; it may have been commissioned by Harrison and given to an associate.

Hints for Collectors
A one-of-a-kind campaign item like this pin is very rare and, if it were auctioned, collectors would compete intensely for it. Ordinary political items may be found in thrift shops and at flea markets. Before investing in specific campaign pieces, learn about their rarity, since this knowledge is all-important in determining value.

69 Surrender at Nashville

Description
Civil War battle scene with 16 Confederate soldiers pursued by 12 Union soldiers; 4 horses. Union soldier at center holding American flag; Confederate commander waving white flag to surrender, his aide carrying Confederate flag. Green meadow with white flowers and 7 bare trees. American flag in background at left. Undulating horizon under blue sky with white clouds. Signed.

Materials and Dimensions
Oil on masonite. Height: 18″. Width: 23⅝″.

Artist, Locality, and Period
Albert Webster Davies (1889–1967), probably New Hampshire. c. 1960.

Comment
Davies was born in Salem Depot, New Hampshire, and held many jobs, from window dresser to theater designer. He is noted for his country and genre scenes and romantic landscapes, though he also occasionally painted historical pictures, such as the one shown here. As it did for many folk painters, the American flag had special meaning for him, and he inserted it in many of his works. He had a fine sense of composition and a feeling for color, which later led him to design textiles.

Hints for Collectors
Since Davies is better known for other types of paintings, this historical work would not command as high a price as his more typical and more popular pictures. It would, however, appeal to collectors specializing in Civil War art. The value of a painting may vary substantially, depending upon where it is sold and the clientele to which it is exposed.

70 Soldier fractur

Description
8 soldiers on parade, shown in profile; all wearing blue coats, tan trousers, brown shoes, and parade hats with red and blue plumes. First soldier carrying raised sword, second beating drum, third playing flute, fourth holding American flag, and last 4 shouldering rifles with bayonets and wearing sheathed swords. Beige background.

Materials and Dimensions
Watercolor and ink on paper. Height: 3¾″. Width: 8¾″.

Artist, Locality, and Period
Unidentified. Pennsylvania. c. 1830–60.

Comment
From about the mid-18th to mid-19th centuries, Pennsylvania-German artists produced a vast assortment of distinctive watercolors that enjoy a unique place in the history of American decorative arts. Working in a tradition directly traceable to illuminated medieval manuscripts, these painters were valued members of their New World farming communities. Fracturs, or calligraphic drawings, served as records of important family events and as decoration for the home. Colored records such as baptismal certificates, hand-drawn and highly ornamented, were created by an educated elite that included schoolmasters and clergymen.

Traditional motifs were unicorns, stags, decoratively drawn mermaids, heraldic lions, and a wide variety of birds including doves, peacocks, distelfinks (stylized goldfinches), and parrots. These designs appear on decorated furniture and objects as well as in works on paper. Today the term "fractur" is applied to most German-style watercolor paintings, whether they have a large amount of calligraphic text or, like this example, none at all. This little watercolor may have been done by a child.

Hints for Collectors
While many art historians and museum curators prefer fracturs with texts that relate directly to family and community events, whimsical examples, such as these painted soldiers, are often more popular with collectors. When a fractur is undated, it is sometimes possible to estimate its time frame by the costumes worn in it. This procedure, however, is complicated by the fact that an artist may have selected costumes, particularly soldiers' uniforms, from an earlier period. Books on the history of uniforms are available in libraries and can aid in dating pictures with a military subject. The example below cannot be so dated because the uniforms are styleless and sketchy, but that hardly matters since the appeal of this work lies in its charm rather than in its value as a historical document.

71 The Heroes of the Revolution

Description
Washington, Lafayette, Steuben, Polasky [*sic*], and other Revolutionary heroes in uniform, standing on snow-covered ground; their names printed beneath them. Soldiers at left holding flag and drum. Bare brown trees at right; mountains, valley, and house in distance at left. Sunset colors in sky. Title inscribed below. Signed.

Materials and Dimensions
Oil on canvas. Height: 36″. Width: 46″.

Artist, Locality, and Period
Louis Mader (c. 1842–92; locale unknown). c. 1860–80.

Comment
Because Americans felt so strongly about their hard-won independence, they acclaimed the paintings of the events and leaders of the Revolutionary struggle, particularly those works by academic painters, such as John Trumbull. Long after the war, folk artists often imitated these famous depictions or created unique visual interpretations of these historical scenes.

Hints for Collectors
While enthusiasts of American history find paintings of this type immensely interesting, some art collectors dismiss them because they were copied from prints or lithographs. Since the collecting public does not pursue them aggressively, it is possible to obtain fine examples of historical painting for surprisingly modest sums. The most desirable examples are richly detailed and brightly colored. Those that display a marked individuality and do not appear to be derivative are most likely to appreciate in value substantially.

72 Andrew Jackson

Description
Full-length portrait of Andrew Jackson in old age, standing on grassy knoll and looking off to his left toward large tree trunk. Wearing glasses, gray cloak, waistcoat, and pants. Right hand holding top hat and cane. Houses, trees, and rolling hills in background. Cloudy sky in white and gray. Slightly yellowed. Title inscribed below. Signed.

Materials and Dimensions
Watercolor, pencil, and pastel on paper. Height: 22″. Width: 16½″.

Artist, Locality, and Period
Ellen T. Harrington, probably Massachusetts. c. 1840.

Comment
Early folk artists often based their designs on popular prints and lithographs or borrowed elements from them. The portrait of President Jackson shown here was probably modeled on a contemporary print, since very similar examples are known. When folk art first began to be collected in the 1920s, works such as this were scorned because they were obviously copied from other sources. Many collectors today, however, are less concerned if the design of a painting was derived from a print, since scholars have established that this occurred more frequently than previously believed.

Hints for Collectors
If you think a painting or drawing was inspired by a print or lithograph, try to trace the source. Refer to books about makers of widely circulated prints, such as Currier & Ives in New York or D. W. Kellogg & Co. in Hartford; also check newspapers of the period, which often featured illustrated advertisements for popular prints.

73 General George Washington on Horseback

Description
George Washington in full officer's parade dress, astride horse; body turned at waist to face viewer. Dressed in blue coat, yellow breeches, and black boots. Black tricorne with prominent red, yellow, and blue feathers. Right hand holding upright sword; left hand holding reins. Brown steed, with black mane, hoofs, and tail, prancing on dirt path edged with grass. Red, yellow, and blue saddle blanket. Tan background. Inscribed "General George Washington."

Materials and Dimensions
Ink, pencil, and watercolor on woven paper. Height: 13⅝". Width: 9¾".

Artist, Locality, and Period
Unidentified. Possibly Pennsylvania. c. 1830–50.

Comment
As the most important figure in the American War of Independence, Washington was revered as a hero and symbol of national unity and became one of the most popular subjects for folk painters. After the Revolution, some extremist factions went so far as to urge the formation of a monarchy with Washington as king.

Hints for Collectors
Collectors who specialize in folk art with patriotic themes are highly competitive at auctions. Exciting pieces may occasionally turn up at small, out-of-the-way auction houses and sell for bargain prices; but if knowledgeable local dealers are present, these works will undoubtedly sell for large sums.

74 Liberty in the Form of the Goddess of Youth

Description
Reverse painting of Liberty, symbolized by standing woman with black hair and eyes and pale complexion, wearing sheer white dress with lacy shawl and blue sash. Left hand holding garland of flowers draped from head, right hand raising gray cup to fierce bald eagle in upper left corner. Right foot resting on symbols of British tyranny. Column behind her. American flag overhead, partially covered with swirling clouds; sunbeams behind eagle. Variegated yellow and green foreground. Distant harbor with red lightning bolts. Signed and inscribed.

Materials and Dimensions
Gouache on glass. Height: 24¼″. Width: 18½″.

Artist, Locality, and Period
Abijah Canfield (1769–1830), Chusetown, Connecticut. c. 1800.

Comment
Prints glorifying the growth of the young Republic were extremely common during the Federal era (1780–1820). Some were shipped to China, where they were used as models for reverse paintings on glass, which were then exported to America. This painting is one of the few American examples of this basic design; in the Chinese versions, Liberty has distinctively Oriental features. Reverse paintings on glass became increasingly popular in America; during the mid-19th century many were backed with foil and called "tinsel pictures."

Hints for Collectors
A broken reverse painting on glass is irreparable and, regardless of how rare or beautiful it may be, will never command a substantial price. Some museums and historical societies will accept and display a damaged piece if it is of significant documentary or historical interest.

75 Liberty

Description
Liberty symbolized by woman wearing full-length dress, black tasseled belt, and plumed and jeweled headdress. She leans on left elbow, has legs crossed, and stands in portico near 2 massive pillars partially covered with drapery. Greek Revival building, trees, and hills in distance.

Materials and Dimensions
Watercolor and pencil on paper. Height: 11½″. Width: 9½″.

Artist, Locality, and Period
Unidentified. New England. c. 1820–30.

Comment
Americans were avidly interested in French politics and society at the end of the 18th century, and Parisian fashions and tastes dominated the American scene into the first decades of the 19th century. As the French, even more than the rest of Europe, took their inspiration from the classical world, so Americans also turned to what became known as Neoclassicism. The Greek Revival architecture in the grisaille watercolor shown here demonstrates this interest. Furthermore, the woman's costume and feathered headdress were probably copied from a French fashion illustration of about 1820–25; this helps date the painting.

Hints for Collectors
Grisaille watercolors were among the most difficult paintings to execute because they were limited to shades of black, white, and gray; thus they are rare and highly desirable. Most are still lifes, and while animals have been depicted in this medium, portraits are relatively unusual. Collectors who specialize in grisailles are generally willing to pay a premium for them.

76 Memorial miniature in locket

Description
Profile of dark-haired woman wearing full-length gown, with right arm raised to signal to distant sailing vessel. Brown foliage and ground; choppy blue-green water. Distant mountains against blue and white sky. Gold oval locket. Initialed "MR" on back.

Materials and Dimensions
Watercolor on ivory. Gold. Height (without frame): 2⅛". Width: 1¾".

Artist, Locality, and Period
Unidentified. c. 1785–1800.

Comment
Mourning or memorial art included needlework, jewelry, and watercolors; it was created primarily by schoolgirls at academies. The painter of this early locket, however, was probably a semiprofessional artist, since the execution is superior to that of most mourning pictures. The departing ship was one of many symbols for death that appeared again and again in memorial art.

Hints for Collectors
Many famous painters executed miniatures, and an attribution to such an artist will of course greatly enhance the value of a piece. Miniature portraits and mourning lockets were sometimes signed by the artist on the reverse of the ivory. A piece should never be allowed to remain out of its case for more than a few moments, since the ivory will soon curl at the edges, making it impossible to reframe. A miniature painting should be judged by the same criteria used in evaluating a large painting, even though miniatures tend to have been less carefully executed.

77 Memorial to George Washington

Description
Woman with long brown hair, black shawl, and flowing white gown, standing on grassy knoll and placing flowers on a tombstone. Tombstone inscribed "Sacred to Washington" and draped with black fabric. Behind monument, willow tree under large oak. Lake at right with 2 men in boat. Mount Vernon and mountains in background. White sky with bluish patches.

Materials and Dimensions
Watercolor on paper. Height: 19¼". Width: 17½".

Artist, Locality, and Period
Unidentified. New England. c. 1820–30.

Comment
George Washington's death was a devastating event for the American people: many considered him godlike and memorialized his passing for decades. Even today, Washington remains a popular subject for folk artists. The excellent memorial picture shown here was almost certainly done at one of the many finishing schools and academies where young women from well-to-do families were taught the polite arts of needlework, music, dancing, and painting. The scene is thought to be based on an unidentified print of the period, since 2 other nearly identical examples are known.

Hints for Collectors
There was little interest in memorial pictures until recently, and even though they are now collected seriously, their subject matter still disturbs many viewers. Watercolors in poor condition can be restored, but the process should be undertaken only by a skilled professional and is generally costly. Since restoration lessens the value of a painting, do not acquire a damaged work unless it has special historical or artistic significance.

78 Woman at Unmarked Tombstone

Description
Brown-haired woman in full-length black dress, standing before unmarked tombstone topped by urn. Large brown tree trunks at right, with gray rock at base. Blue-green weeping willow at water's edge, overhanging tombstone. Grass and marsh, with mountains in distance. White sky with gray patches suggesting clouds.

Materials and Dimensions
Watercolor on paper. Height: 8⅞". Width: 11½".

Artist, Locality, and Period
Unidentified. Possibly New England. c. 1840–60.

Comment
Memorial or mourning pictures first appeared in America in the late 18th century, following a European fashion that was a part of the pervasive Romantic movement in art. These pictures were most often done by students in women's academies, who gave them to friends in mourning or were themselves grieving over the loss of loved ones. Professional artists also executed commissions for mourning pictures. The tombstone in the example shown here has no inscription, suggesting that it was painted for a friend or relative who was still alive. Memorial pictures were often created without a death having occurred; they could be kept on hand and inscribed at the appropriate time.

Hints for Collectors
Few memorial pictures display the highly personal style of this modest example. While unusual works sometimes are not the most valuable, they do tend to attract specialist collectors and to appeal to general collectors as well.

79 Masonic Memorial

Description
Circular scene of woman in white bonnet and blue dress, weeping into dark cloth; 2 boys in orange and black checkered suits before her. At left, tombstone flanked by columns and decorated with Masonic symbols; set atop black and white slab holding 3 candlesticks. 2 large trees against blue and white sky. Off-white background with long inscription below. Signed.

Materials and Dimensions
Watercolor and ink on paper. Height: 14″. Width: 11⅞″.

Artist, Locality, and Period
Eunice Pinney (1770–1849), Windsor or Simsbury, Connecticut. 1809.

Comment
Among all 19th-century American watercolor paintings, Pinney's works stand out for their vigorous originality, fine designs, and robust colors. In contrast to the blatantly derivative and amateurishly executed pieces by schoolgirls in academies or finishing schools, Pinney's paintings were the mature efforts of a middle-aged woman. She was both prolific and versatile, creating landscape, historical, religious, and genre paintings as well as birth registers, memorial pictures, and literary illustrations.

Hints for Collectors
This painting is of great interest not only because it is by a well-known painter, but also because it includes numerous Masonic references. Many collectors specialize in objects of Masonic interest and are often themselves members of the secret order. Do not be surprised when a work of folk art with Masonic symbolism sells for 2 or 3 times as much as a comparable non-Masonic piece.

80 The Annunciation

Description
Oval scene of floating brown-haired angel, in yellow and blue robes, with arm upraised before kneeling Virgin Mary dressed in gray and yellow. Lectern or altar at right, covered in red and yellow cloth, with white scroll on it. Green grass, blue water, and distant rocky slope at right. 3 angels' faces floating in white clouds. Wide brown border. Inscription from Luke (1:30) at bottom.

Materials and Dimensions
Watercolor on paper. Height: 12¾″. Width: 10″.

Artist, Locality, and Period
Unidentified. c. 1830–50.

Comment
The romantic tendencies in European art and literature of the late 18th and early 19th centuries sparked the imagination of many young American women attending academies and finishing schools. There they were instructed in Bible studies and religious obligations, which led many to paint watercolors of biblical episodes. The Annunciation was a popular theme among young ladies who wanted to demonstrate their piety and enthusiasm; the pictures were given away as gifts or traded among friends.

Hints for Collectors
Oval and circular watercolors need to be specially matted, using acid-free matboard available in most art-supply stores. It is also wise to back any watercolor with acid-free paper, since a wood backing can sometimes cause serious discoloration. Modern conservators are able to bleach discolored areas, such as those on the watercolor seen here. Never allow a conservator to go too far, however, because an over-restored painting is less valuable.

81 Christ on the Path

Description
Full-length oversize figure of Christ in red and white robe, standing in the distance on a brown path flanked by 2 brown mountains. 7 white angels flying or walking in the landscape. Sheep, birds, multicolored flowers, mushrooms, and insects scattered over green grass. 3 biblical inscriptions on pale blue sky. Signed.

Materials and Dimensions
Oil on board. Height: 11¾″. Width: 34¾″.

Artist, Locality, and Period
Howard Finster (1916–   ), Summerville, Georgia. c. 1978.

Comment
Reverend Finster turned to painting only recently. A preacher for 40 years, he retired from the pulpit for health reasons and began constructing a massive environmental sculpture called "Paradise Garden" in the small Georgia town in which he lives. This work consists of white concrete walls and walkways inset with an incredible variety of found objects, including sparkling fragments of glass, mirrors, plastic, photographs, hubcaps, and abandoned refrigerators. One of the many hand-written signs on this gigantic jeweled garden explains its essence, "I took the pieces you threw away/ and put them together by night and day./ Washed by rain dried by sun/ a million pieces all in one." He has said of this environment, "Just you and the Lord. And you can talk and He can tell you things to do." His works, like his pronouncements, come from religious fervor; they are the unorthodox visual incarnations of his doomsday preaching.

Hints for Collectors

Many of America's finest contemporary folk painters are southerners who give their works a deeply religious emphasis. Their pictures are often highly personal and said to be based on divine revelation or intervention. Though tending to be crude, they have a boldness and fresh vitality that make them particularly appealing to collectors of modern art, who sometimes cross over into the folk art field. A painting such as the one shown here, however, is often of less interest to conservative folk art collectors who are accustomed to the gentle patina of 19th-century paintings.

As with many artists, Finster's earliest works, created before he achieved national recognition, are the most interesting, for they display a deep conviction that his later pieces, produced for the marketplace, often lack. When considering the acquisition of a work by a 20th-century master, investigate the sales history of his entire output and attempt to buy an example painted within the working period that commands the most respect.

82 Crucifixion

Description
St. Sebastian strapped to bushy green tree, with archer aiming at him. Octopus at left, grouped with 3 figures and spheres. Spaceship with 5 spacemen at top left. Man in black robe with arms outstretched toward large blue eye hovering at top center. Winged creature at top right. Indian, Armenian folk characters, winged man, and other figures below. Islands of green vegetation against pink, blue, and white background.

Materials and Dimensions
Oil on canvas. Height: 32⅝″. Width: 34¾″.

Artist, Locality, and Period
Peter "Charlie" Bochero (c. 1895–1962), Leechburg, Pennsylvania. c. 1960.

Comment
Peter Bochero emigrated from Armenia in 1903 and settled in rural Pennsylvania, where he worked as a handyman but otherwise lived as a hermit. His paintings, not discovered until after his death, belong to the category of contemporary folk art referred to as "isolate" or "obsessive" art. Though lacking the more accessible qualities of realistic paintings, such works are admired for their vitality and individuality. This example depicts 3 themes central to the work of Bochero: biblical lore from his Armenian past, a love of America (expressed here by an Indian), and creatures from outer space.

Hints for Collectors
There are still relatively few serious collectors of "obsessive" folk art painting. Since works of many of the finest such painters—including Mose Tolliver, Sister Gertrude Morgan, and Peter Bochero—are readily available and generally underpriced, they are likely to be worthwhile long-term investments.

83 Choir with Angels

Description
Illustration for Book of Revelations (7:1–3); the passage, written in lower half of painting, foretelling who shall be saved at the end of the world. White-clad figures already saved and brightly robed multitudes chosen for salvation, all surrounded by angels. Angel in center of quotation holding scroll that contains list of the chosen. Plain pink and white background. Inscription continued on back. Signed.

Materials and Dimensions
Watercolor on paper. Height: 14¾″. Width: 19¾″.

Artist, Locality, and Period
Sister Gertrude Morgan (1900–80), New Orleans. c. 1970.

Comment
Sister Gertrude Morgan, an evangelistic street preacher in New Orleans, turned to art to spread the Divine Word when both sermonizing and hymn singing began to seem inadequate. Her unique style of inscribing paintings with either her own stream-of-consciousness prose or a biblical quotation, as shown here, was her hallmark.

Hints for Collectors
Contemporary naive artists whose images—usually of a religious, political, or erotic nature—are drawn from the realm of fantasy have generated a cultlike enthusiasm among certain collectors. If you are attracted to works of this type, look for colorful examples that have been properly protected on both front and back, since such works were often made with inexpensive, fragile materials. This double-sided painting, for instance, is mounted between 2 sheets of glass, so the inscription on the back can be read.

84 Baptismal certificate fractur

Description
Baptismal certificate with inscription in German surrounded by orange, blue, and gold decoration, including heart-shaped wreath of stars with human-faced sun above and emblem below. Inscription at top center, "*Die Lieben Sonne/ Scheint für alle*" (The lovely sun/ Shines for all), flanked by angels in blue loincloths holding horns. Peacocks on branches in lower corners. Golden-brown background.

Materials and Dimensions
Watercolor on paper. Height: 15″. Width: 12½″.

Artist, Locality, and Period
Attributed to Barbara Becker Haman (b. 1774), Shenandoah County, Virginia. c. 1806.

Comment
Though this baptismal certificate, or *taufschein*, was made by a German immigrant living in Virginia, its motifs are similar to those in fracturs of the better-known Pennsylvania Germans. Since such pieces were created to record births, deaths, and marriages, they combined fanciful ornamentation with script. This piece was attributed by comparing the script to that on a signed piece.

Hints for Collectors
The value of a fractur depends largely upon its condition. An example loses much of its value if it has been torn or significantly disfigured or has faded noticeably because of exposure to sunlight. A great deal of research on American fracturs has been completed, and it is often possible to identify an artist on the basis of stylistic similarities; attribution will, of course, greatly enhance the value of a work.

85 Spiritual Chimes fractur

Description
Blue tall-case clock with yellow and black decoration on case and Roman numerals on face. Flanked by angels, birds, chains of fruit, and bowls with diamond designs, all in blue, green, brown, black, and yellow. Ivory-colored background. Inscribed.

Materials and Dimensions
Watercolor on paper. Height: 12¼″. Width: 12½″.

Artist, Locality, and Period
Unidentified. Probably Pennsylvania. c. 1830–60.

Comment
The tall-case clock motif has been depicted in only one other known fractur, signed E.M.M. The artist of the example shown here may have been inspired by the religious verses on it, which refer to the rapid passage of time and the need to pursue one's goals diligently. Although the differences in script suggest that several hands inscribed the message, all parts attest to the virtues of obeying God. The museum of the Bucks County Historical Society in Doylestown, Pennsylvania, contains a paintbox for the production of fracturs, which includes goose-quill pens, cat's-hair brushes, bottles of pigments that were once liquefied with whiskey, and varnish to give paintings such as this one a shimmering effect.

Hints for Collectors
Desirable because of its rarity and fine condition, this fractur would bring a high price in the marketplace. The paper on which early fracturs were executed is often in poor condition because of the corrosive effects of the ingredients in dark watercolors.

86 Tradesmen fractur

Description
4 tradesmen (left to right): smith with hammer over anvil; shoemaker at workbench; baker next to brick oven; innkeeper holding stein over bar. Baker wearing yellow coat with red trim, white apron, and black trousers; others in blue and red; all with black hats and footwear. Roughly patterned border decoration in red, blue, and yellow. Title above each figure and verse below.

Materials and Dimensions
Watercolor on paper. Height: 7½″. Width: 12½″.

Artist, Locality, and Period
Unidentified. Southeastern Pennsylvania. c. 1815.

Comment
When the Colonies were first settled, power and privilege were held by religious leaders, but in the 18th century these gradually passed to merchants and artisans. Enthusiasm for the tradesman as a symbol of American vitality grew throughout the 18th century, and by the time the fractur shown here was executed, his virtues were being extolled in literature, music, and painting. The verses on this fractur boast that each tradesman is capable of making a better living than the one depicted on his left.

Hints for Collectors
Fracturs from Pennsylvania, frequently rich in detail, are valued for the information they provide about the Germans who settled in the New World, as well as for their pictorial artistry. A fractur like this unsigned example will bring a considerably lower price than a piece by a well-known artist such as Lewis Miller, whose thousands of sketches and watercolor books may be seen at the York Historical Society in Pennsylvania, Colonial Williamsburg in Virginia, and at other museums.

87 Fractur book pages

Description
2-page spread with profile of horse and rider on brown stone bridge with red guardrail and 3 arches. Horse-drawn hay wagon entering bridge at lower right; path running diagonally, with house, deer, birds, black snake, and trees above it. Bees and beehives at top. Yellowed paper. Signed and dated.

Materials and Dimensions
Watercolor on paper. Height: 6½″. Width (each page): 3¾″.

Artist, Locality, and Period
Susanna Sibbel (life dates unknown), Pennsylvania. 1808.

Comment
The earliest American fracturs were probably created by members of the religious community founded in 1728 at Ephrata Cloister in Pennsylvania. Schools in Pennsylvania-German communities continued to teach manuscript illumination and fractur writing well into the 19th century, when the function of fracturs was gradually taken over by printed certificates. The pages shown here are from one of the many books that fractur artists filled. The signature page, not shown here, demonstrates the artist's familiarity with standard fractur motifs, though on most pages she chose to picture her surroundings instead. Like so much folk art, this work makes clear that awkwardness of technique does not detract from charm or artistic merit. Its creator followed the folk art convention of depicting subjects in profile to simplify the perspective.

Hints for Collectors
Fracturs appear wherever works of art are sold; they are often found at country auctions in Pennsylvania. Look inside decorated German-style chests; fracturs pasted under their lids should be detached only by a competent conservator.

88 Messiah's Crown fractur

Description
Black rectangular box with spikes along outer border. 2 joined circles inside, one containing fully inscribed heart labeled "conscience," the other a 7-pointed star. Checkerboard decoration on borders. At top, crown with center diamond; "judgment" inscribed below. Inscription along bottom, "The Messiah's Crown/ Anti-Ku-Klux-Klan/ The All Saints Banner/ The Prince of Peace."

Materials and Dimensions
Ink, pencil, and watercolor on woven paper. Height: 15½″. Width: 17″.

Artist, Locality, and Period
Attributed to Franklin Wilder (life dates unknown), Hingham or Leominster, Massachusetts. c. 1870.

Comment
This fractur is one of several by Wilder representing his anti-Ku-Klux-Klan feelings; it was made at a time when membership in the Klan was growing rapidly as a reaction to the emancipation of the slaves after the Civil War. This secret racist society obviously horrified the righteous and religious Wilder, leading him to express his opposition artistically.

Hints for Collectors
New England fracturs are far rarer than those from Pennsylvania, since the tradition was brought to the American colonies by German immigrants who settled primarily in Pennsylvania. Very few American fracturs deal with racism or other social or political issues as directly as this one does. Collectors specializing in art dealing with the struggle for emancipation of black people would pay a premium for such a work.

89 Family record fractur

Description
Page with 3 columns listing, at left, names of Simon Mayberry, wife Mary Hall, and children James and Clara; in center, birth and marriage dates; at right, column reserved for dates of deaths, remaining blank except for tombstone flanked by green trees. Blue scalloped border around inscribed title at top. Date of record and location inscribed at bottom.

Materials and Dimensions
Watercolor and ink on paper. Height: 13½″. Width: 9¼″.

Artist, Locality, and Period
Attributed to the "Heart and Hand" artist (life dates unknown), Saccarrappa (Westbrook), Maine. 1850.

Comment
In the 18th and 19th centuries, there was a sizable production of handmade family records in the German farming communities scattered throughout Pennsylvania. Hand-executed family records were considerably less popular in New England, mainly because professionally printed forms were more available. The so-called "Heart and Hand" artist, though unidentified, was one of the few New England record makers to leave a substantial body of work, which is identifiable by its ornamental borders, tasseled swags, and heart-and-hand designs.

Hints for Collectors
Unlike this work, most family records were not fracturs and were not executed by hand. They were printed in various designs and came with blank spaces to be filled in later. These printed records are of little interest to most collectors unless they were inscribed by their own ancestors or have added decoration. Any example containing information about a well-known family or individual will, of course, have additional value.

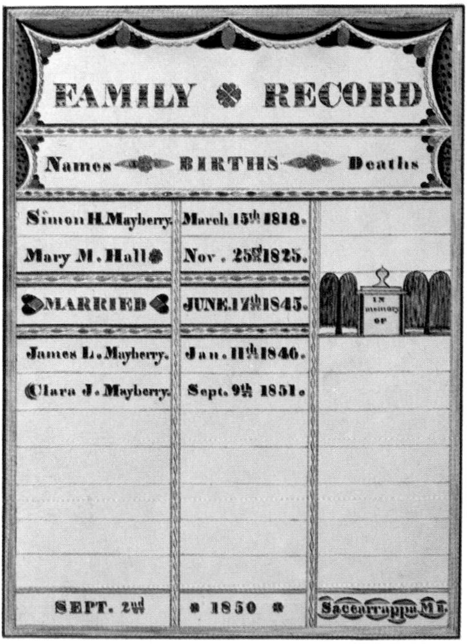

Still Lifes and Animal Pictures

The works in this section depict flowers, fruit, or animals. Many were executed by 19th-century schoolgirls and housewives as gifts for friends or as decorations for their homes. Also included here are calligraphic exercises drawn primarily by schoolchildren, as well as several modern paintings of animals.

Tinsel Pictures and Scherenschnitte
Most tinsel pictures are still lifes. All are reverse paintings on glass backed with crinkled foil to produce a shimmering effect. Though particularly common in the Northeast, they were made in all parts of the country and display regional variations in the flowers and fruit shown.

Scherenschnitte, or scissor cutting, was a tradition brought to America by German-speaking immigrants. Often made as valentines, birth and marriage certificates, or memorial pictures, the more intricate examples required great virtuosity with scissors. The paper, sometimes gilded, was usually mounted on paper or cloth of a contrasting color.

Theorem Pictures
Also favored by 19th-century folk artists were theorem pictures, which flourished especially in New England and Pennsylvania. These still lifes, depicting fruit and flowers in bowls and vases, were symbols of abundance. They were accomplished with stencils, also called theorems, which were carefully arranged and traced, and the outlines then filled with colors. Some, however, were probably copied freehand from instruction books or popular prints. Watercolors on paper as well as oils on velvet or cloth were common mediums. The artists sometimes ground and mixed their own paints and cut their own stencils. Grisaille theorem pictures, executed in shades of gray, were the most difficult to create and are therefore rare.

Calligraphic and Animal Pictures
Art using calligraphic techniques was an outgrowth of new interest in elegant penmanship during the 18th and 19th centuries. Schools taught various techniques and styles of handwriting, most notably the Spencerian method, which features quick curvilinear strokes, or flourishes. Most pictures were inscribed with mottoes or verses that reflected the sentimentality prevalent in the popular arts of the 19th century. Many of these calligraphic works were embellished with animals or flowers.

The 20th-century paintings of animals in this section, unlike the standardized creatures seen in calligraphic drawings of the previous century, are individualistic, colorful folk portrayals.

90 Scherenschnitte

Description
Gold cutout design with symmetrical left and right halves. Pairs of mourning doves above 2 hearts enclosing willow tree, flowers, tombstone, and dove. Overall branches and leaves, with some flowers at edges. Black background.

Materials and Dimensions
Gilt foil. Oilcloth. Height: 10½". Width: 14⅞".

Artist, Locality, and Period
Unidentified. Possibly Pennsylvania. c. 1830–40.

Comment
The ancient art of decorative paper cutting found its way to America through the Germans, who settled primarily in Pennsylvania. They used this artistic mode—called *scherenschnitte*, meaning "scissor-cut"—to embellish birth and marriage certificates as well as lacy Valentines. The elaborate example shown here is somewhat unusual because it is a memorial picture; *scherenschnitte* was used most often for silhouettes in early America.

Hints for Collectors
Early to mid-19th century *scherenschnitte* pictures are generally quite valuable. Do not confuse them with late 19th-century and early 20th-century examples, which have a strong Victorian character. The later pieces, some done even today, are fairly common and very inexpensive, especially in comparison to the early pieces. The rare pieces of *scherenschnitte* that are signed or dated will fetch substantially higher prices. Because fragile, pictorial examples should always be displayed under glass.

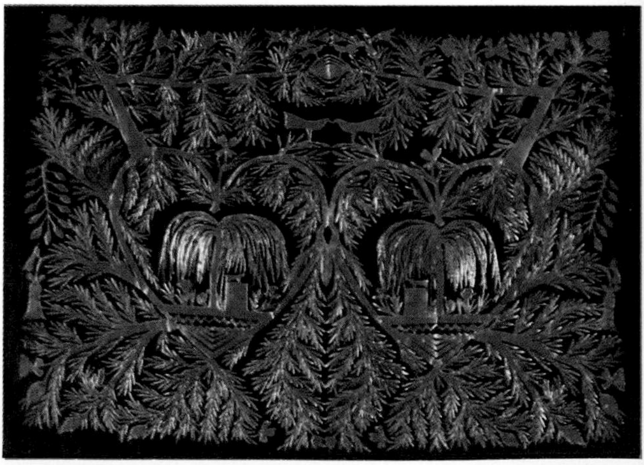

91 Tinsel picture

Description
Central oval daguerreotype of seated child with gray background; encased in gilt frame. Encircled by undulating gold tinsel vine with red flowers and green leaves. 4 gold birds at corners. White background.

Materials and Dimensions
Ink and paint on glass. Tin foil. Hand-colored daguerreotype in gilt frame. Height: 12″. Width: 14⅛″.

Artist, Locality, and Period
Unidentified. Pennsylvania. c. 1850–80.

Comment
The best tinsel pictures display strong regional characteristics. The overall design of this piece includes a floral wreath and 2 pairs of birds, which relate directly to designs found on fracturs and other watercolor drawings from Pennsylvania. Of special interest is the artist's decision to mount a daguerreotype in the composition. Photography was perfected in the 1830s in France. By the mid-1840s, numerous American folk painters, sensing that the camera might ultimately put them out of business, became "folk photographers," advertising their willingness to provide either photographed or painted likenesses. The work shown here combines both mediums as well as tinsel.

Hints for Collectors
Folk pictures combining painting and photography are extremely rare. Rarity, however, does not guarantee demand or substantial value. While this tinsel picture is one of the best examples of its kind, it would not be of great interest to most general collectors and would have a modest market value.

92 Tinsel picture

Description
White, pink, and gold flowers and blue leaves in black and brown vase with flared pedestal. Brown rectangular base with black outlines. Black background.

Materials and Dimensions
Ink and paint on glass. Tin foil. Height: 15″. Width: 13⅛″.

Artist, Locality, and Period
Unidentified. New England. c. 1850–80.

Comment
Tinsel pictures became very popular with folk artists of the second half of the 19th century. Imitative of Chinese works imported in the 18th century, these pictures are reverse paintings on glass, the back side of the glass painted with translucent colors and further embellished with crinkled foil. This adds a shimmering effect to the painted image.

Hints for Collectors
Tinsel pictures with dark backgrounds are not as popular as those with bright backgrounds and are therefore considerably less valuable. Such pictures should have a strong composition and bright colors to compensate for their somberness, as does this example. Because few collectors are attracted to tinsel paintings, they are not likely to increase substantially in value in the near future, even though the best examples are significant expressions of folk art. Tinsel pictures should always be handled very carefully. The painting on glass is fragile, and if the tinsel rubs against it, the paint may flake.

93 Tinsel picture

Description
Multihued flowers and leaves in yellow, silver, and blue vase with flared pedestal. Silver base with black markings. Streaked, pale blue background.

Materials and Dimensions
Paint on glass. Tin foil. Height: 17⅜″. Width: 14″.

Artist, Locality, and Period
Unidentified. Probably New England or Pennsylvania. c. 1840–80.

Comment
Tinsel pictures became common primarily in Pennsylvania and New England during the 1830s and continued to be made by folk painters throughout the century. It is thought that after the mid-19th century tinsel pictures were created almost exclusively by women. The medium gained popularity as women's magazines began publishing articles about how to make such pictures.

Hints for Collectors
Tinsel pictures must be in very fine condition to be valuable. Thus, a piece with broken glass is nearly valueless. Moreover, often the paint did not adhere well to the glass, so that only a few examples remain intact. Tinsel pictures almost always retain their original frames; if not, they may have been restored, which sharply lowers their value. Restoration is usually easy to detect because it is almost impossible for a restorer to match the faded hues. Beware of European examples, which tend to be more elaborate and less valuable in the American marketplace.

94 Grisaille theorem

Description
Footed bowl filled with grapes, peaches, cherries, lilies, and leafy branches, all in shades of gray on white ground. Bowl with wide foliate top, short stem, and circular bottom; set on square base with black trim. Pale background.

Materials and Dimensions
Gray wash and pencil on paper. Height: 14¾″. Width: 10⅞″.

Artist, Locality, and Period
Unidentified. New England. c. 1830–40.

Comment
As early as the 17th century, grisaille still lifes were painted on furniture by Dutch settlers in the Hudson Valley who continued a long tradition of this art form. Few painted pieces from this early period remain. It was during the first half of the 19th century that still lifes gained great popularity, primarily among folk artists. Paintings on canvas as well as watercolors on paper or velvet were most common. Still lifes in grisaille, that is, in shades of gray, are probably the rarest, in part because they were very difficult to execute.

Hints for Collectors
Many naive still lifes are exceedingly crude, but if they have charm they may still be desirable. In general, the more complex a composition, the higher its value. A signature, inscribed date, or other documentation always adds to the value of a piece. While there are countless watercolors of plaited baskets or bowls of fruit, grisaille still lifes are uncommon. Collectors who specialize in grisailles or theorems will pay a premium for them.

95 Theorem

Description
Footed bowl filled with multicolored fruit: peaches, pineapple, berries, grapes, and leaves. Bowl painted in blue and yellow to look like glass, with wide top, tapered stem, and circular orange and blue base. Free-form green ground. Beige background slightly discolored.

Materials and Dimensions
Watercolor on paper. Height: 16″. Width: 19½″.

Artist, Locality, and Period
Unidentified. Probably Pennsylvania. c. 1830–50.

Comment
Theorems can sometimes be dated by the style of the basket or glass container depicted in them. Pressed glass compotes were not produced before the 1830s and were costly appointments for average American households; in this example, the artist was probably attempting to paint such a compote. This appealingly naive theorem—a representation of abundance and opulence—includes a pineapple, the symbol of hospitality and a fruit seldom found in watercolors of this type. Many of the stencils used on theorems may also have been used on carpets, floors, or fabric items such as curtains, pillow shams, bedspreads, or tablecloths.

Hints for Collectors
A theorem should be well framed for best visual effect. Molded gold-painted frames used originally on large portraits from earlier periods can often be cut down and used on theorems. Most frame shops will be able to do this.

96 Theorem

Description
Multicolored flowers and green leaves in oval basket with brown and white weave. Green grass at base. White background. Signed.

Materials and Dimensions
Watercolor on cotton. Height: 18″. Width: 29½″.

Artist, Locality, and Period
David Ellinger (active since c. 1940), Pennsylvania. c. 1970.

Comment
Ellinger is perhaps the best known contemporary painter of theorems on velvet as well as on cotton or paper. He has also executed large oil-on-canvas and fractur paintings. His sensitively stenciled and painted pictures may be mistaken for antique examples, even though he does not try to reproduce period paintings. William Rank is another Pennsylvania painter whose theorems are avidly collected today; Rank's colors are somewhat brighter, and he often fails to achieve the warm hues typical of Ellinger's pieces.

Hints for Collectors
In selecting a theorem, look for a pleasant overall design and clarity of execution. Though lacking in universal appeal, this form is popular with beginning collectors and will probably always maintain a respectable market value. Ellinger's theorems may command prices as high as those paid for many antique works. His original frames, painted and grained in a style virtually indistinguishable from that of antique frames, substantially enhance the value of his theorems.

97 Theorem

Description
Basket of multicolored fruit: grapes, oranges, peaches, and pears; with bird perched on leafy branch and eating berries. Butterfly at left. Brown oval basket atop flat green base. White background slightly yellowed.

Materials and Dimensions
Watercolor on velvet. Height: 16″. Width: 19″.

Artist, Locality, and Period
Unidentified. New England. c. 1820–60.

Comment
Still-life paintings of fruit and flowers were created with stencils, or "theorems," cut out from heavy paper, and were done by young ladies in academies or women at home. The theorem shown here was almost certainly inspired by a design in an art manual or other publication, since numerous nearly identical examples are known.

Hints for Collectors
Collectors tend to prefer watercolor theorems on paper to those on velvet and will generally pay about 50 percent more for them. The disrepute into which contemporary velvet paintings have fallen may bias collectors against examples in this medium. Theorems on velvet, however, particularly those using a pleasing palette, can be quite charming. Complexity of design and originality are characteristics much sought after by collectors attracted to these works. The inclusion of birds, butterflies, or other animals increases the market value of a theorem substantially. Condition is extremely important; examples with tears, stains, or considerable yellowing are less valuable.

98 Hummingbird

Description
Hummingbird with orange head, black beak, white speckled breast, red tail, and gray body and wings, hovering over 2 yellow roses with green leaves. Branches of green foliage hanging from upper right corner. Paler solid green background. Signed and dated.

Materials and Dimensions
Oil on board. Height: 13½″. Width: 7⅝″.

Artist, Locality, and Period
Lawrence Lebduska (1894–1966), New York. 1965.

Comment
Born in Baltimore of Bohemian parents, Lebduska spent his youth learning the craft of stained glass while also studying interior decorating. Primarily a mural painter, Lebduska produced easel paintings in his spare time, taking his themes from childhood memories, Czechoslovak folktales, and children's books. His bright-colored animals, birds, and people were not painted from nature, so that works such as the one shown here have a fanciful quality.

Hints for Collectors
The monetary value of an artist's work depends on the amount of collector and museum interest at any given time: for example, in the 1940s Lebduska's works were in fashion; they were exhibited widely in museums and galleries and were very costly. In his later career he produced a great number of paintings, many of which, though as beautiful and evocative as his earlier pieces, have not found great favor with collectors. Since it is impossible to predict future demand for an artist's output, buying merely for investment is risky.

99 Home

Description
Vivid red hibiscus with 5 petals, large stamen, and green sepals and leaves. Inscribed below is poem entitled "Home," by Robert Southey.

Materials and Dimensions
Ink and watercolor over pencil on woven paper. Height: 8¾″. Width: 7¼″.

Artist, Locality, and Period
Unidentified. c. 1880.

Comment
During the 18th and 19th centuries, Americans were fascinated by exotic fruits, vegetables, and flowers. Diaries such as Ben Franklin's abound in entries enthusiastically describing the importation of rare flowering plants, which were greatly prized and considered status symbols. Professional horticulturists and young women attending finishing schools as part of their cultural training often rendered such plants in watercolor. As the mail-order sale of seeds for fruits, vegetables, and flowers increased in the second half of the 19th century, stenciled and, later, printed catalogues replaced these watercolor depictions. This painting is inscribed with an inspirational poem by the early 19th-century English poet laureate Robert Southey.

Hints for Collectors
Small watercolors of flowering plants attract many beginning collectors because they are still plentiful and relatively inexpensive. Examples that bear elaborate calligraphic inscriptions, such as the poem used here, are more desirable than those without inscriptions. Look for sensitive design, bold color, and decorative quality when selecting such works.

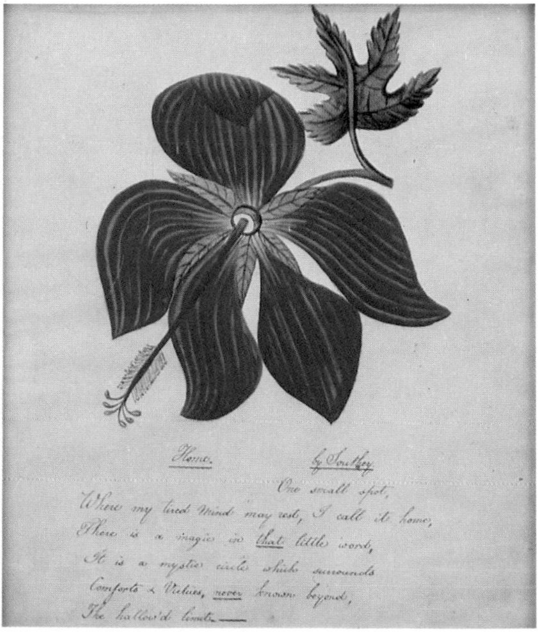

100 Home, Sweet Home

Description
Large red and brown bird and smaller yellow one perched on stylized branches. Small bird carrying inscribed banner in beak. “Home, Sweet Home” in black lettering on elaborate banner below. Inscription across bottom. Beige background slightly yellowed. Signed.

Materials and Dimensions
Ink and watercolor on paper. Height: 10″. Width: 7⅜″.

Artist, Locality, and Period
V. H. Furnier (life dates and locale unknown). c. 1850–90.

Comment
Penmanship was raised to a fine art and became a sign of culture during the 18th and 19th centuries. It was taught at the private academies that, in the 19th century, replaced the tutors who educated children in their homes. Students in academies were encouraged to keep copybooks in which their progress in artistic penmanship could be recorded.

Hints for Collectors
Calligraphic pictures of the late 19th century often reflected the Victorian inclination toward sentimentality. In a society where a man’s home was considered his castle, mottoes such as “Home, Sweet Home” were much cherished. Colorful calligraphic drawings and illustrations, like the one shown here, are more desirable than those executed in a single color of ink. Those with religious connotations are generally less in demand and seldom bring substantial prices.

01 Birds

Description
Large central blue bird with yellow leg resting atop large scroll surrounded by calligraphic feathering in brown and pink; scroll inscribed "Presented to our teacher, Miss Lillian Hamm, by school." 8 rectangular inserts of red, yellow, green, or white birds with scrolls inscribed with students' names.

Materials and Dimensions
Ink and watercolor on paper. Height: 18¾″. Width: 17¾″.

Artist, Locality, and Period
Unidentified. c. 1850–60.

Comment
Calligraphic drawings were done with quills or steel pens and featured the repeated cursive flourishes used in elegant handwriting. Children in a Spencerian writing class probably executed the small cards attached to the large watercolor-and-ink drawing that forms the central design motif of this calligraphic presentation piece. The young artist responsible for the central design was probably the most skillful in the class. "Spencerian" refers to the calligrapher Platt Rogers Spencer, who originated an ornate style of penmanship and created popular copybooks in the mid-19th century.

Hints for Collectors
Unusual works are well worth investigating, but uniqueness alone does not always ensure great value. Overall design, execution, and general appeal remain the major factors in the pricing of a work of art. Run-of-the-mill pieces almost never attract high prices; for instance, calligraphic drawings copied from prototypes printed in drawing books are generally less valuable.

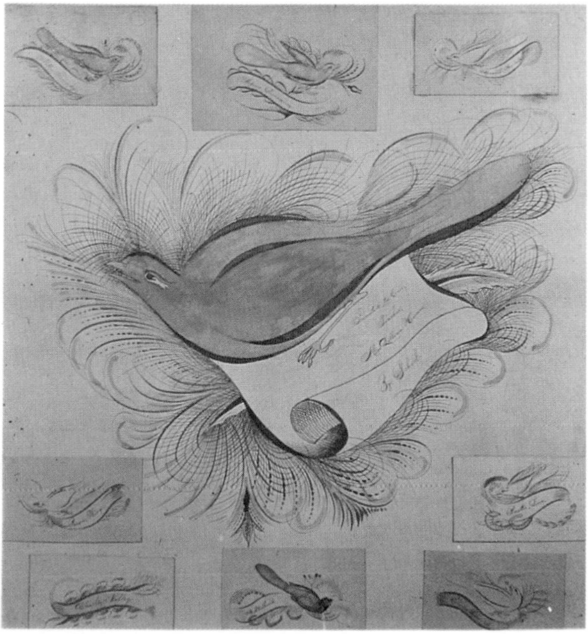

102 Bald Eagle

Description
Open-beaked bald eagle with pale head in profile. Body and strongly contoured wings covered in finely detailed brown feathers. Claws resting on 5 crossed arrows tied with ornate, inscribed scroll at center. Beige background. Signed and dated.

Materials and Dimensions
Ink on paper. Height: 9¾″. Width: 11″.

Artist, Locality, and Period
S. Fagley (life dates and locale unknown). 1872.

Comment
When America's Revolutionary leaders were searching for a national symbol, the Continental Congress established a commission headed by Ben Franklin. He felt strongly that the wild turkey would be the best choice, but other members of the commission preferred the bald eagle, and in time it was adopted as a symbol of America. By the early 19th century, the eagle motif appeared everywhere: on needlework and other textiles, ship carvings, sculpture, glassware, and in many other forms and mediums. Immigrant folk artists were particularly fascinated by this symbol of their adopted country.

Hints for Collectors
Eagles have been depicted in such a variety of poses and in so many mediums that it is difficult to assess which of their qualities are most significant. In general, fierce-looking eagles that are boldly designed and richly patterned command the greatest interest and highest prices.

103 Stag

Description
Large stag with full antlers standing on grassy knoll, surrounded by flowers, bushes, birds, rocks, and a tree stump. White background. Circular border of leafy motifs around central image. Similar motifs forming rectangular border around inscription and signature at lower left corner.

Materials and Dimensions
Ink on paper. Height: 15½″. Width: 19″.

Artist, Locality, and Period
S. R. Baldwin (life dates and locale unknown). c. 1800–50.

Comment
This pen-and-ink drawing may well have been copied from an illustration in an early album of needlework designs. During the 17th and 18th centuries, English books of needlework patterns were eagerly acquired by American families seeking to add a fashionable European look to their furnishings and embroidery. By the early 19th century, such design books had become relics, but some continued to be used for penmanship or calligraphic exercises.

Hints for Collectors
Collectors have always preferred original works of art to those, like the drawing shown here, probably derived from other sources. But it is interesting to note that as scholarship in American folk art broadens, many pieces once thought to be unique or highly original have been linked to earlier designs. Still, for investment purposes, a one-of-a-kind object is most desirable.

104 Tiger

Description
Gold-colored tiger with black stripes, standing on mottled grass. 6 trees and 5 daisies scattered throughout landscape; 3 black birds flying against blue sky with white clouds. Signed and dated in white oval at right.

Materials and Dimensions
Acrylic on board. Height: 17½″. Width: 23½″.

Artist, Locality, and Period
Antonio Esteves (1910–   ), New York City. 1974.

Comment
Antonio Esteves was born in Brazil and came to the United States in 1917 after living for 7 years in Cuba. A building superintendent, he burned his hands in an accident and started to paint as physical therapy. In 1976 he received an award at the Brooklyn Museum's prestigious Fence Show, an annual outdoor exhibition. He has painted more than 150 works, and though he is best known for his religious pictures, he has explored a wide variety of subjects. As seen in this example, his portrayals are intense, dynamic, and colorful.

Hints for Collectors
Because of the great appeal of the subject of this picture, it would bring a substantially larger sum than would most of Esteves's religious paintings, which attract a smaller group of collectors. Depictions of animals are particularly popular with animal lovers and command a premium: cats are most in demand, followed by dogs; owls and turtles are also sought after.

105 Black Cat

Description
Black cat with yellow eyes, lying at a slight angle across background that is blue on bottom and stark pink on top. Signed and dated.

Materials and Dimensions
Oil on canvas board. Height: 12″. Width: 16″.

Artist, Locality, and Period
Vestie E. Davis (1904–78), New York City. 1964.

Comment
Baltimore-born Vestie Davis turned to painting full time in 1947 after having been a circus barker, undertaker, newsstand operator, and church organist. He painted many well-known New York City scenes, from the Plaza Hotel to Coney Island. "I paint what people want and they want what's familiar," he said. "I painted Nathan's hot-dog stand with 300 people, all of them eating or drinking. The more people I put in, the faster they sold." Though he is best remembered for these remarkably detailed images of his beloved city, his animal pictures have wonderful lifelike qualities that appeal to many collectors.

Hints for Collectors
Like many folk artists, Davis depicted the environment around him. Though he is much admired for religious pictures based upon Jewish themes, these never command the considerable prices fetched by his views of New York. Davis painted on both canvas and canvas board. One drawback of pictures on canvas board is that they are difficult to restore; in addition, the corners are fragile and easily crushed.

Signs, Architectural Elements, and Flat Sculpture

The diverse pieces in this section are primarily flat and are painted, carved, or inscribed. A few are three-dimensional but remain pictorial in effect. All together, they present a cross section of American folk art.

Shop Signs and Trade Symbols
Signs were displayed in the first towns settled along the East Coast from Virginia to New England; by the 18th century these early forms of advertising were conspicuous in virtually every town and village. Most were tavern, inn, or trade signs, the latter indicating some kind of retail shop, merchant, or professional service. Toll and roadside signs were also used, but less frequently. Because education was a privilege and literacy rare, most signs were sculptural and depended on their visual appeal rather than on words to attract passersby. (Some trade figures, such as cigar-store Indians, are included in the next section along with other human figures.)
As towns became larger, shops began to compete for customers; consequently, signs became more distinctive and, as literacy spread, they more commonly displayed written messages. Three-dimensional signs gave way to flat signboards, which were often painted by talented artists; unfortunately, few signed their work.

Architectural Elements
Carved embellishments, often placed over doors, on rooftops, and on gateposts, were luxuries seen chiefly on the homes of the well-to-do in colonial times. Because of exposure to the weather, few of these pieces have survived intact or with original paint. Even late 19th-century examples have had a low survival rate. The gate shown here, in the form of the American flag, is an outstanding piece because of its beauty, rarity, and individuality.

Flat Sculpture and Fireboards
The relief carvings in this group, all from the 20th century, at first glance look more like paintings than sculpture. They explore patriotic and religious themes, which have always fascinated folk artists.
Dating from the 18th and 19th centuries, fireboards were essentially utilitarian, though also highly decorative. These custom-made wooden works stood on a base in front of a fireplace, or were attached to it, and were used during the warmer months as decoration and to keep soot from entering a room through a fireplace opening. Subjects ranged from naive still lifes to sophisticated *trompe l'oeil* designs.

Gravestones and Scrimshaw
Gravestones were among America's first sculptures, dating from as early as the mid-17th century. Early New England versions are usually scroll-topped pieces of slate, marble, or sandstone inscribed with portraits of the deceased or such symbols as Death, Father Time, scythes, hourglasses, and winged skulls. After about 1750, larger and more elaborate examples were made. Epitaphs were often misspelled or awkwardly phrased and over the years many have worn away.
The art of scrimshaw flourished and declined with the whaling industry, having its heyday from about 1825 to 1875. Carved and engraved by sailors on long whaling voyages, these objects were most often fashioned from whalebone or whale ivory. The pieces shown here range from common busks, meant to be inserted in corsets, to rare engraved teeth. Other scrimshaw objects are included in the sections on boxes, kitchenware, spinning implements, and animal sculpture.

106 Coffeehouse and shop sign

Description
Double-sided oval sign encircled by metal band and decorated on all sides with projecting metal rods and C-shaped ornaments. Wooden panel painted primarily in dark and light shades of green. On one side, yellow letters shadowed in dark green and red spell "E. FITTS' JR/COFFEEHOUSE"; the date "1832" is in dark green center rectangle. On reverse, interior of store with merchandise on shelves, painted in shades of green and yellow; at top, yellow letters trimmed in red spell "E. FITTS, JRS. STORE"; black-clad storekeeper behind counter. 2 plain rods on top for hanging. Nailed and welded construction.

Materials and Dimensions
Painted wood. Wrought iron. Overall height: 46⅞"; width: 46⅜". Panel height: 22⅜"; width: 34½".

Locality and Period
Vicinity of Shelburne, Massachusetts. 1832.

Comment
The earliest American trade signs were often 3-dimensional sculptures made by woodcarvers. As the level of literacy rose, however, carpenters and sometimes painters began to make flat signboards, such as the one shown here, with painted pictorial and written messages. One of the most notable makers of such signs was Edward Hicks (1780–1849), best known for his series of paintings called *The Peaceable Kingdom;* unfortunately, few other makers signed their work.

Backgrounds on signboards were varied, depicting decor
and patriotic symbols, animals, people, landscapes, or inte
such as this one. Basic types of signs include those to attra
customers to shops, inns, and taverns, identify private home
inform travelers of tolls and provide them with directions. In
signs, especially colorful and inventive, were widely used from
early Colonial times on; some of the earliest portray the English
royal family in a favorable light, which dates the signs at least as far back as the early 18th century.

Hints for Collectors

Trade signs are among the most appealing forms of American folk sculpture. Collectors pay substantial sums for 3-dimensional pieces from the 18th and 19th centuries, provided they are in good original condition. Early painted signs that are highly decorative also arouse great interest among collectors. This particular example is both rare and beautiful; the different advertisements on its 2 sides, original paint, and distinctive ironwork combine to make it very unusual. Because weathering has caused most outdoor signs to fade and suffer paint loss, many have been repainted several times, which substantially diminishes their value. Look for pieces that have refinements such as unusual framing, applied balusters, or handsome wrought-iron embellishments.

avern sign

Description
Semicircular wooden sign with "CENTREVILLE" painted in large white letters trimmed in red. Letters arched over coat of arms in cartouche flanked by white, blue, and American flags. Scrolled decoration under flags; gold-colored background. Gash on white flag at right. Overall weathering. Signed "Richardson Painter." Black pieced-wood frame.

Materials and Dimensions
Pine. Painted. Nails. Height: 16½″. Width: 32″. Thickness: 1½″.

Locality and Period
Painted by Richardson (first name and life dates unknown), Centreville, Pennsylvania. c. 1865.

Comment
American tavern signs dating from the mid-17th century were some of the very first signs to appear in America, and are among the earliest forms of advertising. The size and shape of the sign shown here indicate that it was probably used at the entrance of a tavern in place of the fanlight. Many artists who painted houses, coaches, and portraits also painted signs, which they often signed in large letters to advertise themselves as well as their clients.

Hints for Collectors
The earliest tavern sign extant, by Thomas Child of Boston, is on display at the Bostonian Society. Simple 19th-century examples generally relied on painted decoration alone to convey a message; these must still be in fine original condition to command high prices. The early 3-dimensional signs are most expensive.

08 House sign

Description
Hexagonal wooden sign with painting of pale green house ag beige background. Top floor with 2 pairs of 4-pane windows; main story with door at center, flanked by long glass panels an 2 pairs of screened windows; ground floor with 2 windows under entrance porch. Double staircase from ground level to doorway. 3 trees at left; tall pole at right. The name "HARLSADE" in dark green lettering shadowed by orange. Molded frame painted white, with 2 metal eyelet loops at top.

Materials and Dimensions
Oak. Painted. Steel fixtures. Height: 20″. Width: 26″.

Locality and Period
Connecticut. c. 1910–20.

Comment
The sign shown here, resembling a house in shape, identified a summer cottage. The symmetry of the painted building indicates that it may have been a 2-family house, with the name "Harlsade" a combination of the owners' names. This simple sign was not professionally made, and its frame was probably created from old window moldings. The lack of wear on the reverse side suggests it was hung against a wall.

Hints for Collectors
Early pictorial signs are usually more valuable than those with lettering only. Unusual or charming examples are the best investments. Because trade signs produced before the mid-19th century are rare and costly, collectors often seek fine examples made between 1850 and 1950. Fine craftsmanship and an interesting design compensate for the newness of a 20th-century piece and make it likely to appreciate in value.

Guesthouse sign

Description
Rectangular wooden sign with painting of 6 black trees against white sky. The word "GUESTS" spelled out in worn white sandpaper letters over silhouetted lawn. Front and back identical. Panel crackled and chipped from age. Green frame with mitered corners, broken-pediment decoration at top and bottom, and 2 turned posts at sides. Metal fixtures.

Materials and Dimensions
Painted wood. Sandpaper. Cast iron. Height: 22″. Width: 27½″. Thickness: 2″.

Locality and Period
Manchester, Vermont. c. 1900–10.

Comment
Manchester had many large Victorian homes that served during vacation season as guesthouses and were distinguished by the signs placed on their front lawns. Such signs, like the one shown here, were usually homemade; the turned parts that frequently decorated them often matched those on the porch railings. The lettering style and Art Nouveau design of this example were particularly popular throughout New England at the turn of the century.

Hints for Collectors
Old painted surfaces, especially if exposed to weathering, inevitably become crazed, or crackled, with age. This effect, called "alligatoring" by collectors, is usually caused by abrupt changes in temperature. The presence of a crazed surface is not always a reliable indicator of age, however, for some unethical dealers who find it profitable to sell fakes produce this texture artificially by applying intense heat.

110 Boot trade sign

Description
Tall carved and painted boot with rounded edges and curved top, sides asymmetrically tapered to slim ankle; exaggerated arch, instep, and toe. High heel and protruding sole. Eye hook screwed into center of top for hanging.

Materials and Dimensions
Pine or poplar. Painted. Wrought-iron hook. Height: 33½″. Width: 13″. Thickness: 3″.

Locality and Period
Probably the Northeast. c. 1900–10.

Comment
The first known American shoemaker was Thomas Beard, who came to Salem, Massachusetts, in 1629. Early shoemakers worked by hand at home or in small shops, or traveled from customer to customer. After 1830 the rapid introduction of machinery for making shoes led to the development of factories capable of mass production. The sign shown here might have identified an establishment that made, sold, or repaired shoes. The omission of the owner's name or profession on this sign suggests that the shop was the only shoe-related business in town. Tailors, fishmongers, barbers, butchers, opticians, glovemakers, and other tradespeople also used 3-dimensional trade signs. Later, trade symbols such as this were frequently replaced by signboards.

Hints for Collectors
When buying 3-dimensional trade signs, search for examples that are stylistically striking. The exaggerated profile and humorous quality of this piece make it so appealing that it would probably generate lively bidding at auction.

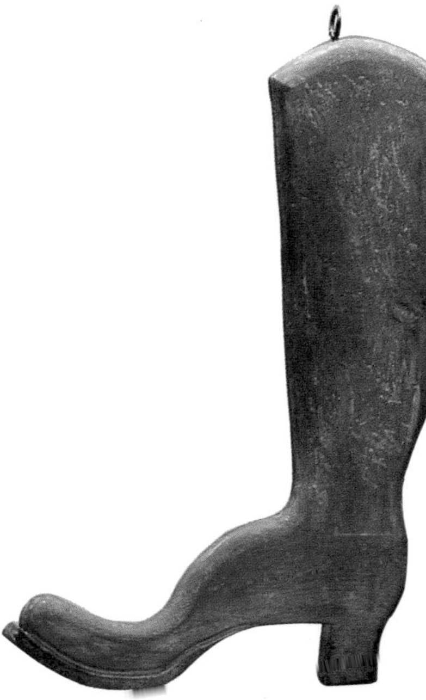

111 Dentist's trade sign

Description
Carved and painted molar with crown (split on side) and 3 root sections made from a single piece of heartwood. Top covered by metal plate tightly nailed around perimeter; rusted iron screw in center for hanging. Overall wear and crazing.

Materials and Dimensions
Pine. Painted. Iron. Tin. Copper. Height: 25″. Width: 12″. Depth: 10¾″.

Locality and Period
New Hampshire. c. 1850–80.

Comment
The trade sign shown here may have been carved by the dentist who displayed it, since it is an enlarged, but otherwise exact, copy of an upper right molar. Dentists, doctors, and lawyers often displayed trade signs until about 1840, when the public began to consider advertising by people in such professions in poor taste and the number of such signs decreased. Other common trade signs included those shaped like watches, teapots, eyeglasses, scissors, and keys, many nearly 3 feet long.

Hints for Collectors
A collector is often attracted to folk art relating to his profession and may be willing to pay a premium for it. Because most trade signs were used outdoors, they will nearly always show signs of age such as rusting of hardware and staining where the metal enters the wood. If there are no such indications of age, the sign is certainly a fake.

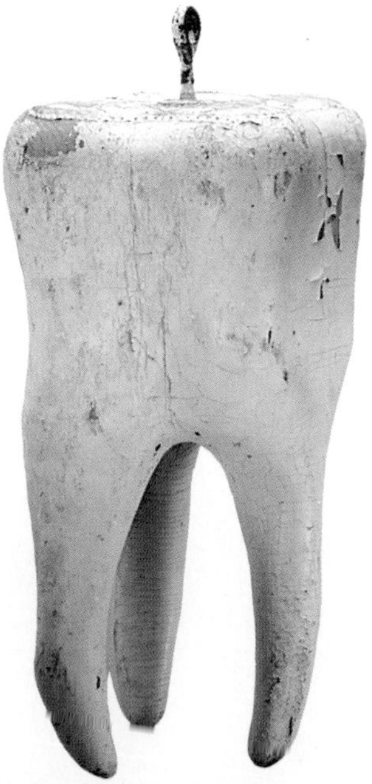

12 **Barber pole**

Description
Barber pole consisting of 8 vertical layers glued together and then shaped like a rolling pin, perhaps on a lathe. Ends painted white; central portion painted white with spiraling red stripe. Holes in top and bottom to permit mounting. Worn overall.

Materials and Dimensions
Pine. Painted. Height: 27¾". Diameter: 5¼".

Locality and Period
Probably the Northeast. c. 1875–1900.

Comment
The familiar barber pole was an early form of advertising popular in both Europe and America. It is said that the red spiraling stripe originally indicated that a barber was also a surgeon or bloodletter; and a black stripe, if present, signified that he was an undertaker as well. In the 20th century, barbers introduced electric poles to attract customers with both light and revolving stripes. While the size and shape of barbers' trade signs may vary—a red-and-white-striped straight razor is also known—instant recognition is proof of their success.

Hints for Collectors
Distinctively designed barber poles are usually of greater interest to collectors than are purely utilitarian ones. Among those fetching the highest prices at auction are freestanding ones mounted on bases sometimes decorated with scissors, clippers, shaving mugs, or other tools of the trade. A beautifully shaped pole will always bring a much more substantial sum than an undistinguished one.

3 Architectural finial

Description
Elongated finial with turned and cut sections. Conical spire above narrow disks and spool-shaped section. Octagonal center segment with 8 applied rectangles, each having pyramidal surface; below center, another spool-shaped segment and 2 disks. Rectangular base with cutout triangles at front and rear of bottom defining feet at corners. Traces of black and gray paint. Nail construction.

Materials and Dimensions
Pine. Painted. Iron-wire nails. Height: 41″. Base length: 8″; width: 8″.

Locality and Period
The Midwest. c. 1900–10.

Comment
Architectural finials have been set atop American buildings since colonial times. Some were geometric in design, such as the one shown here, while others were representational; a pineapple, for instance, a symbol of hospitality, was often placed over doorways and on top of houses, outbuildings, and gateposts throughout the 18th century. These decorations were a luxury and therefore generally appeared primarily on the homes of the well-to-do.

Hints for Collectors
Many folk art collectors find architectural elements appealing. Pieces with highly individualized or inventive designs are the most desirable. If an inexpensive piece has been repainted, you can try removing the later layers of paint to reveal the original surface; this should be attempted only by a professional if the piece is particularly valuable. Some collectors use pieces like this as bases for lamps, whirligigs, or sculpture.

14 Barn-door archway decoration

Description
Triangular architectural element with cutoff bottom corners; flat back made of 3 pieces of wood. 5-pointed star applied in center. Upper edges decorated with 3 rows of applied molding (scalloped, triangular, and plain) placed one atop another. Traces of paint.

Materials and Dimensions
Pine. Painted. Iron-wire nails. Height: 30½″. Length: 38″. Depth: 5½″.

Locality and Period
Connecticut. c. 1880–1915.

Comment
Architectural elements like the one shown here—originally placed over an archway in a barn—are impressive examples of the work of country craftsmen. They often added a whimsical touch to otherwise unadorned rural buildings.

Hints for Collectors
This kind of large wooden piece will not appeal to every collector, but, for those with room to display it, it can add a great deal to a country-style interior. While its decorative elements are quite simple, their well-balanced arrangement combined with the weathered look of the wood make this a very striking design. Architectural elements in all sizes may often be purchased inexpensively when old houses or barns are being torn down. Junkyards and salvage yards are also good sources for this kind of object. During the past decade, many shops specializing in such fixtures, windows, and stairways have opened in larger cities and suburbs, but most charge a premium for their wares.

115 Flag gate

Description
Wooden gate cut out and painted on both sides in American flag design. Solid blue rectangle in upper right corner, with 38 white stars arranged with single star in each corner, 2 concentric ovals of stars, and larger central star. 13 alternating red and white stripes cut in undulating profile. Cross-braces visible between stripes. Yellow wooden ball atop gatepost. Brass ball, at top left, part of latching mechanism.

Materials and Dimensions
Painted wood. Iron. Brass. Height: 39½″. Length: 57″. Depth: 3¾″.

Locality and Period
Jefferson County, New York. c. 1876.

Comment
Around the time of the centennial celebration of American independence in 1876, there was an upsurge of nationalistic feeling that was expressed by the use of patriotic motifs on handiwork ranging from hooked rugs to architectural ornaments. This farm gate, a spirited example of utilitarian folk art, shows the depth of its unknown maker's feelings.

Hints for Collectors
This exceptional gate would be a once-in-a-lifetime find for any collector. As carefully designed and executed as a piece of sculpture, its curving stripes make it look like a flag waving in the breeze, and its round finial atop the hinged post resembles the ball found on many flagpoles. While beyond the budget of most collectors, this object is nevertheless worth studying as an example of the finest folk art. Keep an eye open for such extravagant architectural ornaments when traveling in rural areas and do not hesitate to ask if they are for sale.

16 Abraham Lincoln

Description
Painted relief carving of Abraham Lincoln with red, white, and blue stripes as background. Hair, eyebrows, and beard black with gray flecks. Black pupils set in white and outlined in black. Flat nose; slightly uneven ears. Dark skin tones. Black bow tie covering neck; black coat and white shirt. Disproportionately small body. Hands clasped across chest. Black molded frame. Signed on back.

Materials and Dimensions
Painted wood. Height: 14½″. Width: 9¼″.

Locality and Period
Made by Elijah Pierce (1892–   ), Columbus, Ohio. c. 1975.

Comment
A barber by profession, Elijah Pierce began carving wooden figures in the 1920s—a hobby he continues today. He achieved public recognition only when he was in his seventies; his works have since been exhibited at major museums around the world. His subjects, painted in bold and glossy colors, include biblical scenes, incidents from his youth, his father's tales of slavery, and famous Americans. His highly imaginative imagery is often religious, since he believes that each of his carvings is a message from God.

Hints for Collectors
When acquiring a sculpture by a living artist, be sure to have the craftsman sign and date it. Elijah Pierce generally signs the back of his works in paint or sometimes with a felt-tip marker. A full provenance of a piece can add substantially to its market value.

117 Saint Luke

Description
Painted relief carving of Saint Luke with gold halo and long dark hair and beard; green and maroon robes with gold piping. Seated in low chair and barefooted, holding Greek-inscribed Gospel. Undersize ox at left. Cross joined to alpha-and-omega motif at right. Greek inscription across bottom. Leafy archway enclosing scene; red flowers in corners. Stained outermost frame of carved leaves; inner frame with cross, leaves, and vine-and-grape motifs. Signed.

Materials and Dimensions
Painted wood. Height: 48″. Width: 28″.

Locality and Period
Made by John Perates (1894–1970), Portland, Maine. c. 1940.

Comment
Perates, a Greek-born cabinetmaker who lived in Portland, began carving in 1938. He made a wooden pulpit and a series of large relief panels, including the one shown here, which he donated to a local Greek Orthodox church. Unfortunately, these works were deemed unsuitable by the congregation and remained in the church's basement for many years. Recognized today as significant expressions of folk art, they were influenced by the Byzantine icons that Perates studied for more than 30 years.

Hints for Collectors
Religious wood carvings generally fetch modest prices, since they appeal to comparatively few collectors. However, if a piece, like this example, is monumental or powerful enough, or represents the finest work of an important carver, or has been shown in museums or reproduced in books or magazines, its value will increase considerably.

18 Masonic temple

Description
Painted relief carving of interior and exterior view of Masonic temple. 6 men standing in foreground, wearing gray hats, black coats, and Masonic aprons and pendants. Low altar with 3 carved figural niches in front of men. Masonic symbols in lower left corner. Beige temple façade in left background, with Masonic symbol over door and "MASONIC TEMPLE/Aurora, New York" inscribed around steeple. Vaulted interior behind men, with angels and American flag around portal and Tower of Babel within. Initialed and dated. Narrow green frame part of carving.

Materials and Dimensions
Painted wood. Height: 24¾″. Width: 27″.

Locality and Period
Made by Mary Shelley (1950–   ), Ithaca, New York. 1980.

Comment
Mary Shelley, a young folk artist whose work has been compared with that of Grandma Moses, is both a carver and sign painter. She learned to carve from her father, and what began as a hobby became a major occupation once collectors became interested in her work. Her carvings, which she calls "picture stories," are inspired by important events, places, or people in her life; the Masonic temple shown in this excellent example of her style is located near her home.

Hints for Collectors
When considering the purchase of a contemporary folk carving, assess its aesthetic merit as well as its marketability. Popular appeal and some stylistic continuity with 18th- and 19th-century artistic traditions may justify a high price. The market value of a folk sculpture also often reflects its suitability for decorative display in a contemporary setting.

119 Pictorial fireboard

Description
Fireboard carved and painted to suggest a church interior. White catafalque projecting from center, decorated with carved swags and tassels and topped by 3 white church spires, each with a red cutout window. 6 tall rectangles, suggesting windows, frame landscapes. Black background and white carved trim surround windows. 2 pale rectangles below, flanked by rows of diamond shapes. Black base conforming to curved shape of catafalque.

Materials and Dimensions
Pine. Painted. Height: 43¼″. Length: 47⅛″. Depth: 7″.

Locality and Period
Connecticut. c. 1840.

Comment
During the summer months when a fire was not needed, fireboards stood in front of empty fireplaces. They not only decorated the empty hearth but also prevented soot, birds, or other small creatures from coming down the chimney and entering the room. The owner of the house might select a still life, landscape, or other design, which was often painted by the same artist who decorated the rest of a room. The example shown here was found in a parish house in Connecticut.

Hints for Collectors
This fireboard is unusual because it is not only painted but also carved in low relief to give a 3-dimensional effect. Such an exceptional piece by an anonymous folk artist would be a highly desirable addition to any folk art collection. Though collectors today often hang fireboards as if they were paintings, the comparatively large size and attached base of this example would require that it be displayed on a low platform or in an unused fireplace.

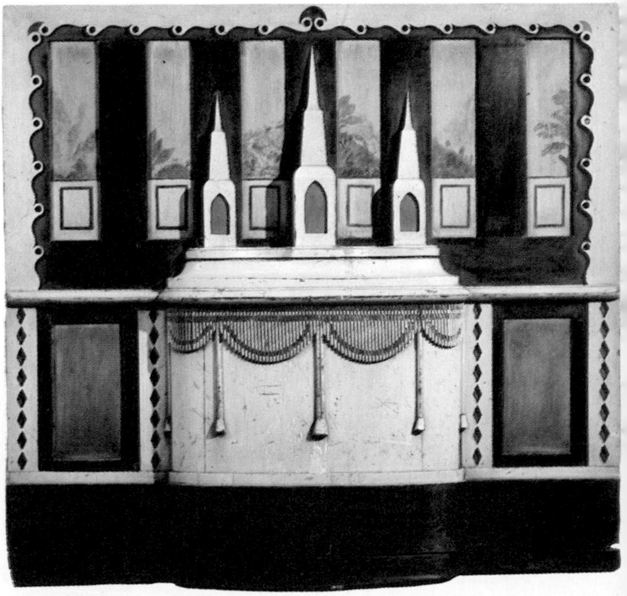

20 Pictorial fireboard

Description
Flat fireboard painted to look like fireplace, with red bricks outlined in white in center section. Tan border along top and sides to imitate wooden mantel; mottled tan section on bottom suggesting stone hearth. Panel made of 4 pieces of wood battened together.

Materials and Dimensions
Pine. Painted. Height: 31½″. Length: 41¾″. Depth: 2″.

Locality and Period
Amherst, Massachusetts. c. 1850–70.

Comment
Fireboards were often constructed of wide boards connected by battens, though sometimes a canvas panel was used. They had freestanding wooden bases or were attached to the fireplace with a turnbuckle; some were notched at the bottom to be fitted over the andirons. They were usually painted, most commonly with *trompe l'oeil* designs, landscapes, floral motifs, or a vase of flowers. Meant to be seen from afar, these subjects were usually executed with heavy outlines and bright colors.

Hints for Collectors
Although not easy to find, fireboards have become much sought after in recent years. Those with detailed landscapes or *trompe l'oeil* paintings, such as this example, are especially desirable. The price of this form of painted folk art has risen considerably over the past decade. Fireboards are most often found in New England, particularly at house sales or when old homes are being torn down.

121 Gravestone

Description
Rectangular slab with stylized head of an angel or the deceased incised in arc atop epitaph, which reads, "Here Lyes [the] body of Ebenez Johnson [the] son of Mr John Johnson and Mrs Sarah Johnson his wife Who died Desebar [the] 1 1727 in [the] ninth year of his age." Rosette-topped borders of geometric designs flanking epitaph. Narrow border at bottom; uncarved free-form base meant for below-ground anchor.

Materials and Dimensions
Granite. Height: 21″. Width: 17″. Thickness: 2″.

Locality and Period
Probably Connecticut. c. 1727.

Comment
Many tombstones from colonial New England bear traditional motifs, such as the angel's face and simple geometric figuration on the example shown here. Incised elements may be difficult to decipher because many soft, locally quarried stones have become badly worn with age. Epitaphs may be awkwardly written, for school attendance was voluntary during colonial times and many stonecutters were therefore almost illiterate. Although most work is unsigned, such a piece may sometimes be attributed by comparing it with a signed one in the identical style.

Hints for Collectors
Collectors of gravestones or gravestone rubbings are particularly interested in symbolism referring to death. Especially popular are stones that show Father Time with a scythe, hourglasses symbolizing the sands of time, trees with broken limbs representing a severed life, or the figure of Death as a skeleton snuffing a candle.

122 Gravestone

Description
Rectangular slab with head of an angel or the deceased incised in arc atop epitaph; partially legible epitaph reads, "Here lyeth the body of Jonathan Hutchison . . . who died Septembar 10 1717 aged 3_ years. . . ." Rosette-topped borders of geometric design flanking epitaph. Scrolled border below. Broken base.

Materials and Dimensions
Granite. Height: 21⅜″. Width: 14¾″. Thickness: 2″.

Locality and Period
Connecticut. c. 1717.

Comment
Now considered part of our national artistic heritage, gravestones are among the earliest dated pieces of American sculpture, with the finest ones usually the work of professional carvers in small New England towns. Carvers in the 17th and 18th centuries used conventional motifs, but in an individualistic manner. Portraits of the deceased were popular during the 18th century. Collectors especially prize gravestones with elaborate and well-executed decoration.

Hints for Collectors
Since relatively few early tombstones are legitimately for sale, the chief risk in acquiring such objects is that they may have been stolen from old graveyards. Without a written guarantee or history of ownership, you may someday have to relinquish your purchase—perhaps at your own loss—if it proves to have been obtained illegally. The dealer who purchased the stone shown here, for example, had to return it when a local historical society informed him that it had been taken from a nearby graveyard.

123 Scrimshaw plaque

Description
Flat rectangular plaque with engraved 3-masted warship under full sail at right; ocean in foreground and land in distance at left. Foliate border incorporating pink roses in corners and at middle of sides. Front surface polished and finished; reverse partly finished, revealing texture of bone and marks from cutting tool.

Materials and Dimensions
Panbone (whalebone). Pigment. Height: 6¾". Length: 10½". Thickness: ½".

Locality and Period
New England. c. 1860.

Comment
Panbone, so named for its flat panlike shape, is a rare and much sought after material taken from the back of a sperm whale's jawbone. Pieces were engraved with a sailmaker's needle or a similar device. Pigment was then rubbed into the crevices to highlight the design. By varying the depth of the engraved line, a skilled craftsman could create shadings and perspective. Though black was the most common color, other pigments, especially red, blue, or green, were used as well.

Hints for Collectors
Collectors are generally more interested in engraved scrimshaw with several pigments than in pieces with black only. Because colorful engraved scrimshaw brings high prices, some people have tried to enhance worn old pieces by adding pigments, so be suspicious of any example that has colors inconsistent with documented, authentic pieces. Panbone plaques are uncommon and expensive because large pieces of panbone are rare.

24 Scrimshaw busks

Description
2 elongated oval busks with engraved vignettes. *Left:* 4 vertical multicolored scenes, crowned by flowers (top to bottom): monument initialed "NC" and flanked by 2 trees; lighthouse with small house adjacent; vase of flowers; 3-masted ship under full sail. All enclosed by linear border. Small split at top repaired at an early date with metal pins and plate. *Right:* 3 horizontal scenes showing ship with iceberg, harpooning of a whale, and ship sailing homeward. Leaf-and-branch borders.

Materials and Dimensions
Panbone (whalebone). Pigment. Length: 13¼″. Width: 1½″. Thickness (left; right): 1⁄16″; ⅛″.

Locality and Period
New England. *Left:* c. 1830. *Right:* c. 1860.

Comment
Though busks were made to be inserted in women's corsets, decorated whalebone busks were rarely worn because they were kept for show. They were prized by women whose whalemen husbands or sweethearts had made them. The careful repair done on the example at the left while it was still fairly new indicates how highly busks were valued. These common scrimshaw items were generally made of panbone or baleen, both taken from a whale's mouth.

Hints for Collectors
Signed scrimshaw is rare, and signed busks extremely so. Many collectors are actually attracted to the anonymity of most scrimshaw, made by unknown whalemen on unknown oceans. Busks may be displayed in narrow shadow-box frames or mounted on lucite stands hung on a wall.

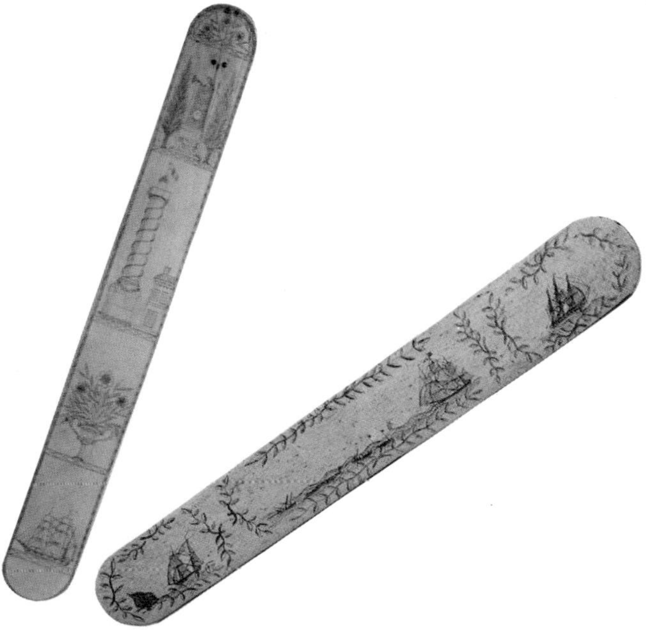

125 Whale teeth

Description
Whale teeth with engraved bust portrait; subject's surname in curved banner above, and 2 crossed branches enclosing sides and bottom. Biblical scenes on reverse. Narrow border across top and wider one across bottom. *Left* (front): George Washington in uniform, with head turned; (reverse): Jesus and Mary Magdalene after the Resurrection. *Right* (front): Lafayette in period dress, with torso and head turned; (reverse): Jesus with woman at well. Vertical cracks resulting from age.

Materials and Dimensions
Whale teeth. Pigment. Height: 5¼".

Locality and Period
New England. c. 1835.

Comment
Usually made for a loved one at home, scrimshaw was a sailor's link with his family and friends. The engraved teeth shown here combine 3 desirable attributes: their main subject is patriotic, their secondary theme is religious, and they are a matched pair. Other common engravings on teeth include nautical, figural, architectural, fashion-plate, domestic, and mythical subjects. Those carved in relief are usually less in demand.

Hints for Collectors
Scrimshaw that is overly decorated may be an old piece with modern embellishments. Look for cohesive design and consistent execution, and seek the advice of experts if you detect stylistic incongruities. Age cracks, unless they ruin the design, do not affect the value of scrimshaw. A pair of teeth should never be split up, since this lessens their interest and value.

126 Whale tooth

Description
Whale tooth engraved horizontally with the ship *Susan*. Banner above ship reads, "The Susan on the coast of Japan"; uppermost inscription, "The Susan of Nantucket/Frederick Swain Master." American eagle and shield to right; eagle holding banner with legend "E Pluribus Unum." Crossed American flags at tip. Inscribed below ship, "Death to the living/long life to the killers/ Success to sailors wives/& greasy luck to whalers" and "This was done by Frederick Myrick for Mr. Prince Coffin, Decem 28th 1828." Reverse shows the crew rendering oil from blubber.

Materials and Dimensions
Whale tooth. Pigment. Height: 5½".

Locality and Period
Made by Frederick Myrick, Nantucket. 1828.

Comment
Because they are the earliest dated scrimshaw engravings and the only dated scrimshaw series, the dozen and a half engraved whale's teeth carved on the *Susan* are the most coveted pieces in this medium. The Peabody Museum in Salem, Massachusetts, and the Nantucket Whaling Museum each have 3 examples. The images and inscriptions engraved on all the *Susan* teeth are almost identical.

Hints for Collectors
Fine engraved whale's teeth are often faked because they are so valuable. An old piece should have a soft beige patina; a yellow or orange cast may indicate an outright fake or a walrus tooth. Teeth may be displayed on imaginatively shaped wooden or wrought-iron stands, with their hollow bottoms resting on a projecting part. They should be placed away from hot lights and in a room neither too dry nor too humid.

Sculpture of People

The human figure has inspired much of the finest and most characteristic American folk sculpture. Dating from the mid-18th century to the present, the examples in this section range in size from 4 inches to 7 feet. They were designed for carnivals and churches, as well as ships and stores. Artists created most by sawing and carving wood, but others were made by chiseling stone, cutting paper, or casting metal or chalky gypsum. Many originally served as utilitarian objects, such as targets, scarecrows, grave markers, religious shrines, or advertisements, though the intended function of some is no longer known. Their early uses are today less important than their artistic merit.

Religious Carvings
From the Southwest comes a uniquely Spanish-American form of religious folk sculpture that blends Hispanic and Indian influences. These religious carvings date from three periods: Spanish Colonial (1692–1820), Mission Republic (1820–50), and American (1850–present). Called bultos, they depict Christ and other religious figures, and were usually gessoed and painted after being carved by their often anonymous makers. Small examples were generally meant for private worship at home; larger ones were placed in churches. This art form has also flourished in Puerto Rico and other Spanish-speaking areas.

Cigar-Store Figures
Among the most picturesque trade symbols are cigar-store Indians. These figures were part of an artistic and literary tradition that had begun in England centuries earlier. Indians did not become the most widely used symbol for tobacco shops in America until the mid-19th century.

The demand for novelty led to the creation of other types of cigar-store figures, from Turks and Africans to racetrack touts and stylish belles. A sign of mercantile success, these eye-catching figures were displayed by virtually every tobacco shop and were often quite costly. They were most commonly used outdoors, where they were bolted to the ground or moved into place on wheels during business hours; others were placed inside shops.

First crafted in East Coast port cities—usually by former figurehead carvers put out of work by the decline of sailing ships—fine examples were soon created in the Midwest as well. Like figureheads, tobacconists' figures were generally made of white pine, with arms executed separately unless carved close to the body. Toward the end of the 19th century, these and other trade figures were banned from the sidewalks of most cities because they obstructed the increasing pedestrian traffic.

Figureheads
Seafarers have traditionally placed symbolic carved figures on the bows of their ships to serve as talismans. Early American figureheads were modeled after English prototypes, usually animals or busts. After the Revolution distinctly American forms evolved, most often full-length human figures wrapped in classical drapery, executed in a simple style much like that of other American folk art. In shipbuilding centers more than 700 carvers produced figureheads of patriotic symbols, such as eagles, statesmen, and heroes, as well as of less-exalted subjects, such as a sea captain's wife. The size of these figureheads was determined by the length of a ship's bowsprit. Ships were also decorated with other carvings, including flat sternboards.

127 Phrenological head

Description
Carved and painted one-piece armless bust of girl with top of head and forehead divided into multicolored free-form sections, each labeled with a phrenological characteristic, such as "Caution," "Sensitiveness," or "Conscientiousness." Carved childlike facial features with traces of paint on lips and eyes. Pleated maroon dress with scoop neck, puffed sleeves, and belt.

Materials and Dimensions
Pine. Painted. Height: 16⅜". Width: 13". Depth: 7⅛".

Locality and Period
Attributed to Asa Ames (1824–51), vicinity of Buffalo, New York. c. 1847–50.

Comment
Phrenology, the analysis of character and mental capacity according to the conformation of the skull, became popular after about 1835. Unlike the carved wooden model shown here, most phrenological heads were molded plaster. This figure has been attributed to Asa Ames (once incorrectly thought to have been named Alexander) on stylistic grounds.

Hints for Collectors
Few folk carvers had an output sizable enough to enable scholars to attribute unidentified pieces on the basis of stylistic similarities. This head, known by connoisseurs of folk art for more than 25 years, was previously attributed to several craftsmen. Its recent attribution to Asa Ames has not enhanced its value substantially, because few of Ames's pieces are known or available. To appreciate significantly in value, an artist's work must come on the market regularly.

28 Carnival target figure

Description
Carved and painted 3-piece bust of bald black man with ears close to skull and caricatured facial features, including browless brown eyes with conspicuous whites, broad nose, and smiling mouth with full red lips. Short neck joined to flat board rounded at top to suggest shoulders. Flat base. Face dented where struck by balls. Screw, nail, and glue construction.

Materials and Dimensions
Oak. Painted. Iron screws and nails. Height: 24″. Width: 13⅞″. Depth: 7″.

Locality and Period
New England. c. 1890–1900.

Comment
Figures such as the one shown here express openly racist attitudes prevalent during the late 19th and early 20th centuries. If the figure itself was not struck by a ball, it often stood above a target that, when struck, caused the figure to react, for example, by blowing smoke out of its ears or mouth. Such targets, by symbolically allowing black people to be struck or ridiculed, emphasized the notion of their inferiority. As these attitudes have been discouraged and have gradually diminished over the past decades, so has this type of folk art.

Hints for Collectors
Carnival figures from ball-toss games, when they are realistic and sensitive representations of the human figure are valued by collectors. Though many collectors avoid objects that are caricatures and represent racial slurs, some collectors find them whimsical and are willing to pay a premium for them.

129 Triple-faced head

Description
Carved male head with 3 brown faces, 2 smiling and one frowning, topped by hat made of a separate piece of wood and painted black. Brass tacks for pupils of eyes. Each nose shaped differently. No ears or neck. Head rests on rough-cut circular platform set on black rectangular base.

Materials and Dimensions
Oak. Painted and stained. Brass tacks. Height without base: 9½″. Diameter of platform: 7½″.

Locality and Period
Possibly the Northeast. c. 1930–40.

Comment
Most American folk sculpture is a product of creativity at the grass-roots level. As survival in the New World became easier and more people had leisure time, whittling became a popular national diversion. Some people carved utilitarian objects such as bowls, while others made pieces meant solely to please the eye and demonstrate the ability of the craftsman. Experts believe that the triple-faced figure shown here is an example of the latter tendency. Any such fanciful object is called a "whimsy." The diversity of modern art has expanded popular acceptance of many kinds of artistic expression, including such 20th-century folk sculptures.

Hints for Collectors
Many conservative collectors of folk art believe that what often passes for folk art in the 20th century is simply craft rather than art, and prefer the yellow patina of antique pieces. On the other hand, many open-minded collectors believe that fine folk art, regardless of its age, is a product of the hand of a craftsman guided by the eye of an artist.

130 Carnival target figure

Description
Carved and painted 3-piece head with caricatured facial features, including oversize almond-shaped eyes with incised pupils, bulbous nose, and slit mouth. Long scratches indicating hair; receding hairline. Kidney-shaped ears; long neck. Worn surface cracked and dented. Nail construction. Mounted on black square base.

Materials and Dimensions
Pine. Painted. Iron nails. Height without base: 13½″. Width: 9″. Depth: 10½″.

Locality and Period
Possibly Mid-Atlantic states. c. 1930–50.

Comment
Carnivals and amusement parks have utilized a rich array of American folk sculpture. While carnival games that used guns featured metal targets (*see* 210), ball-toss games generally had wooden targets like the one shown here, which have only recently been recognized as folk art. Such targets were often badly damaged or were discarded.

Hints for Collectors
Because folk art collecting is a relatively new field, the criteria for evaluating works of art are constantly changing. In the 1970s, folk art attracted a new following; many of these people were already collectors of fine art who prized design, style, and craftsmanship above the folk art historian's traditional concern for age and attribution. Admirers of modern abstract works would probably appreciate this simple stylized piece.

131 Sculptural fragment

Description
Neoclassical metal female head with short wavy hair parted in center; arched triangular tiara with series of vertical openings in front. Expressionless face with high forehead, almond-shaped eyes, long straight nose, high cheekbones, and closed mouth. Short neck with jagged cutoff edges. Rusted and discolored.

Materials and Dimensions
Zinc. Height: 20″. Width: 15″. Depth: 16″.

Locality and Period
Pennsylvania. c. 1876.

Comment
This metal head is a fragment of a 10-foot-tall Neoclassical statue of Justice. Since colonial times, Liberty, Columbia, Justice, and other symbolic female figures have frequently served as subjects for leading folk sculptors such as William Rush of Philadelphia. Courthouses, government offices, and other public buildings of the 19th and 20th centuries were often adorned with such wooden or cast-metal ladies. These figures also appear as ships' figureheads, weathervanes, whirligigs, and in paintings and scrimshaw engravings.

Hints for Collectors
During the last decades of the 19th century, cigar-store Indians, theater sculptures, and a vast array of architectural ornaments were cast in metal and often sold through mail-order catalogues. Strictly speaking, such pieces are hard to classify as folk art, yet many museums, dealers, and collectors accept them as such, and various types are in great demand. Look for well-preserved examples with balanced, innovative designs.

32 Grave ornament

Description
Carved stone head with cadaverous oval face and sunken eyes, long chipped nose, open mouth, small separated teeth, and pointed chin. Band across forehead separating hair from face; shoulder-length hair with chiseled lines.

Materials and Dimensions
Granite. Height: 11½″. Width: 6″. Depth: 4½″.

Locality and Period
New England. c. 1730–70.

Comment
New England gravestones were the first native American sculptures, the earliest known example dating from 1653. The grave ornament shown here may be a representation of Death himself or a portrait of the deceased; the latter custom gained popularity in the 18th century. The lack of writing on many such pieces makes them hard to date and identify. Symbols of death commonly found on early gravestones include a skull, hourglass, angel, and Death with a scythe.

Hints for Collectors
When considering a grave marker, look for a piece with strong individuality. Many 17th- and 18th-century stone carvers, working in cultural isolation, developed highly personal styles and repertoires of motifs, which led to the creation of some extraordinary works of art. During the 19th century, a more standard set of images was used in virtually every stone-carving shop. Still, in some rural areas personally inspired pieces continued to be produced. Because of their sentimental excesses and visual clichés, Victorian grave carvings are less desirable and less valuable than fine early examples.

133 Architectural ornament

Description
Rectangular carved stone face of mythological creature with leaflike hair and beard, and deep eye sockets framed by jutting brows. Long flat nose, full lips suggesting a smile, and flat dimpled chin.

Materials and Dimensions
Marble. Height: 11″. Width: 9″. Depth: 2″.

Locality and Period
New York City. c. 1875–1900.

Comment
Turn-of-the-century architects embellished buildings with wood, stone, concrete, and cast-iron ornaments featuring a wide variety of motifs, including the fleur-de-lis, mythological characters, and patriotic emblems. Many pieces were hand-carved by talented immigrant craftsmen who worked for low wages. Foresighted collectors and dealers often save such architectural decorations from the wrecking ball just before a building is demolished; more often, however, these pieces are destroyed.

Hints for Collectors
Architectural ornaments that are hand-carved are the most interesting examples in this category and command prices as much as 10 times those of cast pieces. Such works can be distinguished by their somewhat irregular surfaces and sharp edges. To develop expertise in this area, study urban artifacts that have been preserved in such public collections as the Brooklyn Museum.

34 Virgin of Montserrat

Description
Carved and painted female figure with ample hood surrounding sculpted head; hood rests on full cape open in front, with full-length robe underneath. Arms, broken off, meant to protrude from cape at waist. Figure set on 2-piece shelf with plain bottom nailed to scalloped back. Overall cracking and wear.

Materials and Dimensions
Painted and stained wood. Wax. Nails. Height: 11″. Width: 6″. Depth: 5″.

Locality and Period
Puerto Rico. c. 1820–40.

Comment
Wherever the Roman Catholic faith gained a following, there has been abundant religious art. In the Spanish-speaking sectors of the New World, the local converts almost always executed such art in wood. Large bultos were intended for churches, while smaller ones, such as the Virgin of Montserrat shown here, were for home devotions. A baroque shell, seen here in a crude version behind this figure, was an important decorative motif signifying the spiritual birth and renewal provided by true faith.

Hints for Collectors
The earliest surviving Spanish colonial carvings have a richer baroque quality than later pieces by local Indians taught by Catholic priests. Many valuable Puerto Rican bultos combine carved wood with fabric and an easily shaped, waxlike substance. Thus, if a bulto has a waxy surface, it may well come from Puerto Rico. It may even be possible to identify the carver of a particular bulto, since much scholarly research has been done in this area of religious folk art.

135 Virgin of Mount Carmel

Description
Carved and painted female figure with brown hood covering hair; deep red face and neck. Dark cape gathered at neck, open in front, and almost full-length in back. Long-sleeved pleated dress in golden yellow. Right arm thrust out from under cape; hand missing. Left arm severed above elbow. Standing on red dome pegged to beveled green base.

Materials and Dimensions
Painted wood. Height: 8″. Width: 3½″. Depth: 3″.

Locality and Period
Soto, Puerto Rico. c. 1885–1900.

Comment
The Carmelite religious order, founded in Syria in 1160, was named after the Virgin of Mount Carmel (a mountain in ancient Palestine). The order was reformed in the mid-16th century by Teresa of Avila, the Spanish mystic and author. When the Spaniards came to the New World, they brought with them their veneration for the Virgin of Mount Carmel. The bulto shown here is a 19th-century expression of that devotion.

Hints for Collectors
Religious carvings are not widely collected, remaining most popular in the areas where they were created. Spanish colonial folk carvings produced in New Mexico, Arizona, and California, for example, always bring significantly higher prices in the Southwest, and the same is true of Puerto Rican religious carvings sold in Puerto Rico. A collector who wishes to sell a piece originally from Puerto Rico should therefore try to do so through an agent there. Fine examples are occasionally available for modest sums in areas of America where Puerto Rican immigrants have settled.

136 The Holy Family

Description
3 carved and painted figures on rectangular base. At left, Mary in full-length red dress trimmed in blue; left hand holds hand of Jesus; right hand reaching forward slightly. Child Jesus at center, wearing blue robe trimmed in orange; arms extended to clasp hands with Joseph and Mary. At right, Joseph in full-length dark robe with red trim and sash; left hand holding staff, right hand holds Jesus' left hand.

Materials and Dimensions
Painted wood. Height: 10½″. Base length: 12″; width: 3″.

Locality and Period
Made by Feliz Lopez (1942–), Espanola, New Mexico. 1979.

Comment
The efforts of southwestern Indians to glorify the Catholicism they adopted from the Spanish colonists has resulted in more than 300 years of religious folk art. More recently, these Spanish traditions have also been carried on by Chicanos. A representation of Christ or some other holy person is called a santo; a 3-dimensional santo, like the one shown here, is called a bulto. Feliz Lopez is a santero, or santo carver, who makes spiritual mementos for devout patrons. *The Holy Family—La Sagrada familia* in Spanish—is representative of the 20th-century primitive religious sculpture of the Southwest now much sought after by folk art collectors.

Hints for Collectors
Spanish colonial folk traditions still persist in isolated areas of the Southwest. Whole families of present-day woodcarvers repeat the imagery sculpted by their ancestors. Carvings by the finest contemporary artisans, highly appreciated by collectors and curators, are very likely to increase in value.

137 Crucifixion

Description
Carved and painted figure of Christ nailed to a cross made of 2 boards with geometric designs; "INRI" (*Iesus Nazarenus, Rex Iudaeorum*—Jesus of Nazareth, King of the Jews) painted on plaque on top. Black hair, eyes, and beard. Extended arms; hands and overlapped feet fastened to cross with wooden pegs. Prominent ribs. Bleeding wounds. Narrow wrap around hips.

Materials and Dimensions
Painted wood. Gesso. Iron nails. Height: 45". Width: 27⅜". Depth: 4¾".

Locality and Period
Attributed to José Ortega (1828–1904), New Mexico. c. 1870–1900.

Comment
Bultos, sculptures either of Christ or other holy figures, express the religious sentiments of Hispanic Americans or Indians whose ancestors were converted to Catholicism by the Spanish. Like many other sculptures in this tradition, Ortega's bultos combine the spare and elongated forms typical of Spanish baroque design with the Indian preference for geometric abstraction. Neighbors and relatives probably served as his models.

Hints for Collectors
Because the soft porous wood takes paint unevenly, most southwestern bultos were first covered with gesso. However, an example with gesso is not necessarily American, for bultos from other countries were often treated similarly. Since very few old bultos remain in private hands and some currently for sale have been stolen from churches, check the provenance of a piece before buying it; if you purchase a stolen work, you may lose your investment. Pieces like this are very valuable.

138 Saint Francis of Assisi

Description
Crudely carved and painted figure fashioned from large log with 2 short plain logs nailed on for arms. Pointed top denoting hood. Face with flat nose and sunken eyes; incised eyebrows, beard, and mustache highlighted in gold. Surface of cylindrical torso suggesting long monk's robe covering feet. Braided clothesline belt tied around center, with ends hanging down at side. Dark weathered paint overall.

Materials and Dimensions
Painted wood. Iron nails. Rope. Height: 48″. Width: 18″. Depth: 9″.

Locality and Period
Attributed to Ben Ortega (1923–), Tesuque, New Mexico. c. 1975.

Comment
The story of Saint Francis of Assisi has been a familiar one in the American Southwest ever since the Franciscans arrived with the Spanish colonial settlers in the late 17th century. The Franciscans urged Indian converts to express their piety in arts and crafts. The rudimentary modern sculpture of St. Francis seen here shows how a folk artist can work with plain materials at hand—in this case, simple logs. Such pieces are often displayed outdoors.

Hints for Collectors
A Chicano who works within a Spanish colonial crafts tradition, Ortega is much respected for his religious carvings. But some collectors find his sculpture excessively crude. A piece of this type is of keenest interest to southwestern collectors and would probably fetch more in Santa Fe than in New York City.

139 Father Time

Description
Carved and painted nude man with pale skin, blue eyes, brown eyebrows, sculpted nose; brown hair and beard attached with glue. Left arm hanging down; right arm holding metal scythe an raised as if to strike bell suspended from metal rod rising from base and curving over figure. Torso and legs made from single pieces of wood (nail holes indicating where short pants hung). Feet attached separately; toes carved. Long gray wings outlined in brown and set into back. Octagonal stand with black top.

Materials and Dimensions
Pine. Painted. Human hair. Brass. Height: 52⅛″. Width: 13⅞″. Depth: 14½″.

Locality and Period
Mohawk Valley, New York. c. 1910.

Comment
The function of this exceptional folk sculpture is unknown. Originally, the figure's articulated right arm could strike the bell with the scythe. Although the unidentified craftsman was not preoccupied with naturalistic representation, his success—like that of imaginative folk artists everywhere—resulted from immediate viewer recognition of the character by its traditional attributes. Stylized representation of the human body was sufficient; no detailing of anatomical features was necessary.

Hints for Collectors
Its remarkable carving and whimsical subject matter lend this piece universal appeal. The best investments in folk art are one-of-a-kind objects that display such artistic imagination.

140 Zozobra or Old Man Gloom

Description
Carved and painted figure with free-form black head, pointed ears, and yellow crown. Eyes with pupils of white flowerlike buttons set in brown and yellow circles. Red mouth; white stars forming teeth. Torso and short triangular arms painted red and green and decorated with tacks and buttons. Yellow legs with white stars. Large black feet with red toenails. Figure supported by metal rod connecting back and rectangular base.

Materials and Dimensions
Painted wood. Paper. Tacks. Celluloid. Metal. Height: 59″. Width: 14″. Depth: 13⅝″.

Locality and Period
Made by "Pop" Shaffer (1880–1964), Mountainair, New Mexico. c. 1935.

Comment
To exorcise misery, a 40-foot-tall effigy of Zozobra is ritually burned at the opening of the annual Fiesta de Santa Fe, which was started in the 1920s by a non-Hispanic painter from the Midwest. Shaffer, the maker of this smaller representation, was a blacksmith who amassed property in Mountainair during the Depression by trading buggies for the land of inhabitants fleeing the drought. Here he built and operated a hotel and farm, which he decorated with some of the 300 to 400 monsters he created from tree roots and branches.

Hints for Collectors
While most serious collectors of 19th-century folk sculpture are not attracted to carvings like this, some do find the odd shape and whimsical nature of such a piece appealing. As 20th-century folk sculpture becomes better understood, these figures may attract a wider audience and appreciate in value.

141 Paper soldiers

Description
Cutout and glued paper soldiers and horses with painted features and clothing. Left figure in Revolutionary uniform consisting of rectangular black hat with red plume, red coat, white breeches, black boots, and white strap holding sheathed sword; musket in left hand. Right figure also a Revolutionary soldier, dressed in black and gold semicircular hat with white plume, blue coat, white breeches, and black boots; gold waistband with sheathed sword. Spotted brown and white horse at left with white and red saddle and blue blanket bordered in yellow. White horse at right with beige mane and tail and blue saddle. Folded supports attached to back.

Materials and Dimensions
Watercolor and ink on paper and cardboard. Soldier height: 4½″; width: 2″. Horse height: 4″; width: 4¼″.

Locality and Period
Probably Boston. c. 1840–50.

Comment
Prior to the 19th century, nearly all children's playthings were handcrafted by relatives or friends. Professional toymakers produced dolls and pewter or silver soldiers and horses, but only for the children of affluent families. Materials often used for dolls included dried moss, pine cones, and even wishbones wrapped in cloth skirts. Other common types of dolls were rag dolls, knitted or crocheted and then stuffed, and rope dolls, which allowed sailors to show off their rope-tying skills.

Since paper was somewhat scarce before the 19th century, paper dolls were rare and therefore highly prized. Being fragile, they were usually preserved between pages of books or in boxes. By the mid-19th century, paper had become plentiful: cutouts made from folded newspaper, for instance, became so common that "how-to" pamphlets were printed in large numbers; and enterprising children often earned money by selling paper dolls and accessories they made at home. The dolls shown here are fine mid-19th-century painted examples; dolls were frequently cut from colored paper instead of being painted. Paper costumes were often attached with sealing wax.

Hints for Collectors
While early professionally made toys appeal primarily to specialist toy collectors, one-of-a-kind handcrafted playthings like the paper soldiers and horses shown here are of greatest interest to folk art enthusiasts. Pieces of this type are rare and seldom come on the market. Cutout toys should be evaluated like other folk art, that is, according to their design, decoration, condition, and originality.

142 The First Suit

Description
Carved and painted anecdotal scene with 4 dark-haired figures. From left to right: slightly stooped, balding man in shirt sleeves and vest, holding measuring tape in both hands; boy in gray-green suit facing parents; tall man in white shirt and blue suit, standing with arms behind back; woman in long-sleeved blue dress, seated on black chair, weeping into handkerchief, and clutching purse on lap. Stained rectangular base.

Materials and Dimensions
Pine. Painted. Height: 17″. Base length: 17″; width: 7″.

Locality and Period
Made by Sol Landau (1919–), New York City. 1981.

Comment
The sculpture shown here depicts the fitting of a boy's first grown-up suit, a rite of passage in the life of a young man. Like other pieces by Landau, this example reveals the emotions of participants in everyday situations. His works, often including children, range from a scene portraying 2 angry mothers, with their sons behind them, arguing over whose son started a fight (*Your Son Started It*), to Jewish themes such as a father showing his child a mezuzah.

Hints for Collectors
American collectors have always favored anecdotal works of art, especially those relating to family events, though they often prefer older folk carvings with their patina of age. Landau's work was first shown in a local bank and in senior citizen facilities in Brooklyn. He brought his work to the attention of a leading folk art gallery, and his pieces are beginning to appear in private and public collections of folk sculpture.

43 Shop figure

Description
Carved and painted life-size man with brown hair, eyebrows, and wide-open eyes. Red jacket open at neck, with black details; shirtless. Arms carved separately and nailed to body; left arm at side, right arm thrust forward, with fist grasping short stick that may have held advertisement. Blue pants; no feet. Deep crack on back; paint crackled overall and chipped at shoulders.

Materials and Dimensions
Pine. Painted. Iron nails. Height: 69″. Width: 20″. Depth: 11½″.

Locality and Period
Maine. c. 1920–30.

Comment
Ever since early colonial times, trade figures and signs have been popular forms of advertising. Like most shop figures, the example shown here was not signed by its maker. Its success lies in its ability to catch the attention of passersby. This type of commercial sculpture is seldom made today because brightly painted or neon signs have taken over its function.

Hints for Collectors
Many traditionalist collectors believe that the work of self-taught 20th-century artists is not true folk art because much of it was created intentionally for decorative rather than utilitarian purposes. Because of this, many naive 20th-century carvings, even very fine ones, sell for relatively modest sums at auctions and in galleries. Beginning collectors may thus be able to assemble a selection of these sculptures at a manageable cost.

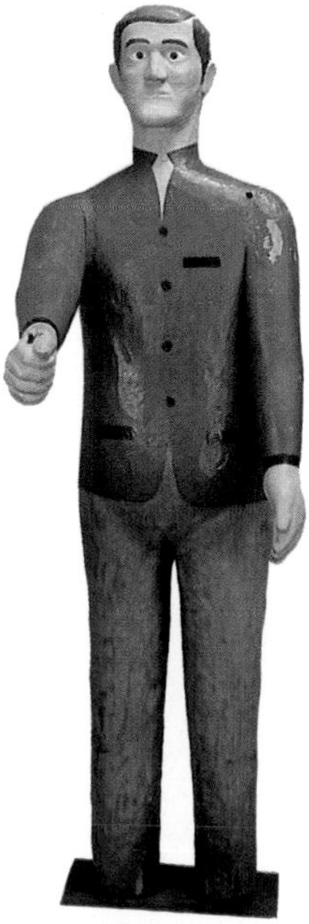

144 Wooden scarecrow

Description
Carved and painted life-size male figure constructed from 18 pieces of wood attached by nails, screws, and bolts of various sizes; all parts nonmovable. Gray hat with separate brim. Head with attached C-shaped ears and long straight nose; black hair, brows, and mouth; eyes are silver-colored tacks inserted in dark painted circles; pinkish-white face and red neck. Upper arms and forearms are individual pieces painted red over gray; flat pink hands. Torso red on top, gray on bottom. Gray legs; black feet.

Materials and Dimensions
Painted wood. Tacks. Nails. Screws. Bolts. Height: 71″. Width: 15″. Depth: 11″.

Locality and Period
Possibly the Midwest. c. 1930–45.

Comment
Most scarecrows were made by decorating a cross with household odds and ends. The unusual piece shown here is a crudely made but sturdy figure in which the illusion of arm movement and the painted tunic are substitutes for wind-blown rags. Its extensive signs of weathering suggest that this figure was used for many years.

Hints for Collectors
Because it is more fully carved than other pieces of this type, this scarecrow is of substantially greater value. Very few have survived, as they were generally used for only one growing season. Check for insect infestation on a piece that has been outdoors for a long time and, if necessary, have it fumigated.

145 Shop figure

Description
Carved and painted male figure with brown hair, tan complexion, black eyes, and red lips; wearing tall black hat, brownish shirt, double-breasted black jacket, pants, and shoes. Inset arms hanging by sides; right hand resting on top of walking stick. Mounted on small rectangle set on domed rectangular base. Overall crazing.

Materials and Dimensions
Painted wood. Height: 23½″. Base length: 7½″; width: 7½″.

Locality and Period
Probably New York State. c. 1870.

Comment
Shop figures, symbolizing either a type of store or one of the types of merchandise sold in it, were sometimes used indoors rather than outdoors. This sculpture of an elegantly dressed gentleman, detailed down to the buttons on his jacket, cuffs on his pants, and walking stick, was probably displayed on a counter or in a case in a men's clothing store.

Hints for Collectors
In recent years folk art has brought prices substantial enough to make the creation of fakes profitable. Collectors should therefore examine each potential acquisition carefully. All painted surfaces should be inspected with a strong magnifying glass. If an object is old, its surface should have hairline crazing caused by shrinkage of the paint's chemical base. But even such a crazed surface can be simulated by a skilled technician, so also look for other appropriate signs of wear.

146 Nodding-head chalkware woman

Description
Elderly woman with movable hollow head and elongated neck attached to body by wire loop. Black hair, eyes, and brows, and red-trimmed white bonnet. Movable lower jaw with white teeth and red lips. Hollow body with full-length black dress. Hands holding open book at waist. Flat bottom.

Materials and Dimensions
Gypsum. Painted. Wire. Height: 9¼″. Width: 4⅝″. Depth: 4⅞″.

Locality and Period
Throughout the United States. c. 1890–1900.

Comment
Chalkware, the poor man's pottery, was produced in Europe during the 18th and 19th centuries and was brought to this country by Italian and German immigrants. Examples like the one shown here are rare not only because they have movable parts but also because, unlike later plaster figures, they are hollow rather than solid. Chalkware went out of fashion at the turn of the century, when the eclectic décor of the Victorian era was replaced by a less cluttered, modern look.

Hints for Collectors
The figure of a woman with a nodding head is the rarest chalkware form, and when one comes on the market it inevitably causes a stir. Beware of the many recent reproductions as well as European imports. To avoid costly errors, collectors should become familiar with authentic American examples on display at the Museum of American Folk Art in New York City, the Henry Ford Museum in Dearborn, Michigan, and other public collections.

47 Figural doorstops

Description
Man and woman with painted facial features and traditional Amish garb. Man dressed in flat-brimmed hat, red shirt, orange jacket, black trousers, and brown shoes. Woman in black and yellow dress, pink apron, and blue bonnet. Cast in 2-piece molds.

Materials and Dimensions
Cast iron. Painted. Height (left; right): 8½″; 7½″. Width: 4″. Depth: 1″.

Locality and Period
The Northeast or Midwest. c. 1880–1930.

Comment
Cast-iron doorstops, called "door porters" in England, have been made in America since the early 19th century. Andrew Jackson, for example, who was elected president in 1828, had cast-iron frog doorstops with the slogan "I croak for the Jackson wagon" as part of his campaign publicity. It was not until after the Civil War, however, that cast-iron doorstops became very popular. Better knowledge of casting techniques by that time enabled factories to make doorstops in almost any design imaginable, often with extraordinary detail.

Hints for Collectors
Since doorstop collecting is a fairly recent specialty, a group may still be put together easily and for a modest sum. These Amish figures are quite unusual, as are any human-shaped doorstops, since most designs were based on variations of a flower basket, ship, or, occasionally, animals. Beware of new doorstops cast from molds recently made from old doorstops; these are usually recognizable by blurred details and new paint.

148 Black dancing figure

Description
Carved figure of black man with exaggerated painted facial features: large red lips, black eyes in prominent, red-rimmed whites, and broad nose; close-cropped curly hair. Unpainted wooden torso clad in remnants of costume, including white collar and tan shirt. Arms attached at shoulder; forearms and hands broken off. Cylindrical legs; straw feet in worn black leather boots with laces. Feet and back of figure connected to trestle base, preventing movement of joints.

Materials and Dimensions
Painted wood. Cloth. Leather. Steel. Wire nails. Straw. Height: 54″. Width: 13½″. Depth: 8″.

Locality and Period
New York State. c. 1890–1900.

Comment
The unknown maker of the figure shown here was undoubtedly white; like many turn-of-the-century artists, he portrayed blacks as socially inferior by caricaturing their facial features and mannerisms. Such distortions occurred not only in folk art such as this piece but also in minstrel shows and in many popular Currier & Ives lithographs.

Hints for Collectors
A carved figure that has lost some or all of its original clothing may be restored, but most collectors prefer unclad, rough-hewn contours. Sculptures showing strong characterization are most likely to appreciate in value.

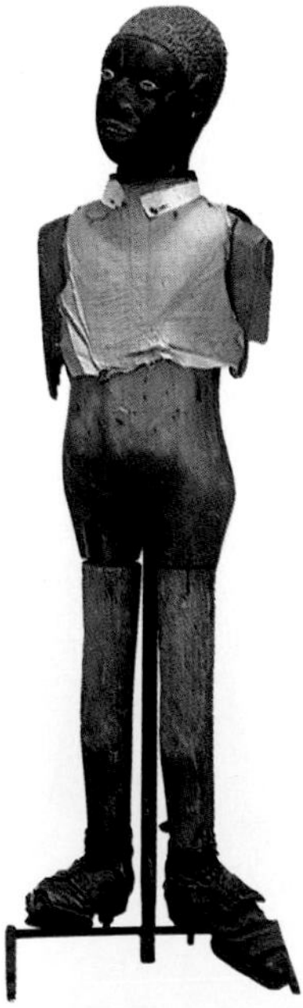

49 Cigar-store Indian

Description
Carved and painted Indian with multicolored headdress atop long black hair. Reddish-brown face, torso, and arms. Black eyes with conspicuous whites. Brass necklace with medallion. Out-thrust arms with clenched fists; detachable cigar in right fist. Remnants of cloth belt. Band and tassel around calf of left legging. Black shoes. Square green base.

Materials and Dimensions
Pine. Painted. Brass. Fabric. Height: 55″. Base length: 17″; width: 16″.

Locality and Period
Massachusetts. c. 1900–20.

Comment
Though probably first used in 17th-century England, only in the 19th century did cigar-store Indians become the most widely accepted symbol for tobacco shops there and in America. Many types of wooden Indians were derived from the romantic images in James Fenimore Cooper's novels, as well as from contemporary engravings and lithographs.

Hints for Collectors
Cigar-store Indians with original paint command the highest prices. Those with paint that was refurbished decades ago, thus showing some fading and wear, are nearly as desirable. A stripped or freshly painted example is of little interest to knowledgeable collectors. Owners of such present-day businesses as men's clothing stores and tobacco shops, however, sometimes purchase early trade signs or figures to advertise their firms or products, and are occasionally willing to pay high prices for recently restored pieces.

150 Cigar-store figure

Description
Carved and painted life-size figure of a Turk wearing a red-crowned gold turban. Dark-skinned face with drooping black mustache and red lips. Ankle-length white coat with half sleeves and ermine-trimmed front; long-sleeved yellow shirt trimmed in green, baggy yellow pants, and red sash at waist. Right arm raised at elbow; left arm hanging at side. Bare ankles; red slippers. Green rectangular base with gold trim.

Materials and Dimensions
Possibly pine. Painted. Height: 77″. Base length: 28″; width: 27″.

Locality and Period
Probably New York City. c. 1890–1900.

Comment
Carvings of Indian chiefs and women, blackamoors, and various other distinct ethnic types functioned as American tobacconists' figures during the 19th and early 20th centuries. Indians, most popular from the 1850s to the 1880s, were followed by many exotic types, of which the Turk shown here is a very fine example. Although this piece was found in Camden, Delaware, and might have been made almost anywhere along the Eastern seaboard, it was probably executed in New York City, the home of many figurehead carvers who turned to making shop figures after the decline of the sailing ship.

Hints for Collectors
The most coveted tobacconist figures either are very realistic, like this Turk, or else highly stylized. Most carved tobacconist figures fall somewhere between these aesthetic poles. Colorful examples in good original condition will fetch the highest prices. A carved wooden figure is more desirable than one of cast metal or plaster of Paris.

151 **Cigar-store figure**

Description
Carved and painted figure of Zouave wearing yellow turban pinned in front with crescent-moon brooch. Golden face with black eyes, eyebrows, and drooping mustache. Long-sleeved maroon cutaway jacket over gray shirt; reddish baggy pants. Yellow sash diagonally across chest and around waist. Dark boots. Right arm upraised with closed fist; left hand slightly lower, with open palm. Right leg advanced in jaunty pose. Tapering rectangular base.

Materials and Dimensions
Possibly pine. Painted. Height: 67″. Base length: 24″; width: 22″.

Locality and Period
Probably East Coast. c. 1890–1900.

Comment
Following the decline of carved Indians as tobacconists' trade figures, characters such as Punch, Columbine, Yankee Doodle, Columbia, British officers, race-track dandies, Bowery belles, and sportsmen became most common. Some shopowners even commissioned likenesses of themselves. One new figure, seen here, was the colorfully garbed Zouave, an Algerian member of the French infantry; some volunteer regiments in the American Civil War adopted the name and dress of these Algerian troops.

Hints for Collectors
Since most carved trade figures were put outside a shop in the morning and taken in at night, some of the largest and best examples were fitted with iron wheels. Many collectors find these fittings unattractive and obtrusive and will not pay as much for figures with them.

152 Cigar-store Indian

Description
Carved and painted Indian woman with pale blue feathered headdress showing traces of gold paint. Cream-colored cape with red border draped over right shoulder and arm, around back, and under left arm. Blue knee-length dress with red border at bodice and hem. Right hand holding rose. White stockings and black boots. Bluish pedestal with pale center panels. Signed.

Materials and Dimensions
Painted wood. Height: 66½″. Base length: 17″; width: 19¼″.

Locality and Period
Made by Samuel Robb (1851–1928), New York City. c. 1875–1900.

Comment
Samuel Robb employed many carvers in his New York City workshop, which produced cigar-store Indians, trade figures, and carvings of circus and carousel figures. Dozens of workshops created images of Indians from tribes around the country; besides wood, these were sometimes made of cast zinc or "white metal" (a mixture of lead and other metals). Cigar-store figures began to disappear around the turn of the century, when they became obstacles in the crowded streets of growing cities. The Indian shown here is called Rose Squaw because of the flower she holds; Robb used the rose as a symbol for his dead wife. His workshops produced many versions of this figure.

Hints for Collectors
Signed cigar-store figures, such as Robb's model of Rose Squaw shown here, are most desirable, particularly if they are by well-known makers. It is sometimes possible to attribute an unsigned figure through its resemblance to signed or otherwise identified examples in style, subject, or painting.

53 Cigar-store Indian

Description
Carved and painted life-size Indian with headdress of multicolored feathers. Shoulder-length black hair; tan face with sculpted facial features. Brown tunic with darker belt and trim. Necklace around open neck; black purse hanging from belt. Left hand extending forward to hold long rifle in vertical position; right hand slightly lower, holding cigars. Brown pants gathered just above black shoes. Square base.

Materials and Dimensions
Painted wood. Height: 87″. Base length: 21″; width: 20″.

Locality and Period
Made by Arnold and Peter Ruef, Tiffin, Ohio. c. 1880.

Comment
This naturalistic figure commands attention and is immediately recognizable, 2 marks of success in a trade sign. Carvers of German, Swiss, and Danish extraction worked in Wisconsin, Illinois, and Michigan, as well as Ohio, so that by the late 19th century local tradespeople no longer had to rely on shop figures made on the East Coast. There is some debate as to whether the ornaments carved on Indian headdresses were meant to be feathers or tobacco leaves.

Hints for Collectors
Few cigar-store figures are as beautiful, imposing, and valuable as this one. The quality of carving, the variety of surface patterns, and the strong characterization add to the richness of this piece. Realistic figures tend to appeal most to people who are not necessarily folk art collectors, whereas folk art connoisseurs prefer highly original designs and stylized forms that transcend simple realism.

154 Cigar-store figure

Description
Carved and painted figure of a black man wearing brown headband with blue diamond-shaped motif at center; short, broad feathers of yellow, green, and red rising from band. Delicately carved features; eyes with prominent whites; reddish lips. Necklace of carved yellow beads. Left arm raised to hold long clay pipe to mouth. Right hand holding 3 tobacco leaves at side. Knee-length brown-belted skirt with red, blue, green, and yellow feathers. 2-tiered rectangular green stand.

Materials and Dimensions
Oak. Painted. Clay. Height: 36″. Base length: 10½″; width: 9″.

Locality and Period
Probably England. c. 1790–1800.

Comment
Early tobacconists' figures depicting blackamoors or exotic Asian subjects were often made in England and imported to the United States. Sculptures such as this one, meant for a table or countertop inside a store, were smaller than those to be set outside a shop. While this figure holds tobacco leaves, others grasped cigars. A detached necklace of metal or wooden beads frequently adorned such objects. Because cigar-store figures were expensive, they were often resold when a shop went out of business.

Hints for Collectors
The bright colors of the feathers making up the figure's headdress and skirt suggest they were painted long after this piece was carved. Added paint is acceptable as long as it is well done and has acquired a patina.

155 Cigar-store figure

Description
Carved and painted figure of a black man with curly black hair, full facial features, and red lips; wearing open-necked cream-colored shirt with ruffles, red wrap belted at waist, and short cream-colored pants. Right arm bent at elbow, yellow snuff box in hand; left arm resting on 3 stacked boxes marked (from top to bottom) "Habana," "Key West," and "Yara." Standing barefoot on 2 coils of yellow rope. Green base curved to match outline of sculpture. Metal hook on back for attaching to wall.

Materials and Dimensions
Pine. Painted. Metal. Height: 40″. Base length: 14″; width: 11″.

Locality and Period
Attributed to James Hamilton (b. 1832), Washington, D.C. c. 1860–70.

Comment
Hamilton's woodcarvings are said to resemble those by the well-known Philadelphia carver William Rush. Hamilton, born a year before Rush died, worked first in Philadelphia and then, in 1859, moved to Washington, D.C. Except for several preliminary drawings and roughly executed, highly stylized cigar-store carvings, little of his work is known. Some pieces may be seen in the Abby Aldrich Rockefeller Folk Art Collection in Williamsburg, Virginia.

Hints for Collectors
It is important to determine whether cigar-store figures are American or English, because the latter are much less valuable in the American marketplace. English figures tend to be more ornate in design and exotic in subject than early American pieces; also, their woods may not be native to this country.

156

Ship's figurehead

Description
Carved and painted life-size figure of young woman made from single piece of wood, with long curly blond hair, blue eyes, and rosy lips; wearing low-cut dress with traces of blue and green paint and short sleeves trimmed in red; red shoes. Holding bouquet of red roses at waist. Full skirt carved longer in back. Left foot forward. Overall wear, crackling, and chipping. Scrolled greenish mount.

Materials and Dimensions
Pine. Painted. Height: 77″. Width: 28″. Depth: 28″.

Locality and Period
Boston, Massachusetts or Portland, Maine. c. 1830–50.

Comment
First carved in animal forms, ships' figureheads in human shapes appeared only after the mid-18th century. In the United States these sculptures were made along the Eastern Seaboard from Maine to South Carolina. The figurehead was placed at the bow of the vessel where port and starboard sides met under the bowsprit. It was regarded by the crew as a kind of talisman; sailors sometimes became concerned if the figurehead of their ship was damaged or replaced.

Hints for Collectors
These sculptures can be visually disorienting when viewed at eye level, for they were carved with an oversize upper section that would appear proportional when viewed from a dock below. Figureheads are best displayed, therefore, high above eye level, so that their proportions are in proper perspective.

57 Ship's figurehead

Description
Carved and painted bust of Ulysses S. Grant with upturned head, black hair, reddish beard and mustache, and blue eyes; wearing gray coat with black lapels and high-collared shirt. Right hand over chest; left arm by side. Separate pieces attached with pegs and nails. Carved drapery around waist. Worn, chipped, and cracked. Square base.

Materials and Dimensions
Pine. Painted. Height without base: 32″. Width: 17″. Depth: 20″.

Locality and Period
Maine. c. 1865–75.

Comment
Ships' figureheads were often modeled after national leaders. The likeness of Ulysses S. Grant shown here has more than 20 coats of paint, the last probably dating from about 1890, when the figurehead was retired after 2 decades on a small merchant sailing ship. Sculptures such as these were painted about once a year because of the ravages of salt, wind, and water.

Hints for Collectors
Old wood carvings that have long been exposed to the elements are likely to become extensively cracked, and their painted surfaces crazed. This condition is acceptable on a figurehead or cigar-store Indian provided it does not occur in a crucial area, such as the face. Many collectors attempt to have large cracks filled; few restorers can do this satisfactorily, however, and unless a crack is totally disfiguring, it is best to leave it as is.

Whirligigs and Weathervanes

Two of the most popular kinds of folk art are whirligigs and weathervanes. Though both are set in motion by the wind and are sometimes related in design, these forms differ in that weathervanes are essentially utilitarian, while whirligigs are made for amusement, and thus tend to be more complex.

Whirligigs

A type of whimsical wind toy, whirligigs were more fully developed in America than anywhere else. There is debate concerning their origin. Some say they began as "Sabbath day toys" in Pennsylvania-German communities, where children were not allowed to play with toys on Sundays; others claim they doubled as weathervanes. In any case, the earliest known reference to these animated sculptures is in Washington Irving's 1819 story, "The Legend of Sleepy Hollow," in which Ichabod Crane, the village "pedagogue," has on his desk "contraband articles . . . detected upon persons of idle urchins, such as half-munched apples, popguns, whirligigs. . . ."

Subjects for whirligigs range from soldiers and illustrious Americans to crowded scenes that convey a story in their lively movements. They were often whittled by amateurs and are appealingly primitive in style and execution. Single-figure whirligigs have rotating paddlelike arms usually mounted on a wooden or metal rod passing through the shoulders of the sculpture. Multifigure whirligigs are powered by a propeller that turns gears and rods that make the figures move. Both kinds have either three-dimensional or silhouette-type figures.

Weathervanes

Though common in Europe for centuries, weathervanes became a quintessentially American form of sculpture in the 18th and 19th centuries. Since weather affected the occupations of most early Americans, weathervanes were placed on top of all kinds of buildings.

Besides being functional, weathervanes were decorative in form and boldly shaped to allow them to be seen from a distance. Popular subjects included arrows, angels, Indians, serpents, grasshoppers, horses and other livestock, and patriotic emblems such as eagles and Liberty. Cocks and fish, because of their symbolism, frequently appeared atop churches, while ships and sea creatures were most common in coastal towns. Some vanes doubled as trade signs.

In the 18th and early 19th centuries, all vanes were handmade. Two types existed: silhouettes and three-dimensional forms, both made of either wood or metal. In the second half of the 19th century, most weathervanes were mass produced. Factory-made vanes tended to be far more sculptural and detailed than handmade examples. They were molded in sheet copper or tin, or, less often, cast in iron. The former process began with a carved wooden pattern from which a metal mold or template was made. A craftsman hammered thin sheets of metal into the mold (or molds, if made in several parts); the results were then soldered together to form the hollow figure. Elements such as tails or ears were either hammered by hand or, to add weight to a figure, cast in iron or zinc. Most factory-made vanes were finished by hand, until later technology rendered handcraftsmanship unnecessary.

Wooden weathervanes were always painted to protect them from the weather and make them more conspicuous. Metal vanes were also frequently painted or gilded. An old vane with its original paint and a rich patina is unusual and particularly desirable.

158 Uncle Sam whirligig

Description
Front and rear views of whirligig of Uncle Sam riding old-fashioned metal bicycle, activated by propeller with white core and 2 red blades attached to front of base. Figure wearing top hat with crown of red and white stripes and blue brim over long white hair; white shirt, red bow tie and vest, blue cutaway jacket, red and white striped pants, and black shoes. Movable legs. Tailpiece with American flag on one side and Canadian flag on other. Base with traces of blue paint.

Materials and Dimensions
Painted wood. Iron. Height: 37″. Overall length: 55½″. Depth: 11″.

Locality and Period
New England. c. 1850–1900.

Comment
The tailpiece of this large handsome whirligig is quite unusual because it bears the American flag on one side and a now out-of-date Canadian flag on the other. The maker of this sculpture probably lived near the Canadian border and wanted to express friendship for his northern neighbor. Wind direction determined which side of the flag was revealed.
Dorothy and Leo Rabkin, the renowned folk art collectors, bought this wonderful wind toy about a dozen years ago from an eccentric dealer near Cooperstown, New York, for approximately the price of a new car. Though many collectors and dealers had seen the piece and were unwilling to pay the asking price, the Rabkins finally purchased it. They have since given it and nearly 100 other whirligigs to the Museum of

American Folk Art in New York City, thereby making its group of whirligigs the most important public collection in the country.

Hints for Collectors

This is a masterpiece of whirligig art: its appealing subject, monumental size, skilled craftsmanship, and imaginative design combine to make it outstanding. Works of such great merit are very costly, but are likely to appreciate in value much more quickly than modest examples; in fact, the prices of many of the finest pieces of folk art have doubled on an annual basis over the last several years. Collectors wishing to restore the broken mechanism of an early whirligig should find a skillful conservator who specializes in such work. Whirligigs are best displayed in out-of-reach places, since they provide an irresistible temptation, especially to children, to activate the mechanism by spinning the propellers, often causing irreparable damage. Collectors asked by a museum to lend a whirligig should insist that it be exhibited beyond the reach of visitors.

159 Early-bird-catches-the-worm-whirligig

Description
2-level whirligig with top level having propeller and blue-clad workmen; outer pair riding seesaw, inner pair sawing wood. Robin mounted on flag that has serrated edge and 2 blue stars over red and white horizontal stripes; robin's beak attached by wire to center pole (worm missing). Bottom level with octagonal revolving platform supporting 4 card-playing workmen seated on 4-legged stools around table. 2 large rotating wheels. Mounted on square block atop octagonal base.

Materials and Dimensions
Painted wood. Wire. Height: 42½″. Length: 36⅝″. Depth: 16¼″.

Locality and Period
The East or Midwest. c. 1880–1900.

Comment
It is said that the whirligig was called a "Sabbath day toy" in Pennsylvania-German communities, where religious beliefs prohibited youngsters from playing with toys on Sunday. To entertain their children on such days, parents often mounted a whirligig in the yard, where the wind would set its figures in motion. Whirligigs were also popular elsewhere, especially in rural areas of New England, New York, and the Midwest.

Hints for Collectors
Few whirligigs are as complicated and have as many moving parts as this exceptional piece, which is also noteworthy because it incorporates silhouette-style as well as 3-dimensional figures. Complexity, condition, and completeness all make this a very desirable work. 20th-century whirligigs are often made of plywood and are rarely as valuable as earlier examples.

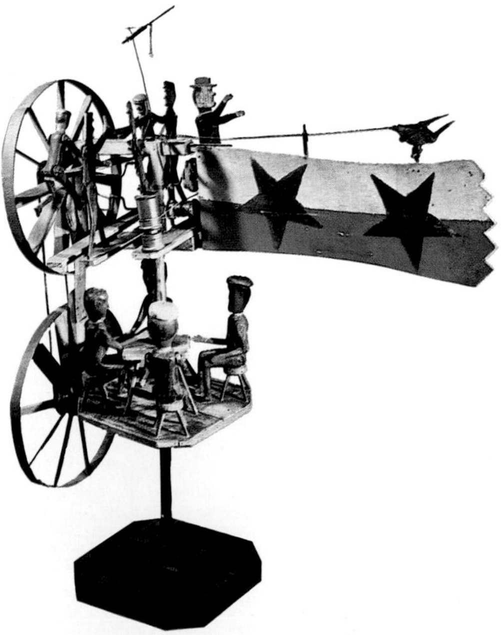

60 Bugler whirligig

Description
Carved bugle boy with painted features; brown-collared smock buttoned at throat, darker brown short pants, and white shoes. Left arm bent at elbow, holding crude metal bugle to mouth; right arm bent at elbow, extended forward. Legs articulated at knees. Figure suspended on metal rod connecting 2 blue stanchions. Propeller at left with red, white, and blue tin blades; tin flag at right with ground of red and white stripes and central 5-pointed yellow star on blue circle with "50" painted in center. Worn overall.

Materials and Dimensions
Wood. Iron. Tin. Painted. Cloth. Height: 32″. Overall length: 48″. Base depth: 9″. Propeller diameter: 23″.

Locality and Period
New York State. c. 1950.

Comment
The red, white, and blue propeller blades, the variation on the American flag, and the bugle boy probably symbolizing the Army are obvious patriotic motifs on this whirligig. The large stationary flag is designed to shift the entire whirligig into the direction of the wind, causing the propeller to rotate and the bugler to march.

Hints for Collectors
Although folk art collectors may judge a work on criteria other than size, the large dimensions of this piece increase its market value. The discoloration on the flag does not detract from the overall appeal and probably should be left as is.

161 Abraham Lincoln whirligig

Description
Abraham Lincoln with prominent eyes, dark complexion, black beard and hair, and large ears and nose. Black top hat with metal brim; black suit over white shirt, black tie, and brown vest with gold chain. Arms attached to wooden rod running through shoulders. Each hand holding paddle stained brown near hands and painted in simplified American flag pattern on both sides. Shiny black shoes. Plain rectangular stand. Signed.

Materials and Dimensions
Honduras mahogany figure. Birch paddles. Tin. Painted. Height of figure: 22½″. Width at shoulders: 5″.

Locality and Period
Made by Janice Fenimore (1924–), Madison, New Jersey. 1978.

Comment
American folk artists often express their patriotic sentiments by depicting famous political figures. Regardless of the profundity of the subject, whirligigs were meant to entertain. The first American whirligig must have appeared before 1819, when Washington Irving mentioned one in his story, "The Legend of Sleepy Hollow." Such devices, battered by the weather, had a limited lifespan and few made prior to 1850 survive.

Hints for Collectors
Fenimore, a carver of whimsical sculpture, has produced many fully functional whirligigs. This simple, yet charming example was the carver's first. To detect an inauthentic whirligig, see if it is, or ever was, capable of movement. Modern fakers can often reproduce only the decorative aspects of whirligigs. Examples that never functioned, whether new or old, are generally classified as fakes.

162 Witch whirligig

Description
Witch with long black hair, black eyes and eyebrows, and red lips; wearing black pointed hat trimmed in yellow, red earrings, black bodice trimmed in red, locket, long skirt vertically striped in red and yellow, and tan shoes. Astride black broomstick with worn twigs at rear end and propeller with 6 tan and red blades in front; center screw.

Materials and Dimensions
Birch or maple. Painted. Twigs. Nails. Screw. Height: 12¼″. Length: 12¼″. Width at shoulders: 5½″.

Locality and Period
New England. c. 1840–60.

Comment
With the coming of the Industrial Revolution, many household necessities once made by hand began to be manufactured by machine; with increased leisure, many Americans turned to handcrafting non-essential articles, such as the whirligig shown here. Whirligigs, in addition to being delightful toys, were useful as well; they could scare birds away from a garden.

Hints for Collectors
Because so many whirligigs have been reproduced or faked, it is important to examine a piece carefully to determine its age. Most whirligigs were originally used outdoors, so they should bear evidence of weathering as well as wear marks where movable parts rub against the body. The connectors of these parts should also be somewhat worn, and metal elements rusted or corroded. Although age generally increases the value of whirligigs, pieces by well-known contemporary artists, such as Edward Larson, sometimes also bring thousands of dollars in urban galleries.

163 Man-in-top-hat whirligig

Description
Man with black top hat and black hair; inset facial features including large concave ears, red-tipped nose, and white eyes. One-piece body in white shirt with 3 black buttons, green vest, red pants, and dark shoes. White paddle-shaped arms with red sockets. Figure standing on green-edged disk atop arrow with red head and green and red circular tail. Black base.

Materials and Dimensions
Painted wood. Iron. Height: 24½″. Length of arrow: 21″. Depth: 6″.

Locality and Period
New England. c. 1925–50.

Comment
Whirligigs, combining the movements of windmills and dolls, reached the height of their popularity and development in 19th-century America. The figures, usually 3-dimensional and brightly colored, may have simple or complex mechanisms. This example is unusual because, in addition to its paddle-shaped arms spinning like a propeller, the entire sculpture rotates when the wind pushes against the tail of the arrow. Though collectors today display these pieces indoors, they are at their best in their intended location—outdoors.

Hints for Collectors
20th-century folk sculpture rarely sells for as much as objects from earlier periods. Collectors should look for well-balanced design, detailed carving, original paint, and charming overall effect when choosing a piece, no matter what its age. The unity of design created by the color scheme and simple geometric forms adds substantially to the value of this figure.

164 Punchinello whirligig

Description
Pair of identical male figures, set between stained and painted stanchions, facing each other with hands joined by metal center rod. Single-piece head and torso; articulated arms and legs. Figures have black top hats, beards, hair, and eyes, yellow coats and stockings, red knickers, and black shoes. Slightly faded paint. 2-piece propeller with 4 blades. Black rectangular base.

Materials and Dimensions
Stained and painted wood. Metal. Height: 19″. Length: 12½″. Propeller diameter: 15½″.

Locality and Period
The East or Midwest. c. 1920–30.

Comment
Punchinello, the ugly bachelor forever pursuing pretty girls, is a stock character from the *commedia dell'arte*, the traditional Italian comic theater. The prototype of Punch, the hero of "Punch and Judy" puppet shows, he is an ideal subject for a whirligig; the wind-produced frantic bowing of the Punchinellos shown here adds to their already clownish appearance.

Hints for Collectors
Most whirligigs with silhouette-type figures were made in the 20th century. Those with many figures and in working order are the most desirable. It is important to oil those with metal mechanisms to keep them running smoothly. An inoperative example should be restored with restraint; otherwise it has little appeal to experienced collectors.

165 Horse-race whirligig

Description
Orange and white windmill with low windows. Propeller with 4 blades causes 2 silhouettes of jockeys on horseback to slide between 2 rails; each jockey and horse made from single piece of wood. Flat orange octagon attached vertically to end of rail. Coin weights glued to 2 propeller blades. Rectangular base.

Materials and Dimensions
Pine. Tin. Painted. Iron hardware. Height: 23″. Overall length: 23″. Depth: 3½″.

Locality and Period
The East or Midwest. c. 1930–40.

Comment
The possible range of subjects for whirligigs was as broad as the carver's imagination. The only requirement was that the pieces have one or more parts that could be set in motion by the wind. When so activated, this example would delight children as well as racing fans, for only a windless moment could end the perpetual contest. While such pieces were made primarily for entertainment, some were incorporated into weathervanes.

Hints for Collectors
Many modern-day whirligig makers copy old designs. Moreover, whirligigs age very quickly, and it may be difficult to distinguish between a piece that has stood outdoors for 20 years and one exposed for much longer. With the experience of seeing and handling a variety of examples and talking to knowledgeable dealers, collectors often develop an instinct for dating whirligigs.

66 Windmill-and-horses whirligig

Description
3-story white windmill with blue roof, black trim, yellow windows, and green door, containing mechanism turned by propeller with 6 blue-striped yellow blades. Man with articulated arms, wearing white shirt and black pants and standing in center of circular movable platform; 2 black and 2 white horses rotate on platform around him. Rectangular base.

Materials and Dimensions
Pine. Painted. Height: 20″. Overall length: 19½″. Depth: 14″. Propeller diameter: 19″.

Locality and Period
The East or Midwest. c. 1900–20.

Comment
Animals such as horses and birds appear frequently on wind toys made around the turn of the century. The charm of these and other whirligigs lies not only in their activation by an invisible force but also in their comical, even irreverent, movements. The horses on the whirligig shown here move jerkily, as in an old-time movie; their master seems to lose his authority, and his arms flail helplessly in the breeze.

Hints for Collectors
Many collectors restrict themselves to objects of one type, such as whirligigs that include buildings, like this example with its windmill. Whatever the category, look for whirligigs with interesting movements and handsome craftsmanship. Parts, especially propeller blades, may be damaged and require restoration; replacement parts should match the design and color of the original. Careful restoration does not seriously devalue a piece.

167 Farm whirligig

Description
Farm scene with large number of separate metal parts. From left to right: brown horse with black markings and articulated head, neck, and tail; man in brown hat, red shirt, and high boots, with articulated left arm pumping water (simulated by rippled colorless glass) into brown bucket; man with left leg resting on sawhorse, sawing log with articulated right arm; 4-story brown windmill (missing propeller) with milk-glass door, fanlight, and windows outlined in black; chicken, with traces of red and yellow paint, pecking worms from tin can; boy in hat, with articulated arms, head, and right leg, sitting on edge of platform and holding fishing rod. Weathered and rusty overall. Reverse is open and unfinished, with mechanisms exposed. Worn paint. Long rectangular base set on 2 pairs of legs.

Materials and Dimensions
Sheet steel. Painted. Glass. Height: 23″. Length: 65″. Depth: 7″.

Locality and Period
The East or Midwest. c. 1900–10.

Comment
This unusually long whirligig was probably made by a farmhand, judging from the accuracy of details such as the water pump. Because the propeller blades of this amazing piece are missing, no amount of wind can possibly set it in motion. Though crudely constructed and painted, the intricate connections of the many articulated parts are fascinating. This example was made to be seen from only one side, but when its pins and flanges are in motion, the reverse side is almost of equal interest.

Hints for Collectors
Metal is an unsatisfactory material for whirligigs because it lacks the sculptural qualities of wood and because it rusts if not adequately protected. Examples in this medium are therefore uncommon and not particularly valuable; however, this large scenic piece is quite desirable. Replacement of the missing propeller blades is a problem since there are no originals to copy; without such guidelines, it is usually best to leave an object like this as is. It is debatable whether a worn whirligig should be repainted; most collectors say no. Poorly crafted modern examples that are weak in design and lack imagination should be avoided, as they will probably never excite much interest in the marketplace. Whirligigs have become very popular with collectors, many of whom find these whimsical artifacts delightful additions to any décor; this has driven up their prices sharply in recent years.

168 Saint Tammany weathervane

Description
Oversize yellow weathervane depicting stern-faced Indian with bow and arrows and feathered headdress. Long hair. Earring and necklace of round beads. Wearing long-sleeved buckskin tunic fringed at knee and belted around waist and across left shoulder. Quiver of arrows attached to belt behind. Right arm extended with hand holding bow; left arm extending downward and grasping arrow. Moccasins on feet; right foot in front of left, both resting on directional arrow. Pockmarked by bullet holes.

Materials and Dimensions
Copper. Painted. Height of figure: 102½″. Length of arrow: 103″. Depth: 12″.

Locality and Period
Found in East Branch, New York. c. 1850–90.

Comment
The enormous dimensions and elaborate workmanship of the weathervane shown here make it quite exceptional. It depicts the symbol of a fraternal organization known as the Improved Order of Redmen; its patron figure, Saint Tammany, was a Delaware Indian chief esteemed by the colonists.

Hints for Collectors
Weathervanes should be sturdy enough to withstand all sorts of weather, yet still be responsive to changing air currents. Sportsmen frequently used large weathervanes like this example for target practice, so bullet holes may be found in old pieces. The presence of many bullet holes decreases market value; restorers often fill these holes with solder, which can be detected with a black light. The most desirable pieces are those in good condition, with original paint or a rich unpainted patina.

169 Archangel Gabriel weathervane

Description
Silhouette of angel blowing trumpet. Head with cutout eye. Graceful wing extending upward from back. Plump, cherubic buttocks and legs. Figure braced by horizontal metal cylinders and vertical straps secured by rivets. Mounted on stand.

Materials and Dimensions
Sheet iron. Wrought-iron straps and cylinders. Iron rivets. Height: 13⅜″. Length: 34″.

Locality and Period
New England. c. 1850–75.

Comment
The archangel Gabriel, God's messenger in the Bible, was a popular weathervane figure during the 19th century. It exists in silhouette and 3-dimensional forms, made of either wood or metal. Sheet-metal weathervanes were particularly common during the third quarter of the 19th century. Some were made from a single piece of metal, others from 3 or 4 small pieces soldered together. When a design became popular, dies cast from a wooden pattern, or model, were used for stamping out the components from which the figure was assembled. Finishing touches were done by hand.

Hints for Collectors
During the last several years silhouette weathervanes from Haiti have flooded the market. These vanes are cut from old oil drums and lack the supporting strapwork of the antique example shown here; thus they are merely decorative. Metal vanes are quite easy to fake, so check the provenance and get a written guarantee of authenticity from a dealer, especially when the purchased piece is costly.

170 Stag weathervane

Description
Leaping stag with 4-horned antlers and thrust-back ears. Illusion of leaping created by retracted front legs and extended rear legs. Erect tail. Hollow molded copper body with worn gilding; cast-zinc antlers and ears. Greenish patina.

Materials and Dimensions
Copper. Cast zinc. Gilded. Height: 23″. Length: 27″. Depth: 3″.

Locality and Period
Manufactured by J. W. Fiske Ironworks, New York City. c. 1885–90.

Comment
During the second half of the 19th century most weathervanes were produced by large East Coast manufacturers and could be purchased in hardware stores or ordered from manufacturers' illustrated mail-order catalogues. Many of these catalogues, now available in libraries, contain pictures and information about dimensions, dates, and original prices. Molded copper weathervanes were cast in iron molds made from wooden patterns. Half of each body part—head, neck, torso, and legs—was made in a mold of corresponding shape, either by hammering a thin sheet of copper into it or by filling the mold with molten zinc, and the results were soldered together to form a partly hollow figure.

Hints for Collectors
Nearly every weathervane manufacturer produced a leaping stag; sensitively modeled and carefully finished molded copper examples are often more valuable than rarer wooden ones. Check the area around the point where the pole enters the body, especially on 19th-century pieces, because continual stress has frequently caused structural weakness there.

71 Stag weathervane

Description
Leaping stag with 5-horned antlers (left antler now lacking 2 horns). Illusion of leaping created by retracted front legs and extended rear legs. Short support wires connecting hoofs to base. Erect tail. Hollow molded copper body with worn gilding; cast-zinc antlers, ears, and tail. Worn patina overall. Bullet hole near tail.

Materials and Dimensions
Copper. Cast zinc. Gilded. Wire. Height: 28″. Length: 43″. Depth: 3¾″.

Locality and Period
New England. c. 1880–1900.

Comment
Unusually large and exceptionally handsome, the weathervane shown here probably stood atop a rural building of ample proportions. Sometimes stags were shown leaping over foliage. Whether whimsical or religious in theme, realistic or freely executed, the success of a vane depended on its maker's artistic ability. The skill of the unknown maker of this piece is especially apparent in the feeling of majesty and motion he imparted to the stag.

Hints for Collectors
Weathervanes designed with a sense of drama and movement are coveted by both novices and experienced collectors. The antlers on these stag vanes were generally made of solid cast metal such as zinc, although some are hollow. Because cast antlers are more durable, they tend to add to the value of a vane.

172 Steer weathervane

Description
Steer with large flat body and head; cast-zinc horns and ears applied separately to molded head. Long tail extending from top of hindquarters nearly to hoofs. Legs resting on flat base, with left legs slightly advanced. Double layer of gold leaf applied in square patches, with layer of yellow paint between; variegated patina on exposed copper and gold leaf. Hollow molded copper body soldered together. Stamped by maker.

Materials and Dimensions
Copper. Cast zinc. Gilded. Height: 18½″. Length: 32″. Depth: 2½″.

Locality and Period
Harris and Co., Brattleboro, Vermont. c. 1870–90.

Comment
Some collectors consider weathervanes the primary form of American nonacademic sculpture in the latter half of the 19th century. Mass-produced weathervanes gradually replaced handmade examples and became so common that by the last quarter of the century the roof of a barn or carriage house looked incomplete without a weathervane. Unlike the piece shown here, which bears its manufacturer's stamp, most vanes were unsigned and unmarked.

Hints for Collectors
Beware of a metal weathervane with a fresh coat of paint, since the new finish was probably meant to disguise repairs and reconditioning. Though collectors will pay a premium for a vane in its original state, they are usually willing to make some compromises about condition when considering a rare and highly desirable form.

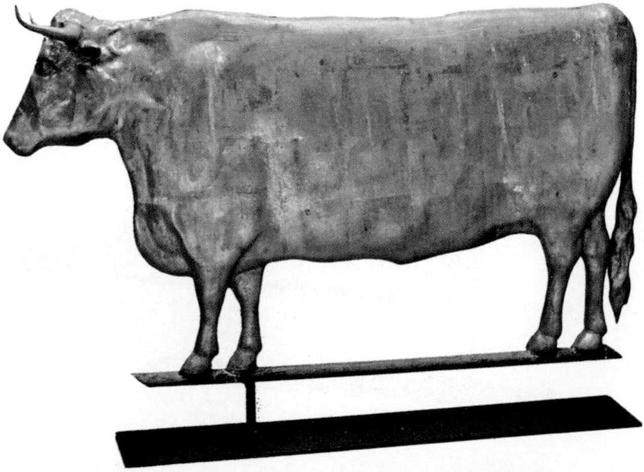

173 Horse-and-rider weathervane

Description
Jockey mounted on galloping horse and holding reins attached to horse's bit and bridle. Illusion of rapid movement created by outstretched tail and legs. Figure connected to base by poles at belly and rear hoof. Jockey's head, cap, shirt, jacket lapels, and boots made of grayish zinc. Hollow molded copper body with greenish patina.

Materials and Dimensions
Copper. Copper wire. Cast zinc. Height: 22″. Length: 42″. Depth: 6″.

Locality and Period
The Northeast. c. 1880–1900.

Comment
The weathervane shown here portrays Dexter, a famous horse in the mid-19th century. First manufactured in 1868 by the Waltham, Massachusetts, firm of Cushing and White, it was adapted from popular lithographs and was also produced in other sizes. It was soon copied by several other companies. Both molded and cast weathervanes, with finishing touches done by hand, are characterized by more finely executed details than were earlier, handmade silhouette types.

Hints for Collectors
This weathervane appears in over 20 versions; however, the makers of most of them have not been identified. This example, though a common type, is notable for its rich patina, which makes it quite valuable. The same oxidation process that results in an attractive patina may, however, eventually cause serious structural weakness.

174 Horse weathervane

Description
Horse with erect ears, flaring nostrils, and short wavy mane. Left foreleg raised; other legs resting on base. Hollow molded body, with halves screwed together at head and legs. Sheet-iron tail, with wavy outline, inserted at hindquarters and fastened with screw. Traces of old black paint.

Materials and Dimensions
Cast and sheet iron. Painted. Screws. Height: 27″. Length: 36½″. Depth: 5½″.

Locality and Period
Probably New England. c. 1840–60.

Comment
American weathervanes, such as the horse shown here, often share aesthetic qualities with some purely decorative sculpture from other countries. In fact, the catalogue of the Newark Museum's important American folk sculpture show in 1931 noted the similarity between the formal, static poses of the horses in weathervanes like this and certain horses by ancient Chinese sculptors. While the bodies were cast, details such as the tail on this horse were handmade and consequently vary in size and shape. Also prized as sculpture are the preliminary wooden patterns used in making the molds for iron weathervanes.

Hints for Collectors
Many vanes such as this one, made of both cast and stamped parts, have been damaged and repaired, lowering their value substantially. Carefully examine parts such as the ears and tail with a black light, which reveals repairs and replacements.

75 Horse weathervane

Description
Silhouette of horse with head, torso, and tail made from single board. Erect ears on small head; strongly arched neck. Rectangular torso ending in arched tail. Squat legs nailed to figure. Cream-colored body dappled with black paint. Chamfered edges.

Materials and Dimensions
Pine. Painted. Height: 20½″. Length: 25″. Depth: 1¼″.

Locality and Period
New England. c. 1890–1910.

Comment
A handmade wooden weathervane usually represented its creator's or owner's special interest; farmers, for example, often chose images of livestock, such as the horse shown here, for their barns. Other weathervanes doubled as trade signs: a gloved-hand vane, for instance, might have been placed atop a glove factory. Wooden vanes, chiseled or sawed from flat boards, were usually painted in solid or contrasting bright colors that have become muted over time. They wear poorly, however, and a piece made before the mid-19th century is a rare find. Examples with original paint are highly prized.

Hints for Collectors
Primitive versions of stylish designs, such as this horse vane, often create great interest at auctions. Check catalogues from previous auctions for vanes similar to the example you are considering, comparing descriptions and prices. A brief catalogue description may fail to mention a vane's restored elements or new paint, so inspect a piece carefully before purchasing it.

176 Peacock weathervane

Description
Silhouette of peacock with plain curved contours; metal ears nailed on. Head and front half of body covered on both sides with tin sheet secured by nails. Tail attached to body by 2 rectangular tin patches and fitted with 3 tin feathers. Wings and feathers delineated by black lines and dashes painted on cream-colored ground.

Materials and Dimensions
Pine. Tin. Painted. Wire nails. Height: 14½″. Length: 23″. Depth: ⅞″.

Locality and Period
New England. c. 1890–1910.

Comment
Weathervanes, more popular in America than in any other country, first appeared here in the mid-17th century and steadily gained favor. By the mid-19th century demand for these wind indicators was so great that they were produced in quantity, at first mostly by New York and Massachusetts firms. Since modern technology provides weather information, handmade vanes, such as this one, as well as mass-produced examples are now coveted solely for their decorative appeal.

Hints for Collectors
Flat wooden vanes—also called silhouette vanes—are extremely fragile; most of the oldest and rarest examples have been repaired with iron straps or other metal reinforcements. Other signs of age are substantial discoloration and wear of paint.

77

Rooster weathervane

Description
Rooster standing atop large arrow. Large molded tail. Legs long and thin, with one advanced. Bullet holes below neck and near tail. Arrow with flat metal feathers inserted in end. Body made of 2 hollow molded sections joined together. Overall gilding worn away in some areas; traces of red paint on comb and wattle.

Materials and Dimensions
Copper. Painted and gilded. Height: 13″. Length of arrow: 14¾″. Depth: 1½″.

Locality and Period
The Northeast. c. 1880–1900.

Comment
Gilded weathercocks, commonly seen on farmhouses, stood atop many churches because the rooster symbolized the cock that crowed 3 times when Saint Peter denied Jesus. Shem Drowne (1683–1774), America's earliest known and most famous professional weathervane maker, fashioned one for Boston's New Brick Church in 1721 (it is now perched on the First Church in Cambridge Congregational) as well as similar ones for other area churches. His designs were much copied by later manufacturers.

Hints for Collectors
This factory-made rooster is rare because it has original paint and gilding; its small scale would make it especially attractive to collectors with limited display space. Most antiques dealers hesitate to attribute a vane to a particular manufacturer or workshop because makers generally did not mark their products and one company often purchased molds from another company going out of business. Vanes with marks of well-known makers, such as Cushing and White, command a premium.

178 Grasshopper weathervane

Description
Grasshopper with long antennae, protruding eyes, and recessed mouth. 6 thin forelegs and 2 broad hind legs with jagged feet; all feet soldered to body and horizontal pole. Hollow molded sections soldered together. Embossed markings; worn gilding.

Materials and Dimensions
Copper. Gilded. Iron. Height: 17″. Length: 35″. Depth: 9″.

Locality and Period
Massachusetts. c. 1880.

Comment
The grasshopper weathervane, handmade or factory-produced, has been popular in America since the 17th century. The one that still stands atop Boston's Faneuil Hall, a copy of one on the London Royal Exchange, was put there in 1749 by its maker, Shem Drowne. Though the vane shown here lacks the green glass eyes of the Faneuil Hall example, its elegant and powerful form makes it a fine 19th-century model.

Hints for Collectors
Because of their long exposure to the elements, not many 18th- and early 19th-century weathervanes have survived. Most examples that appear in the marketplace are from the latter half of the 19th century or are 20th-century reproductions or fakes. An old vane should be worn and weathered overall, particularly the inside of its supporting upright, which fakers may forget to artificially age; surfaces should be oxidized or, if painted, crazed. The end of the horizontal support also provides a clue to age: a round cap is used on many reproductions, while a diagonal cut, as seen here, appears on older vanes.

179 Fish weathervane

Description
Cod with repoussé scales and 2 fins on top and 2 on bottom. Large open mouth; circular eyes with black dots for pupils. 2 side fins hammered in ribbed design. Tail with hammered fin lines. Traces of original yellow paint.

Materials and Dimensions
Copper. Painted. Height: 10¼″. Length: 30½″. Depth: 3¼″.

Locality and Period
Massachusetts. c. 1885–1900.

Comment
Weathervane makers of the 19th century were frequently inspired by local subjects. Thus vanes in coastal towns and villages—some made by whalers, fishermen, and sailors in their spare time—often depicted ships, whales, seagulls, or fish such as the cod shown here. To make weathervanes visible from afar, bold shapes and bright colors were selected. Unpainted copper vanes gleamed brightly in the sun, but since they quickly turned grayish green, many were gilded or painted; yellow-ocher paint was a cheap substitute for gilding.

Hints for Collectors
Since fish were only one of many images used for weathervanes produced in coastal towns, such vanes are comparatively rare. Still, they are not particularly popular with collectors and tend to be underpriced. A fine example in good original condition will probably prove a worthwhile long-term investment, since collecting tastes change over the years and fish vanes will undoubtedly come back into favor.

Animal Sculpture

Perhaps the richest area of American folk sculpture is that of animal figures. This menagerie encompasses virtually every creature of land, sea, and air, and some imaginary ones as well. Representations of eagles are the most common, followed by such domestic animals as cats, dogs, and horses.
The depictions of these animals range from the amazingly realistic to the charmingly naive. Their materials are wood, gypsum, metal, stone, and whale ivory. Their intended uses are as diverse as their subjects, with some functioning as trade signs, carousel carvings, mill weights, coin banks, toys, and grave markers. Decorative figures meant solely to brighten a home, however, constitute the single largest group.
Weathervanes and decoys, two types of sculpture that most often employ animal shapes, are featured in separate sections.

Wood

Most sculptures of animals were carved from wood by local craftsmen or itinerant whittlers, the latter often being European immigrants with a woodcarving background. Though these works are generally anonymous, a few 19th-century carvers are known. Perhaps the most highly regarded is German-born Wilhelm Schimmel, who wandered through the Cumberland Valley in Pennsylvania earning a meager living by selling his impressionistic carvings of eagles, roosters, and other creatures. Aaron Mountz, who as a boy had known Schimmel, continued this tradition into the 20th century and also specialized in eagles. A third carver known for his eagles was John H. Bellamy of Maine, whose realistic works often adorned government buildings and ships.
Other animal carvings, such as carousel figures, were produced in large woodworking shops located primarily in New York City and Philadelphia. Because such pieces were crafted in assembly-line fashion, they often lack the integrated style of a single artist.

Chalkware

In the second half of the 19th century, decorative figures made of gypsum, a chalky substance that is an ingredient of plaster of Paris, became immensely popular. Called chalkware, this inexpensive material was often used for whimsical animal forms, but flowers, fruit, and people were also depicted. Cast in molds, the hollow figures were painted in bright colors.

Metal

At the same time that chalkware flourished, new casting techniques made metal objects available to every American household. Though often given animal or other decorative shapes, these objects were mainly utilitarian, serving as bootscrapers, banks, nutcrackers, hitching-post finials, door stops, targets, or mill weights. Since they were cast in molds made from hand-carved wooden patterns, many of these mass-produced objects are now considered a secondary form of folk art.

Stone and Scrimshaw

Grave ornaments in marble, limestone, granite, and other kinds of stone were sometimes carved in animal shapes. A few even served as gravestones for pets. Stone carvings of animal forms were also used as architectural ornaments.
Whalemen occasionally carved whale teeth into sculptural figures, such as the whale shown here; these were less common than engraved teeth and scrimshaw household utensils.

180 Fish-market sign

Description
Wooden fish with carved head; jaws open, mouth closed at tip. Separate fins set into top, sides, and bottom of body. Scales on body indicated by incised horizontal and vertical lines; tail markings indicated by deep curving lines. Original mustard-color paint. Mounted on 2 wooden rods attached to wooden base.

Materials and Dimensions
Maple. Painted. Height (without stand): 8½″. Length: 30″. Width: 3¾″.

Locality and Period
New York City. c. 1850–70.

Comment
The 3-dimensional sign shown here, possibly modeled after the striped bass, came from a fish market in New York City's South Street Seaport area. Similar signs also hung in front of stores selling bait and tackle. The realistic carving of this fish and its separately crafted fins distinguish it from most other trade signs which are usually simple flat silhouettes made of wood, copper, tin, or iron, and sometimes painted or gilded. Since more and more Americans were becoming literate, after about 1900 shops began to replace such figures with printed signs.

Hints for Collectors
The carved scales on the body of this fish, the meticulous execution of the ribs on the tail, and the sensitive modeling of the head make it an especially desirable piece. Well-shaped and finely crafted folk carvings are generally the best investments.

181 **Sperm whale**

Description
Whale carved from single whale's tooth. Open mouth ¼ length of body; lower jaw with indentations indicating teeth. Relief-carved eyes and flippers just behind mouth. Top tapering from squared front to narrow tail section; bottom nearly flat. Twisted flukes. Highly polished surface. Walrus-ivory base.

Materials and Dimensions
Whale ivory. Walrus ivory. Height (without stand): 3¾″. Length: 7¾″.

Locality and Period
Nantucket. c. 1865.

Comment
This clumsy but charming sculpture was carved from an enormous whale tooth (also called whale ivory). It has acquired a patina that differs noticeably in color from its walrus-ivory base, resulting in an attractive contrast. Since carvings of whales are seldom found and those that do exist usually were made in the early 20th century, this older example is a rarity.

Hints for Collectors
Scrimshaw collectors are faced with a complicated, often changing set of federal and state laws limiting the purchase and sale of whale products. Interstate commerce of many such products was prohibited by the Marine Mammal Protection Act of 1972 and the Endangered Species Act of 1973, though most objects purchased for non-commercial purposes before that date are exempt. Because these and related regulations may change in the near future, collectors should check with dealers, auction houses, or perhaps the Department of Interior or state agencies to avoid investing in embargoed scrimshaw they later may be unable to resell.

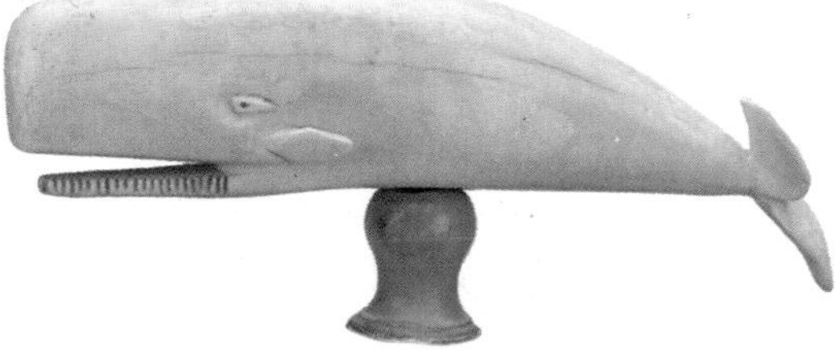

182 **Shark**

Description
Carved and painted shark made of 9 vertically layered wooden slabs glued together. Black top, sides, and fins; gray underside. Open mouth with 17 triangular wooden teeth painted silver and set into jaws. Orange circular eyes nailed to body; zinc nailheads double as pupils. 5 fins set into body. Gills are 3 vertical indentations painted white on each side.

Materials and Dimensions
Pine. Painted. Zinc nails. Height: 18″. Length: 48″. Width: 30″.

Locality and Period
Maine. c. 1920.

Comment
Fish have interested American folk artists since the 17th century. A codfish carving, made around 1760 by John Welch, hangs in the Boston State House, affirming the importance of the fishing industry in Massachusetts. The fish form has also been used for weathervanes, trade signs, decoys, and even doorstops. This dramatic sculpture of a shark may have been carved by a fisherman who had had a memorable encounter with this species.

Hints for Collectors
Many 20th-century folk carvers have created imaginative pieces for decorative rather than functional use, though this practice has often been criticized. Collectors with a traditional point of view generally prefer functional examples and would pass up whimsical carvings such as this shark. In evaluating 20th-century pieces, fine design and craftsmanship are more important than a rich patina, which may be lacking on relatively recent works.

183 **Swordfish sign**

Description
Carved swordfish with sword, 5 fins, and tail all formed from notched board running vertically through center; hollow halves of body surround center board; body opens. Fins and tail with applied starfish and redwood letters reading "SEA FOOD/ BEER & ALE." Drilled hole serving as eye. Inset birch tusks. Doll, with articulated joints, in mouth. Decoration on front only.

Materials and Dimensions
Pine. Birch. Redwood. Nails. Screws. Starfish. Height: 33″. Length: 88″. Width: 8″.

Locality and Period
Made by Bob Self (1946–), New York City. c. 1976.

Comment
According to its maker, this whimsical sculpture is meant to be a swordfish as imagined by a person who had never seen one. Like much folk art, this work was created from found materials—here, wood of various grades left over from other projects. Self has sculpted more than 35 other pieces, including fancifully shaped lamps and boxes.

Hints for Collectors
Decorative carvings like this example are best preserved by being displayed indoors, especially in northern climates. Wood carvings exhibited outdoors should be well finished as well as structurally sound, since wood may split when water seeps into the grain, freezes, and then expands. Old fish-shaped signs are seldom in good condition and very few retain their original painted decoration. Handle painted pieces with care; a rich patina cannot be reproduced once it has been damaged.

184 Frog decoys

Description
Center: Dark green wooden frog with rear legs extended straight back from torso; no front legs. Mouth closed and lined in black. Metal hook at top rear used to attach line. White underside. Weighted. *Right:* Light green wooden frog with linear decoration in dark green and yellow. Tin front legs thrust forward from sides; rear legs forming diamond-shaped opening, with feet bent toward right. White eyes within black circles; red mouth. Wire, curved into 4 circles, set into top, and attached with fishing line to carved wooden reel at left.

Materials and Dimensions
Center: Pine. Painted. Lead weight. Length: 4½″. Width: 1½″. *Right:* Pine. Tin. Painted. Lead weight. Length: 5″. Width: 2¼″.

Locality and Period
Center: The Midwest, probably Wisconsin. c. 1940–50. *Right:* Made by Oscar Peterson (1887–?), Cadillac, Michigan. c. 1940.

Comment
Fish are attracted to frog decoys by their bright colors and sparkling metal appendages. Like most fish decoys, these come from the Great Lakes region and are used exclusively for ice fishing.

Hints for Collectors
Frog carvings are rare and greatly valued by collectors of fish decoys. The example here attached to a reel was made by Oscar Peterson, probably to be sold in a bait store. The small hand-carved example, though displaying great imagination on the part of its creator, lacks the elaborately painted surface of Peterson's decoy and would probably fetch less money.

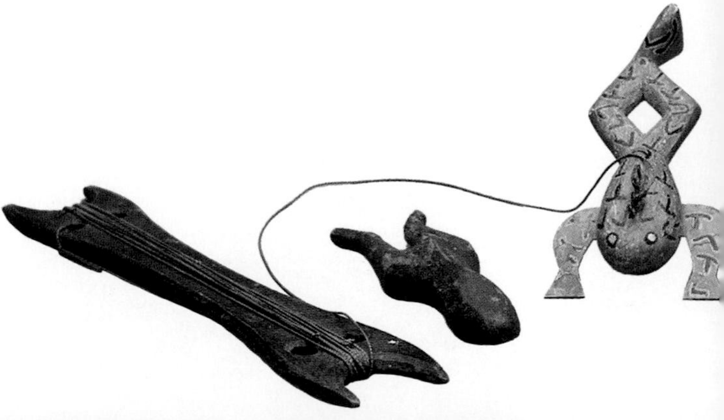

85 Flower holder or frog

Description
Realistic metal figure of frog, with gaping mouth and inset metal eyes. Bumps on skin. Legs thrust outward; toes delineated. 5 holes (¼″ to ½″ wide) through figure. Pebbled surface with worn green paint.

Materials and Dimensions
Cast-metal alloy (pot metal). Painted. Length: 4½″. Width: 3″. Depth: 2¼″.

Locality and Period
Massachusetts. c. 1890–1910.

Comment
By the mid-19th century, American technology had evolved far enough for all kinds of household objects—from match safes and doorstops to inkwells and flower holders—to be mass-produced. Cast-metal flower holders, called "frogs" though not usually frog-shaped, are fine examples of folk art that is utilitarian as well as decorative. They were placed at the bottom of a bowl for flower stems to be inserted in their holes. The design of these pieces must allow them to balance when holding flowers. Modern versions, though also called frogs, are unattractive disks that little resemble their more decorative forebears.

Hints for Collectors
Because such objects were cast in molds, there are probably many in existence, but few reach the marketplace since they are frequently still used by their owners. Look for sharp details when considering a cast piece, because objects made in worn molds tend to lose clarity of line. As with all cast examples, original paint in good condition enhances value.

186 Alligator-shaped nutcracker

Description
Cast-iron nutcracker in form of alligator, with incised eyes, realistic scales on back, and pointed teeth in open mouth. In 2 movable, separable pieces: when mouth is open, tail is raised; when mouth is closed, rear section fits under tail. Traces of old paint.

Materials and Dimensions
Cast iron. Painted. Height: 3½″. Length: 8″. Width: 1″.

Locality and Period
Probably the Northeast or Midwest. c. 1875–1900.

Comment
Nuts are a traditional part of the dessert course at formal meals, and nutcrackers were used in Europe at least as early as the 16th century. They take many different forms; some have a viselike mechanism that is screwed tighter until the nut cracked. By the early 19th century, double-handled brass or iron nutcrackers were extremely popular in the United States and Europe.

Hints for Collectors
The Victorians made nutcrackers in every conceivable shape, including an eagle's head (the beak cracked the nut), a squirrel, and even women's legs (the last shape was also used on the handles of corkscrews and canes). These small objects have become quite popular with collectors, and some forms, including the female legs, are now fairly expensive. But if one turns up in a flea market or in a shop that does not usually carry this kind of Victoriana, it may sell below market value.

87 Dinosaur

Description
Carved and painted dinosaur standing on hind legs. Eyes with red pupils set in prominent whites; indented red mouth; 2 nail-hole nostrils. Spinal column suggested by notched ridge flecked with white paint. Small forelegs and large hind legs, all with metal paws; hind feet each with 5 toes. Pointed tail as long as body, curving slightly upward.

Materials and Dimensions
Pine. Painted. Cast metal. Nails. Height: 9⅜″. Length: 24⅝″. Width: 3½″.

Locality and Period
Made by Fred Alten (1872–1945), Wyandotte, Michigan. c. 1915.

Comment
The dinosaur shown here is representative of the folk art tradition of animal carvings. Like most folk art, it is unrelated to fashionable art of the period or to any art movement. Though the success of this sculpture depends on its whimsical, childlike stylization, it is instantly recognizable as a dinosaur.

Hints for Collectors
Folk sculptors, like folk painters, often used illustrations from books and lithographs as design sources. Many of Alten's pieces were inspired by *Johnson's Household Book of Nature.* In his leisure time, he executed several hundred animal carvings. Most of these are now owned by dealers and collectors around the country and are generally valuable. To develop the ability to recognize the works of a particular artist or examples of a specific style, collectors should focus on one field and study it thoroughly—seeing and handling as many objects as possible and reading widely.

188 **Monkey**

Description
Small seated monkey with head and body carved from single piece of wood. Black eyes outlined in red and set within white circles; black nose and red mouth. Ears are tiny nailheads. Cylindrical body with dark stain. L-shaped leather arms and legs loosely nailed to body to permit movement. Long leather tail pointing upward. Square wooden base stained red.

Materials and Dimensions
Stained and painted wood. Leather. Nails. Height (without base): 4¾″. Length: 1½″. Width (without tail): 2″.

Locality and Period
The Midwest. c. 1925–50.

Comment
Though 20th-century man is somewhat removed from nature, wildlife still fascinates folk artists. Animal-inspired folk carvings range from the very realistic to the unconventional and abstract; some carvers give amusingly human qualities to their animals. The carved monkey shown here was probably fashioned by a carver of fish decoys because its appendages, like the fins and tails of many decoys, are made of leather, and it was found in an old fishing-tackle box containing decoys with leather fins and tails.

Hints for Collectors
Fish decoys and other decorative carvings by midwestern lure makers were, until recently, virtually unknown to collectors outside the Great Lakes area, where they were created and used. Though their prices have recently been increasing rapidly, they are still underpriced and thus worthwhile investments.

89 Piggy bank

Description
Hollow pig with slightly lowered head, erect ears, and long snout. Full rounded body with short legs, right hoofs slightly ahead of left ones. Long curly tail hanging down. Coin slot on back. Painted bright red overall; worn in spots.

Materials and Dimensions
Cast iron. Painted. Height: 5½″. Length: 8″. Width: 2½″.

Locality and Period
The Northeast. c. 1875–1900.

Comment
Among the earliest American toy banks were carved gourds that appeared during the late 1790s. These were followed by glass, pottery, and tin banks, some modeled after animals, buildings, and famous people. Many colorful cast-iron banks, which were both toys and an impetus for thrift, had mechanical appendages that moved when the money was deposited. During their heyday, from about 1860 to 1930, demand for these toys was satisfied by fewer than a dozen foundries. While this bank has to be turned upside down and shaken to remove coins, more expensive examples have a bolt that can be unscrewed to separate the 2 halves; others have a removable stopper or cork.

Hints for Collectors
Cast-iron banks were generally made in metal molds created from hand-carved wooden patterns, or models. Banks with movable parts activated by a coin are the most valuable. Pieces like this example—referred to as "still banks" because they have no movable parts—are usually available for modest sums; this one has been repainted, which significantly lowers its value.

190

Nodding-head chalkware pig and goat

Description
Left: Hollow pale yellow pig with yellow ears, eyes, and mouth all outlined in red; forehead with red and yellow design and black dot; black eyebrows, nostrils, and hoofs. Red collar. Head hung on wire loops inside body. Twisted tail pointing up. *Right:* Hollow white goat with horns, facial features, and collar decorated in red, yellow, green, and black. Front hoofs and tail with black markings. Head hung on wire loops inside body.

Materials and Dimensions
Gypsum. Painted. Wire. Height (left; right): 5⅛″; 7⅝″. Length: 9¼″; 9″. Width: 3¼″; 3⅜″.

Locality and Period
Throughout the United States. c. 1890–1900.

Comment
Chalkware, so named because of the resemblance of its unpainted surface to chalk, refers to ornamental objects made of gypsum, the main ingredient in plaster of Paris. Although chalkware appeared in America as early as 1768 and was created in small workshops during the early 19th century, it was first mass-produced by John Rogers of New York, a railroad mechanic turned sculptor, who sold over 80,000 plaster pieces between 1860 and 1893. Made throughout the latter half of the 19th century by unschooled craftsmen who adapted German and Italian techniques and English pottery designs, chalkware was bought primarily by middle-class Americans who wanted inexpensive ceramic works of art similar to the more costly Staffordshire pieces.

Animals, birds, arrangements of fruit, and even famous people were portrayed; figures of dogs, cats, lions, and deer were the most common, followed by squirrels, sheep, and pigs. Chalkware watchstands, their backs undecorated because they were meant to stand against the wall, were also fashioned in large numbers; the pillared half dome, with a niche for hanging a pocket watch, was one of the most popular forms.

Hints for Collectors
Nodding pieces are prized by collectors of chalkware. The finest examples have fresh and vivid painted decoration. Check the mechanism holding the nodding head in place, since it is delicate and may have been repaired; such restoration is considered major and will lower the value of a piece. Do not confuse authentic, hollow-bodied chalkware with heavier, 20th-century plaster-of-Paris sculptures generally given away as circus and carnival prizes. While chalkware has markedly increased in value in recent years, many collectors still shun it because of its gaudy decoration.

191

Chalkware cat

Description
One-piece hollow figure of seated cat with head slightly turned; pale yellow overall. Erect red-rimmed ears and brown and red eyes. Red mouth and nostrils with 3 brown whiskers at each side. Red and black collar. Body decorated with brown circles and linear markings. Paws set side by side, brown tail wrapped around flank. Long front legs with brown diagonal stripes extending down front. Oval base with brown semicircles.

Materials and Dimensions
Gypsum. Painted. Height: 15⅝". Length: 8¾". Width: 10⅛".

Locality and Period
Pennsylvania. c. 1860–1900.

Comment
This life-size figure of a cat is larger than most chalkware pieces. Its unusual dimensions and imaginative decoration make it a sleek and distinctive sculpture. Though chalkware objects were mass-produced from molds, they were individually painted in bright, even gaudy, oils or watercolors, and thus 2 figures are rarely identical. Many pieces were created in Pennsylvania.

Hints for Collectors
Chalkware cats were made in a variety of sizes; the largest examples are generally the most valuable. Chalkware is easy to restore, and a competent craftsman can hide even severe damage. Turn a piece upside down and inspect the inside of the hollow body; the bright white color may show evidence of glue, indicating repairs. Restoration, if well done, does not lower the value of chalkware as much as it does other forms of folk art. Beware of the many reproductions now on the market.

192

Cat's-head inkwell

Description
Inkwell in shape of a cat's head; hinged top portion. Traces of white paint overall, with red outlines around mouth. Open mouth showing white teeth and red tongue. Sculpted fur and whiskers. Blue ribbon around neck, with ends extending forward to form pen holder.

Materials and Dimensions
Cast iron. Painted. Height: 4½″. Length: 5″. Width: 5½″.

Locality and Period
Probably the Northeast or Midwest. c. 1875–1900.

Comment
While there is some disagreement about whether cast-iron 19th-century objects can legitimately be termed folk art, the fact that they were cast in molds made from one-of-a-kind, hand-carved wooden patterns supports the argument that they can be. Moreover, this particular example is individualized by its hand-painted features, most notably the blue ribbon that seems to disappear beneath the cat's fur. The piece is practical as well as decorative, another characteristic of folk art: the head lifts up to reveal the inkwell, and the ribbon is shaped to hold a pen.

Hints for Collectors
Like doorstops, banks, and other iron designs, this inkwell was undoubtedly made in fairly large numbers. Reproductions, formed in a mold recently created from an old iron object rather than cast from an original mold, may be recognized by blurred or missing details. The sharpness of its smallest details proves this inkwell was from an original casting. Pieces like this may still be bought reasonably, but prices are rising.

193 Cat-shaped bootscraper

Description
Bootscraper in form of a silhouette of a black cat with long outstretched tail. Body with protruding ridge along cat's spine. Drilled hole for eye. Legs fastened to rectangular iron base; no paws. Cast in 2-piece mold.

Materials and Dimensions
Cast iron. Height: 11⅜″. Length: 17¾″. Width of base: 3″.

Locality and Period
Probably the Northeast or Midwest. c. 1880–1915.

Comment
Because unpaved roads turned to mud whenever it rained, scrapers to clean boots or shoes were a household necessity during the 17th to 19th centuries. A bootscraper was usually fastened to the front doorstep of a house; in cities it was often attached to the bricks or cobblestones next to the front steps. Iron, sturdy and relatively inexpensive, was the material most commonly used for bootscrapers, doorstops, and other utilitarian household objects. The design of the bootscraper shown here, sometimes called "Shadow the Cat," was popular in the late 19th and early 20th centuries. Since it was cast in a mold, many identical examples were made.

Hints for Collectors
Due to growing collector interest and demand, naive forms such as this bootscraper are often reproduced today. While reproductions sold in museum shops are clearly marked as such, some may make their way to antiques shops and be passed off as originals. Older cast iron may generally be recognized by an uneven, pitted surface that feels like the skin of an orange. Beware, however, of modern reproductions that have been given an "old" finish by their manufacturers.

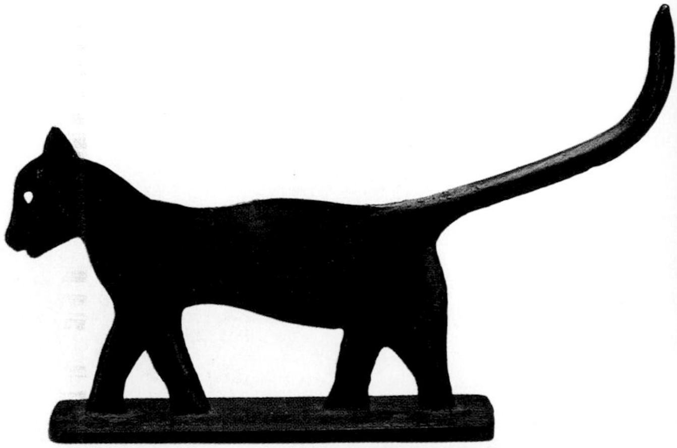

94 Dog-shaped lawn ornament

Description
Silhouette of standing terrier cut out from single piece of wood. Black head with erect white ears outlined in black, white muzzle and black nose, mouth, and whiskers. Brown collar with 5 tan diamond shapes. Black body with white markings on area below collar and at rear; white tail and paws.

Materials and Dimensions
Pine. Painted. Height: 14½″. Length: 11″. Thickness: ¾″.

Locality and Period
Probably New York State. c. 1920–40.

Comment
The portrayal of dogs has had a long tradition in American folk art, appearing in the works of painters such as Ammi Phillips, Noah North, and Jacob Maentel, in pieces by carvers such as Wilhelm Schimmel, and in the wares of many potteries. Dogs often appear in folk art originally designed for outdoor use, including weathervanes, whirligigs, carousel figures, and grave ornaments. The dog shown here, meant to stand on a lawn, displays a distinctively 20th-century style best seen in the cartoon characters of the 1920s and 1930s.

Hints for Collectors
Lawn ornaments have long been collected, but few are old enough to merit the serious consideration of traditional folk art connoisseurs. Examples with distinctive designs, strong colors, and original paint are most desirable. Since these pieces are fairly common and many remain in excellent condition, avoid those with missing or broken parts or excessive wear from exposure to the weather.

195 **Dog's gravestone**

Description
Dog in resting position carved from single piece of gray-veined white marble. Paws extended forward; head turned sideways, resting on right paw. Large floppy ears hanging down alongside head; almond-shaped eyes. Blunt muzzle with mouth closed. Hind legs tucked in alongside body. Long tail curled forward, resting under right leg. Round-cornered base.

Materials and Dimensions
Marble. Height: 3½″. Length: 11½″. Width: 4″.

Locality and Period
New England. c. 1860–80.

Comment
Before animal cemeteries became common in the 20th century, beloved pets—dogs, cats, and even horses—were usually buried on the grounds of their owners' homes. Their bereaved masters sometimes marked the final resting place with carved memorial stones such as the one shown here. One of the most interesting groups of grave markers is in Maplewood Cemetery in Mayfield, Kentucky: life-size figures mark the grave of Colonel Henry C. Wooldridge and include sculptures of himself on horseback as well as of his relatives, friends, and favorite hound, Bob.

Hints for Collectors
Grave markers for pets are rare—in fact, only a handful are known—so they command surprisingly high prices when they come onto the market. They should not be confused with the fairly common lamb-shaped grave markers that were used on children's graves in the Victorian era.

96 Lamb-shaped grave ornament

Description
Lamb in resting position carved from single piece of stone, with head facing left. Wool indicated by incised wavy lines. Plain face with horizontal ears, almond-shaped eyes, and closed mouth. Rounded body with feet tucked under and tail hanging down. Reverse rounded and plain with incised wavy lines. Oval base.

Materials and Dimensions
Limestone. Height: 10″. Length: 13″. Width: 4½″.

Locality and Period
New England. c. 1840–60.

Comment
The lamb, a symbol of gentleness and peace, was a favored form during Victorian times for children's grave markers; such markers were placed at the head or foot of graves or else on top of gravestones. Lambs were usually the choice of middle-class families; poor people marked graves with a plain cross, while the rich commissioned more elaborate works that were often of marble.

Hints for Collectors
When acquiring funerary sculpture, choose examples that are rich in detail and sensitively executed. The 3-dimensional quality that makes this grave marker especially desirable is lacking in many others. Some folk art collectors prefer a more highly stylized representation that stresses overall form above detail. Whether simple or ornate, the piece should be in good condition; a missing ear or hoof will lower the price substantially.

197 Elephant

Description
Carved and painted elephant with body fashioned from solid piece of wood chamfered at corners. Raised trunk flanked by 2 small tusks set into head. 4 stump legs set into underside of body. Flat 2-piece ears attached with nails. Red eyes inside black circles. Rope tail. Cracks from age.

Materials and Dimensions
Pine body. Ash or hickory appendages. Painted. Rope. Nails. Height: 16″. Length: 25″. Width: 8½″.

Locality and Period
Maine. c. 1900.

Comment
Generations of European immigrants brought to America a love of woodcarving. Encouraged by the abundance and variety of woods, they whittled and carved human and animal figures. Their animals ranged from the known to the imaginary, from the serious to the whimsical. Circus and barnyard creatures, monkeys, dogs, and deer were all included in the carver's repertoire. The quaint wooden elephant shown here was probably intended to be a toy. Part of its charm comes from its odd blocky shape: if the tusks and trunk were removed, this carving could just as well be a pig.

Hints for Collectors
For the collector of folk sculpture, condition is usually a prime consideration. There are exceptions, however, such as this example, in which the shrinking of the wood has caused deep cracks in the body; since these cracks do not disfigure the piece or diminish its appeal, its market value remains unaffected.

98 Cow-shaped mill weight

Description
Painted cow with raised beige head slightly tilted to one side, erect ears, and folds of skin on neck. Heavy brown body; right front leg and left rear leg advanced. Long undulating tail with bushy end. Patina of old paint and rust. Mounted on sculpted base.

Materials and Dimensions
Cast iron. Painted. Height: 13″. Length: 14″. Width: 4″.

Locality and Period
The Midwest. c. 1900–20.

Comment
Windmills were used for pumping water to homes and barns throughout the Midwest primarily during the 19th and early 20th centuries. Cast-iron figures of cows, horses, squirrels, chickens, eagles, and buffaloes, as well as some in geometric designs, were used as counterweights for the rotating blades on many simple windmills (*see also* 208).

Hints for Collectors
Many collectors who have never seen a midwestern windmill will not recognize the weights that were used on them. These weights have become highly collectible, rising in value from less than $100 a few years ago to as much as 10 or 15 times that amount today for those pieces with unusual shapes and designs. Learn to recognize the patina of early examples in order to distinguish originals from the reproductions now being made. Mill weights may best be found in the Midwest, where some are still in use.

199 Horse-head hitching-post finial

Description
Realistic hollow metal horse head painted black. Erect ears chipped at top. Wide-open eyes and nostrils, prominent veins and muscles of jaws. Flowing mane. Bit set into closed mouth with 2 movable rings attached at either end. 2 holes in base for attaching to post.

Materials and Dimensions
Cast iron. Painted. Height: 12½″. Length: 11″. Width: 5″.

Locality and Period
Probably the Northeast or Midwest. c. 1865–1900.

Comment
Hitching posts in the form of a plain or decorated wooden upright, often topped by a cast-iron finial, were especially common in the mid-19th century. While the finials were made in a variety of shapes, including floral designs, a black jockey's head, and a fist, the most preferred was a horse's head, such as the one shown here. Cast in a mold created from a wooden model, finials were mass-produced by iron foundries, such as the J. L. Mott or J. W. Fiske Ironworks, and sold through mail-order catalogues. The quality of the designs varied, being emblematic of the owner's station in life. These finials became less popular when one-piece, solid iron posts became widely available.

Hints for Collectors
Nearly all cast-iron pieces were originally painted, usually in black, to prevent rusting. Most hitching posts have been repainted over the years; if well done, this does not lower their value. An example displayed indoors needs no special protection from rusting; if placed outdoors, however, it should occasionally be rubbed with high-grade oil.

200 Horse pull toy

Description
Crudely carved and painted horse standing stiffly with erect head facing forward. Long narrow muzzle, incised eyes and nostrils, and heavy neck (mane missing) made from single piece of wood. Full-chested body made of several horizontal pieces, with carved blanket and English saddle. Straight legs, tapered at center. Short rope tail. Attached to platform set on 2 axles connecting pairs of wheels. Nail construction.

Materials and Dimensions
Pine. Painted. Rope. Iron nails. Height: 18″. Base length: 15″; width: 7″.

Locality and Period
Probably Pennsylvania. c. 1850–70.

Comment
Children's playthings reflect tastes and trends of a period. As a sideline, carvers and carpenters often made toys such as this horse, which is a variation of the rocking horse, the most popular type of toy of the 18th and 19th centuries. Realism was not necessary in such figures, but since children generally prefer toys with movable parts, this horse was placed on a wheeled platform to give it animation.

Hints for Collectors
This simple pull toy is an exceptional folk sculpture with a wonderful patina. The loss of the mane does not seriously affect the overall appeal or market value of this piece. While many sculpture collectors would be eager to acquire such a distinctive piece, collectors specializing in children's toys would probably outbid them if it came up at auction.

201 Carousel horse

Description
Carved brown horse with lowered head, erect ears, glass eyes, white teeth in open jaws, and wavy black mane. Bridle and trappings of red, blue, and yellow cut glass on golden background. Long English saddle with curved sword in scabbard on each side. Red blanket with yellow binding. Horsehair tail. Left foreleg raised and tucked under; other 3 hoofs on ground. Hole for pole through center of underside.

Materials and Dimensions
Painted wood. Glass. Horsehair. Height: 58⅝″. Length: 63″. Width: 14⅞″.

Locality and Period
Attributed to Charles Carmel (life dates unknown), Brooklyn, New York. c. 1914.

Comment
Carousel figures like the horse shown here were often produced in assembly-line fashion in specialty workshops. Partly because many men often worked on one figure, few pieces were signed. Horses were the most common subjects, but tigers, giraffes, rabbits, cows, pigs, camels, and other forms were also made. Few have retained their original paint, since they were usually repainted whenever their surfaces became worn from use.

Hints for Collectors
The original paint and decoration on this carousel horse make it exceptional, since examples in good original condition—which are, of course, most desirable—rarely come on the market. Most collectors of carousel figures approve of restoring pieces that have suffered serious structural damage or surface deterioration; in those cases, skillful restoration adds to the value of a carving.

202 Carousel wagon panel

Description
Panel with head of Uncle Sam in profile and bald eagle, both carved in low relief and painted and set on American flag draped across bottom. Uncle Sam wearing red-and-white-striped headdress; blue band with white stars atop forehead. Sculpted golden face with blue eye set in white and rimmed in black, prominent nose, flowing gray mustache and eyebrows, and long curly black beard. Full-breasted gold-colored eagle with black crown and dark beak on upturned head. Overall feathering carved in low relief. Wings close to body. Back of panel plain.

Materials and Dimensions
Painted wood. Height: 60″. Length: 90″.

Locality and Period
The Northeast or Midwest. c. 1880–1900.

Comment
To accommodate merry-go-round riders who were too young or too sedate to straddle a wooden horse or other bobbing creature, most carousels also had stationary wagons with flat seats. Their sides were decorated with colorful and elaborate designs, such as the panel shown here, that complemented the animals. Like other folk artists, carvers of such pieces often turned to patriotic themes. As in the case of this Uncle Sam, who looks like a pirate, carvers sometimes gave their own interpretation to traditional symbols.

Hints for Collectors
Because carousel wagon panels are large and difficult to display, they often sell for much less than their artistic merit or scarcity justifies. Among the most valuable are those with patriotic or humorous subjects, particularly if they have original paint in good condition.

203 **Eagle**

Description
Carved and gilded eagle with symmetrical wings fully extended as if in flight. Incised feathers. Long graceful neck twisted to one side; open beak. Tail feathers curved under right wing. Large talons curved to grasp American flag (missing). Glue and screw construction.

Materials and Dimensions
Pine. Gilded. Iron screws. Height: 10½″. Wingspan: 35¾″. Depth: 6½″.

Locality and Period
Attributed to John H. Bellamy (1836–1914), Kittery Point, Maine. c. 1860–79.

Comment
John Bellamy began his career as an apprentice to a Boston woodcarver. Because of his skill and facility, he was often commissioned by the government to carve figureheads and other ship decorations, as well as figures symbolizing the United States; among these were his famous sculptures of eagles made to adorn government buildings or ships. The wingspans ranged from 2 to more than 18 feet. Most were carved from pine or, sometimes, mahogany. The birds often gripped an American flag in their beak or talons. The original gilding of the eagle shown here has sand mixed in it, a technique that Bellamy abandoned in his later years.

Hints for Collectors
Though all are relatively expensive, Bellamy eagles vary widely in price. The most desirable are, like the one illustrated, convincingly 3-dimensional and characteristically aggressive in stance. Beware of weathered reproductions painted red, white, and blue, which are sometimes passed off as originals.

204 Eagle on sphere

Description
Eagle perched on sphere on top of stand; each element carved from single piece of wood. Eagle with finely carved raised head; red tongue, mouth, and rims of eyes. Wings raised and spread; braced with U-shaped metal rod attached with nails and screws. Metal hook inserted under lower beak. Carved feathers cover body. Sphere with horizontal rim at center; talons carved on sphere. Mounted on metal rod extending upward from carved wooden base through ball into eagle. Nail construction.

Materials and Dimensions
Painted wood. Iron hardware. Height: 69⅞″. Wingspan: 44″. Depth: 50″.

Locality and Period
Pennsylvania. c. 1905.

Comment
The bald eagle became the American national emblem in 1782 and was used in almost all forms of American folk art. The eagle shown here once perched atop the Fraternal Order of Eagles Lodge in Columbia, Pennsylvania. Folk artists often received commissions from organizations such as this.

Hints for Collectors
This sculpture is extraordinary because it successfully combines handsome design, fine carving, massive proportions, and rich patina. A one-of-a-kind piece such as this would be very expensive if it came onto the market. Though most such large carvings are expensive, less unusual examples at comparatively reasonable prices sometimes turn up at out-of-the-way auctions.

205 Eagle

Description
Carved and painted perched eagle, poised for flight, with outspread wings made from separate pieces of wood pegged to body. Oversize head with red mouth and yellow eyes and beak. Feathers on body and tops of wings carved in close sawtooth pattern; larger feathers on underside of wings. Hunched legs; talons clasping oval base.

Materials and Dimensions
Probably pine. Painted. Gesso. Height: 12½". Wingspan: 17½". Depth: 6½".

Locality and Period
Made by Wilhelm Schimmel (1817–90), Carlisle, Pennsylvania. c. 1870–90.

Comment
Schimmel's sculptures are included in most major collections of American folk art. An itinerant who stayed close to Carlisle and only occasionally wandered into nearby Perry and Franklin counties, Schimmel worked in a highly individualistic and impressionistic style. The pine he often used came from leftovers at barn raisings or from discarded railway ties. He always applied gesso to a carved piece before painting it, usually in bright colors. Though he carved other animals, Schimmel is best known for his eagles, some with wingspans of up to 3 feet.

Hints for Collectors
The quality of Schimmel eagles varies greatly. Examples like the one shown here, characterized by deep, rich carving and bold sinuous outlines, are by far the most desirable and are among the most expensive pieces of American folk sculpture. Repainting a Schimmel piece greatly diminishes its value in today's market.

206 Eagle

Description
Carved and stained perched eagle with crested head, large beak, and indented eyes. Neck, breast, and body carved in diamond pattern; rear edges of wings with carved oblongs. Shaped tail feathers. Thick legs with diamond-shaped carvings above and 3 indented rings below. Each foot with 3 long talons in front and one in back, grasping barrel-shaped support on domed base.

Materials and Dimensions
Pine. Stained. Height: 18″. Length: 16″. Width: 6″.

Locality and Period
Made by Aaron Mountz (1873–1949), Cumberland Valley, Pennsylvania. c. 1893–1918.

Comment
Mountz grew up in the Cumberland Valley, where he spent many hours watching Wilhelm Schimmel carve. Schimmel died when Mountz was 17; Mountz did his best work in his teens and twenties, probably as a result of Schimmel's influence and inspiration. Mountz's eagles, such as the one shown here, are less animated than his mentor's. Mountz produced only a few dozen pieces, and most are now in museums or private folk art collections.

Hints for Collectors
While Mountz is considered a major folk carver, his pieces are more realistic than Schimmel's and generally do not arouse as much collector interest. He painted few of his works; paint added later by someone else decreases the value of a piece.

207 Rooster

Description
Carved and painted rooster with bright red comb. Wings folded against yellow body. Breast with dark blue spots. Hindquarters and arching tail outlined in dark blue. Squat legs ending in long talons that grasp oval painted base.

Materials and Dimensions
Probably pine. Painted. Gesso. Height: 8″. Length: 5⅛″. Width: 2⅝″.

Locality and Period
Made by Wilhelm Schimmel (1817–90), Carlisle, Pennsylvania. c. 1870.

Comment
Wilhelm Schimmel, an immigrant from southern Germany who arrived in America just after the Civil War, wandered through Cumberland County, Pennsylvania, during the mid-19th century. He bartered his whittled wooden figures, such as the one shown here, for room, board, and libation. The homes and taverns he visited became his galleries. This highly individualistic artist, whose only tools were a jackknife, a piece of glass to smooth whittled surfaces, and some paints and brushes, sold his carvings for pennies and died a pauper. He is considered among the most talented of his contemporaries working in the region.

Hints for Collectors
Schimmel carved about 500 roosters ranging in height from 2″ to 12″, but he is also well known for carvings of eagles, squirrels, and some human figures. His most important work, a carving of Adam and Eve in the Garden of Eden, is now in the Philadelphia Museum of Art. Schimmel's large carvings, particularly those with original paint, are very valuable.

208 Rooster-shaped mill weight

Description
Silhouette of rooster with red beak, comb, and wattles. Simple eyes defined by recessed circles. Oversize fanlike tail almost as large as body; "10 ft 110 2" stamped on tail. No legs. Hollow base weighted and attached with screws. Painted white; surface worn and rusted.

Materials and Dimensions
Cast iron. Painted. Iron screws. Height: 15½". Length: 17". Base width: 4".

Locality and Period
Possibly made by Elgin Windmill Power Company, Elgin, Illinois. c. 1880–1910.

Comment
Cast-iron mill weights came in many sizes—weighing from 8 to 85 pounds—and in a variety of barnyard animal forms. The type of windmill on which these weights were fixed was a simple open structure that American farmers employed to pump water into homes and animal troughs. A whirling propeller of fan blades set atop a high trestle was counterbalanced by the mill weight attached at the rear of the propeller mechanism. Sometimes the weight was stamped with the manufacturer's name, but the example shown here, though attributed to Elgin Windmill Power Company, has no such identification.

Hints for Collectors
Unpainted mill weights that have acquired a rusty patina appeal to some collectors. Even more popular are painted examples showing wear and discoloration caused by weathering and those bearing a maker's mark; marked pieces inevitably bring almost twice as much as unmarked ones. The rarest forms, such as certain cows (*see* 198) or squirrels, are most expensive.

209 Folding owl decoy

Description
Great horned owl composed of 3 tin silhouettes (entire body plus 2 halves in front and back), joined by hinges allowing it to be stored flat. Erect ears; black eyes. Front piece with hooked beak. Greenish-tan body with brown and black markings. Rectangular wooden base painted black.

Materials and Dimensions
Painted tin and wood. Height: 20″. Base length: 8″; width: 8″.

Locality and Period
The Northeast or Midwest. c. 1885–1900.

Comment
While most bird decoys are meant to attract the living creatures they simulate, owl decoys are used to attract crows. The crows, which try to drive the owls away, are instead lured into view so that farmers can shoot them, thereby limiting damage to cornfields. Owl decoys usually date from the late 19th or early 20th century, but are fairly rare since most farmers used scarecrows instead for this purpose. Some of these decoys were made of wood or papier-mâché, occasionally with inset glass eyes or leather embellishments.

Hints for Collectors
By the 1880s many small manufacturers were producing tin decoys that could be folded and were light enough to be transported easily. Wooden boxes containing a dozen decoys were sold for 98 cents in 1883 by the Sheboygan Decoy Company of Sheboygan, Wisconsin. If you discover a box with its original contents intact, you have made a terrific find. Since these rarely turn up, they may command well over a thousand dollars.

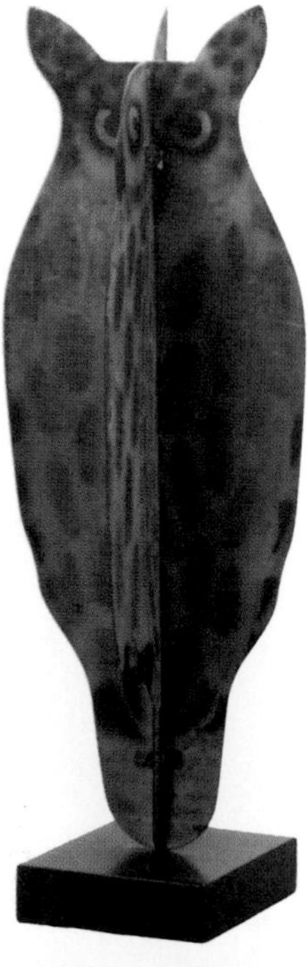

210 Shooting-gallery targets

Description
3 silhouettes of birds with wings raised as if in flight. Notched tail feathers. Figures mounted on 2 triangular flanges, with hole drilled for inserting rod. Painted white and rusted.

Materials and Dimensions
Cast iron. Painted. Height: 3½″. Length: 4″. Base width: 1″.

Locality and Period
Throughout the United States. c. 1900–10.

Comment
Shooting-gallery targets like the ones shown here were manufactured by numerous companies specializing in games of chance for amusement parks. Such targets were commonly arranged in groups: they might be strung on one or a series of rods—either remaining stationary or moving from left to right—or set up in a diorama of a wilderness scene. The player scored points by hitting the target and causing it to fall backward or spin. Among the more unusual targets are leaping stags and birds with a tulip over their backs.

Hints for Collectors
Though still plentiful and inexpensive, these decorative sculptures seem to be increasing in popularity, and their prices may rise. It is preferable to purchase them in sets. This field is not yet well enough known for anyone to be able to attribute specific designs to particular makers, but pieces with fanciful designs are generally most valuable. Target figures are often unpainted, and many collectors prefer them that way; beginning collectors, however, often favor painted targets. Do not confuse American examples with those from South America or Africa, which are in exaggerated animal forms and are usually painted.

Decoys and Lures

The use of decoys to attract wildfowl and, sometimes, fish is a peculiarly American practice. Colonists imitated the Indian method of luring wildfowl with models of these birds, but while Indians made decoys from bulrushes, feathers, or bird skins, the early settlers preferred to carve theirs out of wood. Since colonial times, a great many varieties of wildfowl—including shorebirds, waterfowl, and birds that were hunted for plumage—have served as models for decoys.

The Art of Decoy Carving
Few decoys from the 18th century have survived, and almost none are by identified carvers. Most decoys found today were fashioned in the 19th and 20th centuries by carvers whose aim was to capture the essential features of a species. During the late 19th and early 20th centuries, wooden and tin decoys were also produced by small manufacturers such as the Mason and the Dodge decoy factories in Detroit and the C. W. Stevens Factory in Weedsport, New York. Modern carvings of birds, intended mainly for ornamental use, tend to have more realistic details than the older working decoys.

Hand-carved decoys were made from a well-aged block of wood; the shape was roughed out with a drawknife and completed with a jackknife. The head was usually carved separately and attached to the body.

Among the better known 19th-century carvers are Nathan Cobb, Obediah Verity, and Albert Laing. During the 20th century East Coast makers included Charles "Shang" Wheeler, Lemuel Ward, and John Dawson; in the Midwest, decoys were fashioned by Robert Elliston, Charles Perdew, and Bert Graves. Perhaps the most famous of all carvers was A. Elmer Crowell of Cape Cod, best known for his shorebird decoys. Though many decoys are unsigned, carvers can often be identified by their style.

Waterfowl Decoys
Because waterfowl were the birds most commonly hunted, decoys of them are most available. Decoys of seagoing waterfowl such as the scoter, merganser, and eider may be identified primarily by their white markings as well as their low slanting build and often wide beam. More plentiful are the decoys of waterfowl such as mallards, pintails, and canvasbacks—birds that frequent bays, estuaries, or inland waterways; these decoys are distinguished by an upturned tail and narrow beam. Merganser decoys, which have elegant crested heads, are rare.

Shorebird Decoys
Mounted on sticks that were thrust into the sand, shorebird decoys were wood or tin and either three-dimensional or silhouette types. The most common species of shorebird—sandpipers, yellowlegs, curlews, and plovers—feed along beaches, marshes, and tidal flats. The sandpiper is the smallest, with a pale breast and speckled back. Similar in coloration but somewhat larger is the yellowlegs. The largest is the curlew, which is cinnamon-colored with dark gray accents and has a long bill. The plover is a thickset bird with a large head.

Fish Decoys and Lures
Used around the Great Lakes area for ice fishing, these decoys were usually made of wood and ranged in length from a few inches to several feet. Dangled through a hole in the ice, they lured prey within spearing distance. Cast-iron jigs, lures with hooks protruding from the nose, were used in the rougher waters off Maine and Newfoundland.

211 Turtle decoy

Description
Crudely carved turtle with snub-nosed oval head nailed to flat circular body with rounded edges. Frayed, knotted rope tied through hole drilled in hindquarters. Initials "HM" carved on back. Traces of blue paint on underside. Worn overall.

Materials and Dimensions
Pine. Rope. Iron nails. Height: 5½". Length: 29½". Width: 14¼".

Locality and Period
Probably the South. c. 1895–1910.

Comment
Turtle decoys, widely used as confidence lures in South America, are employed occasionally in the southeastern United States. The turtles climb atop the decoy's broad back to sun themselves; in this relaxed and unsuspecting state, they can easily be netted. American examples are made of southern pine, which has a much wider grain than its South American counterpart. This piece has obviously been much used, since evidence of wear is visible over the entire surface.

Hints for Collectors
Carvings of this type generally interest those decoy collectors who consider aesthetic appeal secondary. Turtle decoys rarely appear on the market, but, when they do, seldom remain available for long. Though the simple abstract form of this piece may appeal to some folk art collectors, examples with painted or carved details are likely to be more valuable. Turtle decoys are best sought in the South, where they are often still in use.

212 White-winged scoter decoy

Description
White-winged scoter crudely carved from solid piece of wood. Small head jutting up at top front; circular white splashes as eyes. Blocky black body with white markings. Short leather strap nailed to underside, with hole in loose end for attaching to anchor, or to other decoys to form a flock.

Materials and Dimensions
Cedar. Painted. Leather strap. Iron nail. Height: 2½″. Length: 14″. Width: 6½″.

Locality and Period
Maine. c. 1885–1900.

Comment
When European colonists arrived in the New World, they found the Indians using waterfowl decoys. The white settlers adopted this and other Indian hunting methods; the Indians also used dead birds as lures, but it is believed that the colonists used only wooden decoys. An example that looks quite primitive because it is blocky and stylized may still be realistic in other respects: the duck shown here, though crude and boatlike, still gives the impression, at some distance, of a bird resting quietly on the water. It also has a vitality and visual effectiveness often lacking in more realistic versions.

Hints for Collectors
There are 2 distinct groups of decoy collectors: one group is made up of specialists primarily interested in the maker, the condition of the carving, and original paint; the other consists of folk art collectors, who generally care less about the maker and original finish than about exciting sculptural form.

213

Canada goose decoy

Description
Goose with projecting inset head and neck carved from single piece of wood. Black beak; gray face with black markings and white cheek patch. Incised and painted eyes. Neck dappled gray and black. Breast and tail with traces of black; center of body gray. Crudely carved and worn overall.

Materials and Dimensions
Cedar. Painted. Height: 8″. Length: 29″. Width: 9″.

Locality and Period
Made by H. H. Ackerman (life dates unknown), Allen Park, Michigan. c. 1965.

Comment
The Canada goose, one of the largest wildfowl, is common throughout North America. During fall and spring migrations, a flock flying in the characteristic wedge-shaped formation is a memorable sight. Decoys of this species are distinguishable by white cheek patches and by the long, or "black-stocking," neck. The one shown here is unusual because the neck is extended in a feeding position. Other species of geese found in decoy form include the brant and rarer snow goose.

Hints for Collectors
Like many primitive pieces of folk art, Ackerman's decoys appeal more to the general collector than to the specialist, who—often a sportsman himself—prefers realistically carved and painted examples. While the more crudely executed decoys may be expected to rise in value, they will never be worth as much as the more finely conceived and realistic pieces.

214 Canada goose decoy

Description
Goose with bill, head, and long neck carved from single solid piece of wood, nailed onto hollow body made of canvas-covered frame. Black bill, head, and neck; dark gray body; white cheek patch, breast, and underside of tail feathers.

Materials and Dimensions
Cedar. Pine frame. Canvas. Painted. Iron nails. Height: 15″. Length: 23″. Width: 9″.

Locality and Period
Chesapeake Bay area or North Carolina. c. 1910.

Comment
Although wild geese use the Atlantic, Mississippi, and Pacific flyways, most goose decoys—varying in size according to species—come from the Atlantic coast. Made of cedar, cypress, pine, or cottonwood, they are shown in varied poses such as swimming, preening, or, occasionally, feeding. Goose decoys can be heavy, made entirely of solid wood; or light, with the body consisting of a canvas-covered wooden frame, as in the example shown here, or hollowed wood, slats, or cork. Set out in the water before the hunting season began, they sometimes remained there until it was over. Although goose decoys were also made by many well-known carvers, most were crafted by anonymous hunters.

Hints for Collectors
Decoys made of canvas over a wooden or wire frame are less appealing than those of solid wood, and consequently never as popular. Until recently they were so little valued that many were left in a very rough state. An example in good original condition is the most valuable; a piece with replaced canvas should command no more than a modest sum.

215 Oldsquaw hen and eider drake decoys

Description
Front: Carved oldsquaw hen with heavy 2-piece body and separate head. Black bill, eyes, and neck; top of head white. Body with traces of white and black paint. Extensively worn. *Rear:* Eider drake with head and bill carved from heavy piece of wood and set into body. Eyes recessed; yellow bill. Black and white body. Worn overall.

Materials and Dimensions
Front: Pine. Painted. Iron nails. Height: 7″. Length: 12″. Width: 6½″. *Rear:* Cedar. Painted. Height: 8″. Length: 19″. Width: 6½″.

Locality and Period
Front: Attributed to Howland Smith (life dates unknown), probably Maine. c. 1920. *Rear:* Made by Harry Wass (life dates unknown), Maine. c. 1910.

Comment
Eider decoys such as the one shown here were used primarily in northern New England and Nova Scotia. Set afloat in large groups, or "rigs," they attracted eiders valued for their down. Since the eider is a saltwater bird whose ocean habitat is frequently rough, its decoy is large and heavy, ranging up to 24″ in length and sometimes made of wood so dense that no ballast is needed. Oldsquaw decoys, found on the northeastern coast but rarely elsewhere, exist in both handmade and factory versions.

Hints for Collectors
The hollow bodies of some decoys allow them to float higher in the water; they may have lead weights nailed to the bottom in order to keep them upright. Although the weight protrudes and makes display more difficult, collectors almost never remove it if it is original.

216 Redhead drake and white-winged scoter hen decoys

Description
Front: Carved redhead drake with black bill and yellow glass eyes with black pupils set into red head; head set into body. Breast and tail black; center white with dark markings. Metal ballast attached to underside; hook on bottom front. *Rear:* Carved scoter hen having wooden head with tan wash on sides, lumpy brown bill, and black glass eyes; head set into cork body. White wing blotches. Metal ballast nailed to wooden rudder on underside. Metal eyelet on bottom front.

Materials and Dimensions
Front: Pine. Painted. Glass. Metal. Height: 7½″. Length: 15½″. Width: 6″. *Rear:* Cedar. Painted. Cork. Glass. Metal. Height: 5½″. Length: 16″. Width: 5¼″.

Locality and Period
Front: St. Clair Flats, Michigan. c. 1930. *Rear:* Made by Charles E. "Shang" Wheeler (1872–1949), Stratford, Connecticut. c. 1930.

Comment
Generally set out in groups, redhead decoys such as the one shown here were common from New Jersey to North Carolina, and farther west. Also shown is a scoter decoy made by Charles E. Wheeler, a respected Stratford carver who specialized in waterfowl decoys, primarily black ducks, scaup, and scoters—species commonly found in the Long Island Sound off Stratford.

Hints for Collectors
This redhead decoy has indications of use—particularly in the white area—which add to its appeal. Refinished decoys, no matter how attractive they are, have very little market value, since experienced collectors avoid them. Even decoys with minor restorations will generally interest only beginning collectors.

217 Miniature redhead drake paperweight

Description
Realistically carved and painted miniature redhead drake. Maroon head with pebbled surface; black eyes, putty-colored beak; black tail and breast. Ocher body with black and gray markings suggesting feathered wings. Lead weight set into center of underside.

Materials and Dimensions
Cedar. Painted. Lead weight. Height: 2½″. Length: 8″. Width: 2½″.

Locality and Period
Made by Frank Adams (1871–1944), West Tisbury, Martha's Vineyard, Massachusetts. c. 1930–40.

Comment
Many 20th-century decoy makers, such as Adams and some other Martha's Vineyard craftsmen, earned their living as woodworkers. They carved birds for both ornamental and utilitarian purposes; Adams made many bird-shaped paperweights, including the one shown here. Such decorative bird carvings were made of the same wood as their utilitarian relatives—aged white pine or cedar.

Hints for Collectors
Modern decoys and carvings of birds often command exceptional prices because they are coveted as works of art. Decoy carvers' guilds maintain high standards and price codes to which members must adhere; unaffiliated carvers, however, often charge less. Some carvers fake old decoys and leave them outdoors for a few years to develop an impressive patina, but these generally remain spiritless reproductions.

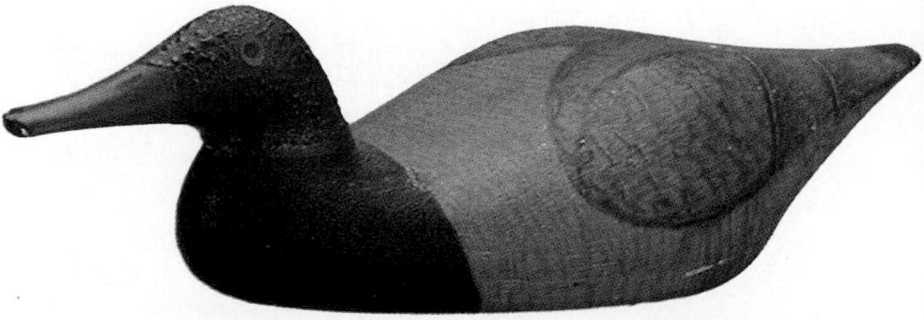

218 Pintail drake decoy

Description
Pintail drake with rounded crown, amber glass eyes with black pupils, high rounded back, and long flat tail extending upward. Black, gray, tan, and white feathering. Original paint. Head repaired.

Materials and Dimensions
Painted wood. Glass. Height: 7⅛″. Length: 18″. Width: 6⅛″.

Locality and Period
Carved by Steve Ward (1895–1976); painted by Lemuel Ward (1896–), Crisfield, Maryland. 1925.

Comment
The pintail decoy, shown here in the popular Humpback model, was a favorite subject for the brothers Lemuel and Steve Ward, the well-known Maryland carvers. For many years, Ward decoys were a joint effort, Steve carving the bold and vigorous figures and Lemuel painting them. The carving was begun with a hatchet instead of the more commonly used saw or knife; capturing the correct body proportions and alert attitude was as important as achieving accurate colors, textures, and patterns. Neither brother carved shorebird decoys.

Hints for Collectors
The damage to the head of this piece significantly lowers its market value. Although this decoy could be fully restored by an expert, even a skilled craftsman might be unable to disguise the break to the satisfaction of a serious collector. For this reason, many damaged decoys are left as is, even though successful restoration might make them more valuable. The Wards made thousands of decoys; these have appreciated greatly over time.

219 Merganser decoys

Description
Front: Carved merganser with red wooden bill notched to separate it from tan head which is set into body; amber blown-glass eyes with black pupils. Wings in low relief. Black body with white markings on wings; white stripe down center of breast. *Rear:* Carved merganser hen with black wooden bill set into crested brown head; carved eyes; head and neck set into body. Cream throat, neck, and breast. Wings in low relief. Dark gray body; wings with white blotches; raised tail. Worn paint.

Materials and Dimensions
Cedar. Painted. Glass. Height (front; rear): 6″; 8½″. Length: 19″; 17″. Width: 4″; 4½″.

Locality and Period
Front: The Northeast Coast. c. 1900–1930. *Rear:* Monhegan Island, Maine. c. 1890–1900.

Comment
Merganser decoys may be either solid carved wood, as shown here, or hollow. When a live merganser, also called a sheldrake, is alone, it is wary and keeps its head high. The variety of characteristic postures is suggested by the positions of these decoys; sizes also vary.

Hints for Collectors
The distinctive appearance of mergansers appeals to those who collect decoys as folk art. Decoys by well-known makers are always of great market value. In areas near migratory flyways, where decoys were used extensively, the few pieces by famous carvers that are still available are generally recognized and, therefore, likely to be expensive. In other locales, where dealers may lack a firsthand knowledge of the best carvers and their work, a well-informed collector may be able to get a good buy.

220

Coot and mallard drake decoys

Description
Decoys with head inserted into body and metal ballast screwed to underside. *Front:* Carved coot with white bill and amber glass eyes with black pupils. Plain black head, neck, and body. *Rear:* Carved mallard drake with tan beak, incised nostrils, and amber glass eyes with black pupils. Green head; red-brown breast; gray body; black tail outlined in white.

Materials and Dimensions
Front: Cedar. Painted. Glass. Metal. Height: 4″. Length: 7″. Width: 3½″. *Rear:* Pine. Painted. Glass. Metal. Height: 6″. Length: 14″. Width: 7¾″.

Locality and Period
Front: Made by Charles Schoenheider (1854–1944), Peoria, Illinois. c. 1880–1900. *Rear:* Delaware River area. c. 1930.

Comment
Mallards, sometimes referred to as "puddle ducks," and coots both use the Atlantic and Mississippi flyways, and decoys modeled after these species are likely to be found in these areas. Although mallards, coots, and Canada geese use the Pacific flyway as well, the art of decoy making was less highly developed on the West Coast. Mallards were also carved in the form of stick-ups to be used in marshes.

Hints for Collectors
Schoenheider was among the most respected makers of decoys. One of his characteristic types has an often beautifully painted wooden body and a cast-iron foot designed for use on ice. He occasionally branded his initials on his work. If you find a coot decoy like the one shown here, research it carefully and have your conclusions checked by a decoy expert. Such a piece may be quite valuable.

221 Long-billed curlew decoy

Description
Long-billed curlew covered with tan burlap wrapped around carved head, neck, and body, and crudely sewn on underside at center. Brown metal bill set into head. Supporting pole inserted into underside.

Materials and Dimensions
Cedar. Burlap. Iron. Height: 8″. Length: 17″. Width: 3½″.

Locality and Period
Probably Virginia. c. 1880–1900.

Comment
Long-billed curlew decoys were both handmade and mass-produced. Also known as the sickle-billed curlew, this species ranges up to 25″ long, making it the largest of the shorebirds. Hunted primarily for sport in the South, the long-billed curlew was considered edible, though not choice; it became even less palatable when its diet included shellfish. Nevertheless, because its large size made it a good target, it was extensively hunted and its population declined; consequently, decoys of this bird are rare. A bona fide long-billed curlew decoy should be large and have its original curved bill.

Hints for Collectors
Decoys with surfaces covered by such materials as burlap, like the piece shown here, or by bird skin, feathers, or other materials are of interest primarily to the advanced collectors of decoys who want an example of every variety. Such pieces have little appeal for novices, and even the most beautiful do not command the high prices paid for fine carved examples. Prices of unusual decoys in original condition vary considerably.

2 Curlew decoy

Description
Carved curlew with inset wire beak slightly down-curved. One-piece unpainted head and body; dark spot on forehead. 2 amber glass eyes. Lightly incised wings. Supporting pole inserted into underside. Worn.

Materials and Dimensions
Pine. Metal wire. Glass. Height: 4½″. Length: 10½″. Width: 1¾″.

Locality and Period
Made by Herman Glick (1895–   ), Havana, Illinois. c. 1970–80.

Comment
Shorebirds, also called beach birds, feed along coastlines and in tidal flats and marshes. To lure these waders, stick-up decoys such as the one shown here come mounted on poles that are pushed into the ground. Curlews are the largest among the various groups of shorebirds, which also include sandpipers, yellowlegs, and plovers. The curlew's most noticeable feature is a slender beak, which can be as long as 8 inches and is used for probing.

Hints for Collectors
The market is flooded with contemporary decoys, but few are realistic representations, because the carver either has chosen to emphasize aesthetic aspects or, unlike Glick, lacks the hunting or birding experience necessary to provide a rich store of firsthand observations. Much of Glick's output is included in museum collections, and this raises the value of his works that come on the market. Since some modern decoys are mistakenly or deliberately sold as antiques, ask a dealer for a written guarantee with provisions for refund.

223 Ruddy turnstone and greater yellowlegs decoys

Description
Left: Carved ruddy turnstone in spring plumage, with black wooden eyes and bill set into head. Reddish head, back, and wings; black breast; cream underside and tail. *Center:* Carved greater yellowlegs in spring plumage, with brown nail-head eyes and black bill set into head. Gray head, neck, breast, and underside; brown back, wings, and upper tail feathers; black markings. *Right:* Carved ruddy turnstone in spring plumage, with black glass eyes and wooden bill set into head. Cream underside and head; black neck and upper breast; brown wings.

Materials and Dimensions
Painted wood. Glass. Iron nails. Height (left to right): 5½″; 6″; 3½″. Length: 9″; 12″; 8¾″. Width: 2½″; 1½″; 3″.

Locality and Period
Left: Virginia. c. 1915. *Center:* Made by A. Elmer Crowell (1862–1952), East Harwich, Massachusetts. c. 1918. *Right:* New Jersey. c. 1915.

Comment
Ruddy turnstone decoys are rare, as these birds were usually shot only for sport. More plentiful are the greater yellowlegs decoys; the piece shown here is representative of the high-quality work of A. Elmer Crowell, one of the most famous decoy makers. His distinctive style is characterized by detailed carving and vivid painting. Crowell also carved thousands of other pieces, including fish, weathervanes, and songbirds.

Hints for Collectors
Crowell's carvings are in great demand and quite costly. His shorebird decoys may be identified by 2 characteristics: separation of the wingtips from the tail and a stippled look (produced by the drybrush technique) around the eyes.

24 Black-bellied plover and sickle-billed curlew decoys

Description

Front: Black-bellied plover in spring plumage with black wooden bill and eyes set into turned head. Cream body; top of tail black, with notches denoting feathers; bottom cream. Black markings. *Rear:* Carved sickle-billed curlew with dark metal bill and black glass eyes set into head. One-piece head and neck set into body. Brown top of head and neck, eye stripe, back, and wings. Rest of body golden with brown markings. Worn.

Materials and Dimensions

Front: Cedar. Painted. Height: 8″. Length: 11½″. Width: 3″. *Rear:* Pine. Painted. Nail. Glass. Height: 10″. Length: 17″. Width: 4½″.

Locality and Period

Front: Made by George Boyd (1873–1941), Seabrook, New Hampshire. c. 1890–1910. *Rear:* Made by the Mason Decoy Factory, Detroit. c. 1910.

Comment

A signature on a decoy may be that of the carver or the owner; the sickle-billed curlew shown here has been cryptically signed "MRIOILBICI," perhaps by the owner for identification purposes. The Mason Decoy Factory, which made this example, was noted for exceptionally fine tonalities and textures.

Hints for Collectors

Shorebirds are among the most appealing decoy forms. Only those in fine original condition are worth buying; a restoration such as the replacement of the bill will substantially decrease the value. Attractive but sometimes inaccurate reproductions of shorebird decoys, for decorative purposes only, are becoming common; unlike the originals, they lack signs of wear and their beaks are wire nails instead of cut nails or wood.

225 Sanderling and black-bellied plover decoys

Description
Shorebird decoys, each made of 2 pieces of lithographed tin joined by wire hinges at top of head and tail. *Front:* Sanderling in spring plumage, with black bill and black eyes with tan circles. Tan breast, rust back, and dark gray wings; feathers painted in contrasting colors; underside off-white. *Rear:* Black-bellied plover in spring plumage, with black bill and eyes. Breast and back off-white and brown, with black feather markings and yellow speckles; underside off-white and gray. Stamped inside "PAT. Oct 27 1874."

Materials and Dimensions
Tin. Iron-wire hinges. Height (front; rear): 3¾″; 5″. Length: 7″; 10″. Width: 1¾″; 2½″.

Locality and Period
Made by Strater & Sohier, Boston. c. 1874–90.

Comment
The tin stick-up decoys patented in 1874 by Herman Strater, Jr., and William Sohier of Boston may have been the first commercially made decoys. Unlike their floating cousins, stick-up decoys are mounted on a stick that is thrust into the mud or sand. As hunting of shorebirds during spring breeding season was outlawed in 1918, it is safe to assume that a decoy painted in spring plumage was made prior to that date.

Hints for Collectors
Although tin decoys are plentiful and inexpensive, and their decorative quality is appealing, they rarely interest collectors who specialize in decoys. If you are attracted to the form, search for well-constructed examples in good condition and with original paint. A slightly worn appearance enhances value; signs of rough treatment, however, decrease it substantially.

226 Bobwhite

Description
Carved bobwhite with brown glass eyes set into head. Black bill; head painted black, olive, and white. Olive back, breast, and wings; gray tail feathers; white underside. Black, brown, tan, and mustard markings.

Materials and Dimensions
Pine. Painted. Height: 3½″. Length: 6″. Width: 3″.

Locality and Period
Made by Herman Glick (1895–), Havana, Illinois. 1970.

Comment
Because today's decoy makers often create decorative carvings rather than utilitarian decoys, they pay particular attention to such eye-catching details as feather markings, an unnecessary finishing touch for working decoys. Since functional models, usually older, are meant to be viewed from afar, they generally have less naturalistic detail and are more abstractly rendered. The bobwhite shown here is intended for collectors rather than for hunters.

Hints for Collectors
Decoys and similar carved birds are widely collected for many reasons. Not only are they attractive as sculpture and tremendously varied in shape and price, but they are also easy to display and more available than other kinds of folk sculpture. A purely decorative carving by a decoy maker, such as this piece, should be judged by more or less the same criteria used for functional decoys: it should be a fine sculptural form with original paint, made by a well-known carver, and preferably in a form typical of that maker. The value of such a piece is very likely to appreciate over the years.

227 Largemouth bass, yellow pike, and sunfish decoys

Description
Left: Carved largemouth bass with inset black metal eyes, red-speckled mouth, and metal loop on top. Body painted black, brown, and white. 3 wooden fins set into body. *Center:* Carved yellow pike with black eyes, red brow and mouth, and pierced finlike insert on top. Yellow body with red gills and black markings. 5 tin fins set into body. *Right:* Carved sunfish with black and red eyes, white mouth, and pierced finlike insert on top. Tan body with black and green markings and red underside. 4 tin fins set into body. All 3 decoys weighted.

Materials and Dimensions
Pine. Paint. Tin. Lead weights. Height (left to right): 2¼″; 1½″; 5″. Length: 9½″; 7″; 7¼″. Width: 1¾″; 1″; 1½″.

Locality and Period
Left and right: The Midwest. c. 1900–40. *Center:* Made by Oscar Peterson (1887–?), Cadillac, Michigan. c. 1905–40.

Comment
Except for the plastic versions produced commercially from about 1930 to 1950, most fish decoys are handmade. Fishermen are often surprised that decoys, which they consider merely utilitarian objects, are judged worthy of being collected for aesthetic and historical reasons.

Hints for Collectors
Fish decoys are generally available for relatively modest sums. Examples by known makers and those in original condition are highly prized. Peterson's work benefited from his detailed knowledge of fishing. Pieces with undistinguished carving and inaccurate detail may not be worth acquiring, since fish decoys appreciate substantially in value only when they have sculptural appeal and original paint, like the examples seen here.

228 **Codfish jig**

Description
Metal fishing lure for cod or pollock; generalized fish form with low-relief mouth, eyes, and gills on both sides. Dorsal fin extending from back of head to tail. Tail with scale markings and hole in center for attaching line. Twin U-shaped hooks protruding from mouth.

Materials and Dimensions
Cast lead. Steel hooks. Height: 2″. Length: 11″. Width: 1″.

Locality and Period
Maine. c. 1880–1900.

Comment
Large numbers of codfish are caught near the Grand Banks off Newfoundland, where currents are so strong that even heavy lead jigs do not sink. Because glittering metal attracts fish, the jig is scraped until it shines before being thrown into the sea. The type of codfish jig or lure shown here is manufactured by pouring lead into a 2-piece mold, 5″ to 11″ long. Fastened at the mouth are 2 to 4 hooks; a hole through which a fishing line may be attached is left in the tail.

Hints for Collectors
Folk art objects with limited appeal will usually fetch a higher price at auctions and shows specializing in a particular category. While some jigs are more detailed or imaginatively stylized than others, all are moderately priced. Large "meets," where both fishing paraphernalia and yarns are swapped, are held each year all around the country.

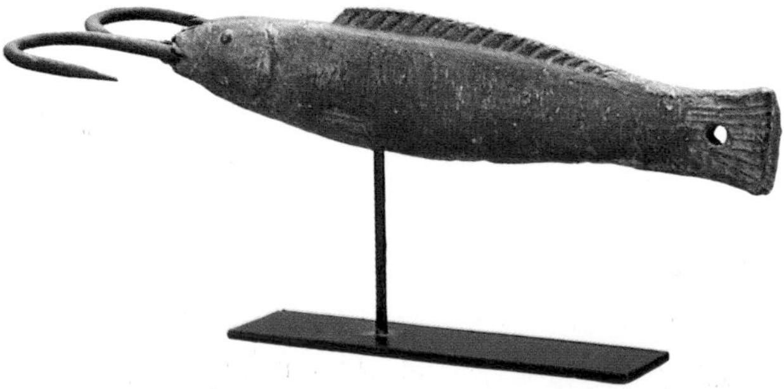

229 **Fish decoy**

Description
Large carved fish with rough surface and 2 tin fins. Grayish-blue on upper section, dorsal fin, and tail; white underside, eyes, and ventral fin. Metal patch attached behind gill by 3 nails. Lead weight on underside, serving as ballast, is held in place by large vertical nail.

Materials and Dimensions
Painted wood and tin. Lead weight. Nails. Height: 10¾″. Length: 41¼″. Width: 6⅜″.

Locality and Period
The Midwest. c. 1900–25.

Comment
Decoys of fish are usually more generalized than those of waterfowl and shorebirds. The bright coloration or glinting metal surface attracts either the decoy's own species or its predator. These carvings often include features not fashioned from wood: eyes may be nailheads or glass, and fins and tails may be metal, as shown here, or leather. A bottle cap may even be used for the mouth.

Hints for Collectors
Fish decoys range in length from 2″ to 48″. Though not common everywhere, they can still be found in the Midwest. Search out older fishermen and visit house sales, for these are the most promising sources. Be certain that the piece you are considering is old: fish decoys are still made and used today, but these newer ones generally lack the fine craftsmanship and signs of wear usually characteristic of older examples.

230 **Sturgeon decoy**

Description
Carved sturgeon painted black. Nose made of 3 small bent nails, eyes of circular nailheads. Wooden fins nailed on top, sides, and bottom. Larger fins of unpainted galvanized tin set into body: fin on top pierced with 5 holes; 2 rounded fins on each side; single fin at bottom rear. Worn paint.

Materials and Dimensions
Painted pine. Galvanized tin. Nails. Height: 4″. Length: 18½″. Width: 5″.

Locality and Period
The Midwest. c. 1900–40.

Comments
Sportsmen who fish through the ice in the Great Lakes area have used decoys since the early 19th century. They set up a shanty over a hole cut in the ice, through which they suspend a decoy on a line, and from the shanty's darkened interior they watch—sometimes for hours—for the shadow of a passing fish. The movement of the decoy lures the fish within range so it can then be speared. Hooks are therefore unnecessary in this sort of ice fishing.

Hints for Collectors
Experienced collectors almost always seek functioning fish decoys rather than purely decorative pieces. Consequently, a rich patina from years of use can add substantially to a decoy's value. As with most folk sculpture, collectors will pay more for fine details and appealing form.

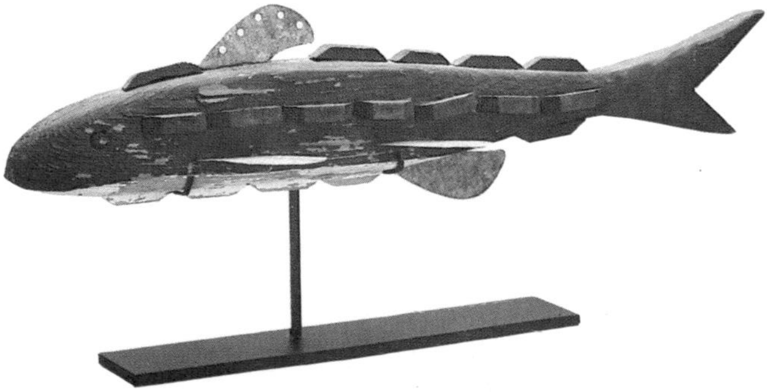

Baskets and Containers

Baskets and other woven objects have been made around the world for thousands of years. In America, woven sandals and food baskets dating from about A.D. 700 are among the remains left by the Basketmaker people, the ancestors of the modern Pueblo tribes. While most baskets fashioned by primitive and modern societies were designed to suit particular needs, such as gathering and carrying fruits and vegetables or storing clothes and utensils, many are aesthetically appealing as well as utilitarian, even if sometimes their only decoration is a simple pattern of interlaced ribs and weavers.

Field, Gathering, and Other Work Baskets
The American Indians and the first colonists found baskets indispensable for most farming activities, from sowing to harvesting. The shapes and sizes of the handles, bottoms, and even rims were determined by the weight and type of objects they were to hold.

Heavy splint field baskets, in round and oblong shapes, were used in picking apples, potatoes, and corn. Because these baskets were constantly dragged along the ground, their bottoms often wore out; to preserve them, replaceable wooden cleats, or runners, were sometimes attached underneath. The bottoms of many baskets meant to hold fragile produce like eggs or peaches had raised centers to keep the contents from rolling around and to distribute the weight toward the sides. Occasionally field baskets had an openwork bottom that allowed air to circulate and rinse water to drain away. Most baskets for gathering are large and heavy, but some, such as the handled ones used in berry picking, are small and dainty.

The shapes of other baskets also provide clues to their use. Elongated baskets functioned as eel traps. Those with an open hexagonal weave, often called a cheese weave today, were used for draining and storing cheese. Oval splint baskets served as feed bags or muzzles for farm animals. Splint baskets on wooden legs held raw wool while it was washed.

Household and Decorative Baskets
Baskets were as common inside the home as in the workplace or on the farm, but they were generally lighter in weight and more delicate. Either open or lidded, they held fruit, nuts, yarn, jewelry, handkerchiefs, and small trinkets. Sewing baskets had a close weave to keep small objects from falling through, and often one or more inside pockets to hold small items.

Many of these baskets are woven of sweet grass, a material named for its persistent aroma and favored by Indian craftsmen. The most common sweet-grass forms are the flat, lidded containers made in many sizes. Other baskets are made of dried pine needles, another unusual material used almost exclusively by the Indians. Also uniquely Indian are such basketmaking decorations as curlicue work, in which thin coils of splint protrude from the surface of the basket to form a series of curls.

Other Containers
Occasionally folk artists have used basketmaking techniques or forms to create containers in materials other than the traditional wood splint, willow rods, or various grasses. Discarded or "found" objects like metal bottle caps, cardboard matchbook covers, small pieces of rolled wallpaper, and even tiny cloves have been strung on wire or thread to create bowls, jars, and miniature tea sets. Other basketlike containers are made of bentwood, wooden slats, or wire.

231 Handled basket

Description
Circular openwork basket with 3 rows of braided rods; rim made of rods extended from middle row. Oversize twisted handle attached to rim by loops of willow. Traces of old red paint.

Materials and Dimensions
Factory-cut willow rods. Painted. Height (with handle): 18″. Diameter: 13½″.

Locality and Period
Eastern United States. c. 1900–30.

Comment
Commonly known as wicker, baskets constructed of thin willow branches—or whips, as they are sometimes called—were made by hand as early as the 17th century. By the end of the 19th, most were produced in factories, where willow was cut and sized by machines. Wicker baskets were produced in varied shapes and for many different uses, including storage of fruit, nuts, or sewing accessories; large baskets were commonly used as laundry hampers.

Hints for Collectors
Factory-made wicker baskets meant as much for display as for use, such as the one shown here, were turned out by the thousands during the late 19th and early 20th centuries, and they are not difficult to find today. Many were painted, and those with original paint are more valuable than similar unpainted ones. Old paint should be worn, particularly on the handles and rim, where the piece would have been handled the most. Baskets like this have been imported from Europe since the late 19th century, and even experienced collectors may sometimes be unable to distinguish an import from a domestic basket.

232 Covered sewing or storage basket

Description
Circular covered basket with sides slanting out toward top. Lid has wide ribs intersecting at center and narrow weavers encircling circumference. Wrapped rim single-bound. Crosshatched weave of medium-width ribs and narrow weavers, except for 2 wide weavers at bottom. Fixed wooden handle inserted in sides and attached at bottom.

Materials and Dimensions
Factory-cut splint. Ash or hickory. Height (with handle): 9″. Diameter: 8″.

Locality and Period
Eastern United States. c. 1900–30.

Comment
A renewed interest in handmade objects was evident in America during the first decades of the 20th century, resulting in the revival of rugmaking, quilting, and basketmaking. People took classes in basketmaking, and a few trailblazing collectors began seeking out fine old baskets. Pieces like the delicate lidded basket shown here were popular items at gift and souvenir shops; they were relatively inexpensive and well suited to a contemporary taste for decorative handmade knickknacks.

Hints for Collectors
Its thinness and regularity indicate that the splint of this basket was machine-cut in a factory—common practice after about 1880, even though the factory-cut splint continued to be hand-woven. The graceful handle, attached in a rather unusual way at the bottom, and the overall delicacy make this early 20th-century basket well worth owning. While most 19th-century baskets are more valuable, fewer have survived, so that good 20th-century examples are also sound investments.

233 Swing-handled basket

Description
Circular basket with crosshatched weave of wide ribs and medium-width weavers. Movable wooden handle attached to rim by carved wooden loops. Wrapped rim single-bound. Bottom with raised woven center.

Materials and Dimensions
Ash splint. Ash. Iron nails. Height (without handle): 8½″. Diameter: 13½″.

Locality and Period
Eastern United States. c. 1885–1915.

Comment
This moderately large basket, with its thick rim and sturdy swing handle, was probably used for gathering eggs or vegetables. Distinctive features such as the raised bottom and swing handle served specific purposes. The raised bottom reduced breakage by keeping objects like eggs from rolling around as much as they would on a flat bottom; it also helped distribute the weight out toward the sides. The swing handle made it easy for the user to bend down while working, since it moved to and fro with his movements.

Hints for Collectors
The current wave of interest in baskets, which began in the early 1970s, continues to be very strong. While any well-made basket with a pleasing form is sought after today, those made for use rather than simply for decoration are generally most in demand. Swing-handled baskets are especially popular and more expensive than many better-made, but more common, baskets.

234 Wool-drying basket

Description
Circular basket on 4 carved wooden legs continuing up to nailed rim. Crosshatched weave with wide ribs and medium-width weavers. 2 carved and notched wooden handles woven into sides and secured with wire at rim. Carved wooden crossbraces underneath. Wires fasten lower part of legs to basket bottom.

Materials and Dimensions
Factory-cut hickory splint. Hickory. Wire. Wire nails. Height: 18″. Diameter of top: 23¼″.

Locality and Period
New York State or New England. c. 1880–1900.

Comment
Known as a wool-drying basket, this unusual type, with its bottom raised several inches above the floor, was used in rinsing and drying flax or wool. Before they were spun, the raw fibers had to be washed, rinsed, and drained. Exactly how these baskets were used is unclear, but the drying process was undoubtedly aided by the air circulating through the splintwork bottom and sides.

Hints for Collectors
Raised wool baskets like the one shown here are quite rare today. Many deteriorated from constant use and exposure to water and strong soap; moreover, the making of these baskets ceased when homespun cloth was no longer produced. The nailed rim and thin factory-cut splint indicate this is a fairly late example; earlier ones usually have a wrapped rim. The hand-carved bottom braces and handles make it more valuable than similar baskets with mass-produced details.

235 Work or storage basket

Description
Painted basket with square bottom and circular top. Plain plaited weave, with ribs and weavers of fairly uniform width and thickness. Openwork bottom. 2 small carved handles on sides fastened between wrapped inner and outer rims. Old orange paint.

Materials and Dimensions
Hickory, oak, or ash splint. Wooden handles. Painted. Height (with handle): 8″. Diameter of top: 13″. Length of bottom: 9½″. Width of bottom: 9½″.

Locality and Period
Probably Maine. c. 1875–1900.

Comment
Splint baskets like the one shown here were frequently made with a square bottom and a circular top. The size, shape, and small handles of this example suggest it may have been meant to hold fairly lightweight objects, such as sewing or darning materials; the openwork bottom, however, suggests it may have been used to store food, since this feature allowed air to circulate through the basket.

Hints for Collectors
The splint in this basket varies slightly in thickness and width, indicating that it was cut by hand rather than by machine; presumably, therefore, the basket was made before the turn of the century, when machine-cut splint began to be widely used. Although the paint may not be original, its condition suggests that it is old, perhaps applied soon after the basket was made. The presence of old paint increases the value of a piece, since most baskets were left with a natural finish.

236 Hexagonal-weave cheese or notions basket

Description
Openwork basket with hexagonal bottom, circular top, and narrow splint in hexagonal weave on sides and bottom. Wrapped rim with raised loop edge. Some weavers and rim loops painted purple or blue.

Materials and Dimensions
Ash splint. Partly painted. Height: 5½″. Diameter of top: 13½″.

Locality and Period
The Northeast. c. 1900–40.

Comment
Baskets with the hexagonal weave seen here are often called cheese baskets, cheese drainers, or cheese strainers. In the 18th and 19th centuries they were used for draining liquid whey as it separated from the cheese curds. They were also used as storage baskets for aging cheese: the cheese was wrapped in cheesecloth, put in the basket, and kept for several months in a cheese cupboard; the cupboard usually had an open front draped with cheesecloth to let air circulate but screen out dirt and insects.

Hints for Collectors
Hexagonal-weave baskets, particularly early examples from the 19th century, are rare today and much in demand. This weave pattern was used primarily for cheese baskets, but also for baskets too small for cheesemaking. This 20th-century example, with its looped rim and painted splint, was most likely made for decorative purposes. The colored splint is unusual in this weave, making this basket more valuable than plainer ones. Its very thin machine-cut splint should prevent collectors from mistaking it for a 19th-century example.

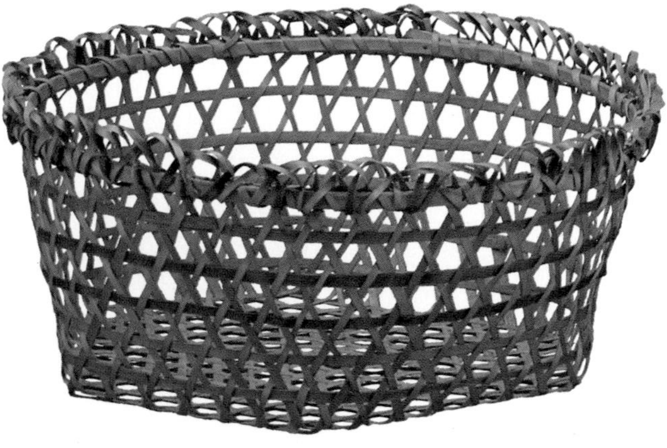

237 Work or storage basket

Description
Basket with sides slanting outward from square bottom to oval top. Crosshatched weave with medium-width ribs and narrow weavers, except for wide top weaver. Some weavers and rim wrapping stained blue. 2 cutout handles at top. Wrapped rim single-bound; hemming at top edge.

Materials and Dimensions
Factory-cut splint, partly prestained. Height: 5½″. Length of top: 13″. Width of top: 14″. Length of bottom: 8″. Width of bottom: 8″.

Locality and Period
Probably New Jersey. c. 1920–30.

Comment
Possibly made by an Indian basketmaker, though the type was also made by non-Indians, the basket shown here is typical of the handwoven work done in the 1920s and 1930s, when prestained splint had become readily available. The oval rim was probably circular originally, having been pulled out of shape from years of being carried by the side grips while filled with heavy contents.

Hints for Collectors
While baskets with colored splint are often called Indian baskets because they were first made by the Indians, this type was soon adopted and made by non-Indian craftsmen; unless the maker is known, it is generally impossible to verify Indian origin. Made in large quantity in the 1920s and 1930s, such baskets are fairly easy to find today. Good overall condition should be accompanied by appropriate signs of age, particularly since 2-tone baskets are still being made in certain regions. Splint dries and becomes brittle as it ages, just as some woods do, and dyes exposed to sunlight fade with time, often unevenly.

38 Shaker sewing basket

Description
Square open basket with trapezoidal compartment hanging inside a corner. Tight crosshatched weave with medium-width ribs and narrow weavers; wider weavers used in bottom. 2 small carved and notched wooden handles at sides. Wrapped rim single-bound and hemmed inside.

Materials and Dimensions
Splint. Wooden handles. Height: 4¾″. Length: 11″. Width: 11″.

Locality and Period
Probably made in a Shaker community in New York State or New England. c. 1880–1910.

Comment
The tight, carefully worked weave of this sewing basket suggests it was made by a Shaker craftsman, though other New England basketmakers also made this type of basket, and often with as much skill and care. Shakers produced baskets commercially from about 1800 to 1880, as well as baskets for their own use before and after these dates. Most baskets made by Shakers display superb workmanship and, like their furniture, are mostly unembellished and well suited to their intended use. This basket, probably meant for storing sewing equipment, was particularly functional, since its tight weave would keep small items from falling through.

Hints for Collectors
Determining whether a basket is of Shaker origin is almost impossible, except in those rare cases when it is marked—generally with the initials "S.C." for Shaker Community or with a number and letter indicating the community room in which it was used. Documentation showing that a piece has come from a Shaker community is, of course, important evidence.

239 Shaker wooden carrier

Description
Painted rectangular carrier with plain slanted sides. Flat handle with curved contour, ends extending down sides. Narrow molded base. Old reddish brown paint. Dovetail construction.

Materials and Dimensions
Ash. Maple. Painted. Height (with handle): 15¾″. Length: 19⅜″. Width: 12⅛″.

Locality and Period
Possibly Enfield, New Hampshire; Harvard, Massachusetts; or Sabbathday Lake, Maine. c. 1860–80.

Comment
By 1820 the Shakers had developed a flourishing business selling the medicinal herbs they grew, and carriers and storage boxes were needed to hold them. Herb carriers like the one shown here were used for gathering and transporting the great variety of herbs from garden to workroom. Such containers were left unfinished, stained, or painted yellow, blue, green, gray, or red. Besides ash and maple, pine was also common in Shaker pieces.

Hints for Collectors
Since simple wooden carriers were made by others besides Shakers, do not pay a premium for a so-called Shaker piece unless it has a label or stamp, a reliable history of ownership, or other evidence of Shaker origin. Stylistic clues may help identify a genuine Shaker object: for example, the graceful wooden handle of this carrier is shaped like those found on many Shaker baskets. The reddish paint, restrained molded base, and dovetail construction make this an excellent, though unmarked, example of Shaker craftsmanship.

40

Field basket

Description
Painted rectangular basket with large wooden hoop handle and nailed wooden rim. Diagonal crosshatched weave of uniformly wide ribs and weavers. 2 external wooden supports running continuously from under rims across bottom. Blue interior; reddish exterior and handle.

Materials and Dimensions
Factory-cut splint. Ash or hickory. Painted. Iron wire and nails. Height (with handle): 12″. Length: 19½″. Width: 12½″.

Locality and Period
The Northeast or Midwest. c. 1900–20.

Comment
The large field basket shown here has wooden supports—also called runners, slides, or feet—that give it added strength and raise it slightly off the ground. The wooden runners are considerably thicker than the woven splint, and enable the basket to withstand such hard use as carrying heavy vegetables in from the fields.

Hints for Collectors
Painted baskets are much in demand and generally command much higher prices than do comparable unpainted ones. This example, however, is relatively late and should cost less than a 19th-century painted piece. The paint should be worn along the edges, handle, and other areas subject to the most wear and tear. Painted baskets should be examined carefully, since some have been recently painted and artificially aged to make them seem more valuable.

241 Double lift-top wallpaper basket

Description
Double lift-top handled basket made of coiled narrow strips of wallpaper. Sides of vertical rows of elongated rolls with wide centers and narrow ends. Lids, bottom, and handle made of smaller rolls set horizontally; radiating design on lids. Rolls strung on wire wrapped with cloth.

Materials and Dimensions
Rolled wallpaper. Cloth. Iron wire. Height (with handle): 7″. Length: 12¾″. Width: 7″.

Locality and Period
New York State. c. 1880–90.

Comment
Middle-class women of the 1870s and 1880s had increasing leisure time in which to pursue a variety of hobbies. They made decorative objects from almost anything—shells, hair, fungi, pine cones, or even, like the basket shown here, tightly coiled strips of wallpaper. Women's magazines like *Godey's Lady's Book* printed instructions for all sorts of items to be made from leftover bits of cloth or pretty paper, but the crudeness of this basket suggests it was produced by an unsophisticated maker probably unfamiliar with such magazines. Shellwork objects may have inspired the creator of this basket, since the small paper rolls resemble certain shells in color and shape.

Hints for Collectors
A basket like this, the imaginative product of a resourceful but untrained person, is a true folk object and quite a find. Its ingenious use of leftover materials is typical of one-of-a-kind objects created by amateur craftsmen working outside the artistic mainstream.

242 **Picnic basket or hamper**

Description
Rectangular double lift-top basket with handle; sides flaring slightly toward top. Crosshatched weave with rods for ribs and narrow splint weavers. Center handle curved and wrapped. Wrapped rim. Double-hinged lids. Wooden bottom. Remnant of loop catch on side underneath rim.

Materials and Dimensions
Split reeds and splint. Pine. Height (with handle): 12¾". Length: 13½". Width: 7¾".

Locality and Period
Possibly made in a Shaker community in New England or New York State. c. 1880–1910.

Comment
Delicate, or "fancy," baskets such as the one shown here were made by the Shakers for sale in their shops, but other craftsmen made similar baskets. Using rods of split reeds gives the weave a very different look from the more common flat-splint ribs. The design source for picnic hampers like this may well have been rice-straw baskets imported from China during the 19th century. Many of these Chinese baskets had painted floral decoration not found on similarly constructed American hampers.

Hints for Collectors
Straightforward design and fine workmanship distinguish Shaker-made baskets, but definite proof of Shaker origin is hard to come by. The best evidence, other than documentation or identifying marks on the piece—both rare—is similarity to authenticated Shaker pieces. Shaker or not, the basket illustrated is a handsomely designed and fairly uncommon type, making it a desirable addition to almost any basket collection.

243 Indian potato-stamped covered baskets

Description
Rectangular baskets with crosshatched weave and lids having single-bound wrapped rims. *Top:* Wide ribs and weavers except for 6 rows of narrow weavers near top. Stamped abstract decoration. *Center:* Wide ribs and weavers except for 3 rows of narrow weavers near bottom and on edge of lid. Freehand and stamped vines and loops. *Bottom:* Wide ribs with alternate rows of wide and narrow weavers. Stamped circles and leaves.

Materials and Dimensions
Factory-cut splint. Natural dye. Height (top to bottom): 11½″; 9″; 12″. Length: 10″; 11″; 16″. Width: 6½″; 8″; 10″.

Locality and Period
New York State or New England. c. 1890–1920.

Comment
Both the freehand decoration on the middle basket and the stamped design on the others are typical of the work of several northeastern Indian tribes, including the Algonquin. A raw hard vegetable such as a potato or turnip, a corncob, or an easily carved piece of softwood was cut in the desired shape, dipped in a dye made from roots or berries, and stamped on factory-cut splint. This kind of basket decoration, usually called "potato stamping," is no longer done.

Hints for Collectors
Given the fragile nature of splint baskets, these examples are in very good condition. Since painted or decorated baskets have been in great demand during the last decade, these would be costly. While it is always difficult to determine the exact age of a basket, their machine-cut splint—characteristically thin and very regular—suggests these were made after about 1890.

244

Indian covered basket

Description
Circular covered basket having crosshatched weave of wide ribs and both wide and very narrow weavers. Some weavers stained. Edge of lid hemmed. 2 narrow splint handles midway down sides.

Materials and Dimensions
Factory-cut ash or hickory splint, partly prestained. Height: 9″. Diameter: 14″.

Locality and Period
New England. c. 1920–40.

Comment
Northeastern Indian tribes, including the Penobscot and Passamaquoddy of Maine and the Algonquin and Iroquois, were already making baskets when the first European settlers arrived. The earliest baskets were probably square or rectangular, but the Indians began producing circular covered baskets to meet the needs of the white men. The hemmed edge of the lid in this example—every other rib is turned back over the top weaver, cut to a point, and tucked in—is a characteristic northeastern Indian technique, although also used elsewhere.

Hints for Collectors
Indian baskets made from about 1800 to 1850 often have freehand decoration in natural dye, while later examples such as this piece have splint stained with synthetic color. Certain tribes continue to make baskets in traditional forms, but use factory-cut splint. The dried appearance and signs of wear on this basket suggest, however, it was not made very recently. Lidded baskets, particularly circular ones, are less common than open ones, and thus usually more costly.

245 Indian covered baskets and pincushion

Description
Flat, covered, circular baskets of woven sweet grass over splint; smallest one made into a pincushion. Largest 2 made of braided sweet grass over splint in crosshatched weave. Other 4 made of woven sweet grass in crosshatched weave over splint. All with wrapped, single-bound rims. Third basket from bottom with traces of green paint. Top basket having velvet cushion (originally yellow) instead of cover.

Materials and Dimensions
Sweet grass. Splint. Partly painted. Velvet. Height (top to bottom): 1½″; ¾″; 1″; 1¾″; 2¼″; 2″. Diameter: 2¾″; 3″; 3½″; 4½″; 5½″; 7¼″.

Locality and Period
Probably Maine. c. 1900–40.

Comment
Covered circular "flatbaskets," such as the ones shown here, were traditionally made of braided sweet grass and ash splint, probably as early as about 1900, by northeastern Indians and some Great Lakes tribes. The thin strands of grass were first braided and then woven, creating a basket with an interesting texture. Many sweet-grass baskets also have splint weavers, often in several colors, including shades of red and indigo.

Hints for Collectors
Since flatbaskets were made in very large quantities, they are readily available today. On most examples, the colored splint on the outside has faded noticeably; but inside, protected from light colors are often as bright as they were originally. These baskets can still be bought quite reasonably; pleasing in both form and texture, they are fun to collect in as many different sizes as you can find. The smallest sizes are least common.

246 Indian covered baskets and pincushion

Description
Left: Small circular footed basket of woven sweet grass and splint in crosshatched weave; stained curlicue decoration on domed lid. Wrapped sweet-grass rim, single-bound with stained lashing. *Center:* Pincushion of woven sweet grass in crosshatched pattern over splint with wide weavers; stained curlicue decoration at bottom. Wrapped sweet-grass rim double-bound. Tan velvet cushion. *Right:* Small circular splint basket with lid and curlicue decoration. Wrapped sweet-grass rims double-bound. Flat sweet-grass handle on top.

Materials and Dimensions
Sweet grass. Splint, partly prestained. Velvet. Height (left to right): 4½″; 2¼″; 3″. Diameter: 5¾″; 3″; 5¼″.

Locality and Period
Probably Maine. c. 1900–20.

Comment
Great skill is required to make these miniature sweet-grass-and-splint baskets. For example, the sweet-grass edging on the rims of 2 of these is double-bound (also called X-bound or cross-bound) —a difficult feat of craftsmanship on such tiny baskets. The curlicue decoration, or curly work, is traditional among the Passamaquoddy and Penobscot tribes of Maine.

Hints for Collectors
Miniature baskets of almost any type are much sought after today, but elaborately decorated older ones like these are especially prized. The footed basket is very unusual, as is the pincushion, which delicately rests on large curlicue supports. Though curlicue pieces continue to be made today, the dry darkened look of the grass and splint visible here is good evidence of age.

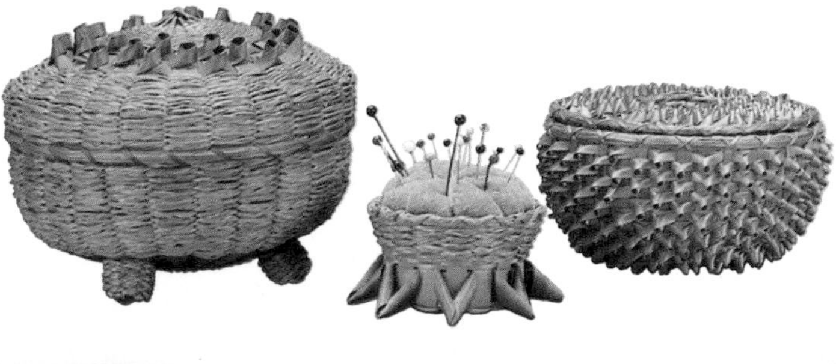

247 **Indian covered baskets**

Description
Covered baskets woven from coiled brown pine needles bound with light-colored grass in decorative stitches. Basket at left with cover overlapping bottom; center and right baskets with flat-topped lids having a center knob. Knob on center basket made of pine needles and grass; knob on right basket, of small pine cones.

Materials and Dimensions
Long-leaf pine needles. Pine cones. Grass. Height (left to right): 2¾″; 1¾″; 3″. Diameter: 8″; 5″; 5½″.

Locality and Period
Florida or Georgia. c. 1900–25.

Comment
Coiled long-leaf, or Florida, pine-needle baskets are still made by several Indian tribes in the South and Southwest, including the Seminoles in Florida and some tribes in Louisiana and eastern Texas. The coils are sometimes bound with imported raffia. The dark brown color of these baskets is the shade the pine needles turn after they are removed from trees and allowed to dry.

Hints for Collectors
The most common pine-needle objects today are trays, usually oval, decorated with seashells and grasses and covered with glass. Most are of recent manufacture, clearly intended for the tourist market; many have inscriptions such as "Souvenir of Miami." The pine-needle baskets shown here, however, with their simple traditional shapes and decoration, are far rarer and of much greater value than the common tourist wares.

248 Indian yarn holders

Description
Left: Jar-shaped holder with crosshatched pattern of splint ribs and alternate rows of braided sweet grass and narrow splint weavers. Long rope handles of braided sweet grass, attached with bowknots and stained splint bands. Lid with center hole and single-bound rim. *Center:* Small acorn-shaped, 2-piece holder closing at middle; wrapped loop catch. Crosshatched weave of braided sweet grass and splint. Wrapped rims single-bound with green lashing. Top hole encircled by stained splint. *Right:* Round yarn holder with crosshatched weave of braided sweet grass and splint. Large loop handle. Top hole edged with narrow splint.

Materials and Dimensions
Sweet grass. Splint, partly prestained. Height (left to right, without handles): 8″; 4½″; 5¼″. Diameter: 8″; 4″; 5¼″.

Locality and Period
Probably Maine. c. 1900–20.

Comment
Made by Indians and sold to tourists, knitting-yarn or string holders like these were popular around the turn of the century, since they allowed women to carry their handiwork with them. In form they are somewhat similar to the oval wicker purses and work baskets made by the Shakers, which were in turn influenced by imported Chinese baskets.

Hints for Collectors
While small covered sweet-grass baskets are still made today, yarn holders like these have not been in fashion since about 1920. Because it is a form no longer being produced, these are well worth collecting. Its elaborate bowknot decoration suggests that the one on the left is probably the oldest.

249 Matchbook bowl with domed lid

Description
Flat-bottomed bowl made from vertical rows of folded, multicolored matchbook covers (matches removed) bound together with string. Sides rounded toward bottom. Folded matchbooks forming dome-shaped lid with red knob, extending over rim of bowl.

Materials and Dimensions
Paper matchbook covers. String. Height: 7½″. Diameter: 12″.

Locality and Period
Throughout the United States. c. 1900–present.

Comment
Folk artists have used almost every conceivable material to make one-of-a-kind objects, many of them functional. Because artists such as the creator of the bowl shown here often lack prototypes made of the materials in which they are working, they must develop their own techniques. In this case, the matchbooks must have been cut in narrow strips and then folded into interlocking segments forming the rows. Great care was taken to use matchbooks of one particular design—a dark blue background with yellow print—to form the edge of the lid.

Hints for Collectors
A marvel of imaginative design and color, this lidded bowl is the sort of piece that may elude a systematic searcher for years, only to turn up unexpectedly at a yard sale or local crafts show. Objects made of 20th-century throwaway materials, just beginning to be considered folk art, can often be bought at a reasonable price, even from dealers specializing in such pieces. Probably the most common items made from leftover scraps are quilts and hooked rugs; small pieces of wood, matchsticks, and cigar boxes are other "found" materials used by folk artists.

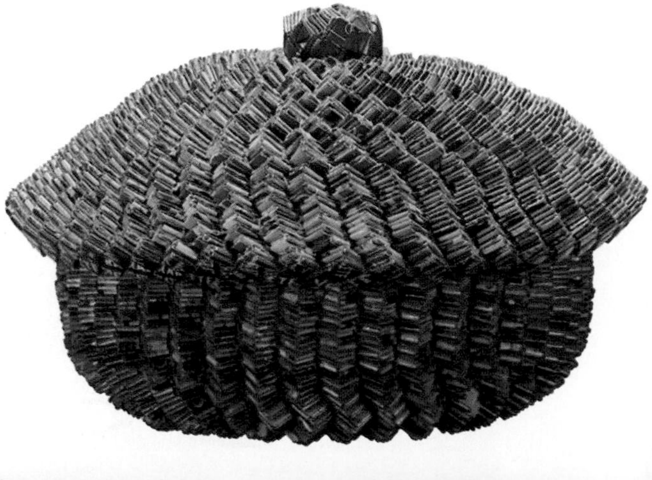

250 **Bottle-cap bowl and cup**

Description
Shallow bowl and cylindrical cup made of multicolored metal bottle caps strung on metal wire and arranged in horizontal or vertical rows. Circular rims made of caps. Coffee-can bottom on cup.

Materials and Dimensions
Metal bottle caps. Metal wire. Tin bottom. Bowl height: 4¾″. Diameter of top: 11″. Cup height: 6⅝″. Diameter of top: 5¼″.

Locality and Period
Pennsylvania, but also throughout the United States. c. 1900–present.

Comment
Coca-Cola was available only at soda fountains before 1899, when the company's first bottling plant was opened in Chattanooga, Tennessee. Once bottled drinks became common, there was a never-ending supply of metal caps, or crowns. Caps were a sturdy and free material that appealed to a number of craftsmen, who fashioned them into a wide variety of forms, ranging from trays and vases to tables and picture frames. Caps were sometimes individually covered with fabric and fastened together to make hot-dish holders. The pieces shown here are typical of utilitarian objects made from bottle caps, though this bowl and cup cannot actually hold liquids.

Hints for Collectors
This sort of folk-art object made from discarded materials does not appeal to everyone; but such pieces are eagerly sought by certain collectors, who are sometimes willing to pay handsomely for them. Nevertheless, bottle-cap objects can sometimes be bought quite reasonably.

251 Work or sewing basket

Description
Shallow circular basket with thin ribs and weavers woven in crosshatched pattern around lower part and openwork diamonds on upper sides. Rim is extension of diamond pattern. Double-woven bottom. Stained brown.

Materials and Dimensions
Factory-cut willow rods. Stained. Height: 4″. Diameter: 11″.

Locality and Period
Throughout the United States. c. 1900–40.

Comment
Though made in America and Europe since at least the 17th century, very few willow, or wicker, baskets made prior to the early 19th century have survived. They are much less common and generally less popular than splint baskets. By the mid-19th century many farmers were growing willow, which was sold to basketmakers after the trees had matured for 5 years. After about 1880, rods were precut to the desired length by machine; most willow baskets found today were fashioned from machine-cut willow.

Hints for Collectors
Since their styles and shapes have changed little over 2 centuries, willow baskets are extremely difficult to date. Intended for general domestic use, this type of basket—also imported from Europe for more than a century and, more recently, from Asia—is almost impossible to distinguish from American examples. Baskets like this are fairly common and inexpensive; if in good condition, they are suitable for storing sewing articles or for serving fruit or bread.

252 Coiled-wood bowls

Description
Open bowls made of bentwood coiled in concentric circles. Sides curving gradually outward toward top. Natural finish. Nail construction. Smaller bowl repaired on bottom with willow strips.

Materials and Dimensions
Bentwood. Iron nails. Height: 4¼″; 3½″. Diameter: 11″; 9½″.

Locality and Period
Probably Pennsylvania. c. 1880–1920.

Comment
Bowls of this shape and size (about 9″ to 12″ in diameter), more often made of coiled rye straw than of bentwood, were called bread-raising baskets, since that was their principal use. They were fashioned primarily by German immigrants in Pennsylvania, Maryland, New Jersey, Delaware, and Virginia. Like the rye-straw baskets or circular tin "bread-raisers," the bowls shown here may have held bread dough while it was rising. Breadmaking was one of the housewife's most important tasks, so bread-raising bowls would have been an important part of her kitchen equipment. These bentwood examples may also have served other purposes, such as holding fruit or storing odds and ends.

Hints for Collectors
Though the technique of wetting or steaming wood and coiling it into a bowl was not very common, bentwood examples do turn up sometimes in the Mid-Atlantic states, where most of these pieces were made. The repair on the small basket does not lessen its value, because it was done well and apparently quite early in the life of the piece and because the basket's shape and appearance remain unaltered.

253 Miniature threaded-clove tea set

Description
Miniature tea set with oval tray, scalloped tray, creamer, cup, and teapot (top missing) made of cloves threaded in rows on string. Curved handles on teapot, creamer, and cup. Oval tray with woven design around inner rim.

Materials and Dimensions
Cloves. String. Oval tray length: 7½″; width: 6¼″; depth: ⅞″. Scalloped tray length: 9½″; width: 9″; depth: ¾″. Teapot height: 3¾″; length: 6¼″; width: 4″. Cup height: 1¾″; diameter: 3″. Creamer height: 3″; length: 5″; width: 3¾″.

Locality and Period
The Northeast or Midwest. c. 1880–1900.

Comment
Objects made of cloves strung on thread or thin wire were not uncommon at the height of the Victorian era, when many unusual materials were imaginatively used for handiwork. Bowls, small baskets, and masted sailing ships were some common clove constructions. Threading the tiny cloves is a difficult task because their small round heads have a tendency to break off under the least pressure.

Hints for Collectors
Threaded-clove objects can often be found in shops specializing in unusual Victoriana. This tea set would be valuable because it is uncommon and a set, but single clove baskets may sell for less than $10. Relegated to an attic or out-of-the-way shelf, many clove pieces have been sitting untouched for years and may have a heavy coat of dust. Careful washing with lukewarm water generally removes the dust and may even restore the spicy scent of the cloves.

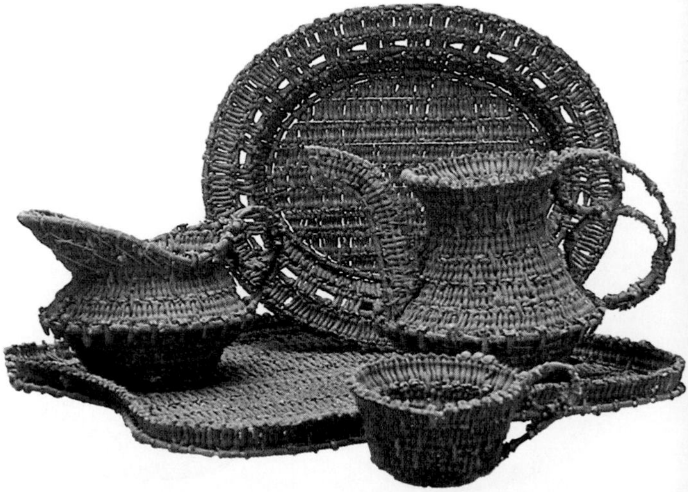

254 **Hanging storage basket**

Description
Flat-backed wall basket in diamond shape, with 3 cutoff corners and loop at top. Triangular pocket in crosshatched weave of matching ribs and weavers. Curlicue decoration on pocket, partially stained brown, and thin brown weaver separating 2 top rows of curlicue. Pocket rim wrapped and single-bound. Flat upper section with stepped profile, having wide ribs and narrow weavers in crosshatched weave.

Materials and Dimensions
Splint. Partly stained. Height: 19¼″. Length: 15″. Width: 5½″.

Locality and Period
New England. c. 1885–1920.

Comment
Hanging baskets such as the one shown here, but with a flat bottom, were called loom baskets, since they were originally hung at the corner of a loom to hold thread bobbins. They continued being made into the early 20th century, well after hand looms had been replaced by mechanical ones. During this later period they were sometimes called comb baskets. Made by many Indian tribes, these baskets often have curlicue decoration, originally characteristic of the work of the Winnebago tribe.

Hints for Collectors
Loom baskets were made over a fairly long period of time; later ones may often be recognized by their wide strips of machine-cut splint. Though the stepped back is traditional, the more steps a basket has, the older and more valuable it is likely to be. Most pockets have a flat bottom, so that the triangular shape of this one is quite unusual. Often the hanging loop (intact here) will have broken off, but if the basket is old and otherwise in good condition, that should have little effect on its value.

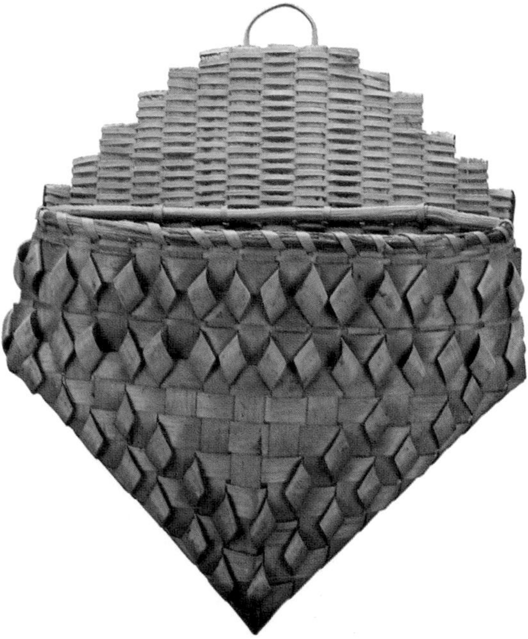

255

Vinegar funnel

Description
Basketry funnel with large mouth and narrow open bottom. Heavy wooden top rim to which ribs are nailed. Plain plaited weave with thick ribs shaped to fit top rim and tapering to sharp points hanging loose at bottom. Narrow weavers around upper two-thirds of funnel.

Materials and Dimensions
Ash splint. Ash. Iron nails. Height: 15″. Diameter of top: 12″.

Locality and Period
New England. c. 1870–90.

Comment
Whether hand-woven or made on a mold, funnels like the one shown here required the talents of a skilled basketmaker. Used primarily in making vinegar and cider, such funnels were lined with cheesecloth before the liquid was poured through. Most have a thin strip of splint laced around the unwoven part at the bottom; this would help keep the points from breaking while maintaining their flexibility. No trace of splint lacing remains on this example.

Hints for Collectors
Because vinegar funnels were fragile and their use was never widespread, they are hard to find today. They are prized for their unusual shape by basket collectors interested in assembling as diverse a collection as possible. General collectors, however, usually prefer the more common forms that can be used for storage or carrying. Baskets in uncommon shapes or with unusual uses (including animal muzzles, clam baskets, and openweave sieves for sifting charcoal) sometimes sell for less than their rarity might seem to warrant.

256 Windsor-type cheese drainer

Description
Open-topped wooden drainer with square bottom and perpendicular rectangular sides, all constructed of wide-spaced parallel rods set into flat frames at top and bottom. Lapped and pegged construction.

Materials and Dimensions
Maple. Length: 27″. Width: 27″. Depth: 8″.

Locality and Period
Pennsylvania. c. 1830–65.

Comment
Although there were cows in the Colonies in the 17th century, butter and cheese did not become common until the 18th century. Cheesemaking was a laborious process, with many steps involving specialized utensils, including cheese drainers like that shown here. At one stage of the process, curds were put in a cheesecloth and set inside the drainer so that liquid whey would drip out and leave a solid block of cheese. The drainer was supported over a large tub by a short wooden horizontal ladder, in some cases permanently attached to the drainer. Drainers were round or square and had straight or slanted sides. Windsor-type drainers such as this are so named because, like Windsor chairs, they are constructed of rods or spindles; other strainers consist of slats or woven splint instead.

Hints for Collectors
Drainers like this one are sought today for their visual appeal. The clean simple lines and geometric shapes make them suitable accessories for either country-style or modern rooms. An old drainer should show evidence of having been used, such as milky white stains on the bottom and sides and wear on the base.

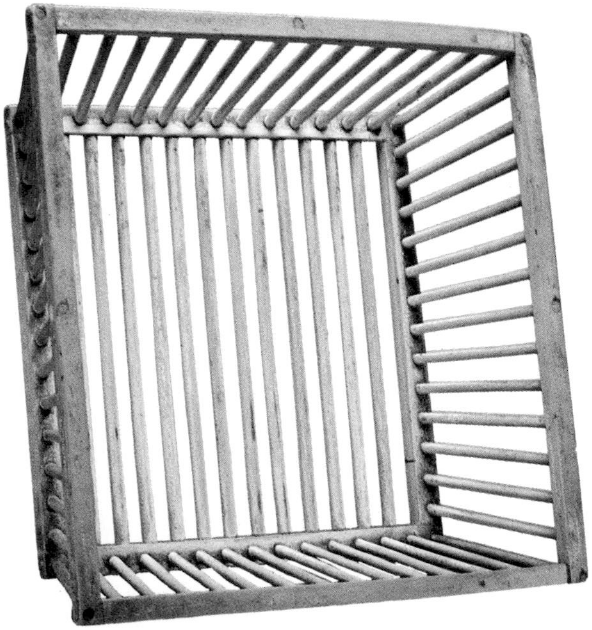

257 Wire field basket

Description
Circular wire basket with sides sloping out from narrow bottom to wide top rim; rims wrapped in wire. Sides made of vertical wires hooked over top and bottom rims. Floor of basket consists of wires radiating from small metal center ring. 2 iron handles looped around top rim and wrapped with thin wire across top.

Materials and Dimensions
Iron wire. Height: 13¾″. Diameter of top: 17″.

Locality and Period
Throughout the United States. c. 1900–25.

Comment
By the early 20th century, factory-made wire baskets like this had become common. Much stronger and more durable than splint baskets, they came in a variety of sizes and were excellent for gathering vegetables—particularly, heavy crops like potatoes—and for general field use. They were also useful for washing fruit and vegetables, since they allowed water to drain off easily and, unlike splint baskets, were not harmed by constant wetting.

Hints for Collectors
Metal baskets of this type are fairly easy to find, so look for one with a handsome, well-defined design and wire in good condition, like this example. Most baskets this large have wider spaces between wires and another metal band set midway between top and bottom for added support. Besides its closely spaced wires, the 2 small handles of this basket are unusual; a larger metal swing handle across the top is more common.

258 **Slat field basket**

Description
Circular basket made of vertical wooden slats slanting out from narrow bottom to wide top rim; slats wide and fairly thick. Double rims nailed to slats at top and bottom. Removable slat bottom with crossed slats underneath for support.

Materials and Dimensions
Hickory. Iron nails. Height: 15½". Diameter of top: 18½".

Locality and Period
New York. c. 1890–1930.

Comment
This sort of moderately large field or gathering basket, sturdy because of its thick slats, was well suited for holding heavy crops like potatoes or corn. The slat bottom, supporting much more weight than did a splint bottom, probably greatly lengthened the life of the basket, as it could readily be replaced if it wore out before the sides did. By the final decades of the 19th century, such baskets were being made in factories all over the country. Though the type shown here has no handles, many factory-made baskets have a single metal bail, or swing, handle instead of the hand-carved wooden kind used earlier.

Hints for Collectors
Baskets made from wooden slats, such as this example, or from factory-produced splint look very different from earlier woven-splint baskets. The overall shape of the basket and size of the slats are always regular, and the splint lacks the imperfections found in handmade examples. Because slat baskets are much easier to find than early splint examples, they are much less expensive. But only those with plain clean lines and in good condition, like this piece, are worth buying.

259 Double peach basket

Description
Tall openwork basket with identical circular mouths at top and bottom; sides sloping inward to narrow middle. Crisscross weave in large diamond pattern. Circular pine "bottom" at narrow center, equidistant from both rims. Nailed splint rings form top and bottom double rims; 3 other rings around middle and at midpoints of both basket-shaped halves.

Materials and Dimensions
Factory-cut ash splint. Pine. Wire nails. Height: 24¾″. Diameter of rim: 13½″.

Locality and Period
Pennsylvania. c. 1920–30.

Comment
This double peach basket is a one-of-a-kind piece; single baskets of similar design and construction were in common use for gathering peaches, but it is hard to imagine how a double basket was used. Since only one end could be filled at a time, perhaps such baskets were used for displaying fruit at market. While at first glance it looks as if made from 2 separate baskets attached in the middle, closer examination shows it to be of one-piece construction, woven of very long strips of splint pulled in by the center rim.

Hints for Collectors
Unusual baskets like the one shown here have a special attraction for some collectors. Part of the fun of owning such a piece is trying to determine how it was used, why it has its shape, and whether related examples have been found. Machine-cut splint baskets from the 20th century used to be available very cheaply, but as collectors have increased in number, prices for almost all baskets in good condition have risen greatly.

260 **Eel trap**

Description
Long cylindrical basket with open bottom and tapering top. Wooden plug attached to top of basket by hooks and cord. Crosshatched weave with ribs and weavers of varied width. Inverted cone-shaped chamber attached to inside of bottom, narrowing to small opening within basket.

Materials and Dimensions
Hand-cut splint, probably oak. Carved wooden plug with iron hooks. Cord. Height: 22″. Diameter of base: 9″.

Locality and Period
Probably Chesapeake Bay area of Maryland or Virginia. c. 1900–10.

Comment
Woven on a mold, this trap, sometimes called a pot, was used to capture eels. Attracted to bait inside, eels wriggle into the wide mouth of the trap and are caught in the narrow chamber at the end, just as lobsters are captured in similar traps. Within a few days the fisherman lifts the trap out of the water, removes the plug at the top, and takes out the eels. The basket shown here was found near Chesapeake Bay and was probably made nearby.

Hints for Collectors
Because of their odd shape and unusual function, eel baskets appeal to a limited number of collectors and thus can occasionally be bought quite reasonably. However, such baskets are rare and do attract collectors of specialty baskets, who are often willing to pay large sums for fine examples. A well-used trap, such as the one shown here, will have a gray, weathered look from continual use in water; this adds to its value unless parts of the trap are actually worn away.

261 Horse feeding basket

Description
Large oval basket with wide mouth at top. Wrapped rim double-bound. Small wooden bow handles, carved and notched, on opposite sides, connected by wide leather strap. Crosshatched weave with wide ribs and narrow weavers. Alternate ribs left longer on top, cut into points, then turned over top weaver and tucked under. Domed bottom.

Materials and Dimensions
Factory-cut oak splint. Wooden handles. Brass-fitted leather strap. Height: 15¼″. Diameter of top: 13½″.

Locality and Period
Connecticut. c. 1880–90.

Comment
Although their use was never widespread, baskets like the one shown here were made in various sizes and were used for feeding horses and other livestock. Farmers also sometimes put basketlike muzzles on their oxen to keep them from feeding while they ploughed the fields.

Hints for Collectors
Few baskets for feeding animals have survived, because most were used until they fell apart. The one shown here is in such good condition because it was probably little or never used. While the uniform width and thickness of the ribs and weavers suggest the splints were cut by machine, this does not diminish the value of the basket, since most splint was machine-cut by the final decades of the 19th century. Besides its excellent condition, this basket's hand-carved handles, graceful shape, and unusual form combine to make it a highly desirable piece.

262 Doll's cradle

Description
Miniature basketry cradle in crosshatched weave. Curved bonnet top consisting of 4 rows of curlicue decoration, with 2 rows painted blue. Main section having wide ribs and wide weavers around top and bottom, and narrow weavers in between. Blue dots painted around top edge. Wrapped rim single-bound. Carved wooden rockers.

Materials and Dimensions
Splint. Pine. Painted. Height: 9½". Length: 14". Width: 6½".

Locality and Period
Maine. c. 1880–1925.

Comment
Miniature baskets of all kinds were popular among tourists visiting the Northeast on summer vacations. The small cradle shown here, however, may have been specially made for a particular little girl. When found recently, it was filled with doll-size bedclothes, including a tiny pillow, sheet, and quilt, all carefully hand-stitched. Similar cradles were made in larger and smaller sizes.

Hints for Collectors
The form, diminutive size, and painted decoration all make this piece rare and quite special. It is likely to be much more costly than more common curlicue baskets in simple circular or rectangular shapes. Too fragile and brittle to be used any longer by a child, it would be an asset to any basket collection, particularly one specializing in pieces with curlicue decoration.

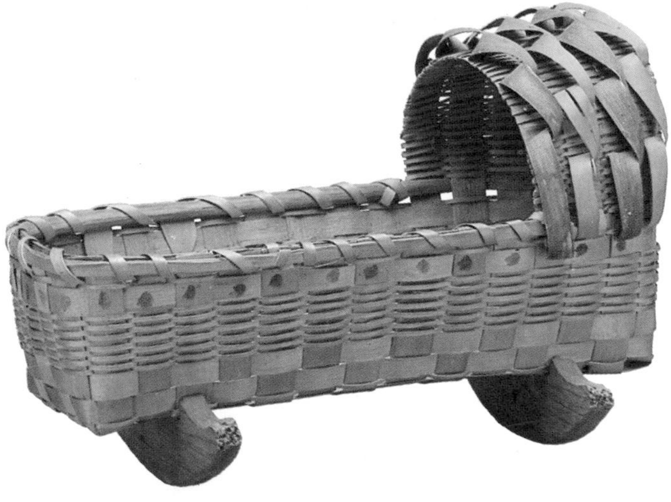

Boxes and Shelves

Early Americans kept many of their possessions in boxes of all sizes, shapes, and materials; many of these containers were imported from Europe. New Englanders of the 17th and 18th centuries seem to have been particularly fond of boxes, which they often crafted in European styles. By the late 18th century, American craftsmen, particularly those in Shaker and Pennsylvania-German communities, had begun to fashion their own distinctive boxes and containers. Boxes were needed not only for storing candles, salt, knives, handkerchiefs, and trinkets, but also for carrying clothes and household goods, for measuring commodities like grain, and for safeguarding documents and valuables.

Wooden, Scrimshaw, and Tin Boxes
Small handmade wooden boxes were painted and decorated in various ways. One of the most popular techniques was grain painting; commonly done on pine or other readily available woods, it simulated the grain of such expensive woods as mahogany. In the first half of the 19th century, fanciful designs were created with the aid of combs, brushes, sponges, and even smoke from a candle flame. Realistic designs, such as patriotic motifs, flowers, ribbons, and the ever-popular swags and bowknots, were also painted on boxes. Finely decorated pieces were often given as gifts to relatives or sweethearts. Whalemen created handsome examples usually out of whalebone; these are called "ditty boxes."
Generally designed to hold documents, tin boxes were made throughout the Northeast. Most were decorated with brightly painted flowers and geometric designs on a black background.

Tramp-Art Boxes
So named because some were produced by hoboes or itinerant artisans who "tramped" from place to place, tramp-art pieces were made of discarded wood, usually mahogany or cedar from cigar boxes or pine from fruit or shipping crates. The soft wood was notched or chipped along the edges and glued layer upon layer to create unusual forms.

Shaker Boxes
As early as the 1790s, the Shakers had begun making their distinctive lidded "pantry" boxes, used for storing food, in many sizes. Circular or oval, these were constructed of thin sheets of wood, which were steamed and then shaped around wooden forms. Characteristic of Shaker boxes are their lapped joints, sometimes called "fingers"; however, these closings were also used by non-Shaker craftsmen. Other wooden containers, such as covered buckets, or firkins, were also made in Shaker communities. After the mid-19th century, similar pantry boxes and firkins were mass produced in factories.

Shelves
Many household objects, including some boxes, needed a place to be displayed, particularly in the Victorian era, when all sorts of souvenirs and specimens were collected. Since woodworking was a popular hobby, shelves of all sizes were crafted at home. Some of the most interesting examples are adorned with carved figures of birds, flowers, or even people. They were often painted as well as saw-cut, carved, or incised. Many of these shelves are too small to have been very useful, which suggests that they were fashioned in large part simply for the woodworkers' pleasure.

263 **Smoke-grained storage box**

Description
Lidded rectangular box decorated overall with light gray paint and black smoke graining. Interior covered with green and white wallpaper. No lock; butt-hinged. Nail construction.

Materials and Dimensions
Pine. Painted. Wallpaper. Cast-iron hinges. Square nails. Height: 7¼″. Length: 14″. Width: 8¼″.

Locality and Period
New England. c. 1830–50.

Comment
By about 1825, boxes were being decorated in a wide variety of colorful designs with techniques such as sponging, graining, and smoking. Each decorative process was executed on a surface that had been painted and allowed to dry only slightly. Smoke graining, the technique chosen here, was accomplished by holding a burning candle close to the wet surface until the carbon from the smoke created an attractive pattern. Smoked patterns varied but were for the most part fairly simple and much less complicated than combed or sponged designs. This box was probably used to hold jewelry or to store linen accessories such as collars and cuffs.

Hints for Collectors
Painted boxes are much in demand today, and those with elaborate designs are particularly valuable. This simple example is interesting because, unlike most boxes of this type, it is lined; the wallpaper covering the interior is an early addition that increases its value. Wallpaper or newspaper lining may sometimes help date a box.

264 Grain-painted sample box and panels

Description
Lidded narrow box, painted and grained on all sides in abstract brownish design on yellow background. Incised red bands around middle of box and edges of lid. 10 sample panels (2 shown). Brass handle, hinges, and 2 hook-and-eye closings.

Materials and Dimensions
Pine. Painted. Brass hardware. Box height: 8¾″; length: 15¹⁄₁₆″; width: 2⅝″. Panel height: 6⅞″; length: 14¹⁄₁₆″.

Locality and Period
Attributed to Moses Eaton (1796–1886), Dublin, New Hampshire. c. 1820.

Comment
Grain painting was done by trained furniture makers or itinerant artists, who used sample boxes like the one shown here to display their skills. It originated as a means of imitating finely grained woods, such as mahogany, on inexpensive country furniture made of pine or other ordinary woods. Graining was accomplished by applying 2 coats of paint of different colors and, while the second was still wet, using a graining brush, comb, corncob, finger, or piece of cut sponge to make an attractive pattern on the wet surface.

Hints for Collectors
This piece is very rare and valuable because it contains all of its original sample panels and because such sample boxes are far less common than grain-painted furniture and storage boxes. The insights it provides about the craft of grain painting also make it highly desirable.

265 Painted trinket box

Description
Lidded rectangular box painted yellow and decorated on top with large brown eagle holding striped shield and branch. Striped ribbon in red, green, and blue draped from eagle's beak across lid and down sides of box. On front of box, pair of small blue doves facing each other, their heads encircled by a pink ribbon extending across front. Edges of lid and sides of box outlined in brown. Inner surfaces sponge-decorated yellow and brown, with 9 small compartments. Small oval escutcheon. Hinged.

Materials and Dimensions
Pine. Painted. Brass hardware. Height: 6⅜″. Length: 14⅞″. Width: 8⅛″.

Locality and Period
New England. c. 1820–40.

Comment
From the 17th through the 19th century, Americans kept their belongings in many types of boxes. Documents, linens, small articles of clothing, ladies' bonnets, candles, knives, and other household items were stored in plain, carved, or painted boxes designed especially for them. About the beginning of the 19th century, stenciled designs on boxes became very popular. Many boxes, painted freehand or with stencils, were decorated with patriotic symbols.

Hints for Collectors
Since boxes were handled a great deal, painted examples in good condition, with colors as bright as those on this example, are unusual. Such boxes bring high prices today, so worn examples are sometimes repainted to make them more desirable; new paint can be recognized by the lack of brittleness and network of cracks that come with age.

266 Painted trinket box

Description
Small lidded rectangular box with dark wooden strips separating pairs of paper-covered panels. Male and female figures, surrounded by birds, trees, and abstract designs, drawn and painted in blue and white on top, side, front, and back panels. Narrow panels on all sides of deep lid decorated with geometric motifs. Metal mountings on lid.

Materials and Dimensions
Wood. Watercolor, pencil, and ink on paper. Brass hardware. Height: 4½″. Length: 8″. Width: 5⅛″.

Locality and Period
New England. c. 1825–35.

Comment
Painted and decorated boxes, extremely popular in the first half of the 19th century, were created by a wide variety of techniques. This box was probably made as a gift, since great care was lavished upon it; its delicate naive paintings perhaps depict members of the artist's or owner's family. Various materials—watercolor, pencil, and ink—were used to draw and paint the portraits on paper.

Hints for Collectors
Painted boxes were especially common in Pennsylvania and New England: those from Pennsylvania tend to be brightly decorated with traditional stylized German designs, such as tulips, birds, and pinwheels; those from New England, such as this one, generally have more muted colors and frequently some kind of painted grain. Its human figures make this particular box very unusual, since most amateur artists would have limited themselves to flowers, trees, swags and bows, or simple geometric designs. The use of paper is also uncommon.

267

Painted dome-top box

Description
Dome-top rectangular box with stenciled and freehand decoration in red, yellow, and orange on black ground. 3 stylized flowers on curved top; circular designs at corners. Initials "DB" at front center of lid. Pair of stylized floral motifs flanking circular design on front. Similar floral motifs on sides. Lid and box edged with solid red border enclosing thin wavy yellow line. Hinged iron lock with rectangular escutcheon framed by wavy yellow line. Iron hinges and handles on sides.

Materials and Dimensions
Pine. Painted. Iron hardware. Height: 11½″. Length: 23¾″. Width: 11¾″.

Locality and Period
New England. c. 1820–40.

Comment
The simple decoration of this box, or miniature chest, is typical of New England designs, closely resembling that found on painted tinware of the period. The wavy yellow lines and red edging were probably done by hand, but the stylized flowers and initials were stenciled. Although many boxes were painted by itinerant artists, others were decorated by amateurs, usually housewives or schoolgirls trying to add a little color to everyday objects.

Hints for Collectors
Even in the 19th century, when painted household wares were very popular, decorated boxes were fairly uncommon. Most household boxes were unpainted or had a coat of solid color—most often green, gray, red, brown, or blue. The painted designs on this example are typical of the decorated boxes that have survived. Domed lids, however, are less common than flat tops.

268 Painted tin document box

Description
Dome-top rectangular box with red, yellow, and green painted decoration on overall black ground. Cherries and leaves on wide white band across upper front, with flowers, fruit, and leaves below. Top with abstract yellow brushstroke border; sides decorated with yellow leaves and stems. Brass swing handle in center of lid; U-shaped hasp latch hanging from bottom center of lid. Tin-wire hinges in rear. Back undecorated.

Materials and Dimensions
Tin. Painted. Brass hardware. Height: 7½″. Length: 9½″. Width: 5½″.

Locality and Period
The Northeast. c. 1830–50.

Comment
The earliest American tinware, made about 1740, was plain; not until about 1810 were painted and decorated pieces, often called toleware, introduced. At first, painted examples were done freehand, but stenciled designs, which required less artistic skill, soon became common. Dome-top boxes of approximately this size were often used for storing documents.

Hints for Collectors
Decorated tinware pieces are still made today. The 1976 Bicentennial celebration spurred a revival of interest in early American crafts, leading many people to take up tin painting; most worked on new trays, pails, or boxes, though some painted old tin pieces as well. Old oil paint should show a network of fine cracks, and the black background some signs of wear. Wear should be greater on exposed parts than on protected areas. Signs of age that are too uniform over the surface of a piece may have been artificially created with lye or acid.

269 Indian pine-needle box

Description
Lidded rectangular box made of pine needles woven to form pairs of square panels on front, back, top, and bottom and a single square at each end. Crocheted pine-needle star in center of each square, and ropelike crocheted pine-needle trim around edges and between squares on front and back. Small crocheted ball protruding at center of front, probably used to fasten loop on lid (missing).

Materials and Dimensions
Pine needles. Height: 4″. Length: 7″. Width: 3¾″.

Locality and Period
The Northeast. c. 1900–30.

Comment
Probably made by an Indian, this woven and crocheted pine-needle box is very unusual. Much more common are baskets made of Florida pine needles by certain southern tribes. This box's square panels are constructed of needles woven at the corners to form diagonal lines that meet in the center. Most interesting is the ropelike crocheted pine-needle trim, which could have been done only while the needles were still green and pliable.

Hints for Collectors
This box is desirable because it combines unusual materials and excellent workmanship. Basically a piece woven of materials traditionally used for baskets, it would appeal to basket collectors as well as to anyone with an interest in textiles or other woven folk art.

270 Carved figural box

Description
Plain rectangular box with overhanging hinged lid having 3-dimensional stag, doe, and fawn in sitting positions, all carved from single piece of wood. Roses and leaves carved in relief at each corner. Nail construction.

Materials and Dimensions
Pine top. Birch base. Shellacked. Brass hinges. Iron nails. Height: 5¼″. Length: 9″. Width: 7″.

Locality and Period
Probably Zoar, Ohio. c. 1900–20.

Comment
This box, probably made by an amateur woodworker as a gift for a relative or friend, may have been used to hold jewelry, handkerchiefs, or small keepsakes. In the 1920s and 1930s, magazines such as *Popular Mechanics* and even the *Ladies Home Journal* ran articles about woodworking projects. While this piece is clearly original in its decoration, the overall design may have been inspired by a magazine article. Objects like this, however, were part of a long woodworking tradition in German communities such as Zoar, Ohio.

Hints for Collectors
The odd combination of Victorian-style roses and crudely carved animals makes this box distinctive. Though made in the 20th century, it is the sort of piece that appeals to collectors of antique folk sculpture because of its naive carvings. Such pieces, often found in rural antiques shops, are generally inexpensive.

271 **Carved box**

Description
Circular wooden box with removable lid having 5 tiers of concentric circles, each with carved triangles or semicircles around the edge. 5-pointed star carved at center of lid, inlaid with smaller star. Outside of box encircled with relief-carved trailing vine. Bottom screwed to sides and carved inside with stars.

Materials and Dimensions
Walnut or hickory. Iron screws. Height: 5¼″. Diameter: 6⅝″.

Locality and Period
Maine. c. 1850–80.

Comment
Though similar to tramp art, this piece differs in construction and material. The lid is lathe-turned from a single piece of wood rather than composed of separate layers of thin wood glued or nailed together. Moreover, it is made of walnut or hickory, whereas tramp art utilized recycled cigar boxes, usually cedar or mahogany, or fruit crates, generally pine. It does, however, have notch carving and wood inlay, as well as star designs, all of which are characteristic of tramp art.

Hints for Collectors
While this box cannot properly be termed tramp art, it is nonetheless a fine example of the woodcarver's art. The graceful trailing vine carved around the sides is particularly distinctive. Collectors should always be on the lookout for this type of unique piece, which is as likely to turn up in a neighborhood yard sale as in a folk art gallery.

272 Tramp-art pedestal box

Description
Hinged lidded box with 10 side panels, each with medallion consisting of concentric layered circles having notch-carved triangles along edges. Similar smaller upright medallions around circumference of lid, with large center medallion topped by layered knob. Small medallions suspended underneath box around carved, layered pedestal. Satin-lined interior. Nail and glue construction.

Materials and Dimensions
Pine. Shellacked. Brass hinges. Iron nails. Height: 11½″. Length: 11″. Width: 11″.

Locality and Period
Probably the Northeast or Midwest. c. 1900–20.

Comment
Typical of carved wooden pieces called tramp art, this piece displays the 2 techniques characterizing such work: layers of thin wood glued or nailed together and chip carving that produces a multifaceted effect. This example, with its protruding layered circles, shows clearly why tramp art is often described as being both additive and subtractive: layers are added one on top of another to build up the piece, and then small V- or Z-shaped notches are gouged out to create patterned surfaces.

Hints for Collectors
The footed, or pedestal, box is a fairly common tramp-art form. Most have 4, 6, or 8 sides, however, so this 10-sided example is quite special. Until the early 1970s, tramp art could be bought very cheaply, but as research focused on the subject, interest began to grow and prices rose considerably, particularly for elaborate examples such as that shown here.

273 Tramp-art storage box

Description
Lidded rectangular box with 2 layered notch-carved pyramids projecting from each side. Lid with large center pyramid serving as knob and smaller ones at corners. 4 inverted layered pyramids serving as feet. Nail and glue construction.

Materials and Dimensions
Cigar-box mahogany. Iron nails. Height: 8¾″. Length: 10½″. Width: 6½″.

Locality and Period
Probably the Northeast or Midwest. c. 1900–20.

Comment
The general technique of notch, or chip, carving used on tramp art was a late flowering of a European tradition that can be traced back to medieval furniture and, in America, to 17th-century chests and Bible boxes from New England. The specific tramp-art type of decoration was brought to America by German and Scandinavian immigrants, many of whom settled in New York and Pennsylvania. Because cigar boxes were produced in these states, their availability as raw materials for handiwork, together with a long tradition of notch carving, made these areas the richest sources of tramp art.

Hints for Collectors
Although large quantities of tramp art were made from the 1860s through the 1920s, almost none were signed. Boxes, particularly numerous, are less valuable than one-of-a-kind pieces that occasionally turn up, such as a model of the Brooklyn Bridge or of a church complete with altar and pews. Though its basic form is common, this piece is noteworthy because of its peculiar feet.

274 Slatted bowl

Description
Open-topped circular bowl with sides consisting of thin diagonal slats with narrow spaces between them. Top and bottom rims formed by series of interlocking notched pieces; bottom rim enclosed by wire hoop. Removable solid bottom fitted into lower rim.

Materials and Dimensions
Cigar-box mahogany. Varnished. Iron wire. Height: 3¾″. Diameter: 12″.

Locality and Period
Probably Massachusetts. c. 1910–25.

Comment
Made of thin strips of mahogany almost certainly from old cigar boxes, this slatted bowl is related to a tramp-art form called "crown of thorns," which features pieces of wood carved and layered to form a lacy openwork design with starlike outlines; the notched top and bottom rims of this piece were produced by a similar technique. Strictly speaking, this bowl is not tramp art, since the wood is neither layered nor notch-carved, but it may well have been made by someone who also carved more typical tramp-art pieces.

Hints for Collectors
The intricate construction of this bowl, particularly of the interlocking rims, makes it unusual. The fact that it is unique and attractive is more important than that it does not fit into any standard category. But because it is not pure tramp art, it would probably cost less than more typical examples.

275 Shaker grain measures

Description
Circular flat-sided containers in graduated sizes. Straight vertical seams. Square-nail construction. Oval Shaker stamp.

Materials and Dimensions
Hickory or ash. Iron nails. Height: 3¾″ to 6½″. Diameter: 6″ to 12⅛″.

Locality and Period
Sabbathday Lake, Maine. c. 1900–10.

Comment
Makers of grain measures were generally required by law to stamp their names on their work, presumably to ensure the accuracy of the measures. This set is stamped "SHAKER SOCIETY, Sabbathday Lake, Me." within a decorative oval. Like early round or oval storage boxes, the measures shown here were shaped by hand on molds and then nailed along a seam. Beginning about 1850, factories in Massachusetts also began producing circular grain measures, which are far more common today than Shaker examples.

Hints for Collectors
The most valuable grain measures are those that are either very small or very large. A complete set, such as this one, will cost considerably more than all of the pieces purchased separately. The unpainted finish of these containers shows the grain of the wood to best advantage and, considering their utilitarian purpose, the results are unexpectedly elegant. Because they were made in a Shaker community, these examples are particularly desirable.

276 Shaker oval boxes

Description
Lidded oval boxes in graduated sizes. Sides and top rim secured by finger laps and nails. Natural finish.

Materials and Dimensions
Maple sides. Pine top and bottom. Copper nails. Height: 1¾″ to 5½″. Length: 4½″ to 13″. Width: 3½″ to 9¾″.

Locality and Period
Probably New England. c. 1870–80.

Comment
Shaker craftsmen were famous for their oval and circular boxes. The sides and rims were first soaked in hot water and steamed, and then shaped around a wooden mold. While the Shakers may have introduced the technique of constructing boxes with the long triangular joints known as "fingers," or "lappers," other craftsmen produced similar pieces. The Shakers first made such boxes as early as the 1790s and continued to do so into the 20th century, when the celibate sect virtually died out. One Shaker craftsman at the community in Sabbathday Lake, Maine, made fine oval boxes and carriers until his death in 1961.

Hints for Collectors
Because this type of pantry box was made by both Shaker and non-Shaker workmen, it is difficult to verify Shaker origin unless a piece is marked or comes with reliable documentation. Complete stacks, usually 3, 4, or 5 boxes, are highly prized by collectors and have thus become very expensive; the set of 7 seen here is particularly rare. Many boxes were painted yellow, green, blue, or red. Those with original paint are generally more valuable than stained or varnished pieces. These boxes are now being reproduced, so beware of modern copies.

277 Bucket or firkin

Description
Circular container with straight-sided lid, wire handle, and wooden grip. Sides made of vertical slats, sloping slightly outward toward bottom. Narrow tin bands encircling rim and base. Inset bottom. Handle attached with wire loops. Yellow paint, not original but old.

Materials and Dimensions
Factory-cut pine. Painted. Tin. Iron-wire handle with maple grip. Iron nails. Height (without handle): 10″. Diameter (bottom): 11¼″.

Locality and Period
The Northeast. c. 1900–20.

Comment
The metal bands on the firkin, or cask, shown here indicate a fairly late date of manufacture. Early 19th-century examples, sometimes called sugar buckets, were reinforced with wooden hoops instead. Firkins similar to the example illustrated were made by Shakers in the 19th century to hold applesauce they produced in New Hampshire and Massachusetts; their lids were usually labeled "Shaker Applesauce."

Hints for Collectors
Firkins became common in the early 19th century and were used well into the 20th century. The type of hoop is a clue to age: the earliest wooden hoops have finger laps or eyelet loops, while later 19th-century examples often have machine-made nails securing the hoops. Recent factory-made firkins, like this one, have wood or iron hoops. Examples with finger laps were made by Shakers and non-Shakers, so this type of construction is no guarantee of Shaker origin. Firkins with original or early paint are worth more than newly painted or refinished ones.

278 Scrimshaw ditty box

Description
Lidded oval box made of baleen shaped around wooden top and bottom. Top painted black; baleen apron secured with finger lap and engraved with boughs. Sides engraved with front and rear views of large house, fence, and trees. Pin construction.

Materials and Dimensions
Baleen. Pine. Painted. Pewter pins. Height: 4″. Length: 8¼″. Width: 6¼″.

Locality and Period
Nantucket. c. 1820.

Comment
Used in all sorts of decorative scrimshaw objects, baleen is a flexible membrane that hardens once removed from a whale's mouth. It ranges in color from brownish-black to beige and off-white. Ditty boxes, most often fashioned from whalebone, were originally made by sailors to hold their small possessions; at home they were used to store anything from jewelry and sewing implements to gloves and seeds. The restrained shape of the box shown here reflects the influence of Quaker life on Nantucket. Its engraved decoration, however, is quite elaborate and elegant.

Hints for Collectors
Ditty boxes appeal to collectors of either scrimshaw or boxes. Their condition is very important, since the apron may be missing or the top or bottom may have been replaced, which lowers a box's value. The tiny holes caused by buffalo worms in baleen do not usually affect value. Engravings do not show up as well on baleen as on whalebone or whale ivory; rubbing powder on the design will help bring them out. Despite possible wormholes and faint engravings, baleen pieces are highly desirable because of their rarity and subtle beauty.

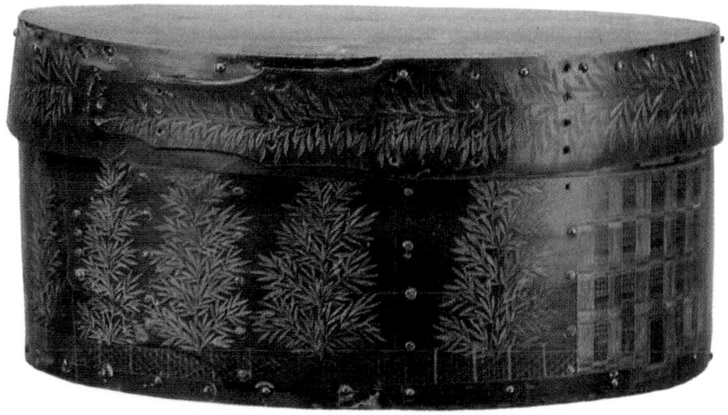

279 Painted open-top box

Description
Plain rectangular box with thick sides slanting in toward bottom. Top edges rounded from wear. Molded bottom protruding beyond sides. Old paint. Nail construction.

Materials and Dimensions
Pine. Painted. Iron cut nails. Height: 4⅞″. Length: 8¾″. Width: 5¾″.

Locality and Period
Probably New England. c. 1840–75.

Comment
Lacking the cardboard cartons or plastic containers found everywhere today, 19th-century housewives and farmers used handmade wooden boxes to store objects for easy access. A box like that shown here could have served any number of purposes in the kitchen, at the workbench, or even in the barn. Though relatively small, its thick walls suggest it was made to hold heavy items.

Hints for Collectors
Since antique painted boxes like this are in great demand and are easy to make, they have often been faked, complete with spurious signs of age. The lack of paint around the top edges and bottom molding of this example, however, is fairly reliable evidence that the piece is old, since those areas should show wear from decades of handling. Its machine-cut nails, instead of the iron-wire ones common later, also suggest a date of manufacture before 1875. This box is so simply constructed that its sides almost appear to be merely resting on the bottom, and much of its appeal results from this straightforward, unembellished design.

280 Painted utility box

Description
Large open rectangular box with center divider separating long compartment from 4 smaller compartments. Carved curving handle set lengthwise over center divider; cutout handhold and 2 incised 6-pointed stars. Old dark red paint. Nail construction.

Materials and Dimensions
Pine. Painted. Iron nails. Height (with handle): 9½″. Length: 28¾″. Width: 16½″.

Locality and Period
Pennsylvania. c. 1850–1900.

Comment
This saw-cut and carved box—probably used for holding tools or household items—displays the turn-of-the-century love of ornament, which found expression on even the most utilitarian objects. Woodcarving was extremely popular not only with men but also women. Several carvers promoted this craft, among them Benn Pitman of Cincinnati, who had 100 women in his first woodcarving class in 1873. Students were taught how to make small objects like the box shown here, as well as carved cabinets, chairs, and even mantelpieces. Similar in design to smaller knife boxes of the time, this piece differs in having several small compartments rather than the 2 large ones commonly found in knife boxes.

Hints for Collectors
Since this box does not have much carved or incised decoration and lacks the more elaborate details found on some slightly earlier pieces, it would be moderately priced. Still, its carved handle, incised stars, and old paint would undoubtedly attract many folk art collectors.

281 Tramp-art writing box

Description
Open rectangular box with sides sloping up toward higher back. Notch-carved trim on most edges. Arched front with 2 applied, layered, notch-carved hearts and 2 small notch-carved drawers. Notch-carved heart at rear of each side. Horizontal slats create compartments, with separate one at right holding 2 ink bottles with tin covers. Nail and glue construction.

Materials and Dimensions
Cedar and pine. Wire nails. Pressed glass and tin (ink bottles). Height: 4½″. Length: 13″. Width: 8″.

Locality and Period
Eastern United States. c. 1880–1910.

Comment
While some may actually have been made by tramps or hobos, most so-called tramp-art pieces were made by miners, lumberjacks, itinerant craftsmen, or anyone who had a penknife and liked to whittle. The maker of this unusual box tried to anticipate all the needs of a letter writer. The 2 small front drawers are just the right size for postage stamps, and the 2 ink bottles fit snugly into their own compartment to help prevent spillage. Objects made in this layered, carved style range from picture frames and boxes to full-size tall-case clocks and furniture.

Hints for Collectors
Boxes of all sorts are the most common type of tramp art, with picture and mirror frames also prevalent. This small desktop box is a one-of-a-kind piece, however, and, as such, is likely to be priced higher than more typical pieces.

282 House-shaped box

Description
Small box shaped and painted like a house. Walls and 2 chimneys with painted brick pattern. Window frames, shutters, front door, and eaves in white. Narrow front porch with 3 white posts supporting overhanging roof; gray porch floor. Peaked gray roof lined to imitate shingles. Roof lifts off to reveal interior. Nail construction. Signed and dated.

Materials and Dimensions
Painted wood. Wire nails. Height: 6⅞″. Length: 5⅝″. Width: 6″.

Locality and Period
Made by M. Rumbaugh, Lancaster County, Pennsylvania. c. 1979.

Comment
Throughout America, people who enjoy woodworking have made domestic objects of amazing variety. Boxes have been fashioned in almost every imaginable form, from a book or a log cabin to a trunk or an egg. The rectangular shape of houses made them particularly adaptable as box designs. Despite their overall primitive design, many were carefully detailed—note the painted front door panels and the tiny door latch on the example shown here.

Hints for Collectors
In the 19th century many folk art objects were hand-carved or whittled. Though this box was cut with modern tools, its charm lies in its meticulous handwork. Such 20th-century pieces are inexpensive, well within the means of beginning collectors. A fine wax may sometimes be used to protect painted and decorated wooden surfaces.

283 House-shaped display case

Description
Large 3-story structure with detachable steeple trimmed in red and blue; golden sphere atop blue spire, open windows and exterior walkways below. Detachable second story in white with red trim and red Spanish-style roofing; open windows and walkways on second floor, surrounded by red, white, and blue balustrade. Bottom story, white with red trim, with paired glass windows on each side. Brightly colored original paint. Nail construction.

Materials and Dimensions
Painted wood. Gesso. Glass. Wire nails. Height: 31″. Length: 15″. Width: 13½″.

Locality and Period
Michigan. c. 1900–10.

Comment
This delightful miniature building, festively painted in patriotic colors, was once displayed on the countertop of a candy store. There it must have delighted many children, particularly the lucky ones allowed to remove the top and fish out the sweets visible through its windows. Its original paint and good condition, however, suggest that this piece was not in use very long.

Hints for Collectors
Charming and unusual pieces are of great interest to collectors, especially if, like this example, they can still be used. If you plan to use a piece of folk art, avoid excessive restoration costs by selecting an object that is still in good condition. What might at first seem an inexpensive acquisition can hold some unpleasant surprises for a collector who does not consider the estimated cost of repairs along with the purchase price.

Showcase

Description
Wooden showcase with 2 circular rotating levels, each fitted with 6 chased-brass frames alternating with 6 ivory half-columns. Topped by large ivory finial in center, 6 smaller urn-shaped knobs around edge, and carved rim; 6 knobs also around second level. Silver handle between levels allows frames to turn. Circular base topped by ivory balustrade. 4 disguised drawers are unlocked by turning finial; ivory pulls on non-opening sections. Raised on 4 scroll-cut ivory feet with tortoiseshell pegs. Label on bottom signed, dated, and inscribed.

Materials and Dimensions
Mahogany. Whale ivory. Brass. Velvet. Silver. Tortoiseshell. Height: 17″. Diameter of base: 11½″.

Locality and Period
Made by William Chappell. New Bedford, Massachusetts. 1855.

Comment
Like most scrimshaw objects, this superb showcase was fashioned at sea. Its maker, on board the *Saratoga*, wrote on its label: "A present to Ephraim Harding, Master of the Ship *Saratoga* of New Bedford, Mass. This miniature 'Show Case' was designed and manufactured by the undersigned during a whaling voyage in the Northern Ocean and under many disadvantages; hence the Charitable will overlook the many imperfections."

Hints for Collectors
Large scrimshaw objects are exceedingly rare and much desired by collectors, so many such pieces have been faked. To imitate the yellow patina of age, new pieces are sometimes stained with oil, tea, or tobacco juice; tinted plastic fakes also exist. Under ultraviolet light, whale ivory will glow, but plastic will not.

285 Cutwork wall box

Description
Hanging storage piece with long open box protruding across bottom. Box front slanting outward, painted green, with 3 applied squares and molded edges in darker shade. One-piece wooden back having cutout inverted crescent above circular hole; at top, 2 large silhouettes of birds with yellow beaks, eyes, and feathers. Nail construction.

Materials and Dimensions
Pine. Painted. Iron-wire nails. Height: 9″. Length: 9″. Depth: 2½″.

Locality and Period
Probably Pennsylvania or New England. c. 1900–30.

Comment
Shelves or storage boxes to be hung on the wall have been common in America as far back as the Colonial era. Early examples include spoon racks, pipe racks, and candle boxes, some elaborately carved and painted. The wall box shown here, though of fairly recent vintage, is a fine folk sculpture that has the kind of traditional folk decoration found on earlier pieces.

Hints for Collectors
This extraordinary wall box is distinguished by its handsome cutout and painted birds. The 2-tone feathering, applied molding, and graceful overall proportions make it more valuable than many similar early 20th-century pieces. Though its iron-wire nails confirm that this box was made in the early 20th century, its fine design and execution might lead a collector to mistake it for a much earlier piece.

286 Cutwork hanging shelf

Description
Hanging shelf with painted cutout decoration; on upper back, red birds with black wings, eyes, and beaks, surrounded by a heart and abstract shapes. Semicircular shelf attached beneath birds, supported by scroll-cut bracket set at right angle to wall and shelf. Hole at top for hanging. Nail construction.

Materials and Dimensions
Pine. Painted and shellacked. Iron cut nails. Height: 17½″. Length: 15″. Depth: 7½″.

Locality and Period
Probably Pennsylvania or New England. c. 1870–90.

Comment
Usually referred to as fretwork, elaborate cutwork like that on this shelf was done with a fretsaw. While fretwork is seen mainly on shelves, it appears also occasionally on boxes and on mirror or picture frames. Wood carving in home workshops, popular during the latter half of the 19th century, was the subject of many articles and manuals; for example, *Fret Cutting and Perforated Carving*, published in 1869, gave patterns for making pieces similar to this wall shelf.

Hints for Collectors
Small fretwork hanging storage pieces, usually with no more than 2 shelves, ranged from elaborate Victorian examples to country-style pieces like this one. Its bird- and heart-shaped forms suggest a Pennsylvania origin, as both motifs occur often on objects made in that region. The hardware on a piece is sometimes helpful in dating it; although designs like the one shown were made in home workshops until the 1930s, the presence of cut nails on this example rather than wire ones suggests an earlier date.

287 Hanging figural cigar holder

Description
Shield-shaped wall plaque with carved figure of black man in blue and white clothes mounted on top; plaque with attached container in form of large yellow acorn with black crosshatched rim, flanked by pair of small black cylinders. "Habanas" (Havana cigars) incised across acorn. At right, sandpaper for striking matches. Hole at top center of shield for mounting. Screw construction.

Materials and Dimensions
Walnut. Painted. Iron screws. Height: 9″. Length: 7¼″. Depth: 2½″.

Locality and Period
Eastern United States. c. 1900–25.

Comment
This small folk object was probably made in a home workshop. The acorn-shaped cup was for cigars, and the side compartments held wooden matches to be struck on the attached sandpaper. Thousands of small objects like this were turned out by amateur craftsmen, but only a fraction of them were as original and eye-catching as this piece.

Hints for Collectors
The hand-carved figure, doll-like and somewhat crude, gives this piece its unique charm. A human form on any utilitarian object—whether a box, shelf, cookie mold, or nutcracker—generally adds to its value as well as to its appeal. Pieces like this sometimes turn up in out-of-the-way thrift shops or at yard sales and flea markets, where they can usually be bought cheaply.

288 **Hanging shelf with drawer**

Description
Saw-cut shelf with rectangular overhanging top having molded edges. Scrollwork brackets flanking single shallow drawer with 2 knobs and vertical center molding. Back decorated with notch-carved edges extending out beyond brackets and forming scalloped skirt at rear below drawer. Holes at sides and in skirt for mounting on wall. Penciled inscription inside drawer, "L. Stevens, W. Derby, Vt."

Materials and Dimensions
Pine and ash. Iron nails. Height: 12¼″. Length: 16″. Depth: 6¼″.

Locality and Period
Vermont. c. 1885–1900.

Comment
An odd combination of elements, this piece combines the elaborate scrollwork and scalloped skirt usually found on earlier high-style furniture with the notch carving typical of tramp art. In the tramp-art tradition, its maker recycled found materials—old wooden boxes that once held lard pails. The boards retain their original stenciled advertisements; the drawer bears the penciled name of the maker or an early owner.

Hints for Collectors
Informal pieces like this, often called "country" furnishings, have great appeal for folk art collectors because of their eccentric mixture of styles. This shelf was made by someone who seems to have adapted prevailing Victorian eclecticism to his own rural tastes. Such small late 19th-century pieces can still be bought quite inexpensively but, like earlier country pieces, they will probably increase in value.

Kitchenware

While countless types of kitchen utensils for cooking, baking, and serving have been produced for American households over the centuries, only some of these practical objects are considered folk art. The pieces included in this section are distinctive in one way or another: some are handmade or fashioned from fine materials; others are particularly well shaped or handsomely decorated.

The first settlers brought with them their utensils from Europe. The greatest changes in kitchenware took place in the 19th century, when these objects began to be crafted in new materials and forms; earlier methods of carving and decoration were influenced by the transplanted traditions of new immigrants and by mass production, which made much handwork uneconomical after about the 1850s.

Woodenware

In the American colonies, where wood was abundant and woodworking a common skill, most early kitchenware, except in some wealthy households, was lathe-turned or carved out of wood. Wooden ladles, scoops, dippers, open salt dishes, bowls, and trenchers (wooden plates) were all used during the 17th and 18th centuries, but few of them have survived outside historical-society and museum collections. Most existing woodenware, also called treen or treenware, dates from the 19th century. The finest examples have either painted or carved decoration or both.

Of all wooden objects, perhaps the most desirable are those made of wood burl, an abnormal growth on certain trees that has a bold irregular grain. Burled-wood objects, such as rolling pins, bowls, and scoops, are particularly desirable. The special wooden molds used by German immigrants for their springerle and marzipan cookies are also in demand.

Metalware

Household utensils made of metals such as tin, iron, copper, or brass were necessary for cooking and other work in which wood was impractical. Teakettles, toasters, waffle irons, and the like had to be wrought or cast in metal to withstand the intense heat of an open hearth. Cooking over an open fire required long-handled tools—spatulas, forks, and ladles to keep the cook some distance from the flames. Early long-handled toasters, mostly made of wrought iron, often had swivel bases so that bread could be toasted on both sides. The best examples were as decorative as they were useful.

Made in America as early as 1740, tinware was unpainted at first, but by about 1810 it was often painted or decorated in many ways. A number of small family-run tinware workshops sprang up, particularly in Connecticut, New York, Maine, and Pennsylvania; these supplied many of the serving and bread trays, teapots, and coffeepots sold or bartered by the numerous peddlers traveling south and west.

Scrimshaw

In the 19th century whale ivory, whalebone, and walrus ivory were all popular materials for kitchen utensils, particularly rolling pins and pie crimpers (also called jagging wheels). The latter were often elaborately carved and occasionally featured brass wheels or silver fittings. Elegant dippers were sometimes made of whalebone or whale ivory combined with fine wood or a carved coconut-shell bowl, producing an exotic effect rarely encountered in American folk art.

289 Painted tin tray

Description
Octagonal tray with angled rim, rolled lip, and 2 cutout handles. Black lacquer overall, decorated with multicolored theorem painting of fruit in brown bowl: watermelon, banana, strawberries, grapes, cherries, apples, peaches, and plums; also foliage. Thin gold outline painted around handles.

Materials and Dimensions
Tin. Lacquered and painted. Length: 26″. Width: 18⅜″. Depth: 1½″.

Locality and Period
Vermont. c. 1870–80.

Comment
Although painted American tinware like the tray shown here is often referred to as toleware, that term refers more accurately to plain or decorated antique French tinware. Household objects of all kinds were decorated in this way from about 1810 to 1900. Most had black backgrounds, but red, yellow, and white grounds were sometimes used. While many designs were executed freehand, the bowl of fruit on this tray was executed with stencils, as were the theorem paintings done on paper or velvet by young ladies during the same period.

Hints for Collectors
Painted tinware has been in great demand since the 1930s and is therefore quite costly today. Since some people try to pass off recent examples as antiques, look carefully for authentic signs of age. The lacquered background on a 19th-century piece will usually have fine scratches and worn areas, and the oil paint will show a network of hairline cracks. Such customary signs of age—unlike loss of a large part of the design—do not appreciably lessen the value of a piece.

290 **Painted tin tray**

Description
Rectangular tray with rounded corners, convex rim, and 2 cutout handles. Black lacquer overall, with central shell motifs stenciled in gold and branchlike lines drawn freehand in bright red; double gold lines as borders. Floral designs and crosshatched rectangles stenciled in gold on rim.

Materials and Dimensions
Tin. Lacquered and painted. Length: 25⅞". Width: 19⅛". Depth: 1⅜".

Locality and Period
Possibly made by Goodrich and Thompson of Berlin, Connecticut. c. 1845.

Comment
About 1740, the brothers Edward and William Pattison came from Ireland to Berlin, Connecticut, where they produced the first American-made tin household utensils. Until about 1900, tinware remained a popular American product, sold all over the country by door-to-door peddlers who got their wares from tinsmiths in New York, Pennsylvania, and New England. The earliest tinware was unpainted, but soon paint and other decoration such as piercing and punching became common.

Hints for Collectors
Whether painted freehand or with stencils, well-decorated antique tinware is comparatively expensive, particularly those rare examples signed by or attributed to specific artisans. Pieces with red or yellow backgrounds are far more valuable than those with the more common black backgrounds.

291 Painted tin bread basket or bun tray

Description
Flat-bottomed oval tray with flared sides and slightly raised ends. Wide white band painted around inside of rim and decorated with red fruit and green leaves. Traces of crystallized decoration below band. Exterior lacquered black.

Materials and Dimensions
Tin. Lacquered and painted. Height: 3″. Length: 12″. Width: 7″.

Locality and Period
Pennsylvania, New York, or New England. c. 1840–60.

Comment
The piece shown here has traits found on tinware made in several areas, but it cannot be attributed to any one maker. Motifs of fruit or flowers painted over a solid white band are characteristic of tinware, or toleware, made in Connecticut as well as of pieces made by the Butler family of Greenville, New York. The shiny traces inside this tray are remnants of a crystallized background made by treating the bare metal with acid, which etches a glistening design into the surface. Crystallized surfaces are often associated with tinware crafted by Pennsylvania Germans.

Hints for Collectors
Experts have begun to identify more and more designs as the work of certain tinware decorators. Determining the maker or decorator of an undocumented piece is, however, still very difficult. The value of a piece is increased considerably only by positive identification. Anyone interested in painted tinware should study the definitive books on the subject and examine pieces at museums and in historic houses in the Northeast.

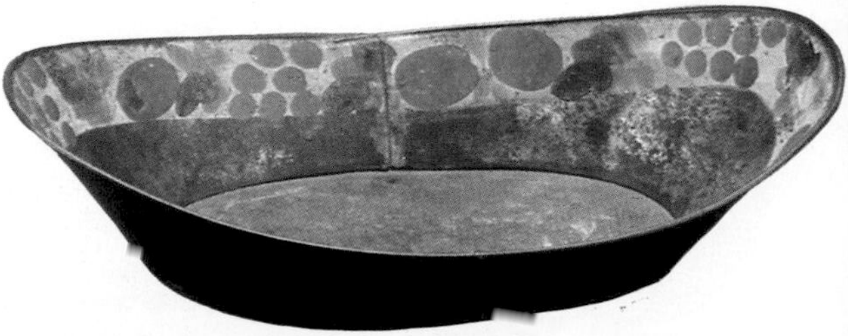

292 Wooden bowl

Description
Hand-carved rectangular bowl with sloping sides and plain rim and base. Crack at one corner of rim repaired with staple. Exterior painted light blue over red.

Materials and Dimensions
Maple. Painted. Wrought-iron staple. Height: 4¾″. Length: 22¾″. Width: 11¼″.

Locality and Period
New England. c. 1840–60.

Comment
The first settlers in America ate from wooden plates called trenchers, but as time passed and life began to allow for small luxuries, pewter and ceramic plates replaced wooden ones. Wooden bowls, however, were still used for preparing and chopping certain foods throughout the 19th century, and oblong examples like the one shown here generally continued to be called trenchers.

Hints for Collectors
Wooden household objects, often called treenware, are among the most difficult to date; a fairly new piece, given hard use, will soon look worn and may easily be mistaken for a much older one. Wooden bowls similar to this piece are still being made, and many have been imported from Europe. This bowl, however, with its early wrought-iron staple, the network of fine lines on its inner surface (the result of much chopping), and brittle paint, is clearly old. Its pleasing shape, satiny texture, and the lightness of its aged wood make this piece particularly desirable.

293 Wooden scoop

Description
One-piece hand-carved scoop with wide shallow bowl shaped like a squared circle. Long thick handle rising at an angle, then tapering slightly to square knob at end.

Materials and Dimensions
Maple burl. Overall length: 9¼″. Width of bowl: 7¼″. Depth: 4¾″.

Locality and Period
New England. c. 1840–70.

Comment
Burled wood, a hard knotty growth or excrescence with a highly mottled grain, is found primarily in elm, ash, and maple trees. Much less common than normal healthy wood, it is quite rare in wooden kitchenware. The decorative grain and interesting texture of the burl make it an attractive medium; thus, the Indians and the colonists as well as many 19th-century Americans prized this wood and used it on some of their finest carved bowls, trenchers, and scoops.

Hints for Collectors
Hand-carved scoops in almost any wood are fairly rare, and those of burled wood exceptionally so. In fact, almost any burled-wood object will command a premium. This outstanding example would appeal to most collectors because of its sculptural quality and unusual rich grain. The more common woodenware pieces, however, are difficult to appraise and should be approached cautiously. With experience, a collector will develop a sense of what old wood should look and feel like. Beginning collectors of early woodenware should start out by buying from one of the many reliable dealers who specialize in such objects.

294 **Wooden spoon and ladle**

Description
Left: Small hand-carved spoon with circular bowl. Rounded handle wider and flatter near bowl. Carved ball-in-cage ornament at end of handle; cage, with circular holes in 4 sides, tapered toward tip. Carved notches on cage and on handle near bowl.
Right: Hand-carved ladle with oval bowl. Thick rounded handle curving back in hook shape at top and tapering to end.

Materials and Dimensions
Left: Birch. Overall length: 7″. Width of bowl: 2½″. Depth: ½″.
Right: Pine. Length: 11½″. Width: 4″. Depth: 2½″.

Locality and Period
Left: Connecticut. c. 1880–1900. *Right:* Ohio. c. 1850–75.

Comment
The first European settlers in America brought wooden plates and spoons with them, but only a few such early pieces have survived; most woodenware now on the market dates from the 19th or, in many cases, 20th century. Metal spoons had largely replaced wooden ones by the end of the 19th century, but manufacturers still offered wooden ladles at about 10 cents each, while country people continued to carve their own.

Hints for Collectors
Both of these pieces exhibit the characteristic roughness of hand carving, as well as certain details, such as the ball-in-cage ornament and the odd-shaped handle, possible only on handmade pieces. Like most wooden kitchen utensils, these are difficult to date exactly. Heavy use and contact with food and water can greatly alter the appearance of wood, so that signs of wear are no guarantee of age. The spoon with the ball-in-cage carving is valuable because some collectors specialize in such "all-of-a-piece" carvings and will pay a premium for them.

295 **Shaker wooden dipper**

Description
Circular bowl with straight sides and flat bottom; vertical seam. Long turned handle with narrow neck and bulbous tip. Section of handle nearest bowl much thicker in diameter. Nail and screw construction.

Materials and Dimensions
Pine, ash, and maple. Iron nails and screws. Overall length: 17″. Height of bowl: 4″. Diameter: 7½″.

Locality and Period
Possibly Canterbury or Enfield, New Hampshire. c. 1880.

Comment
Like the oval boxes made by Shakers (*see* 276), this dipper has a pine bottom and maple sides and is constructed with pliable pieces of wood almost as thin as those used for veneering; this permitted the shaping of the sides. While the bowl surface is fairly rough, the fine craftsmanship and subtle shape of the long handle are characteristic of Shaker pieces. This example was left unfinished, but many similar pieces were painted.

Hints for Collectors
Not all simple household utensils were made by Shakers, so it is hard to be certain that a piece is of Shaker origin unless it is marked or comes with reliable documentation. This dipper's graceful handle and lack of unnecessary ornamentation do, however, strongly suggest Shaker origin. Because they have become so popular with collectors during the past decade, authenticated Shaker objects are almost impossible to find outside of shops specializing in them. Similar but undocumented items generally sell for considerably less.

296 **Scrimshaw dipper**

Description
Dipper with coconut-shell bowl carved with eagle grasping shield inscribed "Union"; other motifs include roses, branches, and 2 birds, and inscription "On board of the whaling bark Stafford. September 1871." Curved wooden handle with inlay of whale ivory and abalone shell attached by pins. Handle joined to bowl by heart-shaped ivory section and pins.

Materials and Dimensions
Coconut shell. Ebony. Whale ivory. Abalone. Copper pins. Overall length: 13″. Height of bowl: 5″. Diameter: 4″.

Locality and Period
New England. 1871.

Comment
Part of the appeal of scrimshaw is its association with the sea and whaling voyages. The carved coconut bowl on this dipper adds to its exotic quality. Few scrimshaw dippers have engraved bowls, as does this piece, but most have fancy handles made of or inlaid with whalebone, whale or walrus ivory, or pewter.

Hints for Collectors
While wooden dippers were a common household object, scrimshaw dippers, particularly those as ornate as this example, were far less common and would probably have been reserved for special occasions in well-to-do households. The one shown here was purchased in the Midwest, where scrimshaw often turns up. Though almost all early scrimshaw came originally from New England—primarily Massachusetts, where most whaling ships were berthed—many whalers migrated to the Midwest and West Coast in the late 19th century, bringing their scrimshaw and other family treasures with them.

297 Copper teakettle

Description
Circular kettle with gooseneck spout, straight sides, and domed lid topped by loop finial. Swing handle with wide flat top, narrowing and curving inward to loops attached at sides of kettle. Dovetailed seams; riveted handle.

Materials and Dimensions
Copper. Brass solder. Lead lining. Height (without handle): 9¾″. Length (with spout): 11″. Diameter: 6¾″.

Locality and Period
Probably the Northeast or Midwest. c. 1860–1900.

Comment
Though copper teakettles were made in America as early as the 18th century, most were imported from England or Scandinavia. A typical American form had a flaring gooseneck spout and a more rotund body than the kettle shown here. The national origin of a kettle can seldom be determined by makers' marks, since these are rare. But European forms do differ from American ones. If this kettle had a hinged cover on its spout, for instance, it would probably be Scandinavian; a letter O stamped on the handle would confirm this attribution.

Hints for Collectors
Distinguishing an American-made copper kettle of the 18th or 19th century from an imported one of the same period is almost impossible for a novice. Even the ability to identify such construction methods as the dovetailing evident here does not guarantee positive determination of age and origin, since similar techniques have been used by coppersmiths here and abroad right up to the present. A beginning collector should rely on a reputable dealer until fully familiar with the forms and subtleties of copper objects.

298

Adirondack or rustic wooden tankard

Description
Plain bark-covered tankard with turned neck and bent twig handle. Circular lid lathe-turned, bark-covered on top, and attached by wooden pin to top of handle. Nail and screw construction.

Materials and Dimensions
Birch. Machine-made nails and screws. Height: 6⅜″. Diameter: 3½″.

Locality and Period
New York State or Great Lakes region. c. 1900–50.

Comment
Because bark-covered furniture and other rustic wooden wares, including tankards such as the one shown here, were made by amateur craftsmen in the Adirondack Mountain region of New York State, they are often called "Adirondack" objects. They were, however, also made in rural areas around the Great Lakes, in the South, and in other parts of the country, and are still being made today. This piece was probably crafted for the maker's own use; others, usually made in professional workshops, were produced for sale to summer tourists.

Hints for Collectors
While many rustic household objects and pieces of furniture were made and sold in the first half of the 20th century (and continue to be sold as souvenirs today), few are as well conceived and executed as this piece. The balance of lid, handle, and turned neck creates a pleasing form, making this a fine example of the so-called Adirondack style. Rustic objects sometimes turn up for very little money at yard sales or flea markets, but shop dealers are usually knowledgeable enough not to let them go cheaply.

299 **Wooden salt dish**

Description
Carved and painted open salt dish on pedestal. Top section circular, decorated with 2 incised stars and heart enclosed by circles; incised zigzag border along top and bottom rims. Conical base with partially flattened sides. Traces of old red paint.

Materials and Dimensions
Ash burl. Painted. Height: 6¼″. Diameter of top: 4¼″.

Locality and Period
Pennsylvania. c. 1780–1820.

Comment
In early America, salt was a precious commodity, derived either from sea water or underground mineral deposits. It was bought in coarse crystals and then ground into fine particles. When used for cooking, it was stored in a rectangular wall box near the fireplace. Salt was also served at the dining table: the first American salt dishes (5″ to 6″ in diameter) were shared by all family members and called "master salts"; only in the late 17th century did individual salt dishes at tables become common. The example shown here was probably used communally. Though some salt dishes had lids, most did not.

Hints for Collectors
The primitive salt dish shown here has the painted and incised decoration typical of pieces made in rural Pennsylvania. Although most of the paint has worn away, the fact that it has handmade decoration in any condition adds to the value of the piece. In addition, the form of this example is unlike that of most open salts, which had sloping sides and shallower bowls; and the base, an optional feature, was usually shorter. It is therefore a fairly valuable piece by virtue of its age, decoration, and unique form. The burled wood adds further to its value.

300

Cast-iron mortar and pestle

Description
Chalice-shaped metal mortar with thick rounded rim and impressed rings around bottom of bowl. Narrow pedestal ending in circular base slightly larger in diameter than bowl. Metal pestle with flattened buttonlike top and smoothly shaped body.

Materials and Dimensions
Cast iron. Mortar height: 4¼″. Diameter of base: 3½″. Pestle length: 4¼″. Diameter of top: 1½″.

Locality and Period
Probably the Northeast. c. 1850–1900.

Comment
Mortars and pestles have been used since ancient times. They were found in almost every 18th- and 19th-century American household and were used to pulverize herbs and spices, crush sugar or salt, mash vegetables, or even grind coffee beans. This cast-iron example is somewhat unusual; brass, wood, marble, or bronze models were more common. Some mortars and pestles were made of ironstone pottery in West Virginia, and others of Parian ware, an unglazed porcelain popular in Vermont in the second half of the 19th century.

Hints for Collectors
Because mortars and pestles were made in diverse materials and had subtle variations in shape, an interesting collection of them can be assembled. Many were imported from Europe, some fairly recently, and these are generally less valuable than examples made in this country. Those rare American pieces that have makers' marks command a premium.

301 Wooden butter mold and stamp

Description
Left: 2-piece mold with cup-shaped case and cylindrical plunger. Circular bottom of plunger incised in wheat-sheaf design (not visible). Lathe turnings around case. Mushroom-shaped knob atop plunger. *Right:* Stamp with incised leaf design bordered by 4 concentric circles. Small turned handle (not visible).

Materials and Dimensions
Left: Maple. Height: 4¼″. Diameter: 4″. *Right:* Birch. Height: 3½″. Diameter: 3″.

Locality and Period
Probably New England or Pennsylvania. c. 1875–1920.

Comment
As early as the 17th century and continuing until the 1920s in some areas, butter was made at home. Both housewives and dairy farmers marked their output with a design both for identification and decoration. Stamps (also called prints) and molds were incised with flowers or leaves that created relief designs on the butter. At first, these patterns were hand-carved by farmers during the long winter; by about 1850 most, including those shown here, were factory-made, with their designs pressed by machines, though some farmers continued to carve their own.

Hints for Collectors
Butter molds and prints were made in a wide range of designs, most commonly cows, flowers, fruit, and wheat sheaves. The most valuable are hand-carved examples with unique designs; these tend to be rougher-looking than factory-made ones, and the tool marks left in chipping away the wood may often still be visible. The current great demand for molds and prints has led to high prices for the best pieces.

302 Tin cookie cutters

Description
Tin cookie cutters with projecting strips shaped like chicken, dog, and dove. Rectangular or shaped backs, solid except for circular hole in center to allow air to escape as dough is cut. Curved handle on top. Soldered construction.

Materials and Dimensions
Tin. Height: 2⅜″ to 2⅝″. Length: 3½″ to 3¾″. Depth: ⅜″ to ½″.

Locality and Period
Pennsylvania. c. 1860–1900.

Comment
Rural Pennsylvania tinsmiths, also called whitesmiths, made tin cookie cutters in a large variety of shapes, the more functional ones with fairly simple outlines that cut out well-defined forms. Housewives cherished their favorite cookie cutters, especially those in unusual designs, and sometimes traded their cookies with neighbors so as to be able to serve as varied an assortment as possible.

Hints for Collectors
Handmade 19th-century cookie cutters, particularly those with human figures or unusual designs such as a peacock or Victorian heart-and-hand, are much sought after by collectors and can be quite costly. The more common animal shapes—deer, horses, birds, or fish—that were often made by machine after about 1900 are relatively inexpensive. Older cutters are generally heavier and have a thick continuous outline or large dabs of solder; more recent ones are usually lighter in weight and have a thinner line of solder attaching the cutting edge to the backing.

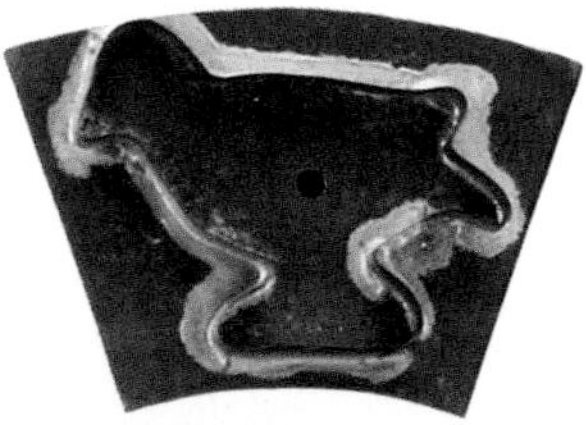

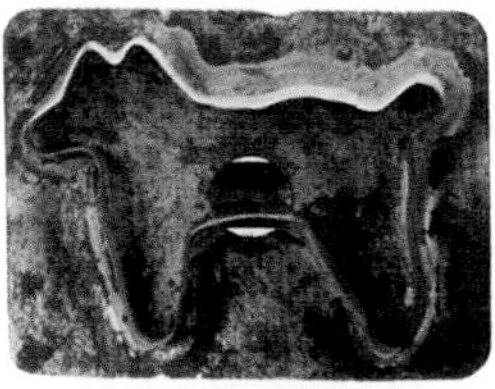

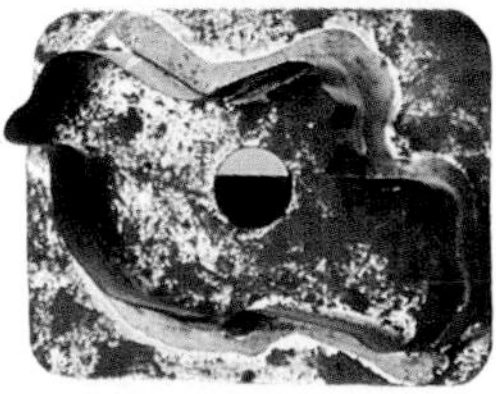

303 Carved springerle board

Description
Long rectangular cookie mold (both sides shown). *Front:* 4 carved men; top 2 carrying shoulder yokes with buckets hanging from ends; bottom 2 wearing plumed hats, one man in profile, the other full front. *Back:* 2 upper blocks each carved with paired men; coat of arms between figures in top panel; third block with fully rigged sailing ship; boar in bottom panel. Name of early owner and date branded on side.

Materials and Dimensions
Walnut. Length: 23½″. Width: 4½″. Thickness: 1⅛″.

Locality and Period
Probably Pennsylvania. 1861.

Comment
Wooden molds of all kinds, including those for making candies, cookies, and cakes, were common in Europe and were brought to this country by the early colonists. The Pennsylvania-German settlers, in particular, baked hard springerle cakes or cookies in molds such as the one shown here. Since dough, like butter, easily took the impression of a mold, beautifully decorated cakes could be created with minimum effort.

Hints for Collectors
Antique springerle molds are fairly uncommon today. Because they were used primarily by German immigrants, not many were made and, being fairly fragile, relatively few have survived. The presence of a date and signature (almost certainly the owner's) make this example especially desirable. While these molds are utilitarian kitchen utensils, they are raised to the level of folk art by the exceptional skill and imagination of their carvers.

304 Carved springerle boards

Description
Rectangular wooden cookie molds. *Left:* 8 carvings of fruit, flowers, animals, and houses, separated by double-line grid; name of early owner branded on back. *Right:* 6 carvings of flower, cherries, deer head, cornucopia, castle, and ship, all separated by grid of 4 incised lines.

Materials and Dimensions
Left: Birch. Length: $7\frac{5}{8}''$. Width: $2\frac{7}{8}''$. Thickness: $\frac{9}{16}''$.
Right: Cherry. Length: $6\frac{1}{2}''$. Width: $3\frac{1}{8}''$. Thickness: $\frac{1}{2}''$.

Locality and Period
Pennsylvania. c. 1850–70.

Comment
Every Pennsylvania-German home had wooden springerle and marzipan molds used to make traditional holiday cakes. Stiff dough was rolled thin and pressed into the mold so that, when baked, the recessed designs came out clearly in low relief. The lines between the individual carvings on the molds shown here make the single large cake easily divisible into 6 or 8 smaller cookies, each with a different design.

Hints for Collectors
Besides the hand-carved springerle molds brought to Pennsylvania by immigrants from Germany, molds for other types of cakes were brought to this country from Holland, Switzerland, and Austria; their long narrow shapes and European woods often distinguish them from molds carved in America. Later in the 19th century, tin molds replaced wooden ones because the latter required more time and skill to craft. Since relatively few wooden molds were made in America, those that come on the market today are generally expensive.

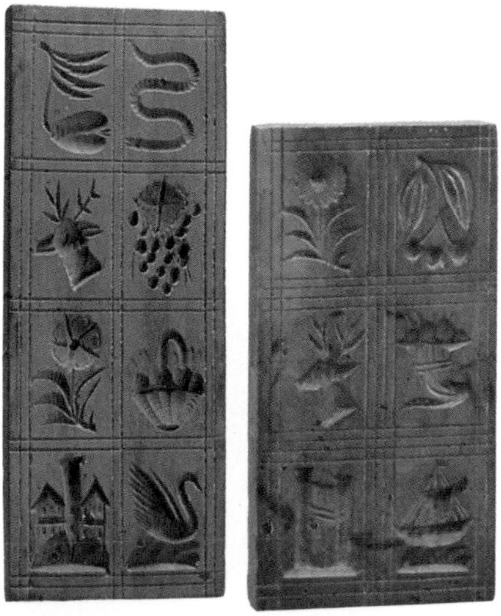

305 Tin candle mold

Description
Tin mold consisting of 2 parallel rows of 6 slender cylinders with tapered bottoms set in rectangular base. Cylinders are open at top and set inside rectangular frame with raised rim. Flat loop handle at top right. Soldered construction.

Materials and Dimensions
Tin. Height: 9¾". Length: 11". Width: 3".

Locality and Period
The Northeast or Midwest. c. 1850–1900.

Comment
Candles were traditionally made in the fall, when animals were slaughtered and their tallow was available. By 1750, candles were already being produced in one Massachusetts factory, but many people continued making their own late into the 19th century. Candles were dipped by hand or formed in molds like the one shown here, either by housewives or by itinerant candlemakers who went from house to house. Most molds were tin or pewter, though pottery ones also existed.

Hints for Collectors
Molds vary in size from those for making single candles to huge frames that hold as many as 8 dozen at a time. Tin molds are the most common, the pewter and pottery forms being rare. The current interest in colonial accessories has led to the manufacture of large numbers of reproduction tin candle molds. Though these generally look new and shiny and have very thin soldering lines, after a few years they begin to dull and might be mistaken for old ones by an inexperienced collector. Originals should have heavy soldering lines and appropriate signs of wear.

306 Redware candle mold

Description
Large wooden frame with 12 tubular pottery molds (7 shown) having threaded tops; bottoms tapering to blunt points. Frame made of 2 wide end planks joined by 2 boards of equal width, with 12 holes to hold tubes. Narrow side strips along top board. Cutout pointed arches on bottoms of end planks. Stamped "MEDLEY."

Materials and Dimensions
Red earthenware; unglazed exterior, clear lead glaze inside. Pine. Iron cut nails. Frame height: 13″; length: 14″; width: 5″. Tube length: 9″; diameter: 1½″.

Locality and Period
Probably New York State; similar examples made in New England and Pennsylvania. c. 1830–50.

Comment
Earthenware candle molds were somewhat uncommon. An 1832 inventory of the potter Ezra Wilcox of Ontario County, New York, for example, refers to a "stand of candle molds," and his son Alvin regularly advertised ceramic molds during the 1850s. Few pottery candle molds have survived, however, and those with their wooden frames intact are particularly rare.

Hints for Collectors
Almost all the known redware candle molds can be traced to upstate New York. The tubes shown here were stamped by an undocumented maker but, since they are very similar to those made by Wilcox, were probably made in New York State. Any redware candle mold is quite rare, and those with a potter's mark are particularly desirable. Single tubes, often overlooked or unrecognized by collectors, are also valuable, though not nearly so high-priced as sets with original stands.

307 Make-do vegetable grater

Description
Tin grater shaped like open-ended cone, having roughly punched surface. Nailed to thick hand-carved wooden handle. Faint V-shaped mark (not visible) where spout was formerly attached.

Materials and Dimensions
Tin. Oak or hickory. Iron nails. Overall height: 13″. Cone height: 5½″. Width of bottom: 4¼″.

Locality and Period
Connecticut. c. 1875–1900.

Comment
One-of-a-kind pieces like this are called "make-do" because their creators made them with whatever materials they had at hand. This utensil, for instance, was created from a discarded tin coffeepot; the spout and bottom of the pot were removed, and the remaining part probably flattened so that holes could be punched from the inside surface outward, thus creating rough edges for grating. This improvised grater is evidence that no object, not even a plain tin coffeepot, went to waste if some ingenious way to recycle it could be found.

Hints for Collectors
Not all collectors are attracted to "make-do" objects, but those with a special interest in how people lived in the 19th century and how resourceful they could be will consider such pieces real prizes. The work of some clever tinkerer, this simple piece has special character—a quality not often found in plain kitchen implements. The appeal here is not just in the object itself but also in the self-reliant instinct that prompted its creation.

308 **Cast-iron meat tenderizer**

Description
Single-handled utensil with roller having continuous rows of pyramid-shaped teeth. Roller revolving on axle set in U-shaped holder. Short rounded wooden handle, shaped to provide a better grip.

Materials and Dimensions
Cast-iron roller and frame; iron axle. Maple. Length: 9¼". Width: 7". Diameter of roller: 3¼".

Locality and Period
The Northeast or Midwest. c. 1880–1900.

Comment
Though the example shown here dates from the late 19th century, implements to tenderize meat were invented much earlier. Colonists in the 17th century utilized one-piece wooden pounders with grooved sides and a flat bottom, as well as wooden mallets with the bottom carved in a raised pattern much like that on the metal roller of this tenderizer. Used to soften a piece of meat before cooking, such tools were sometimes called steak maulers around the turn of the century.

Hints for Collectors
As handmade 18th- and early 19th-century kitchen tools become increasingly rare and expensive, mass-produced mechanical gadgets like this tenderizer have gained in popularity with collectors, though many would deny that these are true folk art. With kitchen objects from as late as the 1920s and 1930s now being collected, those from the late 19th century are rapidly increasing in value. Look for simple utensils with nicely patterned surfaces—like this faceted roller—and for interesting shapes or unusual materials.

309 Wooden rolling pin

Description
Lathe-turned rolling pin made from single piece of wood. Roller with uniform diameter along entire length. Long paired handles with narrow necks and bulbous ends.

Materials and Dimensions
Tiger maple. Length: 18½″. Diameter: 2½″.

Locality and Period
New England. c. 1870–90.

Comment
Wooden rolling pins have been in use in America since the 17th century. The earliest versions had no handles; then came single-handled pins, and finally the double-handled ones still used today. By the 1880s rolling pins with revolving handles were being manufactured commercially; in 1902 Sears Roebuck was offering them at 6 cents apiece. Hollow ceramic rolling pins—some decorated with flowers, others with flour advertisements—were made in the early 20th century; these were good for pastry-making since, like glass examples, they could be filled with cold water to keep the pastry dough cool while it was being worked.

Hints for Collectors
Early one-of-a-kind rolling pins, such as the example shown here, are much rarer than factory-made ones from the late 19th and early 20th centuries. The single-unit construction and beautiful graining accentuating the shape of this roller and its handles make it highly desirable. Examples made of plain maple or cherry would be considerably less valuable. Though such utensils can still be used, this may not be advisable since oils from the pastry dough may further darken the wood, obscuring the grain.

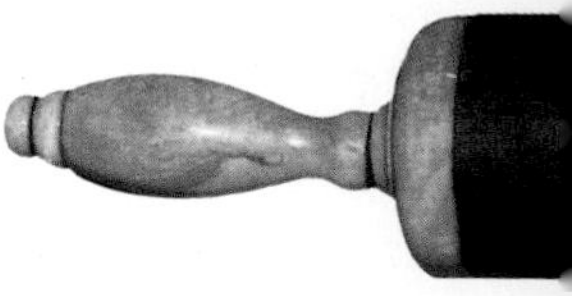

310 Scrimshaw rolling pins

Description
Top: Rolling pin consisting of a solid wooden cylinder, with an ivory disk and a turned ivory handle and knob at each end.
Bottom: Rolling pin carved from solid whalebone, with a turned knob at each end; inscribed lines toward ends and on knobs.

Materials and Dimensions
Top: Rosewood. Walrus ivory. Length: 18″. Diameter: 2½″.
Bottom: Whalebone. Length: 9″. Diameter: 1½″.

Locality and Period
Massachusetts. c. 1850–60.

Comment
Homemade pies were more common in past centuries than they are now; meat pies as well as fruit or custard dessert pies were very popular. Rolling pins, indispensable for preparing pie dough, were made of wood, glass, ceramic, or, like the ones shown here, whalebone or ivory. Many 19th-century pins had only one handle, which left one hand free to press down on and maneuver the pin as it rolled out the dough.

Hints for Collectors
Rolling pins are a common form of scrimshaw, made for shipboard as well as home use. Their simple shape allowed even an inexperienced carver to make one. Not in great demand among collectors, whalebone rolling pins are often relatively inexpensive compared to other scrimshaw forms. Though awkward to display—not many collectors want to put a rolling pin on a coffee table or mantelpiece—they can be beautiful additions to a country kitchen.

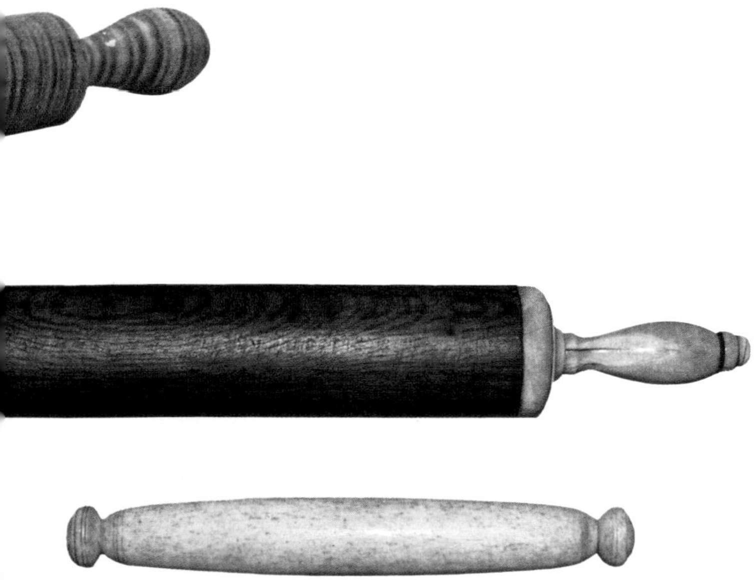

311 Scrimshaw jagging wheels or pie crimpers

Description
Pie crimpers with fluted wheel attached to long handle by pin. Orange patina. *Top:* Handle shaped like hand and cuff (silver cuff link not visible); hand appears to hold squared end of handle; opposite end of handle has engraved leaf and small 6-pointed star with pinhead in center. *Bottom:* Tapered cylindrical handle with flat sides; hole at end for hanging (not visible).

Materials and Dimensions
Top: Walrus ivory handle. Whale ivory wheel. Silver. Length: 5¾″. Wheel diameter: 1⅝″. *Bottom:* Whalebone handle. Whale ivory wheel. Copper. Length: 6¾″. Wheel diameter: 1⅞″.

Locality and Period
Massachusetts. c. 1800–30.

Comment
Jagging wheels, or pie crimpers, have been used since the 17th century, and were a popular form of scrimshaw. These implements trimmed the dough and crimped the edges of the pies that earlier American families ate regularly. They often have a fork at the top to pierce the crust to let out steam. Jagging wheels were commonly made of brass, wrought iron, or steel, as well as wood with brass or ivory wheels.

Hints for Collectors
Jagging wheels are among the most commonly available of all surviving scrimshaw objects. The quality and extent of carving may vary from very plain to extremely elegant; this range is evident in the examples shown here. The difference in value is often tenfold, or even more. One of the best ways to learn about scrimshaw is to visit museums with notable whaling collections, such as the New Bedford Whaling Museum in Massachusetts and the Mystic Seaport Museum in Connecticut.

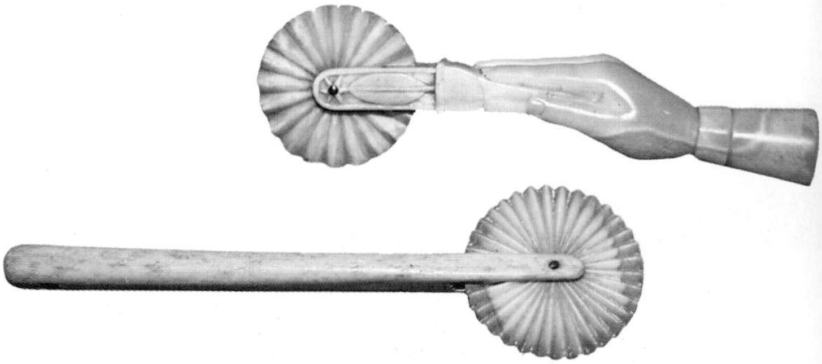

312 Carved crooked knives

Description
Knives with wooden handles carved in shape of a bear, scroll, and hand and attached to steel blade at right angle. Bear with black eyes and small valise at neckline. Scroll marked with incised grid lines. Hand having closed fingers and long straight thumb. Metal collars connecting handles and blades.

Materials and Dimensions
Maple. Steel. Sheet-metal and metal-wire collars. Length (left to right): 7¾″; 6½″; 7¼″.

Locality and Period
Maine and Canadian Maritime Provinces. c. 1880–1910.

Comment
Made by Indians as well as hunters, loggers, and trappers in the northeastern United States and Nova Scotia, so-called "crooked" knives like these were used for work that required pulling the knife toward the holder rather than away. Among their common uses were splitting wood for basket splint, cutting hide for lacings, and skinning animals. Several pieces almost identical to this bear-handled knife (said by some collectors to be a dog with a lunchbox) are known, all the work of a carver from Lunenburg County, Nova Scotia.

Hints for Collectors
"Crooked" knives are somewhat rare and are most often found in the Northeast, where they were made, although these utensils occasionally turn up elsewhere. Fairly expensive because of their rarity, their price is largely determined by the craftsmanship and originality of the carving. Of the knives shown here, the hand and bear types are more valuable than the simpler scroll design.

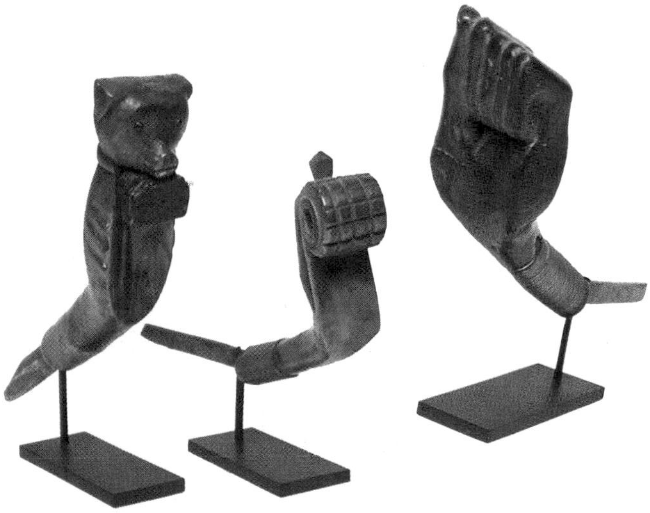

313 Wrought-iron spatula, fork, and serving spoon

Description
Left: Keyhole-shaped spatula, narrowing from wide bottom edge to round center portion. Flat handle with bent loop. *Center:* 2-pronged fork with long handle flattening and widening above neck and ending in curled-back loop. *Right:* Serving spoon, or ladle, with large round bowl and long handle. Handle having notched decoration on neck, then flattening and widening at top and ending in bent loop with curled tip.

Materials and Dimensions
Wrought iron. Spatula length: 10¾″; width: 3½″; thickness: ⅛″. Fork length: 21½″; width: 1¾″; thickness: ½″. Spoon length: 15½″; width: 2¾″; depth: 1″.

Locality and Period
Probably the Northeast. c. 1790–1850.

Comment
Many early kitchen utensils differ from modern versions only in their materials; one exception is the so-called keyhole spatula seen here, a pleasing early form rarely made after the early 19th century. The long-handled toasting (or flesh) fork, also shown here, was used for holding meat or bread over the fire, and the deep-bowled ladle for serving hot soup or porridge.

Hints for Collectors
Spatulas, toasting forks, serving spoons, and skimmers are the most commonly found early kitchen utensils, although such older pieces are becoming more and more scarce. Made of wrought iron, copper, or brass, they vary greatly in price according to materials, workmanship, and ornamentation. Plain wrought-iron pieces, like those shown, are now much in demand and bring high prices; copper and brass examples are priced even higher.

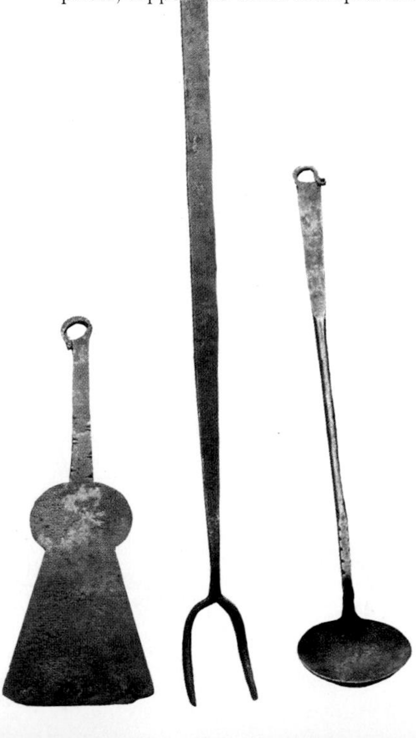

314 Wrought-iron sugar cutters or calipers

Description
Hand-forged cutters with hinged U-shaped head ending in sharp curved pincers. Handles curving out from neck and inward near ends; one tip pierced with hole, the other having a small peg (the catch to link ends is missing). Steel spring on inside of one handle. Steel-rivet construction.

Materials and Dimensions
Wrought iron. Steel. Length: 8″. Width: 3″. Thickness: ⅜″.

Locality and Period
New England. c. 1800–60.

Comment
These pliers-like cutters, known in England as "sugar nippers," were used to cut off pieces from the 10- to 15-pound hard cones or loaves in which cane sugar was often sold. (The loaves came wrapped in dark blue paper so intense in color that it was often kept and later soaked to produce a dye for woolens.) While the wealthy could afford to buy a whole loaf and cut their sugar as needed, poorer people bought only an ounce or two of the expensive commodity and used it sparingly. Sugar was a luxury; maple sugar and honey were the common early sweeteners.

Hints for Collectors
Sugar cutters generally date from the 18th or early 19th century, although some families used them as late as the 1860s. Most were fairly large, utilitarian instruments made of steel and iron, occasionally with incised decoration. Smaller pairs, sometimes used at the dining table, were more elaborately decorated and occasionally made of silver. Sugar cutters of any size and type are rare today, but they do turn up at auctions occasionally. Restoration villages and period houses often have various kinds of sugar cutters on view.

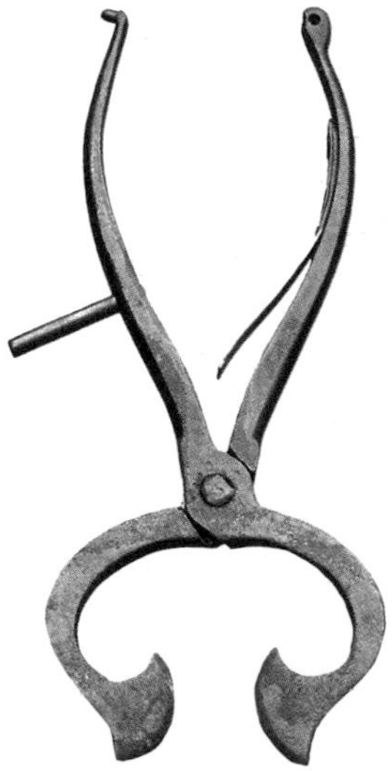

315 Waffle or wafer iron

Description
Double-handled utensil with 2 hinged disks having impressed interior design of central flower with radiating fleurs-de-lis and beaded rim. Long slender cylindrical handles, one ending in rounded finial, the other with small loop and catch. Welded construction.

Materials and Dimensions
Cast and wrought iron. Length: 27″. Diameter of disks: 4¾″.

Locality and Period
The Northeast. c. 1810–40.

Comment
Waffle irons like the one shown were filled with batter, closed, and then held over an open-hearth fire. Made in square and rectangular as well as circular shapes, they often had grids similar to those used on modern waffle irons. The long handles kept the user from being scorched by the fire. Iron is especially good for cooking over an open fire because it distributes heat evenly and retains it, so that food cooks quickly.

Hints for Collectors
Waffle irons made of wrought iron were fairly common in the 18th and 19th centuries, but only a small percentage of these have survived. Like most early kitchen equipment, they are quite expensive because of their rarity and age. The end details of the handles and small catch joining them, refinements not found on most irons, add to the value of this example. In general, the more elaborate the impressed design, the more valuable the piece.

316 Wrought-iron hand-held toaster

Description
Hand-forged iron toaster with scroll-shaped end to hold bread. Long squared rod, spiraled for one-third its length; shaped wooden handle with metal collar. Mounted on flat stand.

Materials and Dimensions
Wrought iron. Sheet iron. Maple. Length: 28¾″. Diameter of rod: ½″. Width of scroll: 4¼″.

Locality and Period
Connecticut. c. 1850–70.

Comment
The earliest toasters were long-handled wrought-iron racks that sat on small feet in front of open hearths. They swiveled so that each side of the bread could be turned toward the fire for toasting. Hand-held 18th- and 19th-century toasters, including the unusual model shown here, were held over an open fire with a slice of bread balanced on the end; they were pulled out to turn the bread over. The spiral design is burned onto the bread just as the lines of a grill are burned onto meats.

Hints for Collectors
Hand-held toasters continued in use even after the invention of the electric toaster in the 20th century. Heavy wrought-iron toasters such as this example dating from the mid-19th century would have been used over an open fire. The striking form and handsome proportions of this piece make it both unusual and desirable. Mounted at an angle on an unobtrusive stand, it would be an attractive addition to any collection of folk art.

317 Wrought-iron swivel-base toaster

Description
Toaster with 2 pairs of parallel semicircular hoops to hold bread slices; each large hoop having a pair of smaller hoops within. Tall iron spiral rising at center of each pair of hoops. All hoops resting on flat rectangle that swivels on 3-footed, T-shaped base. Single foot set below long handle, which flattens and curves upward to rounded end with large hole. Welded construction.

Materials and Dimensions
Wrought iron. Height: 7″. Length of toasting section: 11½″. Length of handle: 20″.

Locality and Period
New England or Pennsylvania. c. 1780–1820.

Comment
Swivel-base toasters like the one shown here were used from Colonial times until the mid-19th century, when open hearths began to be replaced by stoves. Held between the parallel hoops, bread or meat slices were toasted on both sides by rotating the rack. By the turn of the century, hand-held toasters with long metal handles, wooden hand grips, and 2 parallel wire squares to grasp the bread came into use for over-the-stove toasting. Though electric toasters began to be made around the turn of the century, they lacked thermostats and were thus unreliable.

Hints for Collectors
Fireplace toasters were made in both swiveling and nonswiveling versions, with different amounts of decoration. With its 12 hoops and 6 spirals, this piece has a quite elaborate, carefully balanced design. The price of a toaster depends in large part on its craftsmanship and decoration: a simple nonswiveling toaster consisting of 2 rows of plain iron bars would be worth considerably less than this intricate one.

318 Wrought-iron kettle stand

Description
Iron tripod, topped by flat circular ring continuing out on one side as handle with turned wooden handhold. Legs straight in upper half, curving out below, and ending in flat pointed feet. Y-shaped brace connecting 3 legs just above knees. Handle attached to back leg by curved bolted brace. Welded and screwed construction.

Materials and Dimensions
Wrought iron. Pine. Height: 11″. Diameter of top: 8¼″.

Locality and Period
The Northeast. c. 1800–50.

Comment
Cooking over an open hearth often required changing the pots' proximity to the fire, so that every fireplace had several stands or trivets of different heights. Many pots and kettles had their own legs; but for those that did not, a set of stands of various heights enabled a cook to regulate the amount of heat the pots were receiving. Once gas stoves became common, the flame—instead of the pot—could be adjusted, and such stands were no longer necessary.

Hints for Collectors
Most kitchen trivets or stands have 3 legs, but few are as graceful as this example, with its curving legs and dainty feet. Like all early kitchen equipment, such stands are hard to find and fairly expensive today. They are often found in shops specializing in early fireplace or cooking equipment. Several organizations, including the Early American Industries Association (2 Winding Lane, Scarsdale, NY 10583), publish materials of interest to collectors of tools and cooking utensils.

319 Wrought-iron rotating broiler or grill

Description
Iron broiler with grill consisting of 7 flat parallel bars set within circular rim. Grill revolving on central pin inserted at middle of 3-legged base. U-shaped part of base resting on 2 legs. Third leg supporting single bar that curves upward, continuing as flat handle ending in loop. Welded construction.

Materials and Dimensions
Wrought iron. Height: 3½″. Overall length: 22¼″. Diameter of grill: 13″.

Locality and Period
Probably New England, New York, or Pennsylvania. c. 1780–1820.

Comment
A rotating broiler like the one shown here was common cooking equipment during the 18th century and also in the 19th century in homes that still had open hearths instead of stoves. Used to broil meats, fish, or poultry, it was rotated a little at a time so that food would be cooked evenly. Instead of the flat parallel bars of this piece, more elaborate versions had spiral grooves on top to catch drippings, which ran into a receptacle at the bottom and were used for basting.

Hints for Collectors
Early wrought- and cast-iron cooking utensils used over an open fire, such as broilers, toasters, trivets, and skillets, are much sought after today and consequently valuable. Because few have makers' marks, those that are marked bring very high prices. Inexperienced collectors may have trouble determining the age of most iron pieces, but the careful shaping of the handle on this piece, for instance, indicates that it was made by an accomplished early craftsman who took great care in his work.

320 Cast-iron warming shelf

Description
Flat openwork shelf in the shape of a rectangle with rounded corners. Pierced in pattern of large circle surrounded by geometric shapes including 4 circles, each enclosing a 5-pointed star. 2 symmetrical halves hinged at top and screwed together at center.

Materials and Dimensions
Cast iron. Length: 16¾″. Width: 16½″.

Locality and Period
The Northeast or Midwest. c. 1885–1915.

Comment
This shelf was made to fit around the chimney pipe of a cast-iron, wood- or coal-burning kitchen stove. Hinged at the center, it can be opened to be put around the stovepipe and then secured in place at the desired height. Food to be kept warm was set on the shelf, far enough above the burners to keep it from cooking further. Cast-iron cooking stoves were made as early as about 1810, but not until the 1830s and 1840s did they become extremely popular.

Hints for Collectors
Cast-iron stoves, used for heating parlors or cooking in kitchens, were made in a wide variety of designs and shapes, many highly decorated. This warming shelf, probably made to fit a standard-size stovepipe, is a striking design; its bold geometric form, almost Art Deco in feeling, would entice many collectors. Unusual cast-iron pieces like this are just beginning to attract attention; interesting examples can be purchased at moderate prices by collectors able to appreciate their sculptural quality.

Heating, Lighting, and Other Household Items

A comfortable existence, whether in the country or city, has always depended on such essentials as heat and light as well as such luxuries as entertainment. The varied metal and wooden objects in this section all relate to these needs.

Heating

Until the mid-19th century, the main source of heat for warmth and cooking was the fireplace, and a variety of tools were used to maintain the fire efficiently. Andirons and other fireplace equipment such as tongs, pokers, and bellows have changed little since the first settlers brought such objects from Europe. For rich and poor alike, the shapes and styles of these items were similar; the main difference was in the materials—shiny brass implements, rather than dull iron ones, were used in well-to-do households. Bellows, used to fan a dying fire, were frequently decorated with carvings or paintings or both.

Because bedrooms lacked heat in many homes, before going to bed people often inserted warming pans filled with hot coals between the sheets to remove the chill. Portable foot warmers were used in icy carriages and unheated churches. Despite their strictly utilitarian nature, they frequently had handsome punched designs.

In addition to the usual kettles, pots, and pans, cooking at an open hearth required other utensils. Large tin ovens, with open backs that faced the fireplace, contained a spit for turning a large roast or fowl. Long-handled coffee roasters were less common because coffee beans were so expensive. Like warming pans and foot warmers, ovens and coffee roasters usually had punched or engraved decoration.

Lighting

The primary source of light in early colonial homes was the fireplace, though candles and a few rudimentary lighting devices were also used. In the first half of the 19th century, whale-oil lamps came into general use, and in the 1850s kerosene lamps replaced most other forms of lighting. All such devices are of interest both for their forms and their decoration. Early cressets, iron fire-holders that were filled with burning pine knots or twigs soaked in oil, are among the most primitive lighting devices that have survived and are notable for their sculptural forms. Chandeliers and table lamps of every possible material, from brass, tin, iron, and copper to wicker and wood, were handcrafted until the second half of the 19th century, when factories began mass-producing kerosene lamps.

Frames and Gameboards

Men in particular have always enjoyed whittling or carving wood as well as painting their creations. The results have been a wide range of objects, including frames and gameboards, the latter more often painted than carved. Handcarved and painted frames, sometimes made with the tramp-art techniques of chip-carving and layering, as well as frames with elaborate shapes cut with hand tools, were produced in large numbers. Many have appealing one-of-a-kind designs.

Gameboards for chess or checkers were another favorite product of home craftsmen. The decoration on these pieces ranges from checkerboard squares in two contrasting colors to complex multicolored designs, sometimes with painted flowers. Popular with collectors, gameboards are particularly attractive when displayed in country-style rooms.

321

Fireplace baking oven

Description
Tin reflector oven, long and rounded in front and open in back. Hinged rectangular top door that lifts up and latches shut. Flat looped handles at either side of top; 4 looped feet similar to handles. Iron handle protruding on side for turning spit within. Repoussé linear decoration on door and front. Welded construction.

Materials and Dimensions
Tin. Iron. Height: 11¾″. Length: 23¼″. Width: 15″.

Locality and Period
New England. c. 1780–1830.

Comment
Used to roast fowl or meat and sometimes to bake bread, standing ovens like the one shown here were placed in front of fireplaces in well-to-do 18th-century homes. Sometimes called roasting kitchens or reflector ovens, they have a small door, seer open here, through which the meat could be watched or basted. Apple-roasting ovens, which worked on the same principle, were much smaller and shaped like 2 logs set one on top of the other.

Hints for Collectors
Portable baking ovens came in different sizes, all quite rare today. Most stood on legs to raise them above the hearth, but th legs on this piece are especially attractive since they are similar to the handles. Early kitchen equipment is only occasionally found in antiques shops or at shows. Collectors should explore shops that specialize in these objects in order to get a sense of their range and variations in quality.

322 Punched-tin foot warmer

Description
Tin box with punched decoration on sides and top: on all 4 sides, eagle with outspread wings, set within floral wreath. Hinged door on one side. Top decorated with several lines of small punched holes. Tin box set in wooden frame with turned corner posts. Iron-wire handle. Nail and solder construction.

Materials and Dimensions
Tin. Pine. Iron wire. Nails. Height: 7″. Length: 9¾″. Width: 9¾″.

Locality and Period
The Northeast. c. 1800–50.

Comment
While bed-warming pans were used by the earliest Colonists, there is no tangible evidence that foot warmers were in use in 17th-century America. By the 18th century, however, immigrants had brought this European custom to the New World. Since carriages and most churches were unheated as late as 1840, a device to warm the feet—especially in frigid New England winters—was a necessity. Foot warmers were filled with hot coals, which radiated heat through small holes punched in the tin. Worshipers could replenish the coals in their foot warmers during intermissions in the church services.

Hints for Collectors
Foot warmers were among the standard wares carried by Yankee peddlers, who sold them in large quantity. The earliest examples, from the late 18th and early 19th centuries, generally have the finest workmanship, since standards declined as the 19th century progressed. Pieces from 1800 to 1850 are still available at reasonable prices. Punched-tin foot warmers appeal to collectors who value folk objects that are evocative of past life-styles as well as aesthetically pleasing.

323

Fireplace coffee roaster

Description
Rectangular metal box with pattern of small holes in hinged lid. Initials "JJW" punched on lid. Iron rod ending in turned wooden handle with steel collar. Rivet construction.

Materials and Dimensions
Sheet steel. Wrought iron. Maple. Overall length: 22¼″. Length of box: 4¼″. Width: 3″.

Locality and Period
The Northeast or Midwest. c. 1840–80.

Comment
Though coffee was sold in Boston by 1670, at the end of the 18th century it was still a luxury that only the well-to-do could afford. It is said that the earliest American coffee drinkers, unsure of how the beans should be used, boiled them whole and then ate the cooked beans and drank the water. A long-handled roaster like this was set directly on the embers in the hearth, filling the house with the rich aroma of roasting coffee. Similar in shape and size to long-handled corn poppers, coffee roasters differ from the latter in being made of perforated sheet metal rather than wire mesh.

Hints for Collectors
As coffee was fairly scarce and its drinkers few until the 19th century, fireplace coffee roasters were never very common and are quite rare today. The punched initials, probably an early owner's, add to the value of this example, as would any other documentation about the owner or maker.

324 Warming pan

Description
Circular brass pan with hinged lid having ring of punched holes around engraved floral decoration. Ring pull at edge of lid, opposite long turned wooden handle with cylindrical brass collar. Welded and copper-solder construction.

Materials and Dimensions
Brass. Maple. Copper solder. Overall length: 46½". Diameter of pan: 11½". Depth of pan: 4½".

Locality and Period
New England. c. 1820–50.

Comment
Warming pans came to America with the earliest settlers and were used as late as the Victorian era. The pan was filled with hot coals from the hearth and slid back and forth between the bedclothes, which in winter were ice-cold because of the lack of heat in bedrooms. To avoid scorching the sheets, the pan was not allowed to rest too long in any one spot. Usually made of copper or brass, the pans were a prized household possession. Kept brightly polished, they hung by the kitchen fireplace and reflected its glowing light.

Hints for Collectors
Warming pans have long been collected by lovers of Americana and for that reason are fairly expensive. The more elaborate the decoration, the more valuable the piece—with age and condition also contributing to its value. Signed examples are very rare. As with other brass and copper implements, many pans have been imported either recently or as far back as the 17th century; since the imports are hard to distinguish from more valuable American pans, inexperienced collectors should rely on the expertise of dealers specializing in this field.

325 Bellows

Description
Bellows with wooden handles and relief-carved front in form of large urn supported by upraised arms of kneeling man; urn topped by figure of small boy wearing hat and holding flag. Leather side casing attached to wood with brass studs. Brass nozzle and tip. Mounted on display stand.

Materials and Dimensions
Mahogany. Leather. Brass. Length: 17¼″. Width: 6½″. Depth (collapsed): 2″.

Locality and Period
Probably New England. c. 1850–80.

Comment
Bellows, a necessary piece of fireplace equipment, were often decorative as well as functional. Many were painted with scenes in bright shades of red, green, or gold and, like the one shown here, were trimmed with brass studs and given a brass nozzle. One notable painted example, bearing the words "American Artist" and a small figure of a man holding an artist's palette and brushes, was crafted about 1820 by a convict on Welfare Island in New York City.

Hints for Collectors
Made in various sizes, bellows were often carved, painted, or stenciled. The detailed carving on this piece, with its unusually large urn and small figures, makes it a unique, and therefore valuable, example. Elaborately painted pieces are also especially sought after, particularly if they are the distinctive work of a folk painter. Beware of recently repainted examples, which can be detected by a lack of wear.

26 Figural andirons

Description
Pair of andirons, each having an upright in shape of human figure with arms folded at waist. Low-cut shirt indicated by a line. Detailed face and flat hairdo. Legs curving outward to form inverted U-shaped base. Horizontal bar tapering to point at rear, resting on short rear leg.

Materials and Dimensions
Cast iron. Height: 12″. Width: 6½″. Depth: 11″.

Locality and Period
New England, or possibly England. c. 1875–1900.

Comment
Several examples of figural andirons like those shown here have been found, including 2 pairs from Massachusetts. Experts have suggested that they may have been cast in England, since they are similar in form to andirons made there as early as the 16th century. By the 18th century, however, cast-iron andirons were being fashioned in the Colonies in a variety of forms, both animal (owls, dogs, eagles) and human (Hessian soldiers, George Washington), so an American origin is also possible.

Hints for Collectors
While the Hessian-soldier form turns up fairly often, andirons in the shape shown here are much less common, and therefore higher in price. Andirons were often used for many years, so the parts nearest the fire were sometimes worn thin. Because their condition may vary from very worn to almost perfect, identical pairs may range widely in price. Andirons made partly of brass or copper were originally much more costly than those made of iron, and this price differential remains today. Some rare brass examples were signed by makers such as Paul Revere; these are the most valuable.

327 Braided andirons

Description
Pair of andirons, each having a braided upright flanked at top by 2 coils at right angles to smaller coil. At front, upright divided into pair of curved legs ending in small flat feet. Horizontal bar turned down at rear to form supporting leg.

Materials and Dimensions
Wrought iron. Height: 22½″. Width: 11″. Depth: 16½″.

Locality and Period
Probably western Pennsylvania. c. 1870–95. Similar designs created throughout the Northeast and Midwest.

Comment
The fireplace was the only heat source for cooking until stoves of various types came into general use around the mid-19th century. However, open-hearth cooking continued in many households after stoves became available, so that fireplace accessories—andirons, bellows, tongs, brushes, shovels, and pokers—were necessities. Though generally made of wrought iron, highly decorative andirons meant to be used in the homes o[f] the wealthy often had brass or copper uprights set on wrought-iron supports.

Hints for Collectors
The price of a pair of andirons is determined by such factors as condition, age, form, maker, and material. The unusual design o[f] the andirons shown here, with their intricately twisted iron uprights and the simple coiled shapes on either side near the top makes this pair quite valuable, even though crafted of iron rathe[r] than brass or copper. A single andiron is worth only a small fraction of the price commanded by a pair.

328 Loop-topped andirons

Description
Pair of andirons with flat-sided, tapering upright topped by large circular loop. Upright set on widely curved front legs ending in small flat feet. Horizontal bar set through upright; bar bent down at midpoint, then continuing to rear leg (split on right andiron). Welded construction.

Materials and Dimensions
Wrought iron. Height: 20″. Width: 11½″. Depth: 19½″.

Locality and Period
The Northeast or Midwest. c. 1830–50.

Comment
Andirons were usually referred to as "firedogs" in England, probably because some were shaped like dogs. Some European examples from the 17th century, referred to as "spitdogs," had hooks attached to the uprights so that spits could be laid across them; these are also found on some 18th-century American pieces. Another variation had a piece on top for holding a plate or tankard to keep its contents warm. Uprights were topped by ball, urn, lemon, and other finials; legs and feet also varied in shape.

Hints for Collectors
Andirons have been, and continue to be, much sought after by collectors. The simplest, such as the plain wrought-iron pair shown here, frequently have the best lines and most striking designs. Older andirons made in America are usually more expensive than imported ones, but differentiating these may be difficult even for experienced collectors; European models are often more ornate than American ones.

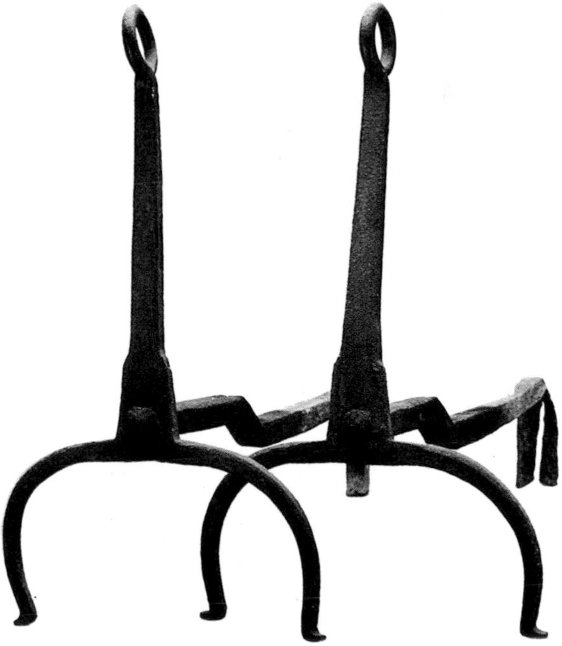

329 Fire holder or cresset

Description
Series of 5 pairs of similar upcurved semicircular ribs, ending in smaller front pair almost closed at peak, all attached to horizontal bar forming right angle at rear with long flat upright support. Rivet construction. Mounted on flat stand.

Materials and Dimensions
Wrought iron. Iron rivets. Height: 21¾″. Length: 16″. Width: 12″.

Locality and Period
Probably the Northeast. c. 1800–50.

Comment
A primitive lighting device, a cresset is an iron vessel or rack meant to hold a burning substance. Generally mounted atop a pole like a torch or suspended like a lantern, cressets like that shown here held bunches of burning twigs or pine knots soaked in oil. Less common than torches, they illuminated night fishing or other outdoor nocturnal activities.

Hints for Collectors
An early lighting device, cressets are rarely found in the marketplace and survive mainly in a few historical-society collections of early tools and lighting equipment. The curved iron ribs give it a primitive or medieval appearance—almost like the skeleton of some prehistoric animal. As boldly appealing as a sculpture, this implement would be striking in almost any setting, whether period or contemporary, and would be a strong addition to any folk art collection. Such a piece should be mounted on an unobtrusive stand like the one illustrated.

330 Eagle-head chandelier

Description
Lighting fixture with 4 upward-curving serpentine arms, each ending in an eagle's head, with sharp beak and a hole for the eye. Circular center section, with 4 curved supports. Rivet construction.

Materials and Dimensions
Wrought iron. Iron rivets. Height: 11½″. Length of pairs of arms: 46½″ and 47¾″.

Locality and Period
New York State. c. 1850–75.

Comment
Most American chandeliers were made of polished brass, wrought iron, or punched tin; early ones held candles, while later examples burned oil (*see also* pp. 28–29). Found in a home adjacent to a blacksmith's shop in the Adirondack region of New York, this ceiling fixture was probably made by the blacksmith himself, clearly an exceptional craftsman. Each of the eagle heads has been carefully wrought by hand; while at first glance they may look identical, closer examination reveals minute differences and tool marks. The lighting fixture hung from long metal chains, and the central metal basket probably held a glass globe and a brass well containing whale oil or kerosene.

Hints for Collectors
Well designed and handsomely crafted, this chandelier is an example of the high level of skill many 18th- and 19th-century blacksmiths achieved. Its graceful, unusual form makes it even more outstanding, and the presence of eagles' heads, a popular patriotic motif, adds to its value.

331 **Wicker lamp**

Description
Wicker table lamp with slender cylindrical stem on convex circular base. Circular shade with wide bottom opening and tapered neck just below flared top rim that curls out slightly. Wicker woven in ribbed pattern. Metal socket and wiring.

Materials and Dimensions
Wicker. Iron and iron wire. Overall height: 16″. Diameter of base: 4¾″. Diameter of shade (bottom): 9½″.

Locality and Period
Probably the Northeast. c. 1915–30.

Comment
The first American-made wicker furnishings date from about 1840. Late 19th-century pieces tended to be most ornate, but in the early 20th century plainer designs like the lamp shown here replaced the intricate, elaborate wicker creations favored by the Victorians. Though most late designs were less elaborate, some inventive pieces, such as a combination planter, goldfish-bowl holder, and lampstand, were still made.

Hints for Collectors
The past decade or so has seen a great rise in the popularity of wicker, both old and new. All sorts of new objects, including table and floor lamps, baskets, and furniture, are readily available even in five-and-dime stores. Most of these pieces, however, are imports from the Far East that are of poor quality in both material and workmanship. The careful tight weave of this lamp, combined with its simple shape and dark, dry look, distinguishes it from new pieces. The exact origin of such a piece would be almost impossible to determine without a label or some other identifying mark; it may also have been an earlier import.

332 Tramp-art cactus lamp

Description
Wooden lamp having green notch-carved base in shape of a cactus with 2 upraised bulbous arms; stepped circular bottom. Shade consisting of 7 chip-carved rings set atop one another, narrowing successively toward top. Nail and glue construction. Metal socket and wiring.

Materials and Dimensions
Pine. Painted. Steel and copper wire. Iron nails. Overall height: 19¼″. Diameter of base: 6″. Diameter of shade (bottom): 9″.

Locality and Period
New York City. c. 1976.

Comment
One characteristic of tramp art is an abundance—sometimes an overabundance—of decoration. Besides layers of elaborate chip carving, some pieces have applied decoration such as paper pictures or photographs, or inlaid bits of mirror, colored glass, or stones. Most examples have geometric shapes, so this naturalistic cactus-shaped lamp is quite unusual.

Hints for Collectors
This lamp is a fine contemporary piece done with the traditional tramp-art techniques of layering and notch, or chip, carving. With its upraised arms and plump curved trunk, it could almost be a Walt Disney character. Recently made tramp art does not usually command as high a price as examples from the late 19th or early 20th century. This unique piece, however, has a whimsical quality shared by many fine works of folk art. A worthwhile addition to a specialized collection of tramp art or one of general folk art, it is likely to rise in value quite rapidly.

333 Tramp-art picture frame

Description
Square picture frame, notch-carved and layered, with heart inset diagonally at each corner. Nail and glue construction.

Materials and Dimensions
Pine. Iron nails. Height: 8¾″. Width: 8¾″. Thickness: 1″.

Locality and Period
New York City. c. 1970–80.

Comment
Though recently made, this frame belongs to a long tradition of tramp art. The earliest known piece is dated 1862 but, because so little tramp art was signed or dated, it is likely that examples were made even earlier. These objects were crafted from the thin-cut mahogany or cedar of cigar boxes, which became abundant in the 1850s; when empty, these boxes were sold cheaply or given away. After about 1925, tramp art gradually faded out, in part because cigar smoking, and thus the number of cigar boxes, began to decline. Also, cardboard boxes were eventually introduced. Some craftsmen today, such as the maker of this frame, still find tramp-art techniques appealing and continue making these layered, notch-carved pieces.

Hints for Collectors
The new pine of this frame is noticeably light in color compared to 19th- and early 20th-century tramp-art pieces made of cigar-box mahogany or cedar, which have darkened from age or shellacking. New tramp art, most commonly small boxes and picture or mirror frames, is less valuable than older pieces but is a suitable addition to rooms with other examples of folk art, both new and old.

334 Carved picture frame

Description
Rectangular wooden frame, painted black, with carved full-bodied figure of whale projecting from each side. Flat inner frame with notch-carved edges and applied starfish and seashells near whales. Nail and glue construction.

Materials and Dimensions
Painted wood. Seashells and starfish. Iron nails. Height: 26″. Width: 25½″. Thickness: 1¾″.

Locality and Period
New York City. c. 1970–80.

Comment
Made in New York City by a contemporary craftsman who undoubtedly loves the sea and all things nautical, this carved and saw-cut wooden frame has the notch carving typical of tramp art. Its highly polished black whales, however, give it a sophisticated quality and take it out of that category, which tends to have a less finished look. These realistic 3-dimensional carvings, with curving tails and slightly open mouths, make the frame itself as interesting as anything it may eventually enclose.

Hints for Collectors
Many talented self-taught craftsmen working today in wood, clay, metal, or paint, like the creator of this frame, utilize traditional techniques. While their work is generally less expensive than 19th- or early 20th-century pieces, some finely crafted and highly original contemporary pieces may be quite costly. Many are made solely for the craftsman's personal satisfaction and are not meant to be sold. Still, for the right price, the maker may be willing to part with a prized piece, especially if he can make another one.

335 Carved checkerboard

Description
Rectangular wooden checkerboard with 10 rows of 8 squares each; alternate squares slightly raised. Narrow area at each end meant to hold checkers; separated from playing board by rounded divider. Entire board framed by molding. Circular and square wooden checkers. Nail construction.

Materials and Dimensions
Pine. Shellacked. Iron-wire nails. Length: 19¾″. Width: 12½″. Thickness: 1¼″. Checkers: ¾″ to 1″ in diameter and 1″ square.

Locality and Period
Probably the Northeast or Midwest. c. 1900–20.

Comment
Made for blind players, this checkerboard has its surface carved in low relief so that the squares can be felt with the fingers. The checkers are in 2 different shapes, circular and square, in order to distinguish opposing pieces. The unknown maker probably fashioned this set for a blind friend who could not play checkers on an ordinary board. It is a mystery why the board has 10 vertical rows rather than 8.

Hints for Collectors
Gameboards have become increasingly popular items during the last decade, but most of those collected are painted rather than carved. This custom-made checkerboard is distinctive because its carved surface gives it a sculptural quality. Though less valuable than a handsomely painted board, it would be an interesting addition to a varied collection of gameboards.

336 Hand-painted checkerboard

Description
Painted checkerboard with gold and red squares outlined in black. Framed by multiple borders in black, red, and green. Short metal feet at corners.

Materials and Dimensions
Maple or birch. Painted. Steel washers and screws (feet). Length: 16″. Width: 16¼″. Thickness: ½″.

Locality and Period
Connecticut. c. 1900–25. Similar designs made throughout the United States.

Comment
Because commercially made games became more and more popular after 1850, fewer gameboards were made by hand. Games such as "Grocery Store" (in which a player could purchase a pound of cheese for 16 cents) and "The Game of Innocence [*sic*] Abroad" were very popular with Victorian Americans and were manufactured in large quantity. Still, there were craftsmen who enjoyed making and decorating their own boards—usually for checkers or Parcheesi—well into the 20th century; some later examples, such as that shown here, were as finely executed as 19th-century ones.

Hints for Collectors
Probably more checkerboards were made than any other kind of gameboard. Many are fairly undistinguished—done in dull colors or lacking decoration—but this brilliantly colored board, an outstanding 20th-century example, has the bold graphic appeal of an Amish quilt. Great care has been taken with such details as the thin black outlines around the squares. The use of gold paint for the squares and green for the border is unusual.

337 Hand-painted reversible gameboard

Description
Gameboard painted on both sides, made in 4 sections battened at top and bottom and rounded at corners. On front, Parcheesi game with black outlines and word "Home" painted in blue at center. Corners decorated with circles enclosing yellow, orange, blue, and green curved segments. On each side, orange strips radiating from center. On back, red and black checkerboard with white borders.

Materials and Dimensions
Birch. Painted. Length: 22¾". Width: 25½". Thickness: ¾".

Locality and Period
Probably New England. c. 1880–1900. Similar designs made throughout the United States.

Comment
This carefully painted, double-sided gameboard may have been created from an old breadboard, since its thickness, battened edges, and rounded corners are all typical of breadboards. The elaborate Gothic lettering of the word "Home" in the center offers an interesting contrast to the simplicity of the board's other decoration. While most boards have plain geometric patterns, a few rare ones are edged with trailing flowers or figural decoration.

Hints for Collectors
Prices for handmade painted gameboards have risen dramatically during the last few years, in part because these boards make attractive decorations in the country-style interiors that have become popular. Even carelessly painted examples with little originality or unattractive designs are sometimes sold for high prices. Collectors should pay large sums only for finely made old boards with original decoration that is in good condition.

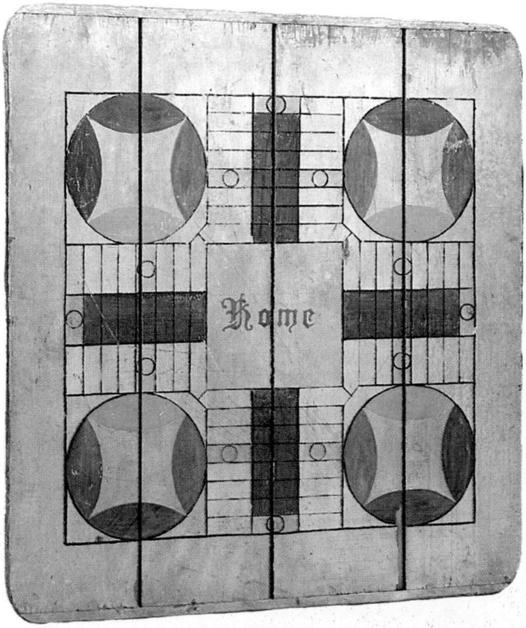

338 Hand-painted Parcheesi board

Description
Painted gameboard with 9 large squares, made in 2 pieces. Large blue square in each corner; blue square at center enclosing white circle with black border and word "HOME." 4 white squares, or playing alleys, with black grid and solid rectangles. Gray border and applied black molding on all sides.

Materials and Dimensions
Plywood. Pine molding. Painted. Wire nails. Length: 29″. Width: 29″. Thickness: 1½″.

Locality and Period
California. c. 1880–1900. Similar designs made throughout the United States.

Comment
Board games have been popular around the world for centuries. Checkers, Parcheesi, cribbage, backgammon, and simple pinball games played with marbles are just a few of the hundreds of games that require boards. In the past, these were often crafted by amateurs for their own use and were thus strictly utilitarian and very plain. Those boards worthy of being called folk art are the exceptions.

Hints for Collectors
Certain features add to the value of any board. A signature and date, usually incised or painted on the back, make a piece more costly. Colors also affect value: boards with blue or red decoration are generally worth more than the more common black-and-white ones. Do not mistake new handmade boards for old ones: modern pieces usually lack the fine detailing and signs of age found on vintage examples.

Spinning and Washing Implements, Canes, and Miscellaneous Tools

During the first two centuries of American history, most households were almost totally self-sufficient. This changed in the mid-19th century, when factory-produced objects replaced many of those made by hand. Some of the early specialized tools devised to help operate a household or farm have obvious functions, but the uses of others are not so evident.

Clothmaking and Sewing Tools

Housewives spent much time spinning wool or cotton thread that they wove into cloth for garments, sheets, and bedcovers. The process of turning raw fiber into cloth required wheels to spin the thread, winders and swifts to measure thread into skeins, looms for weaving cloth, and numerous smaller implements for sewing.

While most spinning wheels and swifts were unadorned, others were clearly made to please the eye as well as to perform a function. Generally, sewing stands, spool holders, and needle cases were made at home with great attention to detail. Whimsical one-of-a-kind pieces were often crafted by a husband or brother as a gift for the family seamstress. However, some, like Shaker spool stands, were designed for sale.

Laundry Implements

Clothes and linens were washed less frequently in the 18th and 19th centuries than they are today, since such work was very time-consuming and exhausting. By the late 19th century, laundry could be washed in primitive types of agitators; though these were similar in principle to automatic washers, they had to be turned manually and required great stamina.

Wooden or metal washboards were made for scrubbing clothes, and wooden wash sticks or forks were used to lift heavy wet clothes from washtubs full of hot water. Ironing was almost as arduous as washing; it required using heavy flat-bottomed irons in various shapes and sizes. Some irons had a hollow interior to hold burning charcoal or a heated iron slug.

Tools for Fishing and Farming

Almost every occupation developed its own special tools, the most appealing of which are handcrafted pieces in bold, even elegant, designs. Some fishing and farming implements are particularly sculptural, such as eel spears and hay forks. Often graceful, hay cutters have a unique shape and handle placement. Various other planting and harvesting tools, such as the wooden dibble boards used to make rows of planting holes, exemplify the kind of simple undecorated objects that collectors seek because of their pleasing forms.

Canes

Walking sticks, or canes, have always appealed to carvers as objects on which to display their skill and ingenuity. Materials for canes include hardy tree roots, branches, ivory, and almost any sticklike form that could be carved. Sculptural forms such as fists, faces, knobs, and animal heads were commonly chosen for cane finials. Handsomely carved or decorated canes have long been prized by collectors.

339 Scrimshaw swift or wool winder

Description
Swift with elongated conical ivory finial set in inverted hemisphere that fits atop another hemisphere to form single ball with black scribe lines. Cage made of slender whalebone slats joined by metal pins and ribbons; attached to shaft by 2 collars. Shaft fitted into sliding ivory collar with screw that adjusts cage size. Fist-shaped ivory clamp holding shaft, with screw mechanism for attaching to table. Engraved "M.E.M."

Materials and Dimensions
Whale ivory. Whalebone. Copper. Silk ribbon. Height: 17″. Diameter of cage: 18″ (open); 5½″ (closed).

Locality and Period
New Bedford, Massachusetts. c. 1845.

Comment
Scrimshaw swifts, marvelously complex, usually have more slats than their wooden or metal counterparts. They come in all sizes and shapes, and clamps and finials were often carved in forms such as barrels or animal heads. Some are footed; others are designed to fit into a hole in a sewing box lid or in the floor.

Hints for Collectors
Though swifts are a relatively common scrimshaw form, those with fine imaginative designs are hard to find. Because swifts are delicate, they often have broken slats, which can sometimes be replaced with pieces of old whalebone. The tiny ribbons can also be replaced. Good scrimshaw examples, whatever their form, are rarer and far more expensive than wooden or metal types. Though a bit awkward to display, swifts can be clamped to a table, shelf, or specially made lucite base.

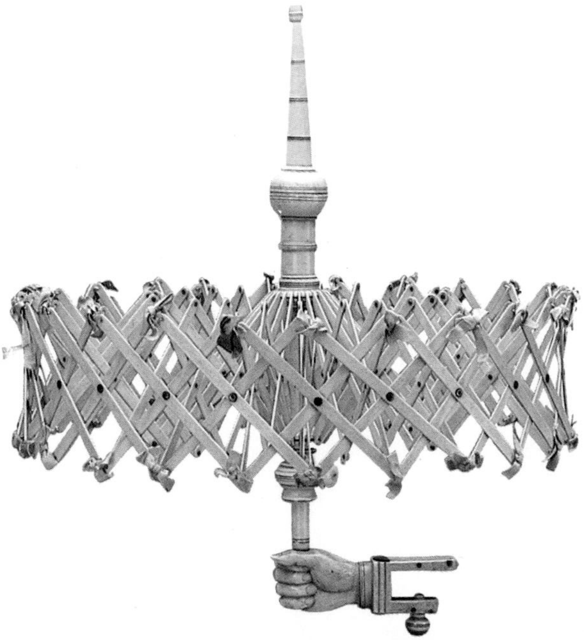

340 Metal swift or wool winder

Description
Swift with revolving metal cage made of red, white, and green slats attached by rings to central pole. Button finial. Circular clamp near middle of pole, with screw and knob to raise or lower slats and adjust their size. Adjustable C-clamp with heart-shaped knob at bottom of pole for attaching to table.

Materials and Dimensions
Wrought iron. Brass. Painted steel slats. Height: 17″. Diameter of cage: 14″ (open).

Locality and Period
Pennsylvania. c. 1880–90.

Comment
Swifts were used to wind skeins of yarn after they were spun, cleaned, and dyed. Most were wooden or metal, but elaborately carved scrimshaw examples, usually the work of sailors on long sea voyages, were also made. While some swifts were made to be set in a heavy block on the floor, others, like the one shown here, were fastened by a large clamp to a table or chair. Because its slats, or ribs, can be opened or closed to adjust to various yarn skein sizes, this type is called an umbrella swift.

Hints for Collectors
The swift illustrated is fairly late and, with its painted steel ribs, quite unusual. The heart-shaped wrought-iron knob is also uncommon and adds to its value. Because of their sculptural form, swifts make attractive display items. Wooden swifts made by the Shakers are particularly in demand.

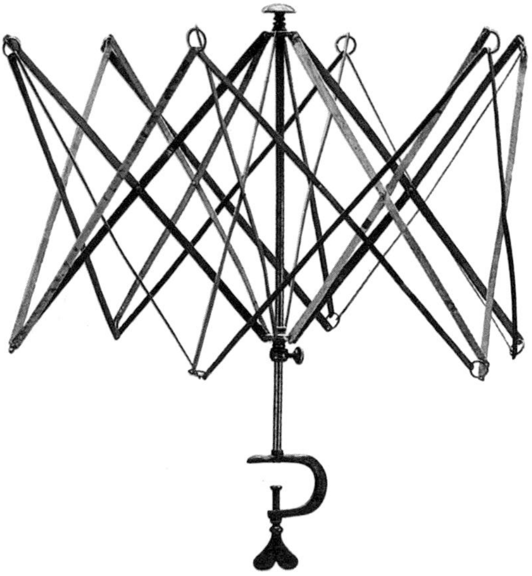

341 **Spinning wheel in cage**

Description
Treadle-driven yellow spinning wheel with 12 spokes; set between 2 slanting boards and enclosed in narrow red case with ladderlike top and ends. One side of case open, other side enclosed by 8 vertical rods attached to horizontal wooden bar in center and fanning out at top and bottom. Winding mechanism at left made of yellow turned cylinders and reels. Treadle with traces of worn gray paint. Nail and screw construction.

Materials and Dimensions
Maple, ash, and pine. Painted. Iron screws and wire nails. Height of case: 33¾". Length: 37¾". Depth: 12". Diameter of wheel: 30".

Locality and Period
New England. c. 1880–1910.

Comment
Wheels for spinning wool into yarn or thread were common in 17th- and 18th-century homes of every class, since the Colonists wove their own cloth to avoid costly English imports. By the mid-19th century, however, factories were turning out so much inexpensive cloth that hardly any had to be made at home. This painted spinning wheel is a late example; its rough construction suggests that it was made in a rural area, where spinning wheels continued in use much longer than in cities.

Hints for Collectors
Though typical unpainted spinning wheels are fairly common and can be bought quite reasonably, few have the distinctive charm and naive quality of this piece. Its bright-colored paint and wooden cage make it a very desirable piece and an excellent addition to a room decorated with simple 19th-century rural furniture and accessories.

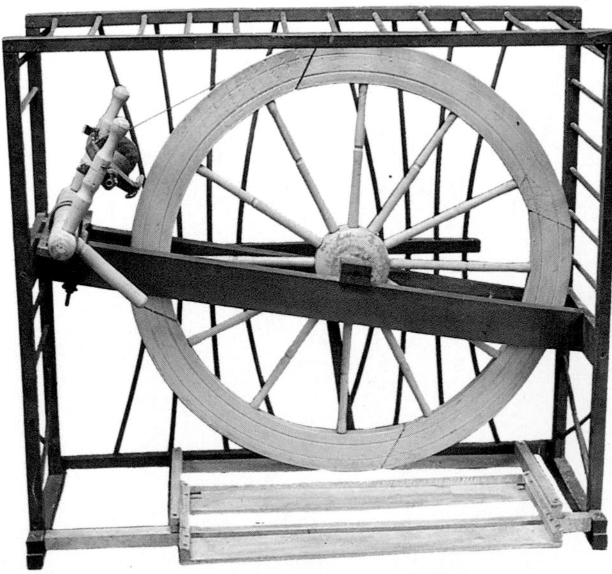

342 Figural wool winder

Description
Wool winder carved in shape of a flat standing woman with a circular face having carved and painted features. Body decorated with abstract designs suggesting a dress and a bead necklace. Flat, notched wheel at center of body painted reddish brown and decorated. Winding arm, with 4 turned spokes ending in short cylinders, attached to body by turned rod. Figure set on rectangular stool with beveled edges and slanted legs.

Materials and Dimensions
Maple and pine. Painted. Height: 39¼″. Width: 16″. Length of winding arm: 26⅛″.

Locality and Period
Connecticut. c. 1875.

Comment
From Colonial times throughout much of the 19th century, wool was spun in almost every home, and many implements associated with making wool cloth were household necessities. After yarn was spun, it had to be wound and measured into skeins. This could be done on several different devices: a yarn winder, such as the figural example shown here; a clock reel, similar to a winder; and a niddy-noddy, a smaller, hand-held wooden device that wound the wool as one rocked one's arm back and forth.

Hints for Collectors
Plain unpainted wooden yarn winders are fairly easy to find, but a carved and painted example like this one is extremely rare. Since the basic shape of a plain winder resembles the human form, the carver of this piece imaginatively transformed a simple utilitarian object into a witty sculpture. A bold and remarkable creation, this wool winder would be very costly if it appeared on the market.

343 Figural spool holder

Description
Flat wooden figure of black woman with painted face, pale eyes, and red lips, dressed in tan blouse, paisley skirt, and red neckerchief. Outstretched arms holding small shelf with 4 metal spool holders. Skirt hem turned up at bottom to form pockets. Wooden base same size as shelf.

Materials and Dimensions
Painted pine. Masonite. Cloth. Iron rods and nails. Height: 12½″. Length: 9″. Depth: 2½″.

Locality and Period
The East or Midwest. c. 1900–40.

Comment
This painted figure is not only charming but also useful, as is evident in the metal spool rods as well as the pockets around the hemline of the dress for holding buttons or other sewing items. While cloth dolls were almost always made by women, most wooden pieces were the work of men, suggesting that this piece may have been a joint effort, with the wood sawed by a husband and the figure dressed by his wife.

Hints for Collectors
Homemade black dolls fashioned from cloth or stockings were very common in the South in the early decades of the 20th century, but a spool holder like this is somewhat unusual. Its charm comes from its vitality: the little figure has a personality of its own, a quality found only in the very best folk art. Imaginative household objects like this may sometimes be found at yard sales or flea markets, where such pieces are usually scooped up quickly by collectors.

344 Shaker spool stand with pincushion

Description
Wooden spool stand with vase-turned center support topped by disk holding blue tomato-shaped pincushion. Support rests on larger circular base. 7 thin iron rods set into base, meant to hold spools of thread. Cake of beeswax on velvet ribbon rests on base.

Materials and Dimensions
Maple. Iron rods. Cotton cushion (not original) stuffed with wool blanket combings. Beeswax. Velvet ribbon. Height: 5⅞". Diameter of base: 5⅝".

Locality and Period
Made in a Shaker community, probably in Maine, New Hampshire, or New York. c. 1900–10.

Comment
Sewing implements and accessories were among the most popular items in Shaker stores, where members of the religious communities sold their handiwork to the public. Spool stands like the one shown here were hand-turned by the brethren, as were the wooden spools sometimes sold with them. Many stands were sold with a woven-poplar needlebook, an emery (to keep needles sharp and free of rust), and a cake of beeswax to coat thread for added strength and to keep it from knotting.

Hints for Collectors
While finely crafted Shaker spool stands were originally inexpensive—a model pictured in a Shaker catalogue of 1908 was priced at $1.75—such items are fairly rare today and, like most Shaker pieces, fetch high prices. Labeled or stamped sewing boxes and accessories generally command a premium. Unstamped examples may sometimes be identified by referring to Shaker catalogues.

345 Scrimshaw bodkins

Description
Bodkins with pointed shafts and handles of varied shapes. Left to right: crosshatched pipe tamper atop openwork cage of 4 round columns, each in 3 segments; clenched fist above 6 square horizontal segments; acorn atop beaded plates, acanthus-leaf decoration, and 2 openwork circles containing small balls; clenched fist above shaft with 3 baleen collars.

Materials and Dimensions
Whale ivory. Whalebone and baleen details. Length (left to right): 4¾"; 4½"; 4¼"; 5⅜".

Locality and Period
New England. c. 1830–60.

Comment
Bodkins are smaller, more decorative versions of the "fids" used by sailors to splice rope, clean their teeth, and stir pipe tobacco. Fancy decorated examples such as the ones shown here were probably gifts for wives and sweethearts. The fist is a common decorative device, found frequently on canes and umbrella handles as well as on sewing implements.

Hints for Collectors
Bodkins are quite common and may often be bought for a modest sum. A collection might be built around bodkins—also made in silver, mother-of-pearl, and plain steel—and related needlework tools, such as the ivory bobbins used for making lace, ivory crochet hooks, and ivory-handled thread cutters. Scrimshaw bodkins may be made into pendants or stickpins by attaching gold wire fastenings to them.

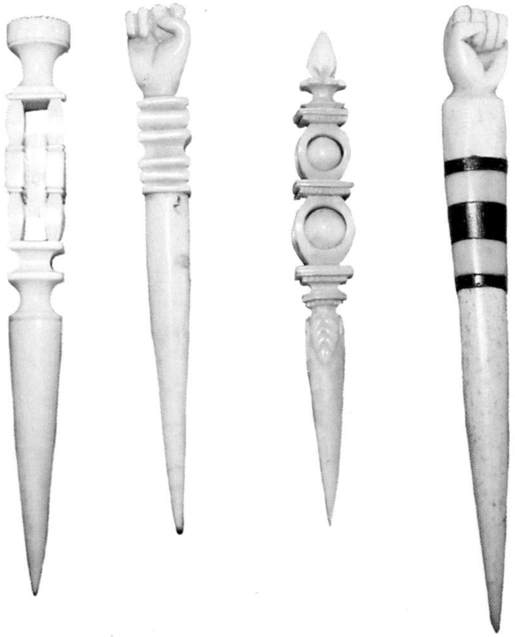

346 # Scrimshaw clothespins

Description
Carved clothespins with faceted tops. Hole drilled near top, connected by narrow slit to arched opening below. Prongs extending from opening, comprising lower third of body.

Materials and Dimensions
Whalebone. Length: 4½".

Locality and Period
Nantucket. c. 1875.

Comment
Whalebone clothespins fashioned by sailors were meant for their own use aboard ship or for family members and friends at home. Such clothespins were superior because they were impervious to weather and their highly polished surfaces did not snag laundry as easily as did the splintery wooden variety. Other common scrimshaw objects included engraved teeth, pie crimpers and kitchen utensils, plaques and figural sculpture, small boxes, canes, swifts, candlesticks, bodkins, and busks.

Hints for Collectors
Though scrimshaw clothespins are not available in quantity, they are prized by collectors. These items sometimes come in their original drawstring bag, which adds to their value. Some examples have engravings on their prongs; these engravings were almost always added later by fakers. Easier to find and much less expensive than the whalebone clothespins are 19th-century hand-carved wooden pins, some made by the Shakers. Clothespins are the kind of small simple object that many collectors overlook, but for that reason they are a good specialty for beginners. An interest in such an object may lead a collector to pursue other tools associated with laundering.

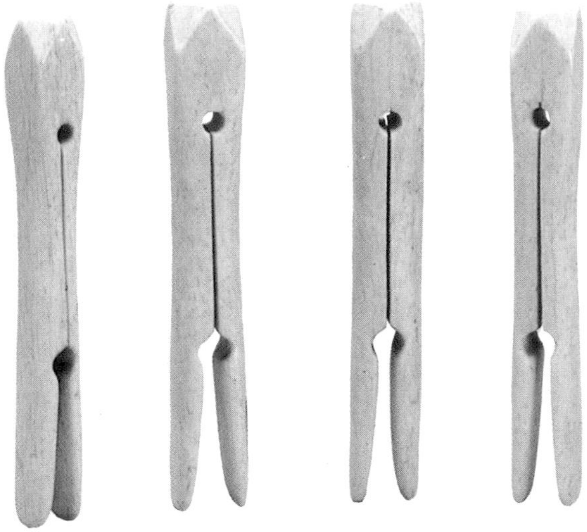

347 Carved wash sticks or clothes forks

Description
Left: Forked stick, tapering gradually from rounded upper half to flatter, wider bottom divided into 2 slightly rounded prongs; topped by cube with diamond-shaped facets. *Right:* Forked stick with long center segment tapering toward top and bottom. Flat-sided cage at top with 4 rectangular openings, separate wooden ball inside, and small button finial. 2 short prongs at bottom. Mounted on flat display stands.

Materials and Dimensions
Probably maple. Length (left; right): 28″; 26¼″. Width: 2½″; 3¼″. Depth: 1⅜″; 1″.

Locality and Period
New England. c. 1880–1920.

Comment
The earliest method of washing clothes used in the Colonies was the age-old one of scrubbing them against a rock in a stream. Wash sticks and wooden tubs soon came into general use, and washboards became popular by the mid-19th century. The wash sticks, or clothes forks, shown here were used to stir the wash and then lift heavy loads of hot laundry out of washing tubs.

Hints for Collectors
Wash sticks were in use for more than 2 centuries. Many were purely utilitarian objects, quickly made and of no artistic value. The sticks shown here, however, are exceptional—bold, simple objects looking almost like primitive human figures. Their elongated forms and smooth surfaces lend them a certain grace and elegance, desirable qualities of the best folk art. Such pieces can sometimes be bought inexpensively.

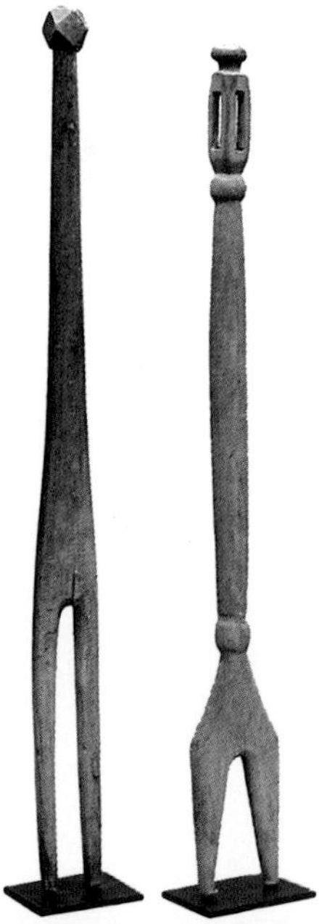

348 Rug beater

Description
Rug beater with looped top made of intricately twisted wire. Section of twisted wire extending vertically from top center to neck. Wooden handle long and rounded; tapered along lower two-thirds. Metal collar connecting handle and wire top. Mounted on flat display stand.

Materials and Dimensions
Steel and steel wire. Maple. Height: 23⅜″. Width: 6½″. Diameter of handle: 1″.

Locality and Period
Throughout the United States. c. 1880–1910.

Comment
Rug beaters were standard household equipment before vacuum cleaners were invented around the turn of the century, and they continued to be used well into the 20th century. A rug was hung on an outdoor clothesline and beaten to get the dust out. Though suitable for factory-made carpets, such treatment tends to damage handmade hooked or braided rugs. Handmade rugs were sometimes cleaned during winter by laying them pile-side down on snow-covered ground until the dirt sifted onto the snow.

Hints for Collectors
Rug beaters are easy to find and generally inexpensive; their varied shapes and designs make them attractive for wall display. Most beaters were made of a single heavy strand of plain untwisted wire bent into a curved or braided shape; this example's many-stranded wire coils are unusual and make it sturdier than most.

349 Bootjacks

Description
Left: Handmade bentwood bootjack, raised on iron support. Oval hoop at top flattens to 2 slats at bottom. Traces of old brown paint. *Center:* Wrought-iron bootjack, U-shaped at top. 2 pierced hearts and 2 diamonds. Undulating sides and slightly curved bottom. 2 iron feet. *Right:* Cast-iron bootjack with loop at top. Lower part elaborately pierced in wheel, half-wheel, and semicircle designs. Curved sides and bottom. 2 iron feet.

Materials and Dimensions
Left: Painted ash. Iron. Length: 22¼″. Width: 5″. *Center:* Wrought iron. Length: 15½″. Width: 5″. *Right:* Cast iron. Length: 20½″. Width: 6″.

Locality and Period
Throughout the United States. c. 1875–1900.

Comment
These handy instruments made it easier to pull off the tall boots that were common footwear in the 18th and 19th centuries. By placing the boot heel in the opening and holding the jack with the other foot, a boot could be removed with a minimum of tugging. Made of many materials, bootjacks were produced in varied shapes—from beetles and frogs to devils and even naked ladies, sometimes referred to as "Naughty Nellies." Though primarily made for men, a few bootjacks made for women are known; these are generally smaller in size and more delicate in shape.

Hints for Collectors
Bootjacks, particularly wooden ones, can often be found in out-of-the-way corners of small shops, especially in the country, and may be quite inexpensive. Older, more crudely made pieces are usually higher priced, and Victorian iron examples in unusual shapes are also in demand.

350 **Sad iron**

Description
Long narrow iron with blocklike base narrowing to a point at front end. Spiraled handle sloping up from front end, then continuing parallel to base; tip of handle turned down slightly before end of base.

Materials and Dimensions
Cast-iron base. Wrought-iron handle. Height: 4¾″. Length: 11¼″. Width: 1⅞″.

Locality and Period
The Northeast. 1785–1840.

Comment
Laundry irons were made in a variety of forms and types. Flounced and ruffled dresses, for example, required special irons for sleeves and pleats; certain fabrics were pressed with special irons that gave them a sheen. Some irons were heated in or before an open fire; others, by an iron slug that was preheated and slipped into the hollow iron. The all-purpose type shown here is called a "sad" iron, a term probably derived from the Old English word "sald," meaning solid. Ironing required a strong arm, since hand irons were effective in part because of the pressure exerted on fabric.

Hints for Collectors
Sad irons of all shapes and sizes are much sought after, and some collectors have been able to amass quite varied groupings. This long thin example, with its hand-wrought twisted handle, is both early and unusual in form, making it valuable. More commonly found and much less expensive are examples from the late 19th or early 20th century, often with removable wooden handles.

351 **Iron washboard**

Description
Flat washboard with rectangular main section of corrugated horizontal rows. Round-cornered top panel with flat rim and paired 6-pointed stars in relief. 2 curved tapering legs with arched profile between. Repaired with rods and rivets where left leg joins body.

Materials and Dimensions
Cast iron. Wrought-iron rods. Iron rivets. Length: 18″. Width: 13½″. Thickness: ⅜″.

Locality and Period
The Midwest. c. 1880–1910.

Comment
Washing clothes has been the homemaker's never-ending chore for centuries. The washboard is thought to have been invented in this country; the earliest versions were of corrugated wood, with planks attached to the sides as feet. By the 1880s, most wooden washboards had been replaced by metal or metal-and-wood pieces. One popular model had embossed circles and bore the legend "Hand-e-washboard, circles do the hard work."

Hints for Collectors
The variety of implements and tubs used over the years for laundering has been immense, and many of these utensils can still be bought inexpensively. Hand-operated wooden wringers, clothes forks, and manual agitators for washtubs are some early pieces often found at farm sales or in out-of-the-way corners of antiques shops. This washboard has a particularly handsome, curving shape that makes it highly desirable.

352 Wooden dibble board

Description
Rectangular board with 12 rows of hand-carved bullet-shaped pegs set in circular holes; rows of 13 pegs alternating with rows of 12 pegs, the latter beginning a short distance from the edge of the board. Peg and nail construction.

Materials and Dimensions
Pine and maple. Cut nails. Length: 17″. Width: 17½″. Depth: 3″.

Locality and Period
Connecticut. c. 1880–1900.

Comment
Dibble boards were used to make a large number of holes in the ground for planting seeds. The board shown here makes 150 holes each time it is pressed into the soil. On a large farm, of course, the use of such boards was too time-consuming and wearying, so other methods were utilized. Many gardeners or amateur farmers still use dibble boards today.

Hints for Collectors
Out-of-the-ordinary farm tools such as dibble boards can often be discovered by rummaging through boxes of tools or what may look like piles of junk at farm or barn sales and at rural estate auctions. Handcrafted utilitarian objects that have great visual appeal are just beginning to become popular among collectors. Old wooden tools, in particular, offer a tremendous variety of interesting designs at reasonable prices. Patience and a good eye are required, however, to select the finest tools in terms of design and condition.

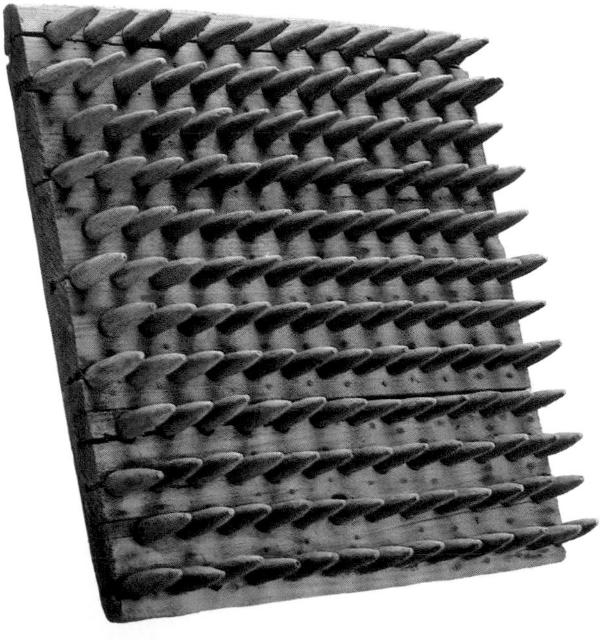

353 Wrought-iron eel or fish spears

Description
Long-shafted pronged spears, seen in detail. *Left:* 2 pairs of flat U-shaped prongs on straight shaft. *Center:* 7 curved prongs with triangular barbs; elongated bulbous neck connecting prongs to round shaft. *Right:* Short spear with 4 broad flat prongs curving inward; neck tapering to flat shaft.

Materials and Dimensions
Wrought iron. Overall length (left to right): 25″; 63″; 21¾″. Width: 2″; 4″; 3½″.

Locality and Period
New England or the Midwest. c. 1860–90.

Comment
Eels, sought for about 2 centuries for both their meat and skin, have been caught in American rivers and coastal waters with spears such as those shown here or with basket traps (*see* 260). The eeling industry was very important as late as the early 20th century, but eels are no longer in demand. Spears were also used by winter fishermen who, sitting in small shanties over holes in the ice, attracted fish with decoys and then speared them.

Hints for Collectors
These iron spears, all wrought by hand, are valuable as historical artifacts as well as decorative objects. Like most folk objects, they are primarily utilitarian; the decorative touches—here, curved prongs and unusual silhouettes—appeal to collectors today but were undoubtedly secondary to their makers. Such fishing spears or other old wrought-iron tools are generally inexpensive and can be handsomely displayed as sculpture.

354 Wooden hay and barley forks

Description
Left: Barley fork with 3 curved, pointed tines held apart by 3 small rods. Flat fourth tine curving outward in front and screwed to iron bracket. Flattened handle. *Center:* Hay fork with 3 flat tines, curved and separated by 3 small rods. Painted and inscribed "JOHN M. REC. 2.02¾." Flattened handle. *Right:* Barley fork with 4 curved tines that are rounded, pointed, and held apart by wedges. Flat fifth tine perpendicular to others, curving upward and tapered. Rounded handle.

Materials and Dimensions
Left: Ash or hickory. Iron bracket and screws. Length: 83″. Width: 14″. *Center:* Maple. Painted. Steel rivets. Length: 61″. Width: 12¼″. *Right:* Maple. Iron rivets, nails, and screws. Length: 74″. Width: 17″.

Locality and Period
Pennsylvania or New England. c. 1875–1900.

Comment
Because wood was lighter and cheaper, many farm tools, including forks, rakes, and grain shovels, were made of wood even after iron became readily available. While these 3 examples are similar, the 2 barley forks have an extra tine in front to hold the barley more securely. The center fork may have been used to pitch hay for a racehorse; the inscription may be his name and his record time for a race.

Hints for Collectors
Wooden farm tools were produced in large numbers, but most eventually wore out or broke from constant use. Beautifully made, graceful tools like these are hard to find today, although they still turn up occasionally at farm auctions, and some folk art dealers have begun to offer fine examples for sale.

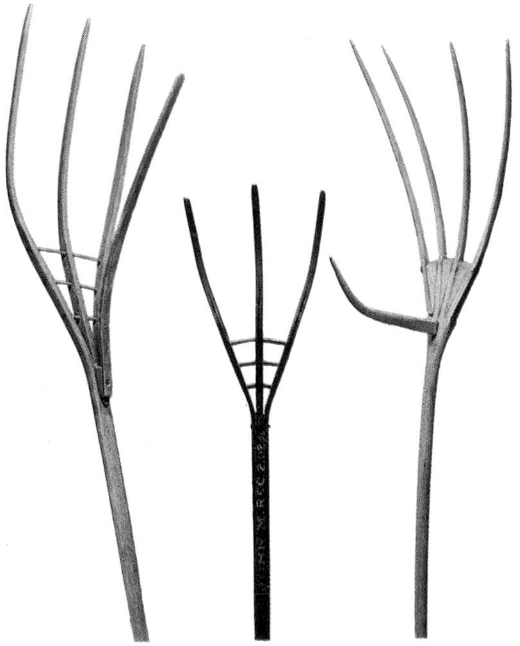

355 Wrought-iron hay cutter

Description
Hay cutter with long pointed blade having grooves incised on one side and serrated edge. 2 long handles, one more strongly curved than the other; rounded wooden handholds with brass collars, attached perpendicularly to handles. Screw construction.

Materials and Dimensions
Wrought iron. Maple. Brass. Iron screws. Overall length: 35″. Width: 10½″. Length of handholds: 5″.

Locality and Period
Connecticut. c. 1850–90.

Comment
Many early tools, including those used by fishermen, carpenters, and farmers, have their own grace and beauty. Hay cutters, always made in this unusual curving shape, are among the most elegant. The proportions and balance of this implement give it a striking sculptural appearance. The example shown here is unusual in having an incised blade as well as the serrated edge found on most hay cutters. Handholds are also subject to variation: on some examples, only one is perpendicular to the cutter while the other is simply a flat extension of the blade.

Hints for Collectors
While interest in early handmade tools has increased in recent years, good buys still abound, particularly at farm or other country auctions where the possessions of several generations of owners are being sold. An example as pleasing as this one, however, may be expensive even at a country auction, particularly if several interested bidders are present.

356 Root cane

Description
Walking stick with free-form root handle continuing down in single slender shaft as barkless rod. Nodules on top of handle.

Materials and Dimensions
Varnished wood. Length: 44″. Width: 9¼″. Depth: 12″.

Locality and Period
Connecticut. c. 1890–1900.

Comment
Around the turn of the century, canes or walking sticks were considered by many as an integral part of a gentleman's outfit. Fashionable urban as well as simpler country versions were common. The one shown here was probably made by a farmer who wanted a distinctly personal walking stick. Some collectors of walking sticks specialize in one-of-a-kind examples such as this; others prefer highly carved pieces, those with gimmicks or gadgets, or canes made by black Americans.

Hints for Collectors
Canes are an affordable specialty, since many fine examples of this form are available for a few hundred dollars or less. Those in usable condition are the most desirable. Pieces that are split, splintered, or altered seldom command substantial sums, so never refinish a walking stick, regardless of its condition. Look for interesting examples in junk shops and thrift shops, since antiques dealers are more likely to charge higher prices. Many dealers, in fact, keep walking sticks for their own personal collections.

357 Carved figural canes

Description
Wooden canes with carved tops. *Left:* Red-stained bald head with long narrow face and large eyes having inset seed pupils. Octagonal shaft with iron-shod tip and brass collar at base. *Right:* Clenched fist with fingers curved around hole probably used for hanging stick on nail; cuff at wrist with V-shaped indentations along top. Cylindrical shaft encircled by snake along entire length, with its head at top.

Materials and Dimensions
Possibly ash or hickory. Stained or painted. Brass. Iron. Overall length (left; right): 36⅞″; 35¼″. Length of top: 2⅞″; 3⅛″.

Locality and Period
Left: New Hampshire. c. 1850–1900. *Right:* The South. c. 1880–1900.

Comment
Canes were made by various types of craftsmen as well as by amateurs. They were particularly popular in the South, where they may have been created first by black carvers continuing an African tradition in which symbolic carved staffs conferred power and prestige on their owners. To be serviceable, canes were usually made of sturdy woods such as hickory, ash, mahogany, or spruce; these were generally given a dark stain, which gradually wore off to reveal glimpses of the lighter wood.

Hints for Collectors
Many collectors specialize in carved canes, and they especially prize sculptural examples showing elaborate craftsmanship. These long, thin objects are difficult to display effectively; some collectors drill a small hole in the bottom of a cane in order to have it stand erect on a spikelike weighted base.

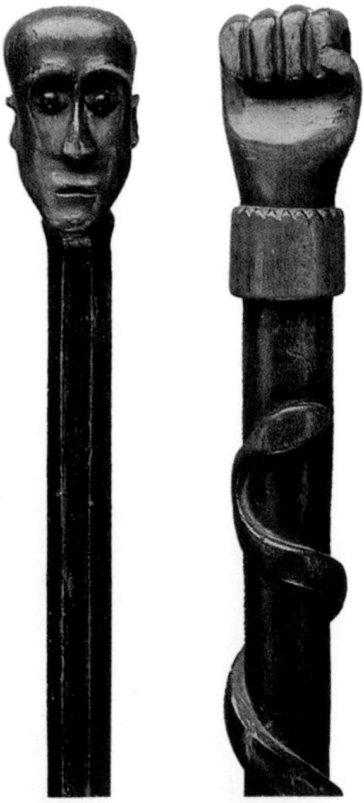

358 Painted and incised cane

Description
Carved cane with painted and incised decoration on straight cylindrical shaft; upper portion shown. Decoration includes seated dog, eagle with tricolored shield, house, barn, flowers, and cats. Inscribed "C. ATKINSON. 1898. Swimming River."

Materials and Dimensions
Ash or hickory. Painted. Length: 33¼″. Diameter: 1¼″.

Locality and Period
Probably New Jersey. 1898.

Comment
Canes were much more common in earlier centuries than today, possibly because gout and other crippling diseases were more prevalent. People took pride in their canes, particularly if finely carved. Sculpted human or animal heads often served as decorative tops. Sometimes a name and date inscribed in the wood identified either the maker or the owner. This example also bears the name of the town where it was made.

Hints for Collectors
While canes with a carved head or handle were fairly common, those with allover carving, such as the example shown here, were not. The painted decoration as well as the carving makes this a fine piece. The patriotic eagle and shield—the latter still bearing much of its original red, white, and blue paint—add to its value. A cane that has been repainted or is too fragile to use is much less valuable. This particular example was purchased for a small sum at a flea market at the end of the day—a particularly good time to shop since vendors are often willing to lower the prices of their remaining merchandise.

359 **Fire warden's staff**

Description
Long painted pole with black bullet-shaped finial having 2 horizontal gilded stripes. Upper third of staff (detail at left) decorated with horizontal black stripe and diagonal black stripe having gilded numerals "1851" (detail at right).

Materials and Dimensions
Maple. Painted. Length: 73″. Diameter: 1¾″.

Locality and Period
Pennsylvania. 1851.

Comment
Although fire-fighting equipment was basically utilitarian, many pieces were elaborately decorated with painted and carved symbols, and volunteer fire departments held competitions to judge which company had the most attractive paraphernalia. The object shown here was a fire warden's staff, a symbol of authority that could be easily seen in a crowd. Often put to practical use as a pointer for directing the fire brigade, the staff also had a ceremonial function at parades and civic events. This pole is probably from a rural area, since those used in cities were more highly decorated.

Hints for Collectors
Objects relating to firemen and other trades or professions are generally of greatest interest to collectors specializing in those fields, who are often willing to pay a premium for authentic examples. Because most of these objects are no longer used today and are thus unfamiliar, it is important to gain background knowledge about 19th-century life to recognize them.

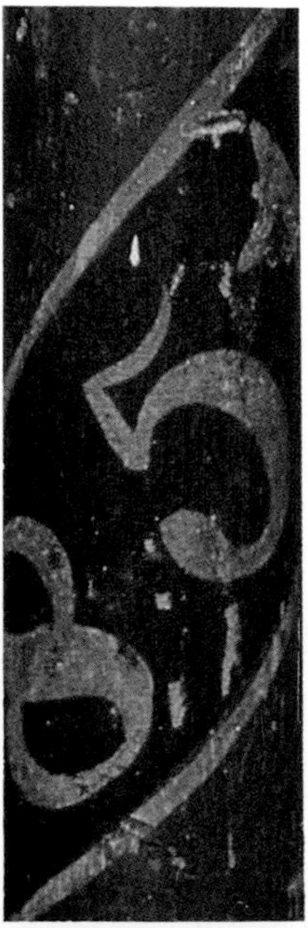

360 Scrimshaw cane

Description
Cane with shaft in 8 sections carved in varied patterns and separated by inlaid rings of diamond-shaped pieces of abalone shell. Larger diamond shapes inlaid around octagonal knob, with 5-pointed star on top and initial "J" on side. Details (left to right): Top section with 4 spiral-carved columns inlaid in baleen; second section from top with 8 vertical grooves; third section from top spiral-carved.

Materials and Dimensions
Whale ivory. Baleen. Abalone shell. Length: 35″. Diameter of knob: 2″.

Locality and Period
Massachusetts. c. 1860.

Comment
Scrimshaw canes, as varied as the whalers who made them, come in all sizes, shapes, and types—from captains' large, scepterlike "going-ashore" canes to men's, women's, and even children's canes. They are generally made of whalebone, whale ivory, or baleen, but other materials—gold, silver, pewter or brass, sealing wax, various pigments, shells, exotic and domestic woods, coins, and parts of fish or mammals—have been used for their inlay or decoration. Tops may vary from a plain round knob or a curved or L-shaped handle to a fist or pair of female legs.

Hints for Collectors
There is great interest in ivory canes; good ones are always in short supply and very expensive. Moreover, since they are delicate, many are chipped or have pieces missing. Handles may have become separated from their original shafts, so beware of "married" examples, those made of segments from several different canes.

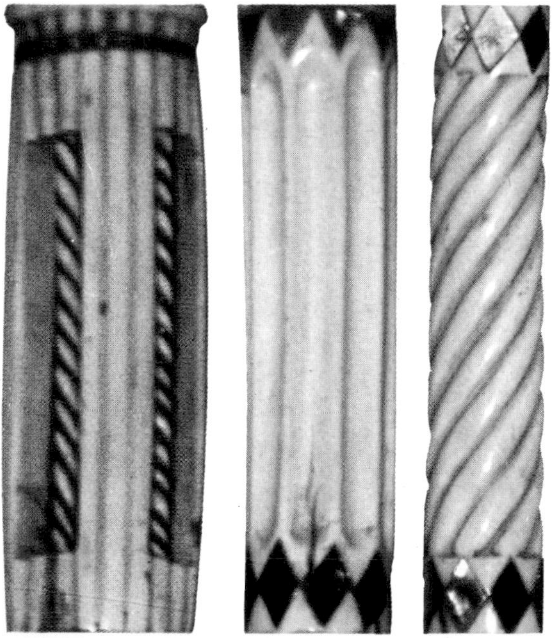

List of Plates by Material

Glossary

Academic A term describing a work executed by an artist who has been formally trained in the techniques of composition, lighting, and perspective. Opposite of naive and primitive.

Acrylic paint Paint made by suspending pigment in a polymer-base emulsion that becomes waterproof upon drying.

Artist's board *See* Canvas board.

Baleen A flexible membrane that hardens once removed from a whale's mouth. Used to make such objects as pie crimpers, swifts, cane handles, and corset busks. It ranges in color from brownish-black to beige and off-white. Also called whalebone.

Batten A strip of wood, used to prevent warping, attached at right angles to the grain of planks that form a flat surface such as a breadboard.

Black light An invisible ultraviolet or infrared light used to detect repairs and alterations on works of art.

Board A flat piece of wood, often pine, on which a painting is executed. Popular among American artists of the 17th, 18th, and 19th centuries.

Bulto A three-dimensional carved and painted image of a religious figure made in the Southwest by Indians and Hispanic Americans and in other areas where Spanish is spoken.

Burl A protruding growth on a tree that, when sliced, reveals beautiful graining. Used for bowls, ladles, and other household objects.

Canvas board Cardboardlike material with a stamped or molded surface that imitates the texture of canvas.

Chalkware Molded and painted ornamental figures cast from processed gypsum and water. Common in America in the late 19th century.

Crazing A network of fine cracks on a painted surface. Usually occurs as the oils in which pigments are suspended dry out; may also be caused by sharp changes in temperature or humidity.

Cross hatching A basket-weaving technique in which pieces of splint are tightly crossed at right angles.

Curly work A traditional Indian basketmaking technique in which excess lengths of splint are formed into curls or points to create a decorative, raised pattern. Called curlicue by some tribes.

Daguerreotype A type of photograph produced by developing an exposed, silver-coated metal plate in mercury vapor. It originated in France during the second quarter of the 19th century.

Finger laps Triangular, overlapping wooden joinings shaped like fingers, frequently used by Shaker craftsmen on wooden pantry boxes and buckets.

Finial A turned or carved ornament atop a shaft or other vertical member.

Fractur A highly stylized, vivid watercolor picture recording an event or depicting a spiritual subject; used by German-speaking Americans for family records or decoration. Often includes a verse in German and standard motifs such as tulips, hearts, and doves. From the German *Fraktur*, an elaborate type of Gothic script.

Genre painting A type of painting that focuses on scenes of everyday life.

Gesso A mixture of plaster of Paris, glue, and water used to prepare a sculpture or canvas for painting. It produces a smooth, nonporous surface.

Gouache Paint made by combining opaque watercolors with a gum preparation.

Grisaille Watercolor painting in shades of gray.

Japanning A painted imitation of Oriental lacquer, usually on wood or tin, in which a solid base coat of japan (a tar-based black paint) is decorated in oil paint with brightly colored flowers or other designs.

Limner A term used for 18th-century American painters, particularly those who were itinerant, with little or no formal training and limited access to materials. Such artists, if unidentified, were sometimes named after their most prominent sitters or the towns where they did their major work.

Naive *See* Primitive.

Obsessive A term describing a modern painter whose images demonstrate a preoccupation with a fixed idea, often religious.

Oilcloth A cotton cloth coated with a finish that usually contains oil, clay, and pigment and renders it waterproof.

Palette The range of colors used by an artist; also the board, usually with a thumbhole at one end, on which colors are mixed.

Panbone A rare and much prized material taken from the back of a sperm whale's jawbone. Named for its flat, panlike shape. Often engraved and shaped into corset busks or plaques.

Panel *See* Board.

Pattern A model, usually wooden, used to produce a mold in which molten metal is cast.

Peg A wooden pin that passes through both units of a joint, binding them together.

Plaiting A basket-weaving technique in which a weaver (horizontal element) is placed over one rib (vertical element) and under the next. Called twill plaiting if pattern is varied.

Primer A base coat of paint or sizing applied to a surface to prepare it for painting.

Primitive A term describing a direct, simple, and unsophisticated style of visual expression, usually employed by a self-taught folk artist; opposite of academic. Not to be confused with "primitive art," referring to the art of primitive peoples in Africa, Asia, and Oceania.

Provenance The history of a work, including its origin and a record of its ownership and where it has been exhibited.

Relief carving Decoration formed by carving away the background to produce projecting figures or forms; called low relief when the decoration projects only slightly and high relief when the background is more deeply cut.

Répoussé A decorative technique in which a raised pattern is created on one side of a thin sheet of metal by hammering or beating the reverse side.

Reverse painting A picture executed on the back of a glass panel. The painting is done in reverse order, from details to background, so that the completed work may be viewed correctly through the glass.

Ribs Vertical elements through which horizontal elements, or weavers, are woven to form a basket.

Sandpaper picture A picture made by drawing on a granular surface, such as sandpaper or marble-dust paper, with charcoal or pastels.

Santo A Spanish term for a carved or painted image of a religious figure made in the American Southwest and in other Spanish-speaking areas. Includes bultos (three-dimensional figures) and retablos (paintings).

Scrimshaw An ornamental or utilitarian article made of whalebone or whale ivory; often carved and sometimes decorated with engravings highlighted by ink or pigments. Usually made by American whalemen.

Splint Thin strips of wood, often varying in width, used to weave baskets. Usually oak, hickory, or ash.

Stretcher A wooden frame over which canvas for a painting is pulled taut.

Tempera Paint made by combining pigment with a glutinous water-soluble substance such as glue, flour, or egg yolk.

Theorem painting A still-life painting that usually depicts fruit and flowers in a bowl or vase. Accomplished with stencils, often called theorems, which were carefully arranged so that outlines could be traced and then filled in with colors.

Tinsel picture A reverse painting on glass that has been backed with crinkled foil to produce a shimmering effect.

Toleware Painted and decorated 19th-century American tinware, including teapots, trays, and bread baskets. Originally referred to 18th-century French lacquered tinware.

Treenware Wooden utensils of all types, most commonly household objects such as spoons, plates, bowls, scoops, and boxes. Sometimes called treen.

Turned Shaped on a lathe; the wood is rotated around a horizontal axis and shaped by fixed chisels.

Weavers Horizontal elements woven through the ribs, or vertical elements, to form a basket.

Whalebone A durable, hornlike material taken from the jaw of certain whales. Carved and engraved by whalemen, and often used for boxes, pie crimpers, plaques, corset busks, and other scrimshaw objects. *See also* Baleen, Panbone, and Scrimshaw.

Whale ivory Whale teeth, often carved or engraved by 19th-century whalemen.

Wrought iron Iron that is hammered, or wrought, into shape, rather than cast. Used in America as early as the 17th century for many kitchen and fireplace implements.

Public Collections

Most large art museums exhibit American folk art. In addition, many of the historic houses, buildings, and restoration villages that are open to the public have fine examples. The sources listed below indicate significant permanent collections.

New England

Connecticut
Hartford: Wadsworth Atheneum. *Mystic:* Mystic Seaport.

Maine
Augusta: Maine State Museum. *Poland Spring:* The Shaker Museum, Sabbathday Lake. *Rockland:* William A. Farnsworth Art Museum.

Massachusetts
Boston: Museum of Fine Arts; The Society for the Preservation of New England Antiquities. *Deerfield:* Historic Deerfield. *Hancock:* Hancock Shaker Village. *New Bedford:* New Bedford Whaling Museum. *Sturbridge:* Old Sturbridge Village.

New Hampshire
Manchester: The Currier Gallery of Art. *Portsmouth:* Strawberry Banke, Inc.

Vermont
Shelburne: Shelburne Museum.

Mid-Atlantic Region

Delaware
Winterthur: Henry Francis du Pont Winterthur Museum.

Maryland
Baltimore: Baltimore Museum of Art.

New Jersey
Newark: Newark Museum. *Trenton:* New Jersey State Museum.

New York
Albany: Albany Institute of History and Art; Museum of Early American Decoration, Inc. *Cooperstown:* New York State Historical Association. *New York City:* Abigail Adams Smith Museum; The Brooklyn Museum; The Metropolitan Museum of Art; Museum of American Folk Art; The New-York Historical Society. *Old Bethpage:* Old Bethpage Village. *Old Chatham:* The Shaker Museum. *Rochester:* The Margaret Woodbury Strong Museum. *Stony Brook:* The Museums at Stony Brook.

Pennsylvania
Doylestown: Bucks County Historical Society. *Harrisburg:* William Penn Memorial Museum. *Lancaster:* Pennsylvania Farm Museum of Landis Valley. *Philadelphia:* Philadelphia Museum of Art. *West Chester:* Chester County Historical Society.

Washington D.C.
National Gallery of Art; National Museum of American History, Smithsonian Institution.

South

Alabama
Mobile: The Fine Arts Museum of the South.

Florida
Sarasota: John and Mable Ringling Museum of Art.

Georgia
Atlanta: Atlanta Historical Society; The High Museum of Art.

Louisiana
New Orleans: Louisiana State Museum.

Mississippi
Oxford: Center for the Study of Southern Culture.

Missouri
Kansas City: William Rockhill Nelson Gallery and Atkins Museum of Fine Arts. *St. Louis:* St. Louis Art Museum.

North Carolina
Asheville: Asheville Museum of Art. *Winston-Salem:* Museum of Early Southern Decorative Arts; Old Salem, Inc.

Virginia
Norfolk: Chrysler Museum at Norfolk. *Williamsburg:* Colonial Williamsburg; The Abby Aldrich Rockefeller Collection of American Folk Art.

Midwest

Illinois
Bishop Hill: Bishop Hill Colony. *Chicago:* Art Institute of Chicago; Chicago Historical Society.

Iowa
Amana: Amana Villages. *Decorah:* Norwegian-American Museum.

Michigan
Dearborn: Greenfield Village and Henry Ford Museum. *Detroit:* Detroit Historical Museum; Detroit Institute of Arts. *East Lansing:* The Museum, Michigan State University. *Grand Rapids:* Grand Rapids Public Museum.

Minnesota
Minneapolis: Minneapolis Institute of Arts.

Ohio
Cincinnati: Cincinnati Art Museum. *Cleveland:* Cleveland Museum of Art; Western Reserve Historical Society. *Columbus:* Ohio Historical Society. *Zoar:* Zoar Village State Memorial.

Wisconsin
Baraboo: Circus World Museum. *Madison:* Wisconsin State Historical Society. *Milwaukee:* Villa Terrace Museum.

Rockies, Southwest, and West Coast

California
Los Angeles: Craft & Folk Art Museum; Los Angeles County Museum of Art. *Oakland:* The Oakland Museum. *San Francisco:* M. H. de Young Memorial Museum.

Kansas
Lawrence: Kansas Grassroots Art Association; Helen Foresman Spencer Museum of Art, The University of Kansas.

New Mexico
Santa Fe: Museum of International Folk Art.

Texas
Beaumont: Spindletop Museum, Lamar University. *Dallas:* Dallas Museum of Fine Arts. *Houston:* Bayou Bend.

Bibliography

Ames, Kenneth L.
Beyond Necessity: Art in the Folk Tradition
New York: W. W. Norton & Co., Inc., 1978.

Andrews, Edward Deming and Faith
Religion in Wood: A Book of Shaker Furniture
Bloomington, Indiana, and London: Indiana University Press, 1966.

Andrews, Ruth, ed.
How to Know American Folk Art
New York: E. P. Dutton, Inc., 1977.

Barber, Joel
Wild Fowl Decoys
New York: Dover Publications, Inc., 1954.

Bishop, Robert
American Folk Sculpture
New York: E. P. Dutton, Inc., 1974.
Folk Painters of America
New York: E. P. Dutton, Inc., 1979.

Bishop, Robert, and Patricia Coblentz
A Gallery of American Weathervanes and Whirligigs
New York: E. P. Dutton, Inc., 1981.

Black, Mary, and Jean Lipman
American Folk Painting
New York: Clarkson N. Potter, Inc., 1966.

Christensen, Erwin O.
The Index of American Design
New York: The Macmillan Co., 1950.

Coffin, Margaret
American Country Tin Ware 1700–1900
Camden, New Jersey: Thomas Nelson, Inc., 1968.

Cooke, Lawrence S., ed.
Lighting in America from Colonial Rushlights to Victorian Chandeliers
New York: Universe Books, Inc., 1976.

Davidson, Marshall B.
The American Heritage History of Colonial Antiques
New York: American Heritage Publishing Co., Inc., 1967.
The American Heritage History of American Antiques from the Revolution to the Civil War
New York: American Heritage Publishing Co., Inc., 1968.
The American Heritage History of Antiques from the Civil War to World War I
New York: American Heritage Publishing Co., Inc., 1969.

Dewhurst, C. Kurt; Betty MacDowell; and Marsha MacDowell
Artists in Aprons: Folk Art by American Women
New York: E. P. Dutton, Inc., 1979.

Downs, Joseph
Pennsylvania German Arts and Crafts
New York: The Metropolitan Museum of Art, 1949.

Earle, Alice Morse
Home Life in Colonial Days
Middle Village, New York: Jonathan David Publishers, Inc., 1975; reprint of 1898 edition.

Earnest, Adele
The Art of the Decoy
Exton, Pennsylvania: Schiffer Publishing, Ltd., 1982.

Ebert, John and Katherine
American Folk Painters
New York: Charles Scribner's Sons, 1975.

Ericson, Jack T., ed.
Folk Art in America: Painting and Sculpture
New York: Mayflower Books, Inc., 1979.

Fales, Dean A., Jr.
American Painted Furniture 1660–1880
New York: E. P. Dutton, Inc., 1979.

Fitzgerald, Ken
Weathervanes and Whirligigs
New York: Clarkson N. Potter, Inc., 1967.

Flayderman, E. Norman
Scrimshaw and Scrimshanders
New Milford, Connecticut: N. Flayderman & Co., Inc., 1973.

Fried, Frederick
Artists in Wood
New York: Clarkson N. Potter, Inc., 1970.
A Pictorial History of the Carousel
New York: A. S. Barnes, 1978.

Gould, Mary Earle
Early American Wooden Ware and Other Kitchen Utensils
Rutland, Vermont: Charles E. Tuttle, 1962.

Hayward, Arthur H.
Colonial Lighting
New York: Dover Publications, Inc., 1962.

Hemphill, Herbert W., Jr., ed.
Folk Sculpture U.S.A.
New York: Universe Books, Inc., 1976.

Hemphill, Herbert W., Jr., and Julia Weissman
Twentieth Century American Folk Art and Artists
New York: E. P. Dutton, Inc., 1974.

Hornung, Clarence P.
Treasury of American Design
New York: Harry N. Abrams, Inc., n.d.

Kassay, John
The Book of Shaker Furniture
Amherst, Massachusetts: The University of Massachusetts Press, 1980.

Janis, Sidney
They Taught Themselves: American Primitive Painters of the 20th Century
New York: Dial Press, 1942.

Kauffman, Henry J.
Early American Ironware
Camden, New Jersey: Thomas Nelson, Inc., 1966.

Ketchum, William C., Jr.
American Basketry & Woodenware
New York: The Macmillan Co., 1974.

Lichten, Frances
Folk Art of Rural Pennsylvania
New York: Charles Scribner's Sons, 1946.

Lipman, Jean
American Folk Art in Wood, Metal and Stone
New York: Dover Publications, Inc., 1972.
American Primitive Painting
New York: Dover Publications, Inc., 1972.

Lipman, Jean, and Tom Armstrong, eds.
American Folk Painters of Three Centuries
New York: Hudson Hills Press, Inc., 1980.

Lipman, Jean, and Alice Winchester
The Flowering of American Folk Art 1776–1876
New York: Penguin Books, Inc., 1977.

Little, Nina Fletcher
Neat and Tidy: Boxes and Their Contents in Early American Households
New York: E. P. Dutton, Inc., 1980.

Lord, Priscilla S., and Daniel J. Foley
The Folk Arts and Crafts of New England
Radnor, Pennsylvania: Chilton Book Co., 1965.

Mackey, William J., Jr.
American Bird Decoys
New York: E. P. Dutton, Inc., 1965.

Pendergast, A. W., and W. Porter Ware
Cigar Store Figures
Chicago, Illinois: The Lightner Publishing Corp., 1953.

Philadelphia Museum of Art
The Pennsylvania Germans: A Celebration of Their Arts 1683–1850
Philadelphia, Pennsylvania: Philadelphia Museum of Art, 1982.

Rumford, Beatrix T., ed.
American Folk Portraits: Paintings and Drawings from The Abby Aldrich Rockefeller Folk Art Center
Boston, Massachusetts: New York Graphic Society Books, 1981.

Sonn, Albert H.
Early American Wrought Iron
New York: Bonanza Books, 1979.

Stoudt, John J.
Early Pennsylvania Arts and Crafts
Cranbury, New Jersey: A. S. Barnes and Co., Inc., 1964.

Teleki, Gloria Roth
Collecting Traditional American Basketry
New York: E. P. Dutton, Inc., 1979.

Welsh, Peter C.
American Folk Art: The Art & Spirit of a People
Washington, D.C.: Smithsonian Institution, 1965.

How to Buy Folk Art

Folk art is available throughout the country at thousands of shops, shows, flea markets, house sales, and auctions. The more valuable works, particularly paintings and sculpture, are most likely to be found in fine galleries and at top-drawer shows and auctions. Many kinds of moderately priced objects, however, are best found at general antiques shops, flea markets, house sales, and rural auctions.

Shops
Most folk art is sold by dealers. These professionals are usually glad to share their knowledge with customers. In an antiques shop or at a dealer's home you have time to examine a piece thoroughly, and you rarely need to make an immediate decision to buy. Since there are dealers who specialize in virtually every kind of folk art and in every price range, you are sure to find one who suits your taste and budget.

Shows
Antiques shows take place regularly in communities of all sizes and give collectors a chance to meet many dealers at one time. Shows featuring Americana almost always include folk art. Because many collectors come to these shows, dealers usually exhibit their finest wares there, making it somewhat easier for collectors to find objects that are hard to locate. But most antiques shows last only a day or two, and since several collectors are often interested in the same item, decisions must be made rather quickly.

Flea Markets and House Sales
Collectors interested in inexpensive folk art, especially household objects, will frequently find what they are looking for at flea markets or house sales. At flea markets, the sellers are rarely professionals. Most of the merchandise is unidentified, and pieces can sometimes be purchased for a fraction of their true value if sellers do not recognize what they have. Here, however, you must depend almost totally on your own knowledge. The same is true of house sales: whether at a tag, yard, garage, or private sale, buyers must be able to distinguish between true bargains and overpriced odds and ends.

Auctions
Auctions, ranging from those at city auction houses to backyard or country affairs, offer a considerable quantity of objects in one place. The unpredictability that makes an auction so exciting, however, is also its major drawback. Buyers have only moments to decide upon a bid, and prices are set by the interest generated in the people who happen to be on hand. Buying at auction requires patience and self-restraint. A particular auction may not offer the specific object you are seeking, and it may be wise to wait until you find exactly what you want at a future sale. (See the following pages for hints on how to buy at auction.)

Shopping Hints
No matter where you buy, be cautious. Although dishonest practices are rare, any seller may occasionally be guilty of poor judgment or excessive optimism; deliberate deceptions are far less common than honest mistakes. Deal with the most reputable people you can find, and if you suspect that an object is not what it is said to be, don't buy. It is wise to get a bill of sale listing what you have bought, its age, attribution, and any repairs done to the piece. Also ask for a guarantee stating that the piece can be returned should any of this information prove untrue.

Buying at Auction

Since some of the finest and most interesting pieces of folk art are sold at auction, it is understandable that sooner or later most collectors try their hand at bidding. Also, tales abound of discovering unrecognized masterpieces or of sought-after objects that fetch half their predicted price. Most of these tales date from the 1920s to 1950s, when bargains were commonplace. Auctions today are attended by an army of sophisticated collectors and dealers, well schooled in what to look for and how much to pay.

Although country and city auctions today offer countless inexpensive objects, they are no longer the place to look for real bargains. Whenever a major work is presented for sale, collectors and dealers usually hear about it beforehand and appear at the auction to battle over its acquisition. Yet because folk art is so varied, and because the field is relatively new, it is likely that from time to time auctioneers will be unacquainted with unusual pieces they are selling—it is then that informed collectors can purchase bargains. At auction, however, knowing the rules of the game can help prevent costly mistakes.

How an Auction Works

An auction is a sale of objects to the highest bidders. The seller, or the consignor, offers goods to prospective buyers through his agent, the auctioneer. The bidder offering the most money for a given item buys the "lot" (one piece or a group of pieces sold together). The auctioneer always tries to stimulate bidding and to get the highest price, since he (or his firm) generally receives a percentage of the sale as payment or commission.

The Viewing and Other Preliminaries

The first step toward informed bidding is to attend the viewing before the auction, an advertised period of a few hours or days during which the objects offered may be examined by the public. Never bid on something unless you have checked it thoroughly beforehand. Compare what you see with the information given in the catalogue, if one is available. If you have any questions about an object, its attribution, or its condition, talk to the auctioneer or the firm's specialist in folk art. If a catalogue is not available, carry a small notebook to jot down the lot number and other information about the object, particularly its condition. If you feel uncertain about the auctioneer's or your own assessment of a piece, especially an expensive one, you may wish to hire a consultant—dealers will often, for a fee, advise you or sometimes even bid for you.

The viewing is also a good time to find out what form of payment the auctioneer requires. Some will take only cash or certified checks; others will accept personal checks with proper identification, or credit cards.

The Sale

At most larger auctions, the auctioneer will provide estimated price ranges for the pieces in the sale. These are usually printed in the auction catalogue or on a separate list. Though pieces quite often sell for more or less than the estimates, these should give you some idea of what the auctioneer expects a piece to fetch. Also, many large auction houses allow a seller to set a "reserve" on a lot—the price below which it will not be sold, frequently close to the low estimate. If bidding does not reach this minimum, the lot will be withdrawn and returned to the consignor for a small handling fee.

 Decide in advance the price you are willing to pay for a particular lot. The Price Guide section of this book provides general guidelines and prevailing market price ranges to help you set your own bidding limit.

The best place to sit at an auction is toward the rear, where you can see more of what is going on. There are two customary ways to bid—by raising a hand or by using the numbered paddle sometimes furnished by the auctioneer. Listen closely; bidding is often extremely rapid. When your pre-established price limit has been reached, stop. This is the key to wise auction bidding.

Patience and persistence are required, since at every auction some pieces may sell for more or for less than most people anticipate. There is almost always a "sleeper" or two, particularly just after or even just before a high-priced lot has captured the attention of the audience.

At many auction houses, someone who has attended the viewing but cannot be present at the auction itself can leave a bid. Such bids will be treated as the maximum the absentee bidder is willing to spend, so that if there is little competition when the auction house bids for you, the final price you pay may be far less than your top bid. An out-of-town collector who has seen an auction catalogue but cannot attend the viewing and auction may sometimes be allowed to place a bid by telephone, but such blind bidding is not recommended unless the bidder delegates someone to examine the object for him prior to the sale.

Collecting Your Purchases

The fall of the gavel and the cry of "sold" mark a successful bid. Now the buyer must pay for the purchase and remove it from the auction premises. Large auction houses will ship items for a fee; most auctioneers do not have such services, however, and the buyer is responsible for transporting a purchase within a stated time limit.

Price Guide

by William C. Ketchum, Jr.

In folk art, as in most fields, experienced collectors are much more likely to find bargains than novices are. To avoid costly mistakes and to make wise purchases, collectors must become thoroughly acquainted with folk art and with today's marketplace. It is also advisable to understand how collecting trends change—why certain types of works suddenly become popular, causing their prices to double or triple within a few years, while other kinds of folk art do not attract a wide audience. To keep abreast of these trends, collectors should study auction reports and talk with dealers about price variations.

Auction Prices versus Dealers' Prices

Dealers' prices are the most accurate guide to what is happening on the market. Because dealers must remain competitive, their prices tend to become relatively uniform over a period of time. Today many collectors look to auctions as the ultimate price determinant, for auctions do offer dramatic evidence of the market in action. A piece is presented, all bidders compete as equals, and the highest bidder gets the piece. Actually, it is not that simple. Anyone who has observed two bidders competing for an object knows that such competition can drive prices well above a reasonable figure. The added attraction of objects with fancy pedigrees may also distort auction records. On the other hand, auction prices can be unrealistically low if, for some reason, attendance at the sale is poor or if doubt is cast on the authenticity of a piece. In general, auction results are good indications of wholesale prices because dealers make many of the purchases, and thus these prices do reflect long-term market trends.

This price guide is based on both auction records and consultations with dealers and knowledgeable collectors. Remember that experienced collectors understand, and we agree, that a price guide is just that, a guide. No two objects are identical, and no two buying situations are the same. Unlike many other kinds of art and antiques, however, folk art brings fairly uniform prices across the country, so that regional price differentials are uncommon.

Attribution, Condition, Scarcity, and Collectors' Tastes

An artist's signature or a strong attribution to a maker will obviously enhance the value of a work greatly. Yet regardless of who executed a piece of folk art or when it was done, the quality of the individual work is a crucial factor. Nearly all folk artists produced only a few great works and even fewer masterpieces. For example, pictures by Ammi Phillips or Edward Hicks, two of the best-known 19th-century folk artists, occasionally bring six-figure prices, but many of their works may still be acquired for sums one-tenth as large.

Condition is also important in determining the value of a piece. If a piece is in poor and irreparable condition, whether from unintentional damage or deliberate alterations, it will be worth only a fraction of its listed price. The prices given here assume that each piece is in good condition, with no major restoration, even if the particular example illustrated shows some damage. Before you buy a repaired, altered, or damaged piece, be sure to adjust the price given here accordingly.

Scarcity also affects value. Rare and early pieces will, other things being equal, command a higher price. If a piece is rare or unusual enough, it is almost impossible to predict what it will sell for. Prices also rise and fall as types increase or decrease in popularity. Changes in taste are hard to predict. Buy what you like, and buy the best. That way you are less apt to be affected by fads.

Price Ranges

The price ranges given here are those for a category of objects represented by the piece illustrated, not prices for the specific objects. Two sets of price ranges are given for paintings: the first is for works of the same quality and by the same artist as the example shown; the second, in parentheses, is either for the entire output of that artist or, if the work is unattributed, for the type of picture.

Portraits

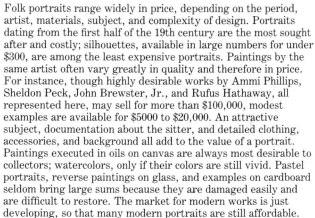

Folk portraits range widely in price, depending on the period, artist, materials, subject, and complexity of design. Portraits dating from the first half of the 19th century are the most sought after and costly; silhouettes, available in large numbers for under $300, are among the least expensive portraits. Paintings by the same artist often vary greatly in quality and therefore in price. For instance, though highly desirable works by Ammi Phillips, Sheldon Peck, John Brewster, Jr., and Rufus Hathaway, all represented here, may sell for more than $100,000, modest examples are available for $5000 to $20,000. An attractive subject, documentation about the sitter, and detailed clothing, accessories, and background all add to the value of a portrait. Paintings executed in oils on canvas are always most desirable to collectors; watercolors, only if their colors are still vivid. Pastel portraits, reverse paintings on glass, and examples on cardboard seldom bring large sums because they are damaged easily and are difficult to restore. The market for modern works is just developing, so that many modern portraits are still affordable.

1 Memorial miniature in locket $2800–3500 ($500–4500)
2 Dorman Theodore Warren $20,000–45,000 ($5000–45,000)
3 Portrait of a Child $35,000–45,000 ($2500–45,000)
4 Young Child with Black and White Cat $8000–14,000 ($2500–14,000)
5 Portrait of a Girl with Basket $8000–12,000 ($5000–12,000)
6 Mary E. Kingman $30,000–40,000 ($10,000–40,000)
7 Boy with a Parrot $5000–14,000 ($3500–35,000)
8 Young Boy Feeding Rabbits $20,000–40,000 ($8500–40,000)
9 Young Boy with Toy Cat $8000–12,500 ($2500–12,500)
10 Boy and Girl $10,000–20,000 ($10,000–40,000)
11 The Tow Sisters $8000–15,000 ($1500–15,000)
12 Lady in Yellow Dress Watering Roses $3000–6000 ($650–6000)
13 Fräulein $650–1000 ($350–5000)
14 Eliza Gordon Brooks $25,000–35,000 ($15,000–50,000)
15 Woman in a Mulberry Dress $12,000–15,000 ($8000–35,000)
16 Lauriette Ashley Adams Peck $12,000–20,000 ($5000–45,000)
17 Woman in Chippendale Side Chair $8000–20,000 ($8000–35,000)
18 Lady from Maine $7500–15,000 ($7500–125,000)
19 Old Woman $2800–3500 ($2500–20,000)
20 The Gossips $1500–2500 ($1500–45,000)
21 Silhouette $200–300 ($150–6000)
22 Silhouette $200–350 ($150–6000)
23 Archer Payne, Jr. $18,000–35,000 ($15,000–45,000)
24 John Jackson $6000–7000 ($6000–100,000)

25 Man with a Pipe $7500–14,000 ($5000–350,000)
26 Reverend Ebenezer Gay, Sr. $45,000–65,000 ($25,000–100,000)
27 Sea Captain $20,000–30,000 ($5000–45,000)
28 Captain Sylvanus Sampson $55,000–75,000 ($15,000–100,000)
29 Gentleman Seated Between Tables $4500–6500 ($3500–7500)
30 Frank Peters, the Tailor $20,000–35,000 ($2500–35,000)
31 Black Man $300–750 ($200–1200)
32 Black Man $650–850 ($650–2000)

Landscapes and Seascapes

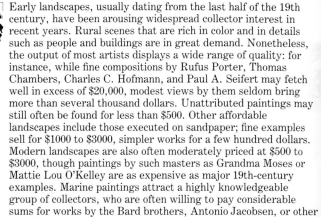

Early landscapes, usually dating from the last half of the 19th century, have been arousing widespread collector interest in recent years. Rural scenes that are rich in color and in details such as people and buildings are in great demand. Nonetheless, the output of most artists displays a wide range of quality: for instance, while fine compositions by Rufus Porter, Thomas Chambers, Charles C. Hofmann, and Paul A. Seifert may fetch well in excess of $20,000, modest views by them seldom bring more than several thousand dollars. Unattributed paintings may still often be found for less than $500. Other affordable landscapes include those executed on sandpaper; fine examples sell for $1000 to $3000, simpler works for a few hundred dollars. Modern landscapes are also often moderately priced at $500 to $3000, though paintings by such masters as Grandma Moses or Mattie Lou O'Kelley are as expensive as major 19th-century examples. Marine paintings attract a highly knowledgeable group of collectors, who are often willing to pay considerable sums for works by the Bard brothers, Antonio Jacobsen, or other popular artists.

33 Mural $6000–12,000 ($6000–65,000)
34 River View $250–450 ($100–650)
35 Romantic Landscape $950–1500 ($600–3000)
36 Hunters in a Hudson River Landscape $10,000–20,000 ($7500–35,000)
37 View of the Genesee Falls When Sam Patch Took His Last Leap in 1829 $2000–3000 ($1000–8000)
38 Slater Mill $4500–6000 ($1000–15,000)
39 Oswego Starch Factory $25,000–35,000 ($10,000–65,000)
40 View of the Schuylkill County Almshouse Property $65,000–90,000 ($35,000–100,000)
41 Residence of Lemuel Cooper $15,000–25,000 ($10,000–35,000)
42 Residence of Mr. and Mrs. John H. Abel $4500–8000 ($1000–8500)
43 Street Scene $7500–10,000 ($4500–15,000)
44 Jackson Square $4000–6000 ($750–8000)
45 Carriage Maker $600–1200 ($500–3000)
46 Reding's Mill $3000–5000 ($2000–10,000)
47 Farm Scene $1200–2000 ($1000–10,000)
48 Dream of a Nudist Camp Wedding $5000–6000 ($2000–10,000)
49 Picking Blackberries by the Creek $15,000–20,000 ($7500–25,000)
50 On a Sunday Afternoon $3000–4000 ($1500–6000)
51 Sledding $1500–2000 ($500–2500)
52 Woman Shoveling Snow $2500–3500 ($1000–8000)
53 Mount Vernon $1200–1500 ($1000–3000)
54 Morris Street and the Strand $800–1000 ($500–2500)
55 The Lighthouse $800–1000 ($500–3500)
56 Harbor Scene on Cape Cod $6000–7000 ($2500–7500)

57 The Sarah Passing Flushing $3500–5000 ($3000–8000)
58 Sailboat and Steamship $4500–6000 ($2500–7500)
59 The America off the Battery $15,000–20,000 ($10,000–45,000)
60 The Mary P. Bates $15,000–20,000 ($10,000–45,000)
61 The Reindeer $100,000–135,000 ($35,000–135,000)
62 The Connecticut $30,000–35,000 ($8000–45,000)
63 The City of Lowell $20,000–25,000 ($10,000–45,000)
64 The Titanic $1000–1800 ($1000–6000)
65 Destroyer $200–400 ($200–1000)
66 Shooting the Polar Bear in the Arctic $3000–5000 ($2500–10,000)

Historical and Religious Paintings

Pictures with historical or patriotic themes have limited appeal for general collectors, but specialists avidly seek them out. Works that are detailed eyewitness accounts of people or events are most in demand, as are original designs; these may sell for anywhere from $5000 to $50,000. The many pictures copied from contemporary prints, however, usually sell today for less than $1000, unless by a well-known artist. Religious folk paintings from any period are not very popular with collectors, so that such works seldom bring prices comparable to portraits or landscapes executed by the same artists. Memorial pictures have fared somewhat better in the marketplace; modest examples made by young women in 19th-century finishing schools often sell for under $1000. Fracturs, on the other hand, have enjoyed great popularity with collectors for many years. Although simple examples may sell in the low to mid-hundreds, fine examples, particularly those by identified artists, usually range from $5000 to more than $10,000, and are likely to continue to rise in price.

67 The Destruction of a Church in Bath, Maine $25,000–35,000 ($25,000–50,000)
68 Painted political pin $1000–1800 ($500–3500)
69 Surrender at Nashville $2500–3500 ($2000–4500)
70 Soldier fractur $2000–3000 ($1500–4000)
71 The Heroes of the Revolution $8000–12,000 ($5000–15,000)
72 Andrew Jackson $600–750 ($500–2000)
73 General George Washington on Horseback $2500–3500 ($2000–5000)
74 Liberty in the Form of the Goddess of Youth $10,000–15,000 ($5000–18,000)
75 Liberty $2000–2500 ($1500–3000)
76 Memorial miniature in locket $1000–1200 ($1000–3000)
77 Memorial to George Washington $2000–2500 ($2000–5000)
78 Woman at Unmarked Tombstone $500–650 ($350–1000)
79 Masonic Memorial $10,000–12,000 ($8500–20,000)
80 The Annunciation $450–600 ($350–1000)
81 Christ on the Path $1000–1500 ($500–3000)
82 Crucifixion $5000–6000 ($2500–7500)
83 Choir with Angels $2000–2500 ($500–5000)
84 Baptismal certificate fractur $6000–10,000 ($2500–10,000)
85 Spiritual Chimes fractur $6000–8000 ($2500–10,000)
86 Tradesmen fractur $5000–7500 ($5000–10,000)
87 Fractur book pages $2500–3500 ($2500–10,000)
88 Messiah's Crown fractur $6000–8000 ($5000–10,000)
89 Family record fractur $2000–3000 ($500–5000)

Still Lifes and Animal Pictures

The folk pictures in this section include some of the least expensive types available today, several of which are likely to rise in value in years to come. Tinsel pictures have never appealed much to collectors; almost all of them sell for between $100 and $1000. Theorem pictures are more popular, and examples with appealing designs and in fine condition may sell for $1000 to $3000. Calligraphic drawings are available in large numbers. Modest designs may be found for less than $100, and even major examples embellished by watercolors seldom cost more than a few thousand dollars. Patriotic themes or depictions of unusual animals are most sought after. Modern folk paintings of animals generally sell in the low to mid-hundreds unless by a well-known artist such as Vestie Davis or Lawrence Lebduska.

90 Scherenschnitte $950–1200 ($200–3500)
91 Tinsel picture $650–850 ($150–1000)
92 Tinsel picture $500–650 ($150–1000)
93 Tinsel picture $650–750 ($150–1000)
94 Grisaille theorem $1500–2500 ($1000–3500)
95 Theorem $3000–4000 ($2500–8500)
96 Theorem $1000–2000 ($500–3500)
97 Theorem $2500–3000 ($1500–6500)
98 Hummingbird $1500–2000 ($500–25,000)
99 Home $250–300 ($50–350)
100 Home, Sweet Home $450–550 ($100–600)
101 Birds $3000–5000 ($1000–6000)
102 Bald Eagle $1500–2000 ($150–3500)
103 Stag $1500–2000 ($500–3500)
104 Tiger $2000–3000 ($1500–4500)
105 Black Cat $750–1000 ($500–10,000)

Signs, Architectural Elements, and Flat Sculpture

The varied pieces in this section range in price from more than $100,000 for unique architectural ornaments, such as the flag gate shown here, to several hundred dollars for simple flat signs from the late 19th or early 20th century. Signs made before the mid-19th century are extremely rare; those with decorative metalwork are especially coveted. A striking three-dimensional example, even if relatively late, may bring several thousand dollars or more. Collectors continue to seek out 19th-century scrimshaw; though a lavishly engraved whale tooth that is signed and dated may fetch as much as $40,000, simpler objects are more affordable at around $1000. While all fireboards are quite rare, flat ones are moderately priced at $2000 or less; a sculptural example may command as much as $20,000. Architectural ornaments, a new collecting category, generally bring $250 to $2000, but many examples sell for less.

106 Coffeehouse and shop sign $30,000–40,000
107 Tavern sign $1000–3000
108 House sign $400–750
109 Guesthouse sign $500–850
110 Boot trade sign $2500–3000
111 Dentist's trade sign $3000–5000
112 Barber pole $850–1000
113 Architectural finial $350–550
114 Barn-door archway decoration $400–750
115 Flag gate $100,000–150,000

116 Abraham Lincoln $2500–3500
117 Saint Luke $20,000–50,000
118 Masonic temple $2000–3000
119 Pictorial fireboard $18,000–25,000
120 Pictorial fireboard $2000–3000
121 Gravestone $1000–3000
122 Gravestone $1000–3000
123 Scrimshaw plaque $2000–4000
124 Scrimshaw busks $1200–1500 each
125 Whale teeth $2000–4000 each
126 Whale tooth $40,000–50,000

Sculpture of People

Folk sculptures of human figures vary tremendously in size, style, and value. In fact, prices vary from less than $100 for cast-iron doorstops and some small carved religious figures to the $20,000-to-$100,000 range for fine cigar-store figures, carnival carvings, and figureheads, all of which are among the most costly kinds of folk sculpture. Collectors of folk art generally seek stylized figures rather than realistic ones; moreover, rich details and sensitively modeled features add significantly to the value of a piece. Unique carvings that are difficult to categorize often excite the most interest and quickly appreciate in value. Religious carvings from the Southwest, called bultos, are usually moderately priced. Whether cigar-store figures or bultos, the works of identified carvers are almost always most valuable, as are those retaining original paint.

127 Phrenological head $25,000–35,000
128 Carnival target figure $1000–1500
129 Triple-faced head $500–600
130 Carnival target figure $850–1500
131 Sculptural fragment $2000–3000
132 Grave ornament $1500–3000
133 Architectural ornament $450–650
134 Virgin of Montserrat $1000–2000
135 Virgin of Mount Carmel $650–850
136 The Holy Family $850–1500
137 Crucifixion $3500–7500
138 Saint Francis of Assisi $250–350
139 Father Time $100,000–150,000
140 Zozobra or Old Man Gloom $6500–7500
141 Paper soldiers $3000–4000
142 The First Suit $800–1000
143 Shop figure $5000–8500
144 Wooden scarecrow $2000–6000
145 Shop figure $8000–15,000
146 Nodding-head chalkware woman $4000–4500
147 Figural doorstops $250–350
148 Black dancing figure $3000–8500
149 Cigar-store Indian $5000–10,000
150 Cigar-store figure $30,000–50,000
151 Cigar-store figure $25,000–45,000
152 Cigar-store Indian $10,000–35,000
153 Cigar-store Indian $50,000–100,000
154 Cigar-store figure $12,000–20,000
155 Cigar-store figure $10,000–20,000
156 Ship's figurehead $35,000–50,000
157 Ship's figurehead $35,000–50,000

Whirligigs and Weathervanes

With prices ranging anywhere from several hundred dollars to more than $75,000, whirligigs are evaluated by five criteria: complexity of design, detail of carving, age, condition, and the amount of surviving original paint. Any example from before 1900 is generally of greater interest to collectors than one from the 20th century. A piece that has been significantly restored or repainted is unlikely to appreciate in value, no matter how wonderful its design. Most of these criteria also hold true for weathervanes, which range in price from $1000 to more than $100,000 for a one-of-a-kind masterpiece, such as the Saint Tammany vane included here. While wooden examples from the 18th and 19th centuries are rarer, they seldom bring the prices commanded by handcrafted or factory-made metal vanes. A vane that has been stripped of its patina is of little value.

158 Uncle Sam whirligig $75,000–100,000
159 Early-bird-catches-the-worm whirligig $65,000–100,000
160 Bugler whirligig $10,000–15,000
161 Abraham Lincoln whirligig $450–550
162 Witch whirligig $8500–10,000
163 Man-in-top-hat whirligig $3500–6000
164 Punchinellos whirligig $900–1500
165 Horse-race whirligig $750–1200
166 Windmill-and-horses whirligig $900–1200
167 Farm whirligig $2000–4500
168 Saint Tammany weathervane $150,000–200,000
169 Archangel Gabriel weathervane $6500–15,000
170 Stag weathervane $3500–5000
171 Stag weathervane $5000–11,000
172 Steer weathervane $3000–7500
173 Horse-and-rider weathervane $4500–7500
174 Horse weathervane $6000–12,000
175 Horse weathervane $2500–4500
176 Peacock weathervane $2000–3500
177 Rooster weathervane $1000–2000
178 Grasshopper weathervane $35,000–50,000
179 Fish weathervane $3000–6000

Animal Sculpture

Folk sculptures of animals have broad popular appeal, largely because these pieces are readily available in a wide variety of mediums and prices. Simple carved 20th-century examples may be found for $50 to $300. At the opposite end of the price spectrum are figures by famous carvers, such as Wilhelm Schimmel, Aaron Mountz, and John H. Bellamy; most of their works sell for $5000 to $50,000. Carousel figures are also costly, usually at $3000 to $20,000. Cast-iron animal sculpture is generally inexpensive, with many modest pieces selling for under $100, and good examples for $100 to $200. However, cast-iron animals in popular forms, such as mill weights and hitching-post finials, generally sell for $500 to $1500.

180 Fish-market sign $3500–5000
181 Sperm whale $600–1200
182 Shark $800–2000
183 Swordfish sign $600–1000
184 Frog decoys $300–400 (center); $600–1000 (right)
185 Flower holder or frog $75–150

186 Alligator-shaped nutcracker $125–150
187 Dinosaur $2500–8500
188 Monkey $250–350
189 Piggy bank $100–150
190 Nodding-head chalkware pig and goat $1000–3500 each
191 Chalkware cat $6000–8000
192 Cat's-head inkwell $200–500
193 Cat-shaped bootscraper $1000–2000
194 Dog-shaped lawn ornament $75–150
195 Dog's gravestone $2000–4000
196 Lamb-shaped grave ornament $2000–4000
197 Elephant $1000–1500
198 Cow-shaped mill weight $750–2000
199 Horse-head hitching-post finial $400–1200
200 Horse pull toy $7500–15,000
201 Carousel horse $12,000–15,000
202 Carousel wagon panel $3000–5000
203 Eagle $2000–5000
204 Eagle on sphere $15,000–35,000
205 Eagle $20,000–40,000
206 Eagle $6000–8000
207 Rooster $4000–6000
208 Rooster-shaped mill weight $600–1200
209 Folding owl decoy $1000–1500
210 Shooting-gallery targets $75–150 each

Decoys and Lures

The prices of wildfowl decoys range broadly from less than $100 to more than $15,000. Fine pieces by well-known makers such as Lemuel Ward or manufacturers such as the Mason Decoy Factory may cost $3000 or occasionally much more. Decoys, such as those of mergansers, that have an arresting overall shape and meticulously executed details often bring prices in the thousands. Whatever the price bracket, a decoy in fine original condition is always most valuable; examples with replaced heads or bills or those with missing parts are severely depreciated, and repainted or refinished decoys are usually of little interest. Decoys of fish have risen dramatically in price, ranging from $75 for small ordinary examples to more than $1000 for some large pieces.

211 Turtle decoy $300–400
212 White-winged scoter decoy $850–1500
213 Canada goose decoy $250–500
214 Canada goose decoy $400–800
215 Oldsquaw hen and eider drake decoys $300–600 each
216 Redhead drake and white-winged scoter hen decoys $100–200 (front); $1500–3000 (rear)
217 Miniature redhead drake paperweight $150–300
218 Pintail drake decoy $3500–7000
219 Merganser decoys $400–800 (front); $5000–10,000 (rear)
220 Coot and mallard drake decoys $150–300 (front); $600–1200 (rear)
221 Long-billed curlew decoy $600–1200
222 Curlew decoy $250–350
223 Ruddy turnstone and greater yellowlegs decoys $250–500 (left); $400–800 (right); $1600–3200 (center)
224 Black-bellied plover and sickle-billed curlew decoys $3500–7000 (front); $5000–10,000 (rear)

225 Sanderling and black-bellied plover decoys $150–300 each
226 Bobwhite $75–250
227 Largemouth bass, pike, and sunfish decoys $300–500 each
228 Codfish jig $100–150
229 Fish decoy $3000–5000
230 Sturgeon decoy $600–850

Baskets

While baskets have been made in a wide variety of forms and materials, collector interest is sharply focused, and prices reflect this. The most popular and valuable examples are generally made of splint and date from before 1900, but baskets from 1900 to 1930 are now attracting high prices as well. Among the most sought-after types are swing-handled, Shaker, painted or potato-stamped, and hexagonal-weave baskets; these often fetch over $200. Because there is less demand for baskets made of sweet grass or willow, many may be obtained for $10 to $50. Prices for baskets made of unusual materials such as matchbook covers, wire, bottle caps, and bentwood are difficult to predict: dealers specializing in traditional baskets may sell them inexpensively, but collectors who recognize their value as folk art are often willing to pay handsomely for them. Since condition is extremely important in pricing any kind of basket, a damaged piece will be sharply devalued.

231 Handled basket $15–30
232 Covered sewing or storage basket $50–150
233 Swing-handled basket $125–275
234 Wool-drying basket $225–300
235 Work or storage basket $75–125
236 Hexagonal-weave cheese or notions basket $100–300
237 Work or storage basket $45–60
238 Shaker sewing basket $200–500
239 Shaker wooden carrier $300–3000
240 Field basket $40–65
241 Double lift-top wallpaper basket $50–200
242 Picnic basket or hamper $100–250
243 Indian potato-stamped covered baskets $300–1200 each
244 Indian covered basket $50–200
245 Indian covered baskets and pincushion $10–35 each
246 Indian covered baskets and pincushion $15–45 each
247 Indian covered baskets $10–30 each
248 Indian yarn holders $25–75 each
249 Matchbook bowl with domed lid $75–200
250 Bottle-cap bowl and cup $50–125 each
251 Work or sewing basket $5–30
252 Coiled-wood bowls $35–60 each
253 Miniature threaded-clove tea set $100–250
254 Hanging storage basket $100–250
255 Vinegar funnel $75–150
256 Windsor-type cheese drainer $200–300
257 Wire field basket $50–200
258 Slat field basket $25–150
259 Double peach basket $80–130
260 Eel trap $500–1200
261 Horse feeding basket $500–1200
262 Doll's cradle $200–400

Boxes and Shelves

Early 19th-century wooden boxes with painted decoration are in great demand, provided they are in good original condition, with the finest examples selling for more than $5000. Carved boxes are also costly, particularly those from the 18th or early 19th century. Tramp-art boxes are fairly inexpensive, with most ranging between $100 and $300, but many selling for even less. Like virtually all Shaker products, boxes and other containers by Shaker craftsmen command a sizable premium; however, these will bring high prices only if they are marked or documented. Painted tin boxes range widely in price, usually from the low hundreds to the low thousands, according to design and condition. Scrimshaw boxes and display cases also vary greatly in price, from $250 for a simple ditty box to more than $10,000 for an elaborate showcase. Small hanging shelves, popular in the Victorian era, are readily available at $50 to $200; several examples included here, however, are far more expensive because of the carved or cutwork decoration that makes them fine pieces of folk art.

263 Smoke-grained storage box $250–750
264 Grain-painted sample box and panels $6000–20,000
265 Painted trinket box $7500–20,000
266 Painted trinket box $6000–15,000
267 Painted dome-top box $2750–4000
268 Painted tin document box $400–1500
269 Indian pine-needle box $75–125
270 Carved figural box $1000–2500
271 Carved box $200–500
272 Tramp-art pedestal box $200–400
273 Tramp-art storage box $150–200
274 Slatted bowl $65–90
275 Shaker grain measures $175–250 each
276 Shaker oval boxes $350–2000 each
277 Bucket or firkin $50–100
278 Scrimshaw ditty box $2500–5000
279 Painted open-top box $50–150
280 Painted utility box $300–700
281 Tramp-art writing box $90–150
282 House-shaped box $200–400
283 House-shaped display case $450–700
284 Showcase $8000–15,000
285 Cutwork wall box $700–900
286 Cutwork hanging shelf $200–450
287 Hanging figural cigar holder $300–400
288 Hanging shelf with drawer $350–1200

Kitchenware

Of the vast number of kitchen utensils and serving pieces produced in this country during the past 200 years, 19th-century pieces made and decorated by hand arouse the most collector interest. Since most types of objects were made in large numbers, the highest prices usually reflect handsome decoration or fine materials rather than scarcity. For example, a plain maple scoop is seldom worth more than $20, but a nicely shaped scoop in maple burl will easily fetch more than $100. Similarly, a tin serving tray painted black with simple gilding may be worth $50, but a similar piece embellished with flowers or a landscape in oils may bring $1000 or even more. Factory-made pieces, such as late 19th-century butter molds, generally sell for a fraction of the price of fine hand-carved examples. Scrimshaw rolling pins and pie crimpers nearly always sell for far more than comparable wooden ones. Wrought-iron utensils are popular with collectors and generally sell in the low hundreds. Because collector interest in late 19th-century cast-iron objects, such as warming shelves and meat tenderizers, is just developing, these items can still be purchased reasonably. Among the least expensive metal utensils are those made of undecorated tin, including cookie cutters.

289 Painted tin tray $1500–2500
290 Painted tin tray $750–1200
291 Painted tin bread basket or bun tray $200–600
292 Wooden bowl $200–325
293 Wooden scoop $100–300
294 Wooden spoon and ladle $50–100 (left); $75–175 (right)
295 Shaker wooden dipper $250–500
296 Scrimshaw dipper $2000–2500
297 Copper teakettle $150–250
298 Adirondack or rustic wooden tankard $40–65
299 Wooden salt dish $300–500
300 Cast-iron mortar and pestle $100–200
301 Wooden butter mold and stamp $40–75 (left); $30–50 (right)
302 Tin cookie cutters $15–25 each
303 Carved springerle board $300–400
304 Carved springerle boards $100–150 each
305 Tin candle mold $100–200
306 Redware candle mold $2500–3500
307 Make-do vegetable grater $35–80
308 Cast-iron meat tenderizer $50–100
309 Wooden rolling pin $100–150
310 Scrimshaw rolling pins $300–400 each
311 Scrimshaw jagging wheels or pie crimpers $2000–2500 (top); $150–250 (bottom)
312 Carved crooked knives $175–350 each
313 Wrought-iron spatula, fork, and serving spoon $50–150 each
314 Wrought-iron sugar cutters or calipers $100–200
315 Waffle or wafer iron $150–400
316 Wrought-iron hand-held toaster $125–200
317 Wrought-iron swivel-base toaster $500–2500
318 Wrought-iron kettle stand $250–300
319 Wrought-iron rotating broiler or grill $250–500
320 Cast-iron warming shelf $100–350

Heating, Lighting, and Other Household Items
Fireplace and heating accessories are priced according to the quality of their craftsmanship and decoration. Foot or bed warmers with punchwork designs, such as eagles or stars, will often bring three to four times the price of a comparable item lacking such decoration. Similarly, bellows with painted decoration may cost well over $300, while plain bellows may be found for less than $100. Figural andirons also command high prices. Elaborate wrought-iron chandeliers or graceful tin ones almost always sell for more than $500; ordinary electric lamps, however, seldom fetch more than $50 to $200. Many collectors today are interested in gameboards because of their bright colors and geometric forms; these boards generally cost upwards of $200.

321 Fireplace baking oven $400–750
322 Punched-tin foot warmer $150–500
323 Fireplace coffee roaster $50–150
324 Warming pan $200–700
325 Bellows $350–750
326 Figural andirons $400–1500
327 Braided andirons $250–1500
328 Loop-topped andirons $300–1000
329 Fire holder or cresset $200–1000
330 Eagle-head chandelier $750–2500
331 Wicker lamp $75–100
332 Tramp-art cactus lamp $150–250
333 Tramp-art picture frame $40–65
334 Carved picture frame $100–250
335 Carved checkerboard $150–300
336 Hand-painted checkerboard $250–500
337 Hand-painted reversible gameboard $300–600
338 Hand-painted Parcheesi board $300–850

Spinning and Washing Implements, Canes, and Miscellaneous Tools

Implements used for sewing and laundering, such as spool holders, washboards, clothespins, and irons, generally sell for under $100. Exceptions are those items with fine carving or other decoration, imaginative forms, or unusual materials. Swifts and spinning wheels tend to be more costly but are still moderately priced; however, an elaborate scrimshaw swift may sell for $3000 to $6000, and a one-of-a-kind figural wool winder may bring more than $10,000. As a rule, Shaker pieces, such as spool holders and clothespins, command a premium. Farm tools may still be purchased reasonably, with most selling for $100 or less, but prices have been rising. Great interest in canes has caused them to increase in value considerably in recent years, so that finely carved examples now bring several hundred dollars; scrimshaw and other rare canes usually fetch even more.

339 Scrimshaw swift or wool winder $3000–6000
340 Metal swift or wool winder $250–500
341 Spinning wheel in cage $650–1250
342 Figural wool winder $10,000–20,000
343 Figural spool holder $50–150
344 Shaker spool stand with pincushion $100–200
345 Scrimshaw bodkins $150–500 each
346 Scrimshaw clothespins $40–125 each
347 Carved wash sticks or clothes forks $75–200 each
348 Rug beater $40–100
349 Bootjacks $75–350 each
350 Sad iron $40–100
351 Iron washboard $100–500
352 Wooden dibble board $100–200
353 Wrought-iron eel or fish spears $25–100 each
354 Wooden hay and barley forks $75–200 each
355 Wrought-iron hay cutter $50–200
356 Root cane $50–200
357 Carved figural canes $300–1200 each
358 Painted and incised cane $300–500
359 Fire warden's staff $350–500
360 Scrimshaw cane $2000–5000

Checklist of Artists and Craftsmen

This table lists the major folk painters, sculptors, and craftsmen whose works are featured in this book, as well as a representative sampling of other important folk artists working in a variety of mediums from the early 18th century to the present. Also included are a number of manufacturers who produced metal sculpture such as weathervanes.

Name	Dates	Locality
Adams, Frank	1871–1944	West Tisbury, MA
Alten, Fred	1872–1945	Ohio; Wyandotte, MI
Ames, Asa	1824–51	vicinity of Buffalo, NY
Aragón, José Rafael	c. 1797–1862	Santa Fe, Cordova, Santa Cruz Valley, NM
Aragón, Rafael	fl. 1840–65	New Mexico
Arning, Eddie	1898–	Texas
Aulisio, Joseph	1910–74	Stroudsburg, PA
Badger, Joseph	1708–63	Boston
Bard, James	1815–97	New York City
Bard, John	1815–56	New York City
Barela, Patrocinio	d. 1964	Arizona, New Mexico
Bartoll, William Thompson	1817–59	Marblehead, MA
Bascom, Ruth Henshaw	1772–1848	Gill, MA
Basye, Joyce	1947–	Baltimore
Beardsley Limner	fl. 1785–1800	New England, New York
Belknap, Zedekiah	1781–1858	Townsend, MA
Bellamy, John H.	1836–1914	Kittery Point, ME, Boston, MA, Portsmouth, NH
Black, Calvin Black, Ruby	1903–72 d. 1980	Yermo, CA
Blackburn, Joseph	c. 1700–65	New England
Blair, John	fl. 1860s	Elleton, MD
Blunt, John S.	1798–1835	New England coast
Bochero, Peter "Charlie"	c. 1895–1962	Leechburg, PA
Boghosian, Nounoufar	1894–	California
Bond, Peter Mason	1882–1971	San Francisco
Boyd, George	1873–1941	Seabrook, NH
Bradley, John	fl. 1832–47; d. 1874	Connecticut, New York City
Brewster, John, Jr.	1766–1854	New England, New York State
Brice, Bruce	c. 1943–	New Orleans
Bridges, Charles	fl. 1735–40	South Carolina
Broadbent, Samuel	fl. 1800–25	Connecticut, New York State
Brown, J.	fl. 1800–35	Massachusetts
Brunton, Richard	d. 1832	Connecticut
Budington, Jonathan	fl. 1792–1812	New York State
Butler, Ann	1813–?	East Greenville, NY

The names of individuals and firms are followed by birth and death dates or the years in which they flourished (abbreviated fl.), primary locality, frequently used materials, and principal types of folk art produced. If an artist or maker has a work illustrated in this guide, the plate number is included under type of work.

Materials	Type of Work
wood	decoys, paperweights (217)
wood	carved animals (187)
wood	carved figures (127)
tempera, gesso; wood	retablos, bultos
tempera, gesso; wood	retablos
crayons, pastel crayons; paper	memory and genre pictures
oils; canvas, board	portraits (30)
oils; canvas	portraits
oils; canvas	ship portraits (61)
oils; canvas	ship portraits
wood	santos
oils; canvas	portraits, landscapes, signs
pastels; paper	portraits, silhouettes
oils; canvas, board	landscapes (54)
oils; canvas	portraits
oils; panel, canvas	portraits (2)
wood	eagles (203) and other carvings
wood, cloth, paints	female dolls, large outdoor sculpture
oils; canvas	portraits
wood	decoys
oils; canvas, tin, wood	portraits, marine and genre pictures, signs, tinware
oils; canvas	religious and obsessive pictures (82)
mixed media	genre and memory pictures
oils; canvas	religious pictures
wood	decoys (224)
oils; canvas	portraits (8), miniatures
oils; canvas	portraits (18), overmantles
acrylics; canvas	cityscapes
oils; canvas	portraits
oils; canvas	portraits, landscapes
oils; canvas	portraits (17)
oils; canvas	portraits
oils; wood panel	landscapes
oils; tin	trays, trunks, boxes

Name	Dates	Locality
Buttersworth, James E.	1817–94	West Hoboken, NJ
Canfield, Abijah	1769–1830	Chusetown, CT
Carmel, Charles	fl. 1910s	Brooklyn, NY
Carpenter, Miles B.	1889–	Waverly, VA
Chambers, Thomas	c. 1808–65	New York State
Chandler, Winthrop	1747–90	vicinity of Woodstock, CT
Church, Henry	1836–1908	Chagrin Falls, OH
Cohoon, Hannah	1788–1864	Hancock, MA
Contis, Peter	fl. 1950s	Pittsburgh
Cooke, Captain	fl. 1910s	New England, Florida
Coyle, Carlos Cortes	1871–1962	Seattle, San Francisco, Florida
Crane, James	fl. 1960s	Ellsworth, ME
Crawford, Cleo	1892–1939	Haverstraw, NY
Crowell, A. Elmer	1862–1952	East Harwich, MA
Cunningham, Earl	1893–1978	Florida
Cushing and White L. W. Cushing and Sons	1867–72 1872–1933	Waltham, MA
Davies, Albert Webster	1889–1967	New England
Davis, Jane A.	fl. 1827–55	New England
Davis, Joseph H.	fl. 1830s	New Hampshire, Maine
Davis, Vestie E.	1904–78	New York City
Day, Frank Leveva	c. 1900	California, New Mexico, Montana, Alaska
Denig, Ludwig	fl. 1780s	Chambersburg, PA
Downes, P. S.	fl. 1880s	New York City
Durand, John	fl. 1766–82	Connecticut, Virginia
Duyckinck, Gerardus I	fl. 1720s	New York City
Duyckinck, Gerret	fl. 1690–1710	New York City
Earl, Ralph	1751–1801	Connecticut
Eaton, Moses	1796–1886	New England
Edmondson, William	c. 1865–1951	Tennessee
Ellinger, David	fl. 1940–80	Pennsylvania
Ellis, A.	fl. 1830s	New Hampshire, Maine
Ellsworth, James Sanford	1802–74	Connecticut, Massachusetts
Esteves, Antonio	1910–83	New York City
Evans, J.	fl. 1827–55	Portsmouth, NH; Boston
Fasanella, Ralph	1914–	New York City, Ardsley, NY
Fellini, William	d. 1965	New York City
Fenimore, Janice	1924–	Madison, NJ

Materials	Type of Work
oils; board, canvas	ship portraits (59)
gouache; glass	Romantic and historical pictures (74)
wood	carousel figures (201)
wood	figural carvings
oils; canvas	landscapes (36) and seascapes
oils; canvas	portraits (26), landscapes, overmantles
oils; canvas; stone	still lifes, portraits, sculpture
oils; canvas	Shaker inspirational pictures
tempera; artist's board	landscapes, memory pictures
oils; sailcloth, canvas	seascapes (58)
oils; canvas	history, evils of marriage, current events
oils; oilcloth, paper	seascapes (64), landscapes
oils; canvas	landscapes
wood	decoys (223), weathervanes
oils; board	landscapes, seascapes (55)
copper	weathervanes
oils; masonite	historical (69) and genre pictures, Romantic landscapes
watercolors, pencil; paper, ivory	portraits (29), miniatures
watercolors; paper	miniature portraits
oils; canvasboard, canvas	landscapes, genre pictures (105)
oils; canvas	Indian mythological pictures
watercolors, ink; paper	fracturs
watercolors; paper	marine pictures
oils; canvas	historical pictures and portraits
oils; canvas	portraits
oils; panel	portraits
oils; canvas	portraits, historical pictures
dry pigments in skim milk; wood, plaster	murals, grain-painted objects (264)
stone	religious carvings
watercolors, oils; velvet, cotton, canvas	theorems (96), fracturs, genre pictures
oils; panel	portraits
watercolors; paper	miniature portraits
acrylics; board	religious and genre pictures (104)
watercolors; paper	portraits
oils; canvas	genre pictures
oils; canvas	landscapes
wood	whirligigs (161), whimsical figures

Name	Dates	Locality
Field, Erastus Salisbury	1805–1900	Connecticut, Massachusetts, New York
Finster, Reverend Howard	1916–	Summerville, GA
Fisher, Jonathan	1768–1847	Blue Hill, ME
J. W. Fiske Ironworks	fl. 1885–90	New York City
Fowle, Isaac	fl. 1807–32	Boston
Frost, J. O. J.	1852–1928	Marblehead, MA
Frymire, Jacob	c. 1770–1822	Pennsylvania
Gatto, Victor Joseph	1890–1965	New York City, Miami
Gier, David	fl. 1960s–	Michigan
Glaser, Elizabeth	fl. 1830–40	Baltimore
Glick, Herman	1895–	Havana, IL
Golding, William O.	1874–1943	Georgia
Goldsmith, Deborah	1808–36	vicinity of Hamilton, NY
Goodrich & Thompson	fl. 1820–50	Berlin, CT
Greenwood, John	fl. 1750s	New England
Haidt, John Valentine	1700–80	Bethlehem, PA
Haman, Barbara Becker	1774–?	Shenandoah County, VA
Hamblen, Sturtevant J.	fl. 1830–56	Maine, Massachusetts
Hamblett, Theora	1895–	Oxford, MS
Hamilton, James	1832–?	Washington, DC
Harley, Steve	1863–1947	Scottsville, MI; West Coast
Harris and Co.	fl. 1870–90	Brattleboro, VT
Hatch, Edbury	1849–1935	Newcastle and Damariscotta, ME
Hathaway, Rufus	1770–1822	Taunton and Duxbury, MA
"Heart and Hand" Artist	fl. 1850s	Maine
Hesselius, Gustavus	1682–1755	Pennsylvania, Maryland
Hicks, Edward	1780–1849	Newtown, PA
Hidley, Joseph Henry	1830–72	Poestenkill, NY
Hillings, John	d. 1894	Bath, ME
Hirshfield, Morris	1872–1946	Brooklyn, NY
Hofmann, Charles C.	1821–82	Pennsylvania
Holmes, Lothrop T.	1824–99	Kingston, MA
Huge, Jurgan Frederick	1809–78	Bridgeport, CT
Hunter, Clementine	c. 1882–	Mississippi
Jacobsen, Antonio	1850–1921	Hoboken, NJ
Jakobsen, Katherine	1951–	Michigan, New York City
Jennys, Richard	fl. 1750s	New England
Jennys, William	fl. 1750s	New England

Materials	Type of Work
oils; canvas	portraits (16), religious pictures
oils; board, canvas, glass, concrete	religious pictures (81), environmental sculpture
ink, pencil, oils, watercolors; wood	portraits, landscapes, engravings
copper	weathervanes (170)
wood	figureheads, ships' carvings
oils; board	marine and historical pictures, landscapes
oils; canvas	portraits
oils; masonite, pressed wood	genre pictures
oils; board	landscapes
watercolors; paper	portraits (12), needlework
wood	decoys (222, 226)
watercolors, crayon; paper	seascapes
watercolors; paper	portraits
oils; tin	painted tinware (290)
oils; canvas, board	portraits
oils; canvas	portraits, religious pictures
watercolors; paper	fracturs (84)
oils; canvas	portraits (27)
oils; masonite	memory pictures
wood	cigar-store and other figures (155)
oils; canvas	landscapes
copper	weathervanes (172)
wood	carved decoration on houses
oils; canvas	portraits (28)
watercolors, ink; paper	fracturs (89)
oils; canvas	portraits
oils; canvas	religious pictures, landscapes, signs
oils; canvas, wood	landscapes
oils; canvas	historical pictures (67)
oils; canvas	nudes, animals, portraits
oils; canvas, zinc	landscapes (40)
wood	decoys
watercolors	landscapes, marine and genre pictures
house paint on cardboard	genre pictures
oils; canvas, composition board	ship portraits (62)
acrylics, oils; canvas	landscapes (43), genre pictures
oils; canvas	portraits
oils; canvas	portraits

Name	Dates	Locality
Jessup, Jared	fl. 1800–20	Connecticut, Massachusetts
Johnston, Henrietta	d. 1728	Charleston, SC
Kane, Andy	fl. 1970s	New York
Kane, John	c. 1860–1934	Pennsylvania, Ohio
Kemmelmeyer, Frederick	fl. 1788–1803	Baltimore, MD
Kitchen, Tella	1902–	Adelphi, OH
Klumpp, Gustav	1902–80	New York City
Krans, Olaf	1838–1916	western Illinois
Labrie, Rose	1916–	Portsmouth, NH
Landau, Sol	1919–	New York City
Larson, Edward	1931–	Missouri, Illinois
Lebduska, Lawrence	1894–1966	New York
Levin, Abram	1880–1957	New York
Lieberman, Harry	1877–	Great Neck, NY
Little, T. J.	1907–	Bellingham, WA
Lopez, Feliz	1942–	Espanola, NM
Louff, Charles	fl. 1880s	Riverside, RI
Lunde, Emily	fl. 1970s–	Minnesota, North Dakota
Maentel, Jacob	c. 1763–1863	Indiana, Pennsylvania
Mark, George Washington	1795–1879	Greenfield, MA
Mason Decoy Factory	fl. 1880s–1910s	Detroit, MI
Mazur, Frank	1910–	Brooklyn, NY
Melchers, Julius Theodore	1830–1908	Detroit
Miller, Lewis	1796–1882	York, PA
Miller, Minerva Butler	1821–1912	East Greenville, NY
Morgan, Sister Gertrude	1900–80	New Orleans
Moses, Grandma (Anna Mary Robertson)	1860–1961	New York State
Moses, Kivetoruk (James)	1908–	Alaska
Mountz, Aaron	1873–1949	Cumberland Valley, PA
North, Mercy	fl. 1820–40	Fly Creek, NY
North, Noah	1809–80	upstate New York, Ohio
Odio, Pucho	1928–	New York
O'Kelley, Mattie Lou	1907–	Georgia
Orme, Albert	fl. 1870s	Southport, ME
Ortega, Ben	1923–	Tesuque, NM
Ortega, José	1828–1904	New Mexico

Materials	Type of Work
oils; wood, plaster	murals
pastels; paper	portraits
acrylics; canvas	genre pictures
oils; canvas	industrial and urban scenes, landscapes, portraits
oils, watercolors; paper	portraits, genre pictures
oils; canvas	landscapes, memory paintings
oils, acrylics; canvas	genre pictures (48), nudes, landscapes
oils; canvas	portraits, landscapes, genre pictures
acrylics; canvas	landscapes, memory paintings, genre pictures (50)
wood	anecdotal scenes (142), figures
oils; canvas	landscapes (46), genre pictures, sculpture, quilts
oils; board, canvas	memory and animal paintings (98)
oils, gouache; canvas, paper	religious and genre pictures
acrylics; canvas	paintings on Jewish themes
wood	whirligigs
wood	santos (136)
wood	carousel carvings
oils; board	memory paintings
watercolors, ink; paper	portraits (7)
oils; canvas	portraits, landscapes, historical scenes, murals, signs
wood	decoys (224)
wood, terra cotta	carvings with Jewish themes
wood	figural carvings, cigar-store figures
watercolors; paper	fracturs
oils; tin	trays, trunks, boxes
acrylics, watercolors, ink; paper	religious pictures (23)
oils; canvas, board, masonite	landscapes, memory paintings
India ink, colored pencils, watercolors; cardboard	Eskimo folk pictures
wood	carved animals (206)
oils; tin	trays, boxes
oils; canvas, wood	portraits
wood	carved human and animal figures
acrylics, oils, watercolors; canvas, paper	landscapes (49), memory paintings, genre pictures
wood	decoys
wood	santos (138)
wood	santos (137)

Name	Dates	Locality
Palladino, Angela	1929–	New York City
Pansing, Fred	1844–1912	New Jersey
Payne Limner	fl. 1790s	Virginia
Peck, Sheldon	1797–1868	Vermont, New York, Illinois
Perates, John	1894–1970	Portland, ME
Perkins, Ruth Hunter	1911–	Pennsylvania
Peterson, Oscar	1887–?	Cadillac, MI
Phillips, Ammi	1788–1865	Connecticut, New York, Massachusetts
Pickett, Joseph	1848–1918	New Hope, PA
Pierce, Elijah	1892–	Columbus, OH
Pinney, Eunice	1770–1849	Windsor or Simsbury, CT
Pippin, Horace	1888–1946	West Chester, PA
Porter, Rufus	1792–1884	Maine to Virginia
Powers, Asahel Lynde	1813–43	Vermont, Ohio, Massachusetts, New Hampshire, New York
Prior, William Matthew	1806–73	Maine, Boston, Baltimore
Raleigh, Charles Sidney	1830–1925	Massachusetts
Rasmussen, John	fl. 1867–79; d. 1895	Berks County, PA
Rice, William	1773–1847	Hartford, CT; Norway, ME
Ritchie, Aunt Cord	fl. 1930s	Hindman, KY
Robb, Samuel	1851–1928	New York City
Robinson, Mary Lou	fl. 1970s–	Pennsylvania
Root, Ed	1868–1959	Wilson, KS
Ruef, Arnold and Peter	fl. 1880s	Tiffin, OH
Rush, William	1756–1833	Pennsylvania
Sampson, Charles A. L.	fl. 1870s	Bath, ME
Sandusky, William H.	1813–49	Texas
Savitsky, Jack	1910–	Lansford, PA
Schimmel, Wilhelm	1817–90	Carlisle, PA
Schoenheider, Charles	1854–1944	Peoria, IL
Scholl, John	c. 1827–1916	Germania, PA
Seifert, Paul A.	1840–1921	Wisconsin
Shaffer, "Pop"	1880–1964	Mountainair, NM
Sheboygan Decoy Company	fl. 1880s	Sheboygan, WI
Sheffield, Isaac	1798–1845	New England
Shelley, Mary	1950–	Ithaca, NY

Materials	Type of Work
acrylics; wood	history, nudes, genre pictures
oils; canvas	ship portraits (63)
oils; canvas	portraits of Payne family (23)
oils; panel, canvas	portraits (24)
enamel paint; wood	painted religious carvings (117)
acrylics; canvas	landscapes (51)
wood	fish and frog decoys (184, 227)
oils; canvas	portraits (25)
oils; canvas (paint textured with sand, earth, rocks, shells)	landscapes
wood	religious carvings (116)
watercolors, ink; paper	memorial (79), historical, genre, and religious pictures, landscapes
oils; canvas	narrative and genre pictures
watercolors, oils; plaster, paper, canvas	murals (33), landscapes, portraits, silhouettes
oils; wood, canvas	portraits
oils; canvas, glass, cardboard, board	portraits (3), historical scenes, landscapes
oils; canvas	ship portraits (60)
oils; tin	landscapes
oils; wood	signs, portraits
white oak, hickory, willow	baskets
wood	cigar-store (152) and carousel figures
acrylics; canvas	landscapes
concrete	environmental sculpture
wood	cigar-store figures (153)
wood	ships' figureheads, decorative carvings
wood	figureheads
oils, watercolors; canvas, paper	landscapes
oils; board, canvas, masonite	genre pictures
wood	carved animals (205, 207), figures, toys, household ornaments
wood	decoys (220)
wood	fanciful carvings
watercolors, oils, tempera; glass, canvas, cardboard, paper	rural landscapes (41)
wood	carved figures (140)
tin	decoys
oils; canvas	portraits (15)
wood	relief carvings (118)

Name	Dates	Locality
Shute, Ruth W. Shute, Samuel A.	1803–82 1803–36	New England, upper New York State
Sibbel, Susanna	fl. 1800–10	Pennsylvania
Smibert, John	1688–1751	Massachusetts
Smith, Ben	fl. 1850s	Monhegan Island, ME
Smith, Fred	1886–	Wisconsin
Stettinius, Samuel E.	1768–1815	Pennsylvania
Steward, Joseph	fl. 1750s	Connecticut, Massachusetts
Stock, Joseph Whiting	1815–55	New England
Strater & Sohier	1874–90	Boston
Sweetser Family	fl. 1850s–	Vermont
Theus, Jeremiah	1719–74	South Carolina
Tolliver, Mose	fl. 1970s–	Alabama
Tolson, Edgar	1904–	Campton, KY
Vanderlyn, Pieter	c. 1687–1778	Kingston and Albany, NY
Vogt, Fritz G.	fl. 1850–1900	vicinity of Albany, NY
Walker, Inez Nathaniel-	1911–	New York State
Walton, Henry	d. 1865	Ithaca, New York; California; Michigan
Ward, Lemuel	1896–	Crisfield, MD
Ward, Steve	1895–1976	Crisfield, MD
Ward, Velox	1901–	Texas
Waters, Susan C.	1823–1900	Pennsylvania, New York State
Wentworth, P. M.	fl. 1930–45	California
Wetherby, Isaac Augustus	1819–1904	Maine, Massachusetts, Iow
Wheeler, Charles E. "Shang"	1872–1949	Stratford, CT
Wiener, Isidor "Pop"	1886–1970	New York City
Wilder, Franklin	fl. 1870s	Massachusetts
Willey, Philo "Chief"	1886–1980	New Orleans
Williams, William	c. 1710–90	mid-Atlantic states
Willson, Mary Ann	fl. 1810–25	Greenville, NY
Wilson, Elder Delmer	1873–1961	Sabbathday Lake, ME
Wright, Thomas Jefferson	1798–1846	Texas
Yoakum, Joseph	1886–1973	Chicago
Zeldis, Malcah	1931–	New York City
Zeller, George	1818–89	Pennsylvania
Zook, J. W.	fl. 1880s	Illinois

Materials	Type of Work
watercolors, pastels, oils; paper, canvas	portraits (14)
watercolors; paper	fracturs (87)
oils; canvas	landscapes
wood	decoys
concrete, glass, mirrors, found objects	sculpture of people and animals
watercolors; paper	portraits
oils; canvas	portraits
oils; canvas	portraits (10)
wood	decoys (225)
splint	baskets
oils; canvas	portraits
house paint; cardboard	portraits
wood	religious carvings
oils; canvas	portraits
crayon, pencil; paper	rural landscapes (42)
crayon, marker, pencil; paper	portraits (31)
watercolors; paper	portraits, town views, maps
wood	decoys (218)
wood	decoys (218)
oils; canvas	western and memory pictures
oils; canvas	still-life and animal pictures, portraits (6)
pencil, crayon, gouache; paper	religious pictures
oils; canvas	portraits
wood	decoys (216)
oils; canvas, wood; plastic wood	paintings of Jewish subjects, animal carvings
ink, pencil, watercolors; paper	fracturs (88)
acrylics; board, canvas board	landscapes (44), genre pictures
oils; canvas	portraits
watercolors; paper	historical, religious, and fanciful pictures
wood	Shaker boxes and carriers
oils; canvas	portraits
pastels, crayon, pen; paper	memory pictures
gouache, oils, acrylics; canvas, masonite	landscapes (47), religious and genre paintings
watercolors, ink; paper	fracturs
watercolors; paper	fracturs

Picture Credits

Numbers in boldface refer to entries. Numbers in italics refer to pages.

Photographers

All photographs were taken by Schecter Me Sun Lee with the exception of the following: 2, 4–12, *10–17*, 14–18, 21, 23, 25, *25* (bottom), 26, *27* (top and bottom), 28, 29, *29*, 33, 35, 36, 39–42, 52, 53, 59–63, 67, 68, 70, 71, 74–76, 79, 84–89, 91, 92, 95–97, 101, 106, 115, 119, 125, 126, 132, 137, 140–142, 145, 146, 153, 158, 159, 168, 190, 191, 200–202, 204, 218, 229, 260, 261, 265–267, 284, 285, 312, 326, 342, 345, 360. Chun Y. Lai photographed 21, *27* (top), 52, 53, 67, 70, 75, 95, 96, 132, 142, 200, 285, 312, 326. Helga Photo Studio photographed 5, 10, 14, *14*, 15, *16*, *17*, *27* (bottom), 29, 35, 39, 41, 68, 76, 79, 88, 89, 91, 92, 97, 101, 106, 115, 119, 137, 140, 141, 145, 146, 158, 159, 168, 190, 191, 201, 204, 218, 229, 260, 261, 265–267, 342.

Collections

The following individuals, galleries, and institutions kindly allowed us to reproduce objects from their collections:

Abigail Adams Smith Museum, New York City: 297, 300, 301, 305, 313–315, 317–319, 321–324, 328, 350.
Marna Anderson Gallery, New York City: 326.
Aarne Anton, American Primitive Gallery, New York City: 111, 185, 208, 210, 228, 241, 244, 249, 250, 256, 257, 271, 274, 286, 294, 308, 316, 320, 325, 327, 329, 330, 340, 341, 347–349, 352, 354–356.
Nancy and Jim Clokey, Massapequa, New York: 312.
Gary Davenport, New York City: 21, 52, 53, 70, 75, 95, 200.
Diamant Gallery, New York City: 283.
Henry Ford Museum, The Edison Institute, Dearborn, Michigan: *29*, 74, 153, 202.
Pie Galinat and Bob Self, New York City: 183, 242, 245–248, 251, 253, 254, 269, 273, 281, 331–335.
Frank Ganci, Schooley's Mountain, New Jersey: 113.
The Hall Collection: *15*.
George Hammel: 306.
Barbara Johnson: 123, 124, 125 (courtesy Sotheby's), 126 (courtesy Sotheby's), 181, 278, 284 (courtesy Sotheby's), 296, 310, 311, 339, 345, 346, 360.
Jay Johnson, America's Folk Heritage Gallery, New York City: 22, 67, 142, 180, 196, 243, 268, 270, 276, 280, 287, 288, 291, 293.
Kelter-Malcé Antiques, New York City: 108, 109, 114, 182, 232–234, 236, 238, 240, 252, 255, 258, 259, 262, 272, 277, 307, 336–338, 343, 351.
William C. Ketchum, Jr.: 65, 289, 358.
Bernard and S. Dean Levy, Inc., New York City: 132.
Made in America, New York City: 112, 359.
Maine State Museum, Augusta, Maine: 33.
Frank Maresca, New York City: 157.
Hermine Mariaux: 192.
Grandma Moses Properties, New York, © 1979: *13*.
Museum of American Folk Art, New York City: 1, promised gift of Howard and Jean Lipman; 3, promised gift of Robert Bishop; 5, gift of Mrs. Jacob M. Kaplan; *10*, gift of the City of New York Department of Parks and Recreation; 13, courtesy of Terry Dintenfass, Inc.; 14, Museum of American Folk Art purchase; *14*, gift of Mr. and Mrs. M. Austin Fine; 15, gift of Ann R. Coste; *16*, bequest of Effie Thixton Arthur; *17*, gift of Amicus Foundation, Inc.; 19, *25* (top), gifts of Mrs. Jacob M. Kaplan; *25* (center), gift of Mr. and Mrs. William Wiltshire III; 27, promised gift of Robert Bishop; *27* (bottom), gift of Mrs. Adele Earnest; 29, Eva and Morris Feld Folk Art Acquisition Fund; 30, gift of Arnold B. Fuchs; 35, promised gift of Cyril I. Nelson; 38, gift of Mr. and Mrs. William Wiltshire III; 39, 41, Museum of American Folk Art purchases; 56, promised gift of Robert Bishop; 57, gift of Toby and Martin Landey; 68, Eva and Morris Feld Folk Art Acquisition Fund; 73, promised anonymous gift; 76, 79, Museum of American Folk Art purchases; 80, gift of Dorothy J. Kaufman; 88, 89, gifts of Mr. and Mrs. Philip M. Isaacson; 90, promised gift of Robert Bishop; 91–93, gifts of Mr. and Mrs. Day Krolik, Jr.; 94, promised gift of Cyril I. Nelson; 96, gift of Mr. and Mrs. Howard Lipman; 97, promised anonymous gift; 99, gift of Margery G. Kahn; 100, gift of Herbert Waide Hemphill, Jr.; 101, promised gift of Cyril I. Nelson; 102, gift of Dr. Lillian Malcove in honor of Adele Earnest; 103, gift of Mr. and Mrs. Howard Lipman; 106, gift of Margery and Harry Kahn; 115, gift of

Herbert Waide Hemphill, Jr.; 119, Museum of American Folk Art purchase; 120, gift of Mrs. Jacob M. Kaplan; 127, bequest of Jeanette Virgin; 129, 130, promised bequest of Dorothy and Leo Rabkin; 134, 135, gift of Mrs. Richard Valelly; 136, gift of Steve Miller, American Folk Art; 137, anonymous gift; 138, gift of Edward M. Meyers; 139, gift of Mrs. John H. Heminway; 140, promised bequest of Dorothy and Leo Rabkin; 141, gift of Pat and Dick Locke; 143, promised bequest of Dorothy and Leo Rabkin; 144, gift of Dorothy and Leo Rabkin; 145, Joseph Martinson Memorial Fund, Frances and Paul Martinson; 146, bequest of Effie Thixton Arthur; 147, promised gift of Robert Bishop; 148, promised bequest of Dorothy and Leo Rabkin; 152, gift of Sanford and Patricia Smith; 158–160, promised bequests of Dorothy and Leo Rabkin; 161, gift of Jeanne R. Eisele; 162, 164–167, promised bequests of Dorothy and Leo Rabkin; 168, Museum of American Folk Art purchase; 187, gift of Mr. and Mrs. Joseph A. Dumas; 190, 191, bequests of Effie Thixton Arthur; 193, gift of The Friends Committee of the Museum of American Folk Art; 201, gift of Laura Harding; 204, gift of William Engvick; 207, promised anonymous gift; 214, 215, 216 (rear): gifts of Alastair B. Martin; 216 (front): gift of Merle H. Glick; 218, gift of Herbert Waide Hemphill, Jr.; 219, 220 (rear): gifts of Alastair B. Martin; 220 (front): gift of Merle H. Glick; 221, 223–225, gifts of Alastair B. Martin; 226, gift of Merle H. Glick; 229, promised gift of Robert Bishop; 260, 261, promised gifts of Judith A. Jedlicka; 263, gift of Margery G. Kahn; 264, anonymous gift and gift of the Richard Coyle Lilly Foundation; 265, Eva and Morris Feld Folk Art Acquisition Fund; 266, Museum of American Folk Art purchase; 267, gift of Mr. and Mrs. Howard Lipman; 290, gift of Mrs. A. C. Howell; 309, gift of Mrs. Gertrude Schweitzer; 342, Eva and Morris Feld Folk Art Acquisition Fund; 344, promised gift of Robert Bishop.
Carol Nehring: 303, 304 (left).
Maze Pottinger, Highland Beach, Florida: 198.
Private Collections: cover, 11, 20, 24, 31, 32, 34, 37, 43–51, 54, 55, 58, 64, 66, 69, 72, 77, 78, 81–83, 98, 104, 105, 116–118, 121, 122, 133, 149–151, 154, 156, 163, 178, 184, 186, 188, 189, 194, 195, 206, 209, 211–213, 217, 222, 227, 230, 231, 235, 237, 239, 275, 279, 282, 285, 292, 295, 298, 299, 302, 304 (right), 353.
Susan and Sy Rapaport, Great Neck, New York: 199.
George Schoellkopf Gallery, New York City: *27* (center), 107, 128, 169–177, 179, 197, 203, 205, 357.
Sanford and Patricia Smith, New York City: 61, 62.
Smith Gallery, New York City: 59, 60, 63, 155.
Sotheby's, New York City: 2, 4, 6–12, *12*, 16–18, 23, 25, *25* (bottom), 26, 28, 36, 40, 42, 71, 84–87, 125, 126, 284.
Robert Stuart: *27* (top).
George Walowen & Michael Schneider, Walker Valley, New York: 110, 131.

Index

Numbers in boldface refer to entries. Numbers in italics refer to pages.

The Knopf Collectors' Guides to American Antiques

Also available in this unique full-color format:

Chairs, Tables, Sofas & Beds
by Marvin D. Schwartz

Chests, Cupboards, Desks & Other Pieces
by William C. Ketchum, Jr.

Glass Tableware, Bowls & Vases
by Jane Shadel Spillman

Pottery & Porcelain
by William C. Ketchum, Jr.

Quilts, Coverlets, Rugs & Samplers
by Robert Bishop

Staff
Prepared and produced by Chanticleer Press, Inc.
Publisher: Paul Steiner
Editor-in-Chief: Gudrun Buettner
Managing Editor: Susan Costello
Project Editor: Michael Goldman
Assistant Editor: Constance V. Mersel
Art Director: Carol Nehring
Art Assistants: Ayn Svoboda and Karen Wollman
Production: Helga Lose, Amy Roche, and Alex von Hoffmann
Picture Library: Edward Douglas
Drawings: Paul Singer
Design: Massimo Vignelli